Farmers, Monks and Aristocrats: the Environmental Archaeology of Anglo-Saxon Flixborough

EXCAVATIONS AT FLIXBOROUGH

Vol. 1 The Early Medieval Settlement Remains from Flixborough, Lincolnshire: The Occupation Sequence, *c.* AD 600–1000 *by Christopher Loveluck and David Atkinson*

Vol. 2 Life and Economy at Early Medieval Flixborough, *c.* AD 600–1000: The Artefact Evidence *edited by D. H. Evans and Christopher Loveluck*

Vol. 3 Farmers, Monks and Aristocrats: The Environmental Archaeology of Anglo-Saxon Flixborough *by Keith Dobney, Deborah Jaques, James Barrett and Cluny Johnstone*

Vol. 4 Rural Settlement, Lifestyles and Social Change in the Later First Millennium AD: Anglo-Saxon Flixborough in its Wider Context *by Christopher Loveluck*

Farmers, Monks and Aristocrats: the Environmental Archaeology of Anglo-Saxon Flixborough

by
Keith Dobney, Deborah Jaques, James Barrett
and Cluny Johnstone

with contributions by
Christopher Loveluck, Allan Hall, John Carrott,
Jerry Herman, David Slater, Courtney Nichols,
Susan Haynes, Amanda Bretman, Beverley La Ferla,
Gundula Muldner and Vaughan Grimes

OXBOW BOOKS

Published by
Oxbow Books, Oxford, UK

ISBN 978-1-84217-290-2

A CIP record for this book is available from the British Library

This book is available direct from

Oxbow Books, Oxford, UK
(Phone: 01865-241249; Fax: 01865-794449)

and

The David Brown Book Company
PO Box 511, Oakville, CT 06779, USA
(Phone: 860-945-9329; Fax: 860-945-9468)

or form our website

www.oxbowbooks.com

This book is published with the aid of a grant from English Heritage.

Front cover: Agricultural scenes taken from a ninth-century illuminated manuscript
(*Historiche, chronologische astronomische Schfriften, Salzburg vor 821.*
Copyright Austrian National Library, picture archive, Vienne Cod. 387, fol. 9v)

Back cover: Section of central ditch showing dark soil ash fill with concentrations of
bone (courtesy of Terry O'Connor)

Printed in Great Britain by
The Short Run Press Ltd, Exeter

This book is dedicated to those whom Anton Ervynck has fondly called…

"…. The Former Inhabitants of Flixborough…"!

Contents

1   INTRODUCTION AND RESEARCH OBJECTIVES
     by Keith Dobney and Christopher Loveluck

2   THE ARCHAEOLOGICAL BACKGROUND
     by Christopher Loveluck

3   CHRONOLOGY, RESIDUALITY, TAPHONOMY AND PRESERVATION
     by Christopher Loveluck, Keith Dobney, Deborah Jaques, James Barrett, Cluny Johnstone, John Carrott, Allan Hall, Amanda Bretman and Susan Haynes

7   THE AGRICULTURAL ECONOMY
      by Keith Dobney, Deborah Jaques, Cluny Johnstone, Allan Hall, Beverley La Ferla, and Susan Haynes

8   EXPLOITATION OF RESOURCES AND PROCUREMENT STRATEGIES
      by Keith Dobney, Deborah Jaques, James Barrett, Cluny Johnstone, John Carrott, Allan Hall,
      Jerry Herman, Courtney Nichols, Gundula Muldner and Vaughan Grimes

9   EVIDENCE FOR TRADE AND CONTACT
    by Keith Dobney, Deborah Jaques, James Barrett and Cluny Johnstone

10   ZOOARCHAEOLOGICAL EVIDENCE FOR THE NATURE AND CHARACTER OF THE SETTLEMENT
     by Keith Dobney, Deborah Jaques, James Barrett and Cluny Johnstone

APPENDIX 1. RECORDING PROTOCOL FOR MAMMAL AND BIRD REMAINS

List of Figures

List of Tables

List of Plates

Appendices – List of Tables

List of Contributors to the Flixborough Volumes

ARCHIBALD, MARION, Formerly Dept. of Coins and Medals, British Museum.

ATKINSON, DAVID, Senior Project Officer, Humber Field Archaeology.

BARRETT, JAMES, McDonald Institute for Archaeological Research, University of Cambridge.

BLINKHORN, PAUL, Northamptonshire Archaeology Unit.

BRETMAN, AMANDA, University of Leeds (biological work on geese bones).

BROOKS, MARGARET, English Heritage project conservator, Wiltshire Conservation Centre.

BROWN, MICHELLE P., Dept. of Manuscripts, British Library.

†CAMERON, KENNETH, Formerly Professor Emeritus, School of English, University of Nottingham.

CANTI, MATTHEW, English Heritage Archaeological Science.

CARROTT, JOHN, Palaeocology Research Services.

COPELAND, PENELOPE, Illustrator for much of Vol. 4.

COWGILL, JANE, Lindsey Archaeological Services.

CRAMP, ROSEMARY, Professor Emeritus, Dept. of Archaeology, Durham University.

DARRAH, RICHARD, Freelance consultant on historical uses of wood in buildings.

DIDSBURY, PETER, Freelance pottery consultant.

DOBNEY, KEITH, Dept. of Archaeology, Durham University (co-ordinator of the bioarchaeological research 1995–2000).

†EDWARDS, GLYNIS, English Heritage Archaeological Science.

EVANS, D. H., Archaeology Manager, Humber Archaeology Partnership. Joint editor of Vol. 2, and assistant editor for Vol. 1; project manager 2000–2005.

EVERSHED, RICHARD, Dept. of Biochemistry, University of Bristol; organic residue analysis.

EVISON, VERA L., Professor Emeritus, Institute of Archaeology, UCL, London.

FOOT, SARAH, Dept. of History, University of Sheffield.

FOREMAN, MARTIN, Assistant Keeper of Archaeology, Hull Museums and Galleries.

FRANKLAND, MICHAEL, Humber Field Archaeology; principal illustrator for these volumes.

GAUNT, GEOFFREY, University of Bradford; formerly British Geological Survey.

GEAKE, HELEN, Dept. of Archaeology, University of Cambridge.

GRIMES, VAUGHAN, Max Planck Institute, Leipzig (oxygen isotope analysis of dolphins)

HALL, ALLAN, Dept. of Archaeology, University of York.

HAYNES, SUSAN, UMIST (DNA research on geese bones).

HERMAN, JERRY, National Museum of Scotland, Edinburgh (cetacean remains).

HINES, JOHN, School of History and Archaeology, Cardiff University.

HUGHES, MICHAEL, Freelance specialist on ICPS analysis of pottery.

JAQUES, DEBORAH, Palaeoecology Research Services.

JOHNSTONE, CLUNY, Dept. of Archaeology, University of York.

JONES, JENNIFER, English Heritage conservator, Dept. of Archaeology, Durham University.

KENWARD, HARRY, Dept. of Archaeology, University of York.

LA FERLA, BEVERLEY, Dept. of Biological Sciences, University of York (linear enamel hypoplasia in pigs).

LOVELUCK, CHRISTOPHER, Dept. of Archaeology, University of Nottingham. Principal author and series editor; project manager 1996–2000.

MAKEY, PETER, Freelance lithics specialist.

MARSDEN, BILL, BM Photographic Services, Hull (detailed finds photographs).

MARSHALL, JOHN, Formerly Senior Illustrator with the Humber Archaeology Partnership.

MAYS, SIMON, English Heritage Archaeological Science.

MORTIMER, CATHERINE, Freelance archaeo-materials analyst.

MULDNER, GUNDULA, University of Reading (stable isotope analysis of dolphins).

NICHOLS, COURTNEY, Dept. of Biological Sciences, Durham University (DNA analysis on the dolphins).

O'CONNOR, SONIA, Conservation Laboratory, Dept. of Archaeological Sciences, University of Bradford.

O'CONNOR, T. P., Dept. of Archaeology, University of York.

OKASHA, ELIZABETH, Dept. of English, University College, Cork.

OTTAWAY, PATRICK, York Archaeological Trust.

PANTER, IAN, Head of Conservation, York Archaeological Trust.

PARKHOUSE, JONATHAN, Warwickshire Museum Field Services (Archaeology).

PATTERSON, ZOE, Freelance illustrator (Anglo-Saxon pottery).

PAYNE, ANDREW, English Heritage Archaeological Science.

PESTELL, TIM, Curator of Archaeology, Norwich Castle Museum & Art Gallery.

†PIRIE, ELIZABETH, Numismatic specialist.

ROFFE, DAVID, Dept. of History, University of Sheffield.

ROGERS, N. S. H., York Archaeological Trust.

ROGERS, PENELOPE WALTON, Anglo-Saxon Laboratory.

SITCH, BRYAN, Keeper of Archaeology, Hull Museums and Galleries.

SLATER, DAVID, Dept. Biological Sciences, University of York.

SMITH, LINDA, Formerly illustrator with the Humberside Archaeology Unit.

SMITH, REBECCA, Former Contract Illustrator, Humber Field Archaeology.

STARLEY, DAVID, Royal Armouries, Leeds (formerly Ancient Monuments Laboratory, English Heritage).

THOMAS, GABOR, Dept. of Archaeology, University of Kent (Canterbury).

TURNER, LESLIE, Former Contract illustrator, Humber Field Archaeology.

VINCE, ALAN, Freelance ceramic consultant.

WASTLING, LISA M., Senior Finds Officer, Humber Field Archaeology.

WATSON, JACQUI, English Heritage Archaeological Science.

YOUNG, JANE, Lindsey Archaeological Services.

YOUNGS, SUSAN M., Dept. of Prehistory & Europe, British Museum.

Abstract

Between 1989 and 1991, excavations adjacent to the former settlement of North Conesby, in the parish of Flixborough, North Lincolnshire, unearthed remains of an Anglo-Saxon settlement associated with one of the largest collections of artefacts and animal bones yet found on such a site. Analysis has demonstrated that the excavated part of the settlement was occupied, or used for settlement-related activity, throughout what have been termed the 'Mid' and 'Late' Anglo-Saxon periods. In an unprecedented occupation sequence from an Anglo-Saxon rural settlement, six main periods of occupation have been identified, with additional sub-phases, dating from the seventh to the early eleventh centuries; with a further period of activity, between the twelfth and fifteenth centuries AD.

The seventh- to early eleventh-century settlement remains were situated on a belt of windblown sand, overlooking the floodplain of the River Trent, eight kilometres south of the Humber estuary. The windblown sand had built up against the Liassic escarpment, to the east of the excavated area. The remains of approximately forty buildings and other structures were uncovered; and due to the survival of large refuse deposits, huge quantities of artefacts and animal bones were encountered compared with most other rural settlements of the period. Together, the different forms of evidence and their depositional circumstances provide an unprecedented picture of nearly all aspects of daily life on a settlement which probably housed elements of the contemporary social elite amongst its inhabitants, between the seventh and eleventh centuries. Furthermore, and perhaps even more importantly, the detailed analysis of the remains also provides indications of how the character of occupation changed radically during the later first millennium AD, when the area of what is now North Lincolnshire was incorporated, in chronological succession, within the Kingdom of Mercia, the Danelaw, and finally, the West Saxon and then Anglo-Danish Kingdom of England.

The publication of the remains of the Anglo-Saxon settlement is achieved in four volumes, and will be supported by an extensive archive on the Archaeological Data Service (ADS) for the United Kingdom. The excavation, post-excavation analysis and publication phases of the project have been funded principally by English Heritage, and the project has been run through the Humberside Archaeology Unit – now the Humber Archaeology Partnership.

The different volumes within the series of publications serve slightly different purposes. This volume presents an integrated analysis of the environmental remains. A broader thematic social analysis of the site is presented in Volume 4. There, interpretation of the settlement remains relating to themes such as the agricultural economy, craft-working, exchange, and problems of defining settlement character is (of necessity) viewed through the filter of site taphonomy and discernible patterns in the discard of artefacts and faunal remains. The undertaking of the thematic social analysis presented in Volume 4 depended on the extent to which deposits and their contents could be shown to be representative of the settlement as a whole, or the excavated area alone. Furthermore, analysis of changing trends through time could be achieved only through establishment of the existence of like deposits in different periods of the occupation sequence. Assessment of the parameters of interpretation possible in different periods of occupation rested on a range of factors. These comprised the refuse disposal strategies used; the extent of artefact residuality and re-deposition; survival factors relating to particular types of evidence: for example, artefact fragmentation and animal bone taphonomy; and the presence of intact occupation surfaces, within or in association with structures, e.g. floors within buildings.

The excavated settlement remains were both located upon, and sealed by blown sand; and the sealing deposits were up to two metres deep in places. Below this sand inundation, post-excavation analysis has identified evidence of six broad periods of settlement activity, with definable phases within them, dating from at least the early seventh century AD until the mid fourteenth/early fifteenth century. The overall stratigraphic sequence can be summarised as a series of phases of buildings and other structures, associated at different periods with refuse dumped around them in middens and yards, or with a central refuse zone in the shallow valley that ran up into the centre of the excavated area. Several of the main structural phases were also separated by demolition and levelling dumps and it is this superimposition that has resulted in the exceptional occupation sequence. The majority of the recovered finds, approximately 15,000 artefacts and hundreds of thousands of animal bone fragments, were found within these refuse, levelling and other occupation deposits. The high wood-ash content of a significant number of the dumps, their rapid build up, and the constant accretion of sand within them, formed a soil micro-environment which was chemically inert - the alkalinity of the wood-ash and sand accretion preventing acid leaching. It was this fortuitous burial environment that ensured the excellent preservation conditions for the artefact and vertebrate skeletal assemblages.

The environmental archaeological evidence from the site of Flixborough (in particular the animal bone assemblage) provides a series of unique insights into Anglo-Saxon life in England during the eighth to tenth centuries. The research reveals detailed evidence for the local and regional environment, many aspects of the local and regional agricultural economy, changing resource exploitation strategies and the extent of possible trade and exchange networks.

Perhaps the most important conclusions have been gleaned from the synthesis of these various lines of evidence, viewed in a broader archaeological context. Thus, bioarchaeological data from Flixborough have documented for the first time, in a detailed and systematic way, both site-specific and wider transformations in Anglo-Saxon life during the ninth century AD, and allow comment on the possible role of external factors such as the arrival of Scandinavians in the life and development of the settlement. The bioarchaeological evidence from Flixborough is also used to explore the tentative evidence revealed by more traditional archaeological materials for the presence during the ninth century of elements of monastic life. The vast majority of bioarchaeological evidence from Flixborough provides both direct and indirect evidence of the wealth and social standing of some of the inhabitants as well as a plethora of unique information about agricultural and provisioning practices associated with a major Anglo-Saxon estate centre.

The environmental archaeological record from Flixborough is without doubt one of the most important datasets surviving from the early medieval period, and one which will provide a key benchmark for future research into many aspects of early medieval rural life.

Zusammenfassung

Von 1989 bis 1991 fanden in der Nähe des aufgegebenen mittelalterlichen Dorfes North Conesby in der Gemeinde Flixborough, North Lincolnshire, Ausgrabungen statt, die eine angelsächsische Siedlung mit einem der umfangreichsten Spektren an Kleinfunden und Tierknochen, dass je an einem vergleichbaren Fundplatz entdeckt wurde, aufdeckten. Die Auswertung des Fundmaterials zeigte, dass der ergrabene Teil der Siedlung während der „mittleren" und „späten" angelsächsischen Zeit durchgehend bewohnt oder für siedlungsähnliche Tätigkeiten verwendet wurde. Anhand einer für eine ländliche angelsächsische Siedlung bisher einmaligen Nutzungsabfolge konnten sechs Hauptperioden mit mehreren Phasen identifiziert werden, die schwerpunktmäßig vom 7. bis zum 11. Jahrhundert, mit einer jüngsten Nutzung vom 12. bis in das 15. Jahrhundert, reichen.

Die Ansiedlung des 7. - 11. Jahrhunderts befand sich ca. acht Kilometer südlich des Humbermündungsgebiets in der Flussebene des Trent auf einer Erhebung aus Flugsand. Dieser hatte sich vor einem östlich der ergrabenen Fläche gelegenen liassischen Geländeabbruch angesammelt. Während der Ausgrabungen konnten die Reste von ca. 40 Gebäuden und anderen Strukturen, sowie Überreste von Abfallgruben, die im Vergleich mit ähnlichen Siedlungen erstaunlich große Mengen an Kleinfundmaterial und Tierknochen enthielten, identifiziert werden. Insbesondere wegen ihres guten Erhaltungszustands bieten die verschiedenen Fundmaterialgattungen einen einmaligen Einblick in fast alle Aspekte des täglichen Lebens einer Siedlung des 7. bis 11. Jahrhunderts, in der unter anderem Angehörige der damaligen sozialen Elite wohnten. Von größerer Relevanz ist jedoch, dass die detaillierte Analyse des Fundmaterials deutlich macht, wie drastisch sich die Nutzungscharakteristika der Siedlung im Laufe des ersten Jahrtausends nach Christus veränderten. Während dieser Zeit gehörte das heutige nördliche Lincolnshire nacheinander zum Königreich Mercia, dem Danelag und dem westsächsischen, später anglo-dänischen, Königreich England.

Die Publikation der Ausgrabungen der angelsächsischen Siedlung umfasst vier Bände, und wird durch ein umfangreiches Archiv im digitalen *Archaeological Data Service* (ADS) Großbritanniens ergänzt. Ausgrabungen, Auswertung und Publikation des Projekts wurden finanziell hauptsächlich von *English Heritage* getragen und von der *Humberside Archaeological Unit*, jetzt *The Humber Archaeology Partnership*, durchgeführt. Die verschiedenen Bände der Publikation erfüllen je unterschiedliche Rollen: Band 3 enthält eine integrierte Auswertung sämtlicher botanischer Überreste.

Weiterreichende Analysen der soziologischen Entwicklung des Fundplatzes sind in Band 4 enthalten. Dort werden archäologische Daten der Ausgrabungen auf der Basis taphonomischer Studien und erkennbarer Abfallentsorgungsstrategien im Rahmen verschiedener Thematiken wie agrarwirtschaftlicher Entwicklung, Materialverarbeitung, Handelsstrukturen und Problematiken der Definition des Siedlungscharakters aufgearbeitet. Die Aussagekraft derartiger thematischer Analysen hängt jedoch direkt davon ab, ob einzelne Schichten und deren Inhalte für die gesamte Siedlung oder nur deren ergrabenen Teil repräsentativ sind. Eine weiterreichende Diskussion gradueller Veränderungen in der Nutzung des Fundplatzes war nur anhand von Vergleichen ähnlicher Befunde in verschiedenen Siedlungsperioden möglich. Mehrere Faktoren bestimmten dabei, in welchem Maße Aussagen für einzelne Perioden gemacht werden konnten: Parameter, nach denen Abfall zu verschiedenen Zeitpunkten deponiert wurde, Verfälschung des Fundbilds durch Altfunde und Umlagerung, spezielle Erhaltungsfaktoren für bestimmte Fundgattungen wie Kleinfundzerfall oder Tierknochentaphonomie und die Existenz von intakten Siedlungsschichten wie existierenden Laufniveaus, die innerhalb von Strukturen gefunden wurden oder mit diesen assoziiert waren.

Die ergrabenen Siedlungsreste waren auf eine Schicht aus Flugsand gesetzt. Eine ähnliche Wehschicht, teils bis zu 2m tief, bedeckte sämtliche Funde. Unter dieser Sandmenge konnten 6 Hauptperioden der Ansiedlung mit zugehörigen, gut definierbaren Unterphasen identifiziert werden. Insgesamt datieren diese vom frühen 7. bis zur

Mitte des 14. Jahrhunderts, bzw. in das frühe 15. Jahrhundert. Die gesamte Schichtenabfolge kann als eine Reihe verschiedener Gebäude und anderer Strukturen mit zugehörigen Höfen und Abfallhäufen bzw. -gruben sowie einer zeitweise genutzten zentralen Abfallgrube im Bereich des flachen Tals im Zentrum der Grabungen zusammengefasst werden. Mehrere der Hauptbesiedlungsperioden sind durch Zerstörungsschichten und deren Planierungen klar trennbar, wodurch sich eine außergewöhnlich klare Nutzungssequenz ergibt. Der größte Teil der ungefähr 15.000 Kleinfunde und unzähligen (100.000+) Tierknochenfragmente stammt aus diesen Abfall-, Aufschüttungs- und anderen Nutzungsschichten. Eine bemerkenswerte Anzahl der Abfallgruben enthielt große Mengen von Holzasche. Dieser Faktor, sowie der schnelle Aufbau der Schichten und die konstante Ablagerung von Sand erzeugten ein konservierungstechnisches Mikroklima mit chemisch inaktivem Boden – die alkalische Holzasche verhinderte ein Zersetzen durch Säuren, die durch die Sandschicht drangen und deren Alkalinität aufhoben. Aufgrund dieses glücklichen Umstands waren sowohl Klein- als auch Knochenfunde außerordentlich gut erhalten.

Durch das botanische Fundmaterial der Ausgrabungen in Flixborough und insbesondere die Tierknochenfunde ergibt sich eine ganze Reihe erstaunlicher Einblicke in das tägliche Leben einer angelsächsischen Siedlung in England während des 8. bis 10. Jahrhunderts. Die Auswertung dieser Funde ermöglicht nicht nur Aussagen über lokale und regionale Flora und Fauna, sondern auch über verschiedene Aspekte der örtlichen und regionalen Agrarwirtschaft. Anhand botanischer Überreste konnten ferner Veränderungen in der Nutzung vorhandener Ressourcen sowie im Bestehen und Ausmaß von Handels- und Austauschnetzen festgestellt werden.

Die wahrscheinlich interessantesten Resultate des Projekts ergaben sich aus der Synthese dieser verschiedenen Fund- und Befundgattungen, die in einem weiteren archäologischen Rahmen untersucht wurden. So konnten anhand der bioarchäologischen Überreste zum ersten Mal sowohl fundplatzspezifische als auch weiterreichende Veränderungen im täglichen Leben einer angelsächsischen Siedlung des 9. Jahrhunderts n. Chr. systematisch und detailliert festgestellt werden. Weiterhin ermöglichten diese Daten Aussagen über mögliche externe Einflüsse, wie z. B. die Ankunft skandinavischer Siedler, auf das Leben und die Entwicklung des Fundplatzes. Das bioarchäologische Fundmaterial aus Flixborough bietet zudem einen weiteren Ansatzpunkt zur Diskussion einer anhand traditionellerer Fundgattungen nur andeutungsweise erkennbaren Präsenz monastischer Elemente im 9. Jahrhundert. Der Grossteil des bioarchäologischen Materials aus Flixborough liefert sowohl direkte als auch indirekte Nachweise des Reichtums und sozialen Status einiger Einwohner, sowie unzählige Informationen zu den landwirtschaftlichen Nutzungs- und Versorgungsstrategien eines wichtigen angelsächsischen Siedlungszentrums.

Das botanische Fundspektrum Flixboroughs ist somit zweifelsohne eines der wichtigsten Datensets des frühen Mittelalters. Als solches ist es wahrscheinlich, dass dieses Forschungsprojekt auch in Zukunft für Forschungsarbeiten zu verschiedenen Aspekten des ländlichen Lebens im Frühmittelalter maßgeblich bleiben wird.

Translated by Christoph Rummel

Résumé

Entre 1989 et 1991, des fouilles adjacentes à l'ancien établissement de North Conesby, dans la paroisse de Flixborough, North Lincolnshire, mirent à jour les vestiges d'un établissement Anglo-saxon associés à l'une des plus larges collections d'artefacts et d'ossements animaux jamais trouvée sur un tel site. Les analyses ont montré que la partie fouillée de l'établissement était occupée, ou utilisée pour des activités liées à l'établissement, pendant ce qu'on a appelé le « Milieu » et la « Fin » de l'époque Anglo-saxonne. Grâce à cet exemple sans précédent de séquence d'occupation d'un établissement Anglo-saxon rural, on a identifié six périodes d'occupation principales, avec des sous phases supplémentaires, qui vont du septième au début du onzième siècle ; avec une autre période d'activité située entre le douzième et le quinzième siècle après JC.

Les vestiges de l'établissement datant du septième au début du onzième siècle se trouvaient sur une région de sablon, qui dominait la plaine inondable de la rivière Trent, située à huit kilomètres au sud de l'estuaire de la rivière Humber. Le sablon s'était accumulé le long de l'escarpement liasique, à l'est de la zone fouillée. On mit à jour les restes d'environ quarante bâtiments et autres structures ; et, grâce à la présence d'importants dépôts de détritus, on a découvert de grandes quantités d'artefacts et de restes animaux, contrairement à la plupart des autres établissements ruraux de la période. Les différentes formes de preuves, ainsi que les circonstances de leur déposition, fournissent une image sans précédent de presque tous les aspects de la vie quotidienne dans un établissement qui comptait certainement, entre le septième et le onzième siècle, des membres de l'élite sociale de l'époque parmi ses habitants. De plus, et peut-être surtout, les analyses détaillées des vestiges fournissent aussi des indications quant au changement radical du caractère de l'occupation pendant la fin du premier millénaire après JC, quand la région de l'actuel North Lincolnshire fut incorporée, chronologiquement, au Royaume de Mercie, au Daneslaw, et enfin au Royaume d'Angleterre Saxon de l'Ouest, puis Anglo-Danois.

La publication des vestiges de l'établissement Anglo-saxon se compose de quatre volumes, et s'appuiera sur les nombreuses archives du Service de Données Archéologiques (*Archaeological Data Service,* ou *ADS*) du Royaume-Uni. Les fouilles, analyses post-fouilles, et les phases de publication du projet ont été financées principalement par English Heritage (organisme Britannique de protection du patrimoine historique), et le projet fut mené à bien par l'Unité Archéologique du Humberside (Humberside Archaeology Unit), désormais connue sous le nom de Humberside Archaeology Partnership. Les différents volumes qui composent la série de publication ont des objectifs qui diffèrent quelque peu. Ce volume-ci présente une analyse intégrée des restes environnementaux.

Une analyse sociale thématique plus large du site est présentée dans le Volume 4. L'interprétation des restes de l'établissement par rapport à des thèmes tels que l'économie agricole, l'artisanat, l'échange, et par rapport aux problèmes quant à la définition du caractère de l'établissement, y est nécessairement vue à travers le filtre de la taphonomie du site et des schémas discernables de déposition d'objets et restes animaux. Le déroulement de l'analyse sociale thématique présentée dans le Volume 4 dépendait de la possibilité de montrer à quel point les dépôts et leurs contenus étaient représentatifs de l'établissement entier, ou de la zone fouillée seule. De plus, les analyses de l'évolution des tendances à travers le temps n'ont été possibles qu'après avoir déterminé l'existence de dépôts similaires à différentes périodes de la séquence d'occupation. L'évaluation des paramètres d'interprétations possibles à différentes périodes d'occupation reposait sur plusieurs facteurs. Ceux-ci comprenaient les stratégies d'élimination des détritus utilisées; la quantité d'artefacts résiduels et redéposés; les facteurs de survie de certains types de preuves: par exemple, la fragmentation des artefacts, et la taphonomie des ossements animaux; ainsi que la présence de surfaces d'occupation intactes, à l'intérieur ou associées à des structures, comme par exemple les sols à l'intérieur de bâtiments.

Les vestiges de l'établissement qui ont été fouillés se situaient sur le sablon, et ils en étaient également recouverts. Ce dépôt de couverture mesurait jusqu'à 2 mètres de profondeur par endroit. Sous cette épaisseur de sable, les analyses post-fouilles ont pu identifier 6 périodes d'activités de l'établissement, qui comprennent leurs propres sous-phases, et qui dataient au moins du début du septième siècle et allaient jusqu' au milieu du quatorzième/début du quinzième siècle après JC. La séquence stratigraphique générale peut se résumer à une série de phases de construction de bâtisses et autres structures, associée au cours de différentes périodes à des détritus répandus ou amassés autours des structures, ou encore à une zone centrale d'amoncellement de détritus dans la petite vallée qui s'étendait jusqu'au centre de la zone de fouilles. Plusieurs de ces phases structurelles principales étaient aussi séparées par des couches de gravats provenant de démolition et de nivellement, et c'est cette superposition qui rend la séquence d'occupation exceptionnelle. La plupart des découvertes (environ 15000 artefacts et des centaines de milliers de fragments d'os animaux) provenaient de ces amas de détritus, couches de déblaiement, et autres dépôts liés à l'occupation. Un nombre significatif de ces amas se distinguent par une forte proportion de cendre de bois, leur formation rapide, et l'apport constant de sablon, ce qui a provoqué la formation d'un microenvironnement du sol qui était chimiquement inerte: Les cendres de bois alcalines et l'apport de sablon ont empêché le lessivage acide. Cet ensevelissement fortuit a permis d'excellentes conditions de conservation des artefacts et d'ensembles d'ossements articulés.

Les preuves archéologiques environnementales du site de Flixborough (en particulier les ensembles d'ossements animaux) nous ouvrent des perspectives exceptionnelles sur la vie Anglo-saxonne en Angleterre du huitième au dixième siècle. Les recherches révèlent des preuves détaillées de l'environnement local et régional, maints aspects de l'économie agricole locale et régionale, l'évolution des stratégies d'exploitation des ressources, et l'étendue d'éventuels réseaux de commerce et d'échange.

Les conclusions les plus importantes furent peut-être obtenues grâce à la synthèse de ces différents ensembles de preuves, vues dans un contexte archéologique élargi. Ainsi, les données bioarchéologiques de Flixborough ont montré pour la première fois, d'une manière détaillée et systématique, des transformations à la fois spécifique au site et d'autres plus générales de la vie Anglo-saxonne pendant le neuvième siècle après JC, et elles ouvrent la voie à une réflexion sur le rôle possible de facteurs externes tels que l'arrivée de Scandinaves dans la vie et le développement de l'établissement. Les preuves bioarchéologiques provenant de Flixborough sont également utilisées pour explorer les preuves expérimentales révélées par des matériaux archéologiques plus traditionnels de la présence d'éléments de vie monastique au cours du neuvième siècle. La grande majorité des preuves bioarchéologiques de Flixborough fournit des preuves à la fois directes et indirectes de la richesse et position sociale de certains des habitants, ainsi qu'une foule d'informations uniques sur les pratiques agricoles et d'approvisionnement associées à un établissement Anglo-saxon de grande importance.

Les archives archéologiques environnementales de Flixborough font sans aucun doute partie des ensembles de données les plus importants qui subsistent du début de l'époque médiévale, et elles fourniront un point de référence incontournable pour la recherche future sur de nombreux aspects de la vie rurale du début de l'époque médiévale.

Traduit par Sterenn Girard-Suard

Preface and Acknowledgements

This monograph is the culmination of over 13 years of punctuated work which began shortly after I began work at the Environmental Archaeology Unit, at the University of York in 1991. Despite a number of setbacks and changes in fortunes of a number of the organisations, research groups and individuals involved, the project (funded by English Heritage) was kept alive by the efforts and sheer determination of a range of dedicated people, all of whom shared a common goal: to explore and bring to the attention of others the significant (and many of us would argue unique) archaeological and biological record from one of the most important early medieval sites ever excavated in England.

It was clear from the early 'assessment' phases of the project that the sheer scale of the bioarchaeological evidence from Flixborough (specifically the vertebrate assemblage) had the potential to significantly improve and even alter our understanding of the middle to late Saxon period, in a way (dare I say), rarely attempted. This assertion only grew stronger throughout the duration of the project as more of the evidence was revealed, and as I hope this final publication attests.

The goal throughout has been to research the bio-archaeological evidence in detail, in a way that went beyond the mere reconstruction of dietary preferences of the inhabitants (although this has obviously remained a central tenet), to one which placed the evidence at the heart of a wider archaeological narrative. The more broadly 'themed' structure of this monograph may, therefore, not appeal to some bioarchaeological colleagues, who perhaps would prefer a more traditional 'environmental report' – although in this respect we have also tried to provide as much detailed evidence as possible in order to satisfy those wishing to explore the bioarchaeological record in more depth. Such a traditional structure has been deliberately avoided in an attempt to a) do the evidence justice in a wider archaeological context and b) help those outside our so-called specialist field explore the bioarchaeological evidence within a much broader interpretative archaeological (and thus more familiar) framework. Whether we have succeeded in either of these goals, can only be judged by those who read it!

A great many individuals and organisations have been involved over the last decade in helping to bring the Flixborough bioarchaeological project to its conclusion. Although there is not space enough in this volume to list them all, the following deserve special thanks for their efforts and support:

Firstly the principal authors would like to acknowledge the work of the additional contributors to the volume: Chris Loveluck (now of the University of Nottingham) for archaeological input and textual references to Continental sites; Allan Hall (University of York) for the archaeobotanical analyses; John Carrott (Palaeoecology Research Services) for the molluscan analyses; David Slater (University of York) for his contribution to Chapters 5 and 8; Jerry Herman (National Museum of Scotland, Edinburgh) for the identification of the Flixborough cetacean remains and for his contribution to Chapter 8; Courtney Nichols (Durham University) who undertook the ancient DNA work on the Flixborough bottlenose dolphins and for her contribution to Chapter 8; Gundula Muldner (University of Reading), and Vaughan Grimes (Max Planck Institute, Leipzig), for isotope analyses of the Flixborough bottlenose dolphins; my PhD student Susan Haynes (now of UMIST) who undertook the ancient DNA research on the geese bones and Amanda Bretman (now of the University of Leeds) for undertaking the histological work on the geese remains and both their contributions to Chapters 6 and 7; Beverley La Ferla (University of York) for her study of linear enamel hypoplasia in the pigs and her contribution to Chapter 7.

Thanks are also due to the numerous other students who undertook a variety of dissertation topics on the Flixborough animal bones – especially: Thadsin Panithanarak (Dept of Biology PhD student at York University) who recently completed ancient DNA research on the crane bones from Flixborough – soon to be published; my PhD student Ian Barnes (now of Royal Holloway) who began the aDNA research on the geese; John Harwood and Deborah Petterson (University of York) for their work on the introductions and extinctions of mammals into the North of Britain; Alex Tams

(Durham University) for his work on pig tooth wear.

Others who deserve special mention are; Anton Ervynck (The Flemish Heritage Institute and University of Ghent) and Umberto Albarella (University of Durham), both of whom have provided valuable advice and insight into various aspects of analyses and interpretation over the last years; their input has been greatly appreciated (although we still agree to disagree over several of the conclusions). Anton Ervynck has also had the unenviable task of reading this first draft, whilst Umberto has kindly allowed unpublished data to be used for comparative purposes in Chapter 10 (data regarding use of bird signatures). Ingrid Mainland (University of Bradford) and several MSc students of the University of Sheffield also provided valuable technical assistance by systematically sorting and providing basic data from the many wet-sieved samples. Thanks are also due to Kathryn Johnson (Palaeoecology Research Services), whose tireless and valuable editorial assistance ensured the eventual submission of the first manuscript.

Others who deserve special mention for their support and encouragement throughout the project include Tim Williams (now of the Institute of Archaeology), Chris Scull (English Heritage), Simon Davis (now of Instituto Português de Arqueologia), Peter Young and Jeremy Searle (Department of Biology, University of York) and Dave Evans (Humber Archaeology Partnership – the current project manager).

Institutions and organisations whose support has also been invaluable include The Humberside Archaeological Unit (now Humber Archaeological Partnership – HAP), University of York Biology Department and its former Environmental Archaeology Unit (where most of the bone sorting, identification and recording was carried out), staff at the British Library for providing hours of stimulating references to falconry and wildfowling, and most importantly English Heritage who provided long-term major funding for the assessment, analytical and publication phases of the bioarchaeological research.

With regard to the analysis of the fish bone assemblage, special thanks are owed to the many colleagues who have assisted with the provision of (often unpublished) reports, not all of which could be explicitly cited: Alison Locker, Ruby Cerón-Carrasco, Rebecca Nicholson, Sheila Hamilton-Dyer, Dale Serjeantson, Polydora Baker, Terry O'Connor, Inge Enghoff and Jane Richardson. Inge Enghoff and Andrew Jones kindly helped with several difficult identification issues.

A special thanks is due to Chris Loveluck, friend and colleague (and erstwhile project manager of the entire Flixborough post-excavation project), whose continued (and at times dogged) support of the bioarchaeological research programme (even after he had left to take up a British Academy Fellowship at the University of Southampton), kept the whole logistical and intellectual academic process on track.

I would specifically like to acknowledge the continued financial support of the Wellcome Trust, who have funded my wider research activities over the last 4 years and who have (indirectly) ensured the completion of this project after I left English Heritage. I would also like to thank the Department of Archaeology, Durham University for providing me with a new research home.

Finally, I would like to thank the most important contributors to this research project, whom Anton Ervynck has often referred to in more lighthearted moments as *"the former inhabitants of Flixborough"*. Without their vast appetite for meat, fowl and fish, and their desire for organised refuse disposal, there would be no evidence to discuss. I dedicate this book to them.

Dr Keith Dobney
Durham University
29th April 2007

1 Introduction and Research Objectives

Keith Dobney and Christopher Loveluck

1.1 Introduction

Between 1989 and 1991, excavations within the parish of Flixborough, North Lincolnshire, uncovered the remains of an exceptionally wealthy Anglo-Saxon settlement, 8km south of the Humber estuary, overlooking the floodplain of the River Trent (Fig. 1.1). Analysis has demonstrated that the excavated part of the settlement was occupied, or used for settlement-related activity, throughout the Middle and Late Saxon periods (see Loveluck and Atkinson in Volume 1, Chapter 4). In an unprecedented vertical stratigraphic sequence from an Anglo-Saxon rural settlement, six main periods of occupation were identified, with additional sub-phases, dating from the early seventh to the early eleventh century, and a further period of High Medieval activity. The remains of approximately forty buildings and other structures were uncovered, and vast quantities of artefacts and animal bones were retrieved. Together, the different forms of evidence and their depositional circumstances provide an unprecedented picture of nearly all aspects of daily life during the Middle and Late Saxon periods, on a settlement which probably housed elements of the contemporaneous social elite amongst the spectrum of its inhabitants. Furthermore, and perhaps even more importantly, the detailed analysis of the remains also provides indications of how the character of occupation changed radically during the second half of the first millennium. The reasons for these changes are a matter for detailed debate in both this and the other volumes of the Flixborough publications (see particularly Volume 4).

The bioarchaeological evidence, the principal focus of this volume, addresses a variety of issues, many of which, not surprisingly, relate to economic and environmental aspects of the settlement itself. This traditional view of the role of environmental archaeology has, however, sadly hampered the realisation of its broader potential in addressing a much wider range of important archaeological questions. The full exploration and subsequent integration of bioarchaeological evidence is, therefore, still rare in many reports and publications. This volume attempts to move away from the rather standardised presentation and discussion of bioarchaeological data (usually as distinctly separate classes of information – i.e. by species or higher taxa) that has been the norm for some considerable time. Although much of the same evidence is still presented, the structure of the volume is set out in such a way as to further explore broader archaeological themes, many of which have relevance beyond the so-called perceived 'specialist' fields of zooarchaeology or archaeobotany.

1.2 Research Objectives

Despite the existence of written sources, and decades of excavation, our current, somewhat limited, knowledge of the dynamics of Middle and Late Saxon economics in England, render any research into the archaeology of this period of national priority. The quality of the archaeological evidence contained within the settlement sequence at Flixborough is, therefore, particularly important for both the examination of site-specific issues, and for the investigation of wider research themes and problems currently facing Middle and Late Anglo-Saxon settlement studies. For example, with regard to site-specific research, the remains provide an exceptional opportunity for reconstructing the changing character of the settlement's economy, and aspects of its relationships with its surrounding landscape and region. Whereas, at a broader level, amongst other themes, the wider comparison of the traits evident at Flixborough enables a re-assessment of the problems of defining the status and character of Middle and Late Saxon rural settlements from their archaeological remains. At the same time, it is also possible that certain observable trends in the evidence reflect the changing relationships between rural and urban settlements in the period between the eighth and eleventh centuries.

A range of broad and more specific academic objectives which the various bioarchaeological (and other) remains could help to address, were outlined in the original material assessment report (Whitwell 1994). These can be summarised as follows:

– determine structural details of buildings through surviving structural materials such as wood and roofing materials
– establish the range of activities represented by the various bioarchaeological remains recovered from the site
– determine the extent to which individual buildings or areas can be associated with specific activities or functions
– establish fluctuations in the character of occupation
– determine any evidence for planning or organisation of the site
– consider the status of the settlement, particularly in relation to the suggested religious and/or aristocratic connections
– determine the place of Flixborough in the local manorial, administrative and ecclesiastical hierarchy
– attempt to 'place' Flixborough into its local topographic context by understanding the contemporary surrounding environment
– establish Flixborough's position in the regional economy of Lindsey (including consideration of locally and regionally traded goods
– establish 'finds profiles' for Flixborough and other relevant sites in the UK and on the continent
– elucidate evidence for cultural trading and political links with Lindsey and further afield
– conduct a re-assessment of the concept of 'high-status' Mid-Saxon sites.

More specific avenues of potential for the bioarchaeological remains were highlighted in the updated project design subsequently submitted to English Heritage (Loveluck 1996). These included investigation of:

– the various components of the agrarian economy (animal husbandry as well as the arable and horticultural aspects)
– the exploitation of woodland resources (for construction purposes and fuel)
– the environmental conditions in the vicinity of the settlement
– the relationship between the settlement and its immediate hinterland
– the patterns of consumption
– the character and status of the settlement as a producing and/or consuming community within the local Mid-Saxon settlement hierarchy.

The nature and extent to which the various bioarchaeological groups of material (animals and plants) can address these questions rests on the quality of the surviving evidence, which, in the case of Flixborough, is extremely variable. The identifiable charred plant assemblage was very small and represented in only a few restricted contexts. As a result, charred plant remains have provided very little information on arable and horticultural practices at the site (Chapter 7). They did, however, provide invaluable evidence (along with molluscs) for a specific resource exploitation of the nearby coastal saltmarshes (see Chapter 8). Charcoal provided some useful hints as to what kinds of wood were used for fuel and for structural purposes (Chapter 8), whilst (with the animal bones), molluscs and charred plant remains enabled a plausible (and in some cases detailed) view of aspects of the early medieval environment to be reconstructed (Chapter 5).

As previously mentioned, however, it is the zooarchaeological assemblage (including marine molluscs) which has provided the most comprehensive basis for addressing the greatest number of the research questions outlined above. For Britain as a whole (and particularly the north of England), well-dated vertebrate assemblages of early medieval date are somewhat limited in number and distribution. Problems with site visibility, context integrity, scale of excavation, length of occupation sequences and dating have rendered many of these assemblages of limited interpretative value, whilst the study of specifically Middle to Late Saxon animal bones has also been biased by the rarity of sites, and by a focus towards the excavation of monastic centres. Sites where large vertebrate assemblages can be linked with good vertical stratigraphy and dating evidence, and where material has been recovered using systematic procedures involving sieving and sampling (as at Flixborough), are, therefore, extremely important.

The vertebrate remains are of particular value for the investigation of the specific facets of the economy of such a settlement, especially animal husbandry (Chapter 7), exploitation of wild vertebrate resources (Chapter 8), and trade and exchange links (Chapter 9). However, these and more fundamental questions relating to the nature and character of the settlement (Chapter 10) can only be framed and subsequently addressed within an established research framework linked to our current understanding of the Middle to Late Saxon period in England – a brief summary of which follows.

Rural settlements

Although it is still uncertain how, or if, Mid-Saxon (7th-8th centuries AD) rural estate holdings were different to those of the Early Saxon period, it is generally assumed that a similar territorial structure to that of the Late Roman period still existed. By the Mid-Saxon period, extant documentary evidence appears to confirm this assumption and indicates the existence of the large estates incorporating within them a mosaic of resource areas. However, during the Mid-Saxon period we see, not only an increase in general size of these estates, but also

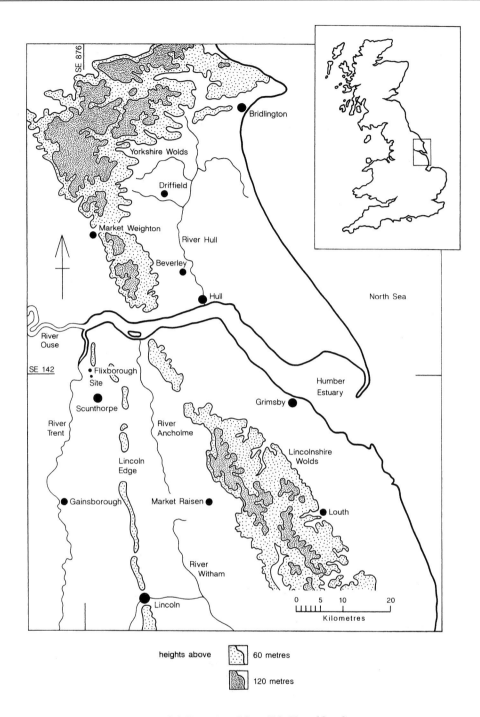

FIG. 1.1 Location Map (M. Frankland).

increasing complexity in land-holding with the introduction of *bocland*. This development witnesses the
beginnings of ecclesiastical estates under charter,
whereby Kings and secular aristocrats donated large
estates or portions of them to the church. As a result, the
new monastic estates, as well as old established secular
aristocratic land-holdings, subsumed large adjacent
territories, as well as smaller far-flung holdings, with
rights of access to certain resources (e.g. domestic
livestock, wild terrestrial and marine resources, and
woodland).

From *circa* mid ninth century AD, (Late Saxon/Anglo-
Scandinavian period), these large monastic and secular
estates began to be broken up into smaller territorial
holdings. In the north of England, this occurred as a
result of a combination of factors. The first and perhaps
most obvious, was the settling of the 'Great Army' in AD
876. However, the jealousy of the secular aristocrats
towards large ecclesiastical estates may have contributed
in some degree to their reduction in size, perhaps through
the deliberate confiscation of land in areas not affected
by Viking raids. Changes in the patterns of land-holding,

however, appear to have already begun in the early ninth century, heralding a period of major social and economic upheaval.

During the tenth century (by and large), the pattern of land ownership appears to be reflected by much smaller secular estate holdings and monastic estates than those of the Mid-Saxon period. Direct consequences of this must have been the dislocation from previous far-flung holdings and rights of access to a range of resources. This would have resulted in a change in the production/ subsistence pattern towards a more intensive system and the need for more trade. Through the 10th–11th centuries, elite groups (Anglo-Scandinavians in the north) were linked with enlarged secular aristocratic estates.

The historical evidence for hierarchies of sites bound together on large estates provides ideal opportunities to study their inter-relationships. The movements of products (such as domestic and wild animals) in the form of taxation/renders to high-status estate centres like Flixborough, is certainly something that can help explore further the nature and character of Anglo-Saxon 'clientship'. The presence of numerous wild species (particularly birds and fish) in the Flixborough assemblage, as well as providing a superb opportunity to explore the palaeoecology of the vicinity of the site, allows a more thorough definition of the different territories that were exploited by its inhabitants.

The emporia and urban development

Our understanding of so-called 'proto-urban' settlements in the north of England is severely hampered by extremely small numbers of sites and their associated samples of vertebrate remains. For the Mid-Saxon period, the only such site is Fishergate, York – assumed to be the *wic* or emporium (trading centre) known as Eoforwic. Archaeological evidence of *wics* throughout England indicates direct evidence of trading and craft specialisation. The nature of occupation at these sites is not well understood, and it is not clear whether they were occupied permanently, or at intervals throughout the year, or even who inhabited them. It appears to be the case (from documentary evidence on tenurial structure) that these were externally provisioned from their rural hinterlands. A tenuous case for this has been made for the vertebrate remains from Fishergate (O'Connor 2001).

The nature of the relationship between the Mid-Saxon emporia and their rural hinterlands, whether with high-status monastic or secular estates such as Flixborough, is still unclear. A number of clues can be gleaned from, for example, specialist craft activities which although present at *wic* sites, can also be demonstrated at rural sites such as Flixborough (for more detailed evidence of these see Volume 4). Luxury imported commodities (e.g. pottery and lava quernstones) were also reaching a wide range of sites in the immediate hinterlands of the *wics*, especially so-called high-status centres (such as Flixborough). This almost certainly reflects direct contact occurring along the coast and major estuaries (in the case of eastern England, both north and south of the Humber). It is, therefore, likely that the movement and importation of luxury commodities in the region was directly controlled by Anglo-Saxon kings and their trading posts. These emporia or *wics* were probably trading settlements partly fulfilling a customs and excise role, (in order to control supplies of important commodities and, at the same time, levy duties upon them), as well as being limited production centres.

The development of the major urban centres such as Jorvik (York) and Lincoln, during the Late Saxon/Anglo-Scandinavian period in the north of England, and the role they played in transforming the political and economic status of the Saxon estate structure, is still not well understood. During this period, it is apparent that a major decrease in specialist craft activities occurs in the rural estate centres, with large-scale specialist craft activities and production shifting into the developing towns. At the same time, imported luxury commodities also become concentrated in these new urban centres, and do not appear to be widely dispersed into the hinterland, even at high-status rural settlements such as Flixborough. This implies that perhaps the importation and distribution of luxury commodities were at that time controlled by Scandinavians within the towns. This could also be the case for agricultural surplus and access to higher-status resources such as wild game.

At the same time, expressions of wealth and status by rural estate holders may have altered significantly. Aspects of this could well be reflected in changes in the consumption of regional resources from more local estate holdings (e.g. increased numbers of livestock and/or of more commonly occurring wild resources such as wildfowl). Comparisons between the vertebrate assemblages from Flixborough and Anglo-Scandinavian York and Lincoln would help resolve these questions.

In certain aspects of material culture therefore, the Anglo-Scandinavian towns could be said to be more 'divorced' from their hinterlands than their predecessors (i.e. Mid-Saxon *wics* or emporia) in terms of their control and distribution of a range of resources. Although both Middle and Late Saxon systems reflect methods of control and taxation, the growing bodies of diverse archaeological evidence (including animal bones) may indicate that the systems were very different. Contrasting the complex interaction between rural and urban occupation dynamics for the later 9th and 10th centuries could further refine our views on the relationship between two kinds of contemporaneous consumer economies. It is, therefore, obvious that we should utilise bioarchaeological evidence in broader studies which aim to explore aspects of the social and economic infrastructure of these periods and settlement types.

2   The Archaeological Background

Christopher Loveluck

2.1 Topographical setting and circumstances of discovery

The Anglo-Saxon settlement at Flixborough was situated on a belt of windblown sand which had built up against the Liassic escarpment, immediately to the east of the excavations (see Gaunt in Volume 1, Chapter 1). Until the seventeenth and eighteenth centuries, this belt of windblown sand was located on the interface between two environmental zones. These comprised the wetlands of the lower floodplain and delta areas of the River Trent, situated to the west and north, and the well-drained soils of the Lincoln Edge, on the escarpment to the east (Gaunt 1975, 15; Lillie 1998, 51–52; see also Gaunt in Volume 4, Chapter 4). Descriptive impressions of this landscape, with its meres, marshes, sand belts of pasture and arable land, together with occasional woodland, can be gleaned to a certain extent from the Domesday survey of 1086 (Foster and Longley 1924; Darby 1987, 103–108). They can also be visualised more fully from John Leland's account of his journey of 1544, from Gainsborough through to the Isle of Axholme (Chandler 1993, 294–297).

The excavated part of the Anglo-Saxon settlement was located upon and adjacent to a spur on the sand belt, with a shallow valley extending into the central part of the site. Derrick Riley first identified settlement remains in this area in 1933, following the recovery of Maxey-type pottery and loom-weights. Unfortunately, this type of pottery was not identified as Mid-Saxon in date until Addyman's excavations at Maxey, in Northamptonshire (Addyman 1964). Consequently, Riley concluded (in his unpublished notebook) that the settlement was Romano-British in date. Harold Dudley also referred to his recovery of Anglo-Saxon remains from nearby Conesby, although the exact geographical relationship of these finds to the excavated settlement evidence is unclear (Dudley 1931, 44).

Prior to the quarrying of sand on the site, the settlement was confirmed as dating from the Anglo-Saxon period, during an archaeological evaluation in 1988 by Dr Kevin Leahy, Keeper of Archaeology and Natural History, at Scunthorpe Museum. This evaluation uncovered the remains of eleven east-west aligned inhumation graves, without grave-goods (Leahy FX 88 archive; Leahy 1995). Some of the burials were interred in coffins or chests, with iron fittings identical to those from other Anglo-Saxon cemeteries in the surrounding region, dating from the period between the seventh and ninth centuries AD (Mortimer 1905, 254–257; Ottaway 1996, 99–100). The partial foundations of possible buildings were also uncovered during this evaluation. As a consequence, therefore, English Heritage funded the Humberside Archaeology Unit (now Humber Field Archaeology) to conduct further evaluations, which resulted in a two-year programme of excavations on the settlement, from 1989 to 1991 (Plate 2.1).

Between 1991 and 1995, further geophysical, magnetic susceptibility and surface collection surveys were undertaken, and additional evaluation trenches were excavated. They demonstrated that Middle and Late Saxon archaeological evidence, as well as scatters of Romano-British and medieval artefacts, extended both to the north and south on the sand belt, and also eastward towards the limestone escarpment. The remains from the Flixborough excavations, therefore, represent only a sample of the multi-period settlement activity in the vicinity (Loveluck and McKenna 1999; see also Loveluck Volume 1, Chapter 2 and Andrew Payne's contributions to Volume 1, Chapter 2).

2.2 The Anglo-Saxon occupation sequence

The evidence for Anglo-Saxon settlement was sealed by windblown sand, up to two metres deep in places. Below this sand inundation lay evidence of six broad periods of settlement activity, with definable phases within them, dating from at least the early seventh century AD until the mid fourteenth century. The overall stratigraphic sequence can be summarised as a series of structural phases, often associated with refuse in middens or yards around buildings, or with larger refuse deposits, which were cast into a shallow valley that ran up into the centre of the excavated area (FIG. 2.1). Several of the main structural phases were also separated by demolition and levelling dumps, and it is this superimposition, that has resulted in the survival of an exceptional Anglo-Saxon occupation sequence. Most of the approximately 15,000 artefacts and 200,000 animal bones recovered were found within these refuse, levelling, and other occupation deposits. The high wood-ash content of a significant

number of the dumps, their rapid build up, and the constant accretion of sand within them, formed a burial micro-environment which was chemically neutral – the alkalinity of the wood-ash and sand accretion preventing acid leaching (Canti 1992, 18; Canti, Volume 1, Chapter 2). It was this fortuitous burial environment that ensured the excellent preservation conditions for the artefact and zooarchaeological assemblages.

The earliest period of activity, ascribed to the seventh century comprised the remains of three buildings on two building plots (see FIGS 3.1 and 3.2, Volume 1)). The early buildings, in the south of the site, had post-hole foundations, although ghosts of posts or planks were absent. The fills of the post-holes from the southern buildings contained predominantly mid to late fourth-century Romano-British pottery; Early Saxon local wares; and Early Saxon Charnwood-type ware from Leicestershire; the post-hole fills of the demolished buildings of Phase 1b also contained the first Maxey-type ware from the settlement sequence (Williams and Vince 1997, 219–

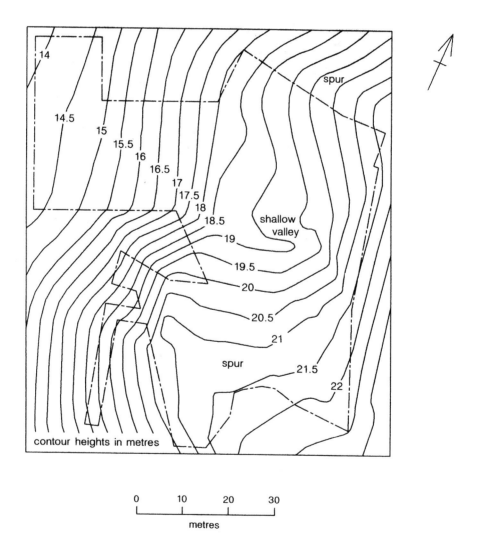

FIG. 2.1 *Contour map of the excavated area, 1989–1991, showing the sand spurs and the central shallow valley* (M. Frankland).

220; see Volume 2, Chapter 12; see also Chapter 3, this volume). The spout of an oxidised (red-orange) pottery pitcher, possibly imported from northern France during the seventh century, was also recovered from a post-hole of the latter phase (see Vince in Volume 2, Chapter 12). The location of the earliest buildings in the south-eastern part of the excavated area suggests that they represent the periphery of an Early Anglo-Saxon settlement focus, in the immediate vicinity. The recovery (as residual finds) of fragments of small-long brooches, annular brooches, and a mid sixth-century Great square-headed brooch, also hints at the presence of an Early Saxon settlement focus, and possibly a cemetery nearby (Hines, Volume 2, Chapter 1; Rogers, Volume 2, Chapter 1).

Between the late seventh and mid eighth centuries (Periods 2 to 3a), most of the excavated area was utilised as a habitation zone, with buildings located to the north and south of the shallow valley running through the centre of the site. The new buildings were constructed on different alignments to those of Phase 1b, most of them on new building plots, aligned on variations between approximate east-west and north-east to south-west alignments. The end of Period 1 and the re-planning of activity in the excavated area upon the onset of Period 2 also coincided with the first occurrence of Maxey-type pottery ware at Flixborough, as noted above – the earliest production of this type of pottery in the East Midlands is dated between the late seventh and early eighth century (Vince and Young, Volume 2, Chapter 12 and ADS archive). Sometime between the late seventh and mid eighth centuries, a large boundary ditch was also dug; it ran on an approximately east-west alignment, from the shallow valley straight down the slope towards the Trent floodplain. It is extremely difficult, however, to date the creation of this feature, prior to its filling in with material, which provided *termini post quos* of the early to mid ninth century (see also Chapter 3 this volume). By that time, the ditch had been re-cut at least once.

Two buildings and their associated archaeological features are particularly noteworthy from the late seventh to mid eighth century, namely buildings 6 and 21. These structures had post-hole foundations, and stone-lined 'soakaway' gullies which ran from the exterior of the central post along one of the short-walls of each of these buildings. Both seem to have had a drainage function, taking water into the shallow valley, presumably prior to the construction of building 11 – stratigraphically the earliest building in the central part of the site. As a consequence, certain materials – particularly small vertebrate remains – seem to have been carried in suspension, and eventually collected in these features. Refuse dumping strategies in this period comprised the deposition of rubbish immediately outside the buildings.

Sometime in the first half of the eighth century, building 20 was replaced by an exceptional building amongst those from the Anglo-Saxon settlement, constructed on what appears to be a gravel foundation for a sill beam and timber superstructure. This building (1a) was divided into two halves by an internal division, with a fired-clay hearth at its eastern end (FIG. 2.2). The 'soakaway' gullies were also filled during this period, and both buildings 6 and 21 were rebuilt or renovated on the same plots. The fills of the post-holes of these buildings yielded both pieces of decorated glass vessels, imported from the Continent, which could date from the seventh to ninth centuries; as well as sherds of two imported wheel-thrown pottery vessels dating from the seventh and seventh to eighth centuries respectively and made in the Vorgebirge region of the Rhineland, near Cologne, and northern France or Belgium (Evison, Volume 2, Chapter 2; Vince, Volume 2, Chapter 12). Although it is difficult to be certain, at some point during the first half of the eighth century building 11 – represented by its partial foundations – was built in the central part of the site; a collection of post-holes to its west may reflect the presence of another building. Refuse organisation also changed slightly, in that material was dumped to the north of the southern buildings, extending down a slope of the spur, into the central shallow valley bottom.

Exceptionally amongst the excavated structures, building 1a also contained the graves of four individuals, buried along its long-walls, on an east-west alignment. Two additional burials were also placed outside the building to the south and south-east. Examination of the skeletal remains has shown that all but one of the burials were juveniles, between the ages of three and twelve years old. The exception was the skeleton of a woman, aged between 20 and 30 years, who had been buried in close association with the skeleton of a peri-natal infant, possibly reflecting the death of mother and infant in childbirth (Mays, Volume 1, Chapter 8).

During the middle decades of the eighth century, the buildings on either side of the shallow valley were replaced, most on the same or broadly similar plots as those of the first half of the eighth century (FIG. 2.3). Notably, however, new buildings – for example 13 and 23 – were also constructed on previously unused plots. The former building was a substantial structure, built on the gently inclining northern slope of the shallow valley. It was constructed immediately in front of the plot used by the former building 21, and the replacement of the latter structure – building 8 – was set further back to allow sufficient space from building 13. It is also possible that the three buildings represent a linear chronological succession, in that building 8 replaced 13 and 21, in that order. The buildings themselves were earth-fast constructions, predominantly within continuous trench foundations, although buildings with post-hole foundations also existed, in the form of building 13. Several, such as buildings 1b and 2, also contained internal fired-clay hearths. The former represented a complete re-building of building 1a, without any obvious reference to the locations of the burials within it.

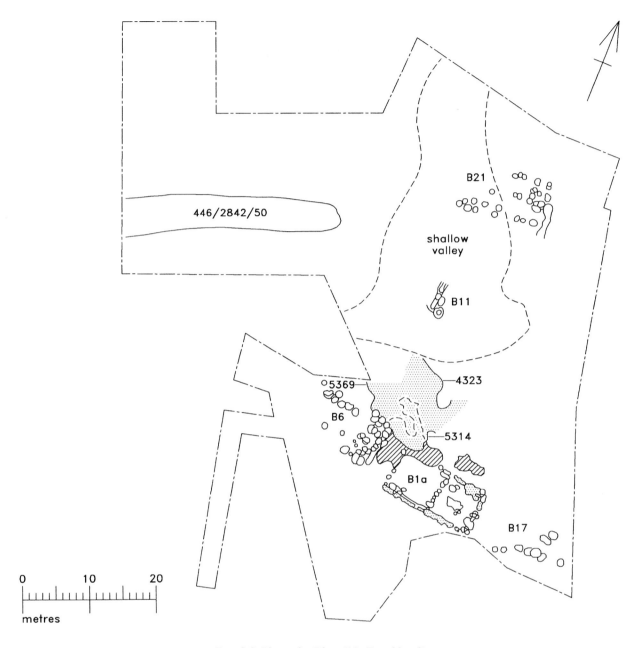

446/2842/50

B21

shallow
valley

B11

○5369
B6
○
○

4323

5314

B1a

B17

0   10   20

metres

FIG. 2.2 Phase 3a Plan (M. Frankland).

Between the mid eighth and the early decades of the ninth century, the central part of the excavated site became the focus for cyclical episodes of construction and refuse disposal around buildings (FIG. 2.3). This was followed by combinations of demolition and refuse deposits (FIG. 2.4), and episodes of larger-scale refuse dumping, with indications that this area was being used as a possible communal refuse zone (FIGS 2.5 & 2.6; see also Chapter 3). It is also possible that the latter episodes of large-scale dumping represent levelling and site clearance, prior to re-planning and new phases of building, within the excavated area (see Loveluck and Atkinson, Volume 1, Chapter 4). Significant quantities

of imported glass vessel fragments were recovered from these demolition and refuse deposits, together with several sherds of continental pottery vessels; the earliest stratified coin was recovered from deposit 8200 (Phase 3biii) in this period – an imported silver *sceat* (a series E 'porcupine' type), thought to have been minted in the Rhine mouths area of Frisia, between AD 700 and 730 (Archibald, Volume 2, Chapter 13). Overall, however, most of the finds comprised craft-working debris, domestic utensils, and Maxey-type pottery, with a small number of dress accessories. Significantly, however, the deposits defined within the depositional Phases 3biv and 3bv also contained large quantities of vertebrate remains.

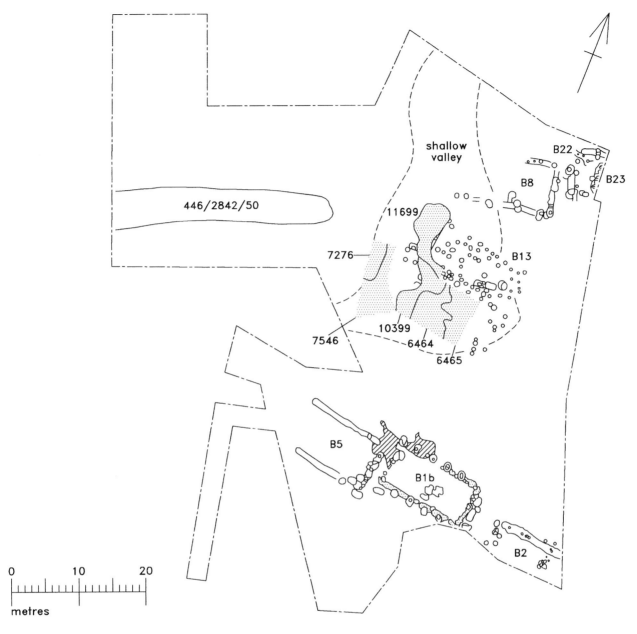

Fig. 2.3 Phase 3bii Plan (M. Frankland).

At some point between the early and mid ninth century (Period 4), the physical character of occupation within the excavated area was altered, with the construction of three lines of buildings, encompassing both the broad re-use of former building plots and new sites for construction in doing so. Refuse dumping around these buildings seems to have been limited, although there are indications that some material was discarded, and became incorporated into the uppermost demolition and levelling dumps of Phase 3b, which formed the activity surface around the buildings, during Period 4. New types of artefact, deposited for the first time during the early to mid ninth century included several styli, a piece of window glass and two lead window cames, and sherds of Ipswich ware, imported from the emporium in Suffolk, together with a local pottery ware, early Lincoln Fine-shelled ware, which appears to have been made from the early decades of the ninth century (Loveluck and Atkinson, Volume 1, Chapter 4; Blinkhorn, Volume 2, Chapter 12).

Subsequently, during the middle decades of the ninth century, the buildings in the centre of the site were demolished, and both the central shallow valley and the ditch became foci for large-scale refuse dumping: here were found the largest quantities of craft-working evidence from the settlement sequence – especially those

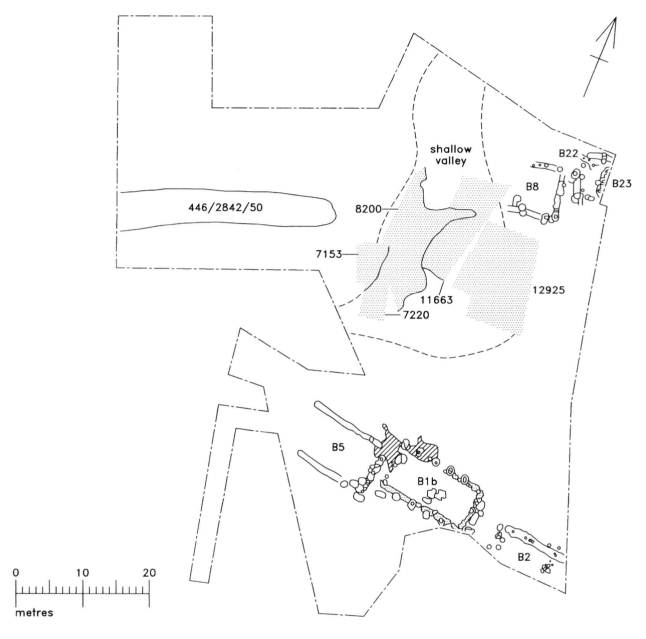

Fig. 2.4 Phase 3biii Plan (M. Frankland).

relating to textile manufacture (Fig. 2.7). The central
dumps contained over 200 un-fired clay loom-weights,
and other weaving debris, and large numbers of animal
bones, all shielded from acid leaching by the highly
alkaline wood-ash content of the dumps. The broadly
datable artefacts included Early Lincolnshire Fine-shelled
ware pottery and a late eighth- or early ninth-century gilt
silver disc brooch. The well-preserved loom-weight
fragments and late eighth- to ninth-century artefacts from
the dumps in phase 4ii reflect a high proportion of
material contemporary with the phase. Both demonstrably
residual and potentially contemporaneous sherds of
continental pottery and vessel glass were also present, as
were imported continental *sceattas*, minted between the

early and mid eighth century. The ditch also contained
residual artefacts, in the form of coins and pottery,
alongside dress accessories and coins datable to the period
between the early and middle decades of the ninth
century, within both its lower and uppermost fills. In the
latter, two silver pennies of Aethelberht, King of Wessex,
minted between AD 858 and 865 (Archibald, Volume 2,
Chapter 13) were recovered. Like the central dumps, the
ditch also contained significant quantities of animal bones
(Plate 2.2). Again, several styli and pieces of window
glass and lead came were found in these refuse or site
clearance deposits.

Following the site clearance possibly reflected by Phase
4ii, the building plots of the previous period were

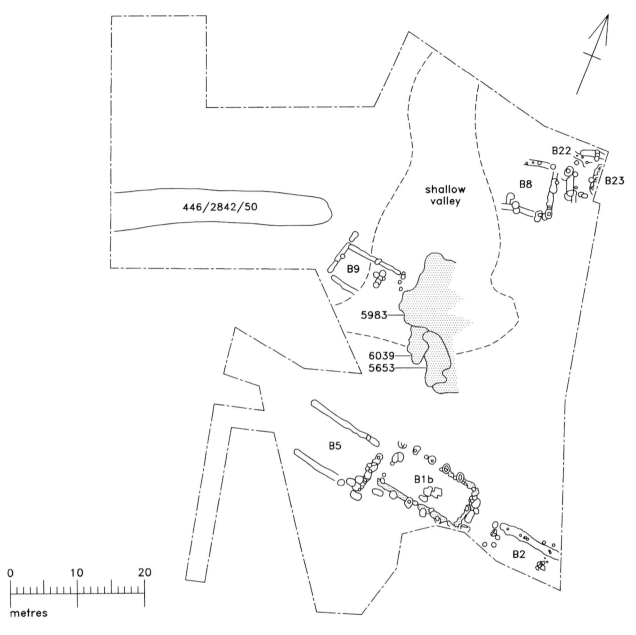

FIG. 2.5 Phase 3biv Plan (M. Frankland).

abandoned. In their place, small buildings with post-hole foundations were constructed – some with fired-clay hearths – in the southern part of the excavated area, during the mid to late ninth century (Period 5 of the occupation sequence: FIG. 2.8). The former shallow valley in the centre of the site was again used as a refuse dumping zone; whilst several buildings were constructed cutting the line of the former ditch. On the basis of parallels with similar structures in Mid- to Late-Saxon phases on other settlements, such as Wicken Bonhunt, Essex, and West Heslerton, North Yorkshire, it is possible that the latter buildings were granaries or haylofts (Wade 1980, 97–98; D. Powlesland pers. comm.). To the north of the refuse dumping area was a zone of domed fired-clay ovens. These ovens were linked with the buildings to the south by gravel paths, which crossed the central refuse dumps. The presence of the paths and the varying characteristics of the dumps themselves suggest that the central part of the site acted as an open midden for an extended period, and that they were not deposited in one episode of levelling. Between the late ninth and early tenth century, some of the small buildings were replaced, whilst others were also constructed over the central midden, cutting through the former gravel paths (FIG. 2.9). Parts of both the southern and northern sectors of the site were then used as refuse dumping zones. Features and deposits of the latter phase contained small quantities of pottery, which seems to have been produced in the

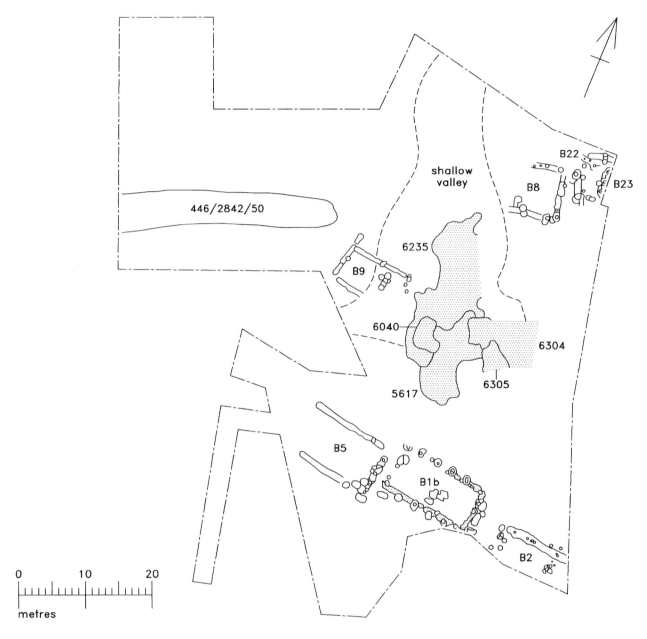

Fig. 2.6 Phase 3bv Plan (M. Frankland).

East Midlands from the late ninth or early tenth centuries: namely, Torksey ware, Lincoln Kiln-type ware and Late Saxon local wares (Young, Volume 2, Chapter 12). Significant quantities of animal bones were recovered from the dumps of Phase 5a, although very few were retrieved from the deposits of Phase 5b.

At some point between the early and mid tenth century, the small buildings and possible granaries were completely demolished, and were replaced by the largest buildings seen within the occupation sequence, all of which had continuous trench foundations (FIGS 2.10 & 2.11). None of the new buildings were positioned to respect earlier building plots. The largest structure, building 7 – almost 20m by 6.5m in size – cut across the

central part of the site, and building 12 cut through the demolished ovens and dumps of Phases 5a and 5b. The other buildings of this phase are noteworthy for the fact that they all continued under the eastern edge of the excavations. The latest buildings (numbers 32 and 33) also had different alignments, having been placed on a north-south axis.

During the mid tenth century, building 7 was also demolished, and was covered by refuse dumps, one of which (3891) contained a vast quantity of animal bones. A small range of tenth-century pottery types was also recovered from the refuse deposits, again comprising Torksey, Torksey-type and Lincoln pottery wares, alongside examples of a new heavier form of loom-weight

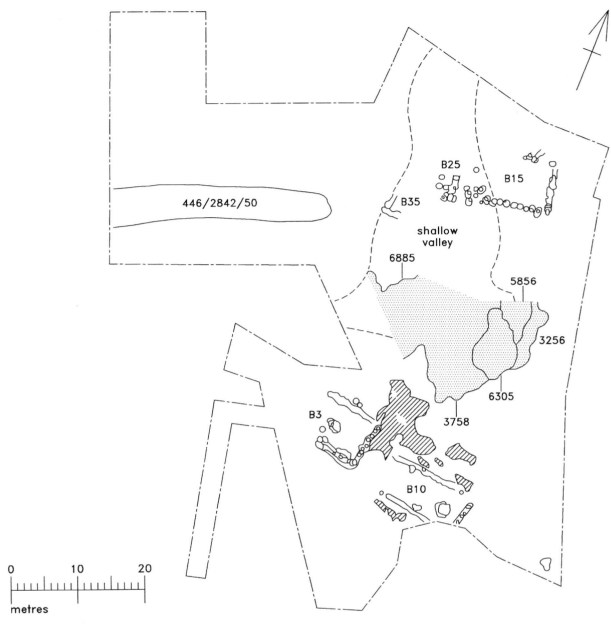

FIG. 2.7 Phase 4ii Plan (M. Frankland).

for weaving (which had appeared in Phase 5b). The largest collection of iron-working debris from the Flixborough sequence was also recovered from this phase, including the first major collection of iron-smelting evidence. The dumps, such as 3610 and 3891, may have accumulated at the same time as building 33 was in use, although deposits such as 6300, running down the eastern edge of the excavated area, were created after the latter building had been demolished. The impression given by the evidence, therefore, is that during the tenth century the habitation area of the settlement was shifting eastwards, towards the ironstone escarpment. Between, the mid tenth and early eleventh century, the whole of the excavated area was then used as a refuse dumping zone, and large quantities of artefacts and animal bones were recovered from these deposits (FIG. 2.12). This change of land-use, from a settlement zone associated with habitation, craft-working and dumping, to an area associated only with refuse disposal, is consistent with the view that the settlement had shifted to the east, and that the excavated area was henceforth on its periphery.

This migration immediately eastward would place the late tenth- and eleventh-century settlement in the vicinity of All Saints' Church and the deserted medieval settlement of North Conesby. The church is documented from the thirteenth century (Roffe, Volume 4, Chapter 8.2); and it was also known both as North Conesby and Flixborough Old Church (Coppack 1986, 51). The place-

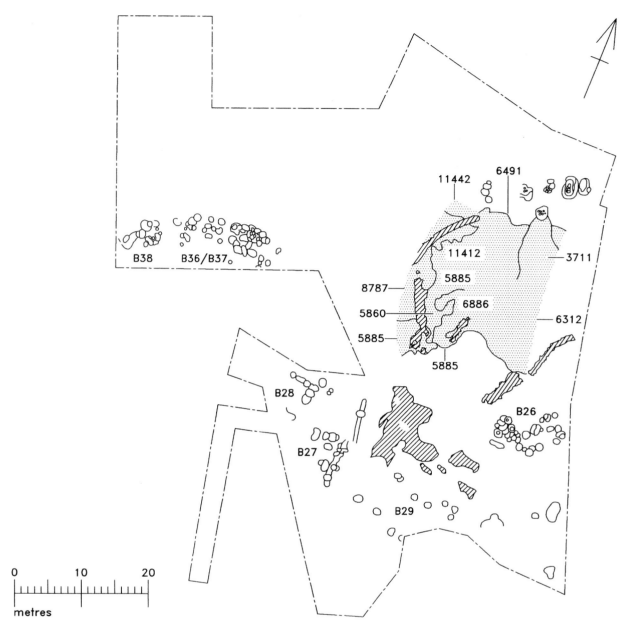

Fig. 2.8 Phase 5a Plan (M. Frankland).

name 'Conesby' is particularly interesting since it comes from the Old Danish *Kunungrsby*, meaning 'King's Farm or settlement' (Cameron 1998, 33; Cameron, Volume 4, Chapter 4.2). Like Flixborough, North Conesby was mentioned in the Domesday survey, and Foster and Longley noted that a moated enclosure, to the east of the church, was buried under iron slag in the early 1920s (Foster and Longley 1924, liii and 149). The place-name Conesby may have been associated with the excavated Anglo-Saxon settlement from the tenth century, if not slightly earlier. The gradual eastward shift of the settlement would account for the linkage of the name with the deserted medieval site, which may have been defined by the church and Anglo-Norman manor house,

at the two extremities of the settlement.

An explanation for the settlement shift could relate to the church. During the mid to late tenth century, the first stone churches such as that at Burnham, were built on other nearby settlements in north Lincolnshire; it has been suggested by Coppack (1986, 47–50) that these were linked to aristocratic proprietors and estate centres It is possible that a Late Saxon stone pre-cursor also exists below All Saints' Church, just as at Burnham.

Interestingly, however, the Domesday survey does not mention any churches either at Flixborough, North Conesby or Burnham (Foster and Longley 1924, 148–151). The construction of a new stone church on the stable foundation of the Liassic ironstone escarpment,

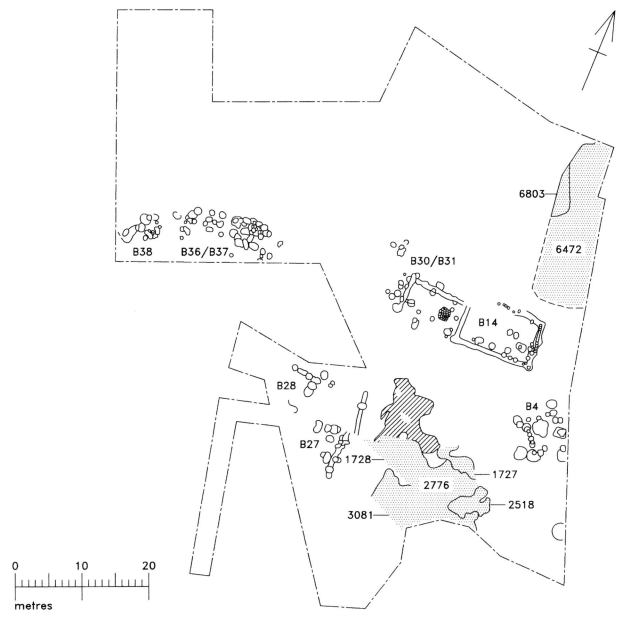

Fig. 2.9 Phase 5b Plan (M. Frankland).

rather than on the unsuitable windblown sand, could provide one reason for the eastward shift of the main settlement during the second half of the tenth century. Subsequent, peripheral settlement features such as an oven, pits and a drainage ditch, in use between the twelfth and fifteenth centuries, also support the idea that the heart of the medieval settlement focus lay to the east of the excavated area.

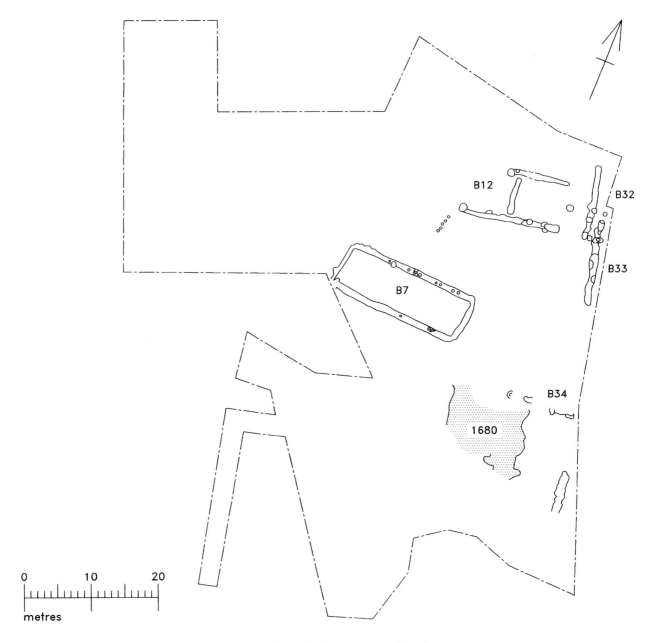

Fig. 2.10 Phase 6i Plan (M. Frankland).

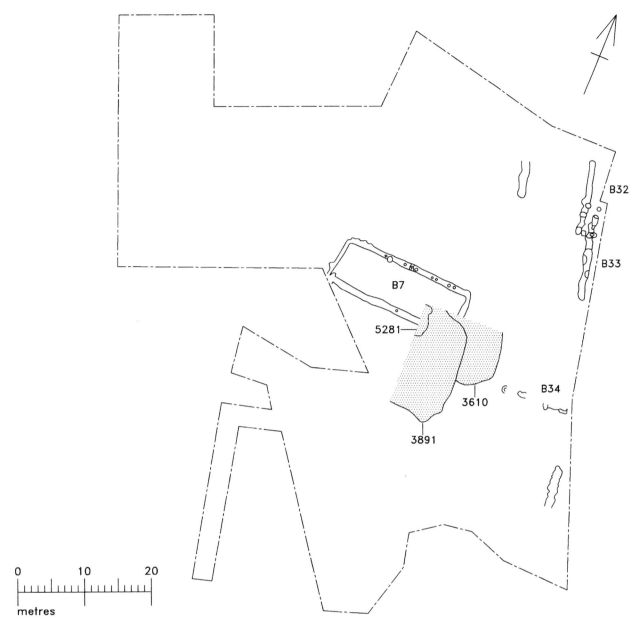

Fɪɢ. 2.11 Phase 6ii Plan (M. Frankland).

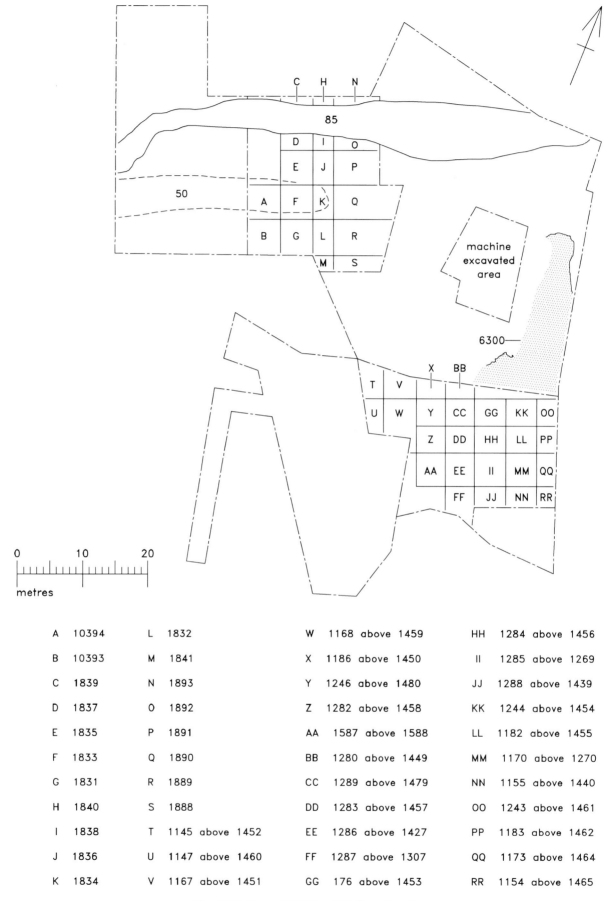

0   10   20
metres

A	10394	L	1832	W	1168 above 1459	HH	1284 above 1456
B	10393	M	1841	X	1186 above 1450	II	1285 above 1269
C	1839	N	1893	Y	1246 above 1480	JJ	1288 above 1439
D	1837	O	1892	Z	1282 above 1458	KK	1244 above 1454
E	1835	P	1891	AA	1587 above 1588	LL	1182 above 1455
F	1833	Q	1890	BB	1280 above 1449	MM	1170 above 1270
G	1831	R	1889	CC	1289 above 1479	NN	1155 above 1440
H	1840	S	1888	DD	1283 above 1457	OO	1243 above 1461
I	1838	T	1145 above 1452	EE	1286 above 1427	PP	1183 above 1462
J	1836	U	1147 above 1460	FF	1287 above 1307	QQ	1173 above 1464
K	1834	V	1167 above 1451	GG	176 above 1453	RR	1154 above 1465

FIG. *2.12 Phase 6iii Plan (M. Frankland).*

3   Chronology, Residuality, Taphonomy and Preservation

Christopher Loveluck, Keith Dobney, Deborah Jaques, James Barrett, Cluny Johnstone, John Carrott, Allan Hall, Amanda Bretman and Susan Haynes

3.1 Introduction

by Keith Dobney and Christopher Loveluck

Within the seventh- to eleventh-century phases of the Flixborough occupation sequence, with their extensive (and in some cases massive) refuse dumps of artefact and vertebrate remains, significant similarities appear to have existed in the refuse strategies of different periods (see Chapters 4 & 6 for more details). Some deposits seem to reflect dumping immediately outside buildings, whilst others represent more organised, larger refuse heaps, often in the central part of the site. Consequently, a potentially exceptional, and currently unparalleled, resource of well-dated deposits forms the basis from which to examine a range of themes relating to the economy and character of the settlement, through much of the Middle and Late Anglo-Saxon periods. Before any attempt can be made to analyse and interpret the contents of these deposits, however, it is essential to establish the limits of inference from the evidence. That is to say, it is necessary to assess whether material from deposits of different periods can be used as a basis from which to draw conclusions on the settlement as a whole, or merely the excavated area, through the course of the occupation sequence.

To establish the extent to which remains resulting from apparently similar refuse strategies are representative of the overall settlement, or merely the excavated area, it is necessary to examine the nature of the varied refuse deposits, the circumstances of their formation, and the derivation and date of material within them. This involves summarising the indicators of deposit movement, predominantly provided by artefact remains, but also animal bones.

For this summary discussion designed to establish a baseline from which to ask questions of the archaeological data, it is not possible or appropriate to analyse each major deposit within the chronological framework provided by the occupation sequence; detailed expositions of the various components of the deposits are considered elsewhere (Loveluck and Atkinson, Volume 1, Chapters 3–7). Nevertheless, a summary of the overall constituents and the character of deposits in different periods is presented below, in order to establish their value for the interpretation of different aspects of life on the settlement. This background account relating to archaeological site formation, and the integrity of deposits as a basis for wider interpretation, provides a description of overall trends in the deposition of archaeological remains, against which those evident amongst the bioarchaeological remains can be compared and integrated. The combined value of the analysis of the varied forms of artefact and biological evidence for shedding light on subjects such as the settlement's agricultural base, patterns of craft-working and exchange, and the character of the settlement itself, are then discussed at greater length in this volume and Volume 4 of the Flixborough publications.

3.2 Parameters of interpretation: a chronological framework for analysing the bioarchaeological remains

by Christopher Loveluck and Keith Dobney

Analysis of the components of the deposits, and the circumstances of their formation, allows us to produce broad profiles of the deposition of artefacts and (primarily, for the purposes of the present discussion) animal remains, relating to four broad periods of the

Anglo-Saxon occupation sequence at Flixborough – namely, for Periods 3, 4, 5, and 6 respectively. For certain classes of evidence, however, such as the vertebrate remains in this volume, availability of data makes it more appropriate to examine the material from Periods 4 and 5 (the ninth century approximately) as an integrated whole. This relates to the likelihood that material from Phase 5a could reflect remains broadly contemporary with Phase 4ii, and also the general paucity of animal bones from Phase 5b.

Quantities of finds prior to the late seventh century are too small to provide a basis for drawing wider conclusions. Similarly, the practice of dumping refuse outside houses between the late seventh and mid eighth centuries makes it difficult to be sure that the finds are representative of the settlement as a whole during that period. Nevertheless, the nature of the evidence for exchange, certain animal husbandry and provisioning regimes, and craft-working practices is still of key importance in assessing aspects of the character of the settlement, and the social relations of its inhabitants with the wider landscape and beyond at that time. Therefore, consideration is also given to the evidence from the late seventh to mid eighth centuries for the light it may shed on aspects of settlement character – not least because much of the identifiably residual material in later contexts was produced, and probably re-worked, following use in this period.

As a result, the analysis of the vertebrate remains in this volume will proceed in the main by examining observable trends from four broad periods, taking into account the limits of inference imposed by the nature of the deposits. The chronological parameters of this analytical framework are defined as follows: the late seventh to mid eighth century (Period 2 and Phase 3a); the mid eighth to the early decades of the ninth century (Phase 3b); the ninth century (Periods 4 and 5); and finally, the tenth century (Period 6). For ease of understanding these chronological groupings will hereafter be referred to as the following: Phase 2–3a, Phase 3b, Phase 4–5b and Phase 6. The period at the end of Phase 6 (i.e. late 10th/early 11th century) – principally represented by 'dark soils' – will also be treated separately and referred to hereafter as Phase 6iii.

3.3 Aspects of site formation processes and residuality

by Christopher Loveluck and Keith Dobney

What was recorded?

Detailed preservation records were made for the vertebrate remains from a total of 98 contexts. These represented only about 10% of the total number of contexts but well over 80% of the bone fragments recorded. Additionally, material from 104 wet-sieved samples, representing 95 contexts, was examined to make preservation and fragmentation records – only mammal remains were utilised for this analysis. Unfortunately, there were few obvious patterns observable in the wet-sieved material, so the following discussion deals almost exclusively with the hand-collected/dry-sieved assemblage. However, separate sections are also included for fish bones, large mollusc shells and archaeobotanical remains (see further this chapter).

Semi-subjective records of the state of preservation, colour of the fragments, and the appearance of broken surfaces ('angularity') (see Appendix 1 for an outline of the different categories) were made. In addition, semi-quantitative information was recorded concerning fragment size, dog gnawing, burning, butchery and fresh breakage. These data were then used in an attempt to identify assemblages that might have contained material which was residual or re-worked based on the assumption that poorly preserved, eroded and battered material found in the same deposit as fragments that had very angular broken edges and good preservation was likely to be of different origin. What was difficult to deduce was whether these variations in preservation resulted from the mixing of contemporaneous material which had been utilised and disposed of in a different manner, or whether there were combinations of bones of widely differing dates. Conclusions drawn from these data are compared and contrasted with the broader archaeological evidence, all of which are summarised by major period (see further below).

Phase 2–3a (late 7th to mid 8th century)

During the later seventh or early eighth century, there was a greater concentration of activity within the excavated area than in Period 1, exemplified by the construction of buildings 6, 17, 20 and 21, and the possible digging of the Mid-Saxon boundary ditch (Fig. 3.1), although, the temporal span of the latter feature is hard to define, prior to it being filled in during the mid ninth century. The patterns of discard from this phase were broadly similar to those of that preceding it (Phase 1b), in that refuse deposits accumulated outside the buildings – particularly in the southern part of the site. Re-working of sherds of the Late Roman lid-seated jars (vessels 1 and 2), already seen in earlier phases, demonstrates the local derivation of much of the material in the southern sector. Yet the importation of material from other parts of the settlement is also reflected in the occurrence of a sherd of the Rhenish Walberberg pot (vessel 13) in a post-hole fill of building 21; a sherd of continental grey-burnished ware (vessel 42); and decorated, imported glass vessel fragments from post-hole fills of building 6. The 'soakaway' gulley features, associated with buildings 6 and 21, also reflect washing down of earlier material – again the Roman lid-seated jars; and they acted as particularly good collection points for small animal bones (especially the southern soakaway

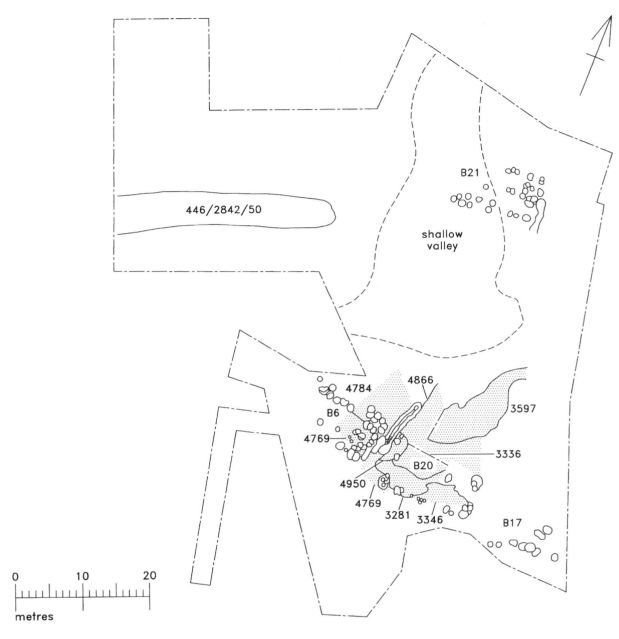

FIG. 3.1 Period 2 Plan (M. Frankland).

– feature 3967 / 970). Unlike the earlier seventh-century phases, more animal bones were also deposited within the refuse deposits, as were other tools and artefacts, although numbers were still smaller than for the later eighth, ninth and tenth centuries. In summary, therefore, it is possible to conclude that most of the material in the deposits from Period 2 reflects activity in the excavated area, although significant elements in the finds assemblages also indicate links beyond the settlement, as well as aspects of craft-working, animal husbandry, and exploitation of the landscape around the settlement.

In character, the deposits from the first half of the eighth century (Phase 3a) hold many similarities with those of the preceding phase (Period 2). Indeed, with the

exception of the construction of building 1a on its gravel sill foundation, and the use of the building as a selective burial focus for a certain element of the settlement's population, the rebuilding of buildings 6 and 21 reflects a considerable continuity in the use of space. Refuse dumping, however, extended further into the centre of the site. The re-working of sherds of the Romano-British lid-seated jars (vessels 1 and 2) probably reflects the cutting of earlier deposits, during the renovation [and/or replacement?] of buildings. It is also possible that the Walberberg vessel fragment may have arrived in this part of the site in this period, during the re-modelling of buildings 6 and 21. Further craft-working evidence was recovered from the refuse dumps and fills of post-holes –

mainly textile-manufacturing tools. Further fragments of imported trail-decorated glass vessels were deposited within the floor deposits and post-hole fills of buildings 1a and 17. The vessel glass found in the fill of a post-hole from the earlier incarnation of building 6 may also have become incorporated at this time (FIG. 3.10*, Volume 1). This occurrence of imported luxuries in association with particular buildings is a key feature of the early to mid eighth-century buildings in the southern part of the site (Loveluck and Atkinson, Volume 1, Chapters 3 and 4; Evison, Volume 2, Chapter 2.1). Later, finds such as glass vessel fragments were recovered predominantly from refuse dumps. During this period, the refuse dumps beyond an area of gravel hard-standing, between buildings 1a and 6 provided the majority of the animal bones. Unfortunately, however, the filling in of the earlier 'soakaways' with gravel resulted in the removal of optimum conditions for the build-up of small vertebrate remains. Consequently, the absence of certain types of deposition context has no doubt affected the archaeological visibility of certain possible procurement strategies (see Chapter 8, this volume).

Overall, therefore, structural Phases 2 and 3a form a coherent period of similar discard activities, between the late seventh and mid eighth centuries. Most of the dumped refuse, which lay immediately outside the buildings, contained re-worked material from the same broad building plots, primarily in the form of the Romano-British vessels 1 and 2 (Didsbury, Volume 2, Chapter 14). This suggests that the vast majority of animal bone and craft-working detritus was derived from consumption and processing activities in the adjacent buildings. However, the presence of small quantities of iron-smithing debris, and one possible fired-clay mould or crucible fragment, indicate the importation of some industrial residues into the excavated area, since no *in situ* indications of iron or non-ferrous metalworking were recovered (Loveluck and Atkinson, Volume 1, Chapters 3 and 4; Wastling, Volume 2, Chapter 11). The glass vessels also reflect consumption of imported luxuries and, alongside the relatively small numbers of imported Continental pottery vessels, they can be regarded as signs of the integration of certain elements of the settlement's population within long-distance exchange routes with northern France, the Low Countries and the Rhineland – probably reflecting their social standing. In this sense, the material from the late seventh to mid eighth centuries holds a complex mix of traits linked to the immediate excavated zone, and to the settlement as a whole.

The vertebrate remains and finds from most contexts representing this phase (i.e. 3968, 4621, 4638, 4963, 5088 and 5391) showed little or no evidence of residuality, with the exception of Context 3968, which contained a residual Roman pot sherd. As already discussed, this is likely to represent re-deposition of locally-derived material and, although the colour of the bones from this deposit was somewhat variable, the

preservation was good, suggesting that the bones, at any rate, were homogeneous in origin. In Contexts 5314 and 4323 the small quantity of particularly poorly preserved, rounded and eroded fragments may reflect the continued re-working of deposits between Phases 1a and 3a, as shown in this area from joining sherds of Roman vessels. Other contexts possibly containing residual bone were 748, 2784, 4487 and 5390. Intrusive elements, in the form of rabbit bones, were recovered from several deposits (685, 875, 956, 4172 [part skeleton] and 11033.

Phase 3b (mid 8th to early 9th century)

Between the middle of the eighth century and the early decades of the ninth century, patterns of refuse dumping became more centralised within the shallow valley (see Chapter 2, above). This progressed initially from the continued practice of dumping around standing buildings – particularly buildings 13 and 8, prior to the formation of central middens to the east of building 9. During this period, the artefact component and elements of the high-temperature manufacturing debris reflect a complex mix of material derived from local actions, and from outside the excavated area. The quantities of refuse from this period are also much larger than for the preceding phases of activity, reflecting the onset of the use of the shallow valley as a communal midden zone, possibly for the settlement as a whole.

Elements of the deposits around building 13 were certainly heavily re-worked, and probably imported from outside the excavated area. For example, deposit 6465 contained small, highly fragmented pieces of fired-clay moulds, one of them for a decorated artefact, together with a possible crucible fragment (Wastling, Volume 2, Chapter 11), and no signs of non-ferrous metalworking were found locally in the excavated area. Deposit 6465 also contained a large number of loom-weight fragments (weighing 3 kg and including over 50 recorded weights), in large and small pieces, possibly reflecting both locally-derived and transported elements (see FIG. 2.3). Furthermore, this refuse deposit also contained a sherd of samian ware, of the mid to late second century, and a sherd of an Iron Age pot (vessel 20) was also discovered in a post-hole of building 8. These pottery sherds probably reflect the importation of material from an un-excavated part of the settlement which had disturbed early Romano-British settlement evidence (Loveluck and Atkinson, Volume 1, Chapter 4; Didsbury, Volume 2, Chapter 14; see also Volume 2, Chapter 12).

Subsequently, a phase of dumping around building 8, after the demolition of building 13, saw the first occurrence of coinage within the stratified deposits, in the form of an imported continental series E 'porcupine' *sceat*, from the Rhine mouths area of Frisia, minted in the early decades of the eighth century, and deposited in the refuse dump 8200 (see FIG. 2.4 this volume; Archibald, Volume 2, Chapter 13). A continuing local derivation for some of the dumped material was reflected by a sherd of the late fourth-century lid-seated jar (vessel 1), found within the occupation / refuse deposit 7220. During the larger-scale dumping of material during sub-phases 3biv and 3bv, the re-organisation of existing refuse from within the excavated area is again reflected, alongside the further importation of finds from other parts of the settlement (Loveluck and Atkinson, Volume 1, Chapter 4; see also FIGS 2.5 and 2.6 this volume). Material disturbed from earlier deposits, and found within these dumps included sherds of Walberberg vessel 13, and the greensand vessel 21. Large quantities of vertebrate remains were deposited in these refuse dumps, and separate refuse pits were also dug in certain instances. One of these pits – feature 6709 – contained a fill (6710) consisting almost entirely of animal and bird bones (see Chapter 6). Between the mid eighth century and the early decades of the ninth century, therefore, the organisation of refuse disposal, and the indices of the origin of material from both inside and beyond the excavated area, enabled tentative suggestions on the character of life to be made on the settlement as a whole.

Most vertebrate assemblages from this phase contained varying (mainly quite small) proportions of rounded or eroded fragments, with variability of colour also prominent. Fresh breakage was observed on a higher proportion of fragments than in the two previous phase groups, affecting up to 20% of the fragments in ten of the deposits and over 50% in the remaining three contexts. Assemblages from Contexts 4322, 6710 and 11699 were all recorded as containing mostly poorly preserved fragments, perhaps reflecting a greater frequency of re-worked material within these deposits. Despite a uniformity of colour, the preservation of material from Context 6710 was generally worse than for material from other contexts in this phase group, again suggesting a higher degree of re-working before a single discrete act of burial. Moreover, material from several of the dump deposits (Contexts 5617, 5653, 5983 and 6235) was characterised by the presence of small amounts of poorly preserved bones. The presence of pot sherds from a single vessel in both Context 5653 and the overlying deposit 5617 indicates the re-working of some material within these two dumps. However, this could largely have resulted from localised reorganisation of the refuse dumps as discussed above. In contrast, material from contexts 6039, 6040 and 6136 was uniformly well preserved, indicating that these may have been relatively undisturbed primary deposits.

Phase 4–5b (9th century)

In some ways, the refuse patterns associated with the three lines of buildings of Period 4 (FIG. 3.2), constructed sometime between the end of the eighth and the mid ninth century, exhibited some similarities to those current between the late seventh and mid eighth century, in the sense that significant finds were found apparently in association with buildings or within their floor deposits.

For example, fragments of imported glass vessels were recovered from within buildings 3 and 10, and a stylus was found in a deposit to the north of building 3 (Evison, Volume 2, Chapter 2; Pestell, Volume 2, Chapter 3). Artefacts such as styli, and also a small number of window glass and window lead came fragments, were only deposited from the early decades of the ninth century, and they have a particular concentration in Period 4, with the fewer later examples probably representing residuality. One piece of window glass and two lead cames were also recovered from the latest central refuse deposits, probably formed at the end Phase 3b (Cramp, Volume 2, Chapter 4).

These deposits from the end of phase 3b formed the activity surfaces around the buildings of Period 4, and the presence within two of the uppermost refuse contexts of Phase 3b of several artefacts which made their appearance predominantly between the early and middle decades of the ninth century, could reflect two possible scenarios of deposition. They were either discarded at the end of Phase 3b, during site re-modelling, or they were thrown away during Period 4, and hence were incorporated within contemporary surface deposits by trampling and deposit truncation, in this case worked into the uppermost dumps of Phase 3b (Loveluck and Atkinson, Volume 1, Chapters 3 and 4). Limited disturbance of earlier deposits, probably through renewed building in the central part of the site, is also suggested by the occurrence of a sherd of the hand-made greensand vessel 21 within a fill of post-hole 6324, from building 39.

Overall, however, during the main structural phase of Period 4, with its three lines of buildings, the excavated area seems to have been kept relatively free of refuse, with only limited amounts of occupation and refuse deposits accumulating around the buildings. Such a pattern of discard provides a stark contrast to the picture of large-scale refuse disposal, possibly associated with the demolition of all the buildings within the excavated area, potentially within a short period, during the middle decades of the ninth century (FIG. 2.7). This phase of refuse dumping (4ii), or even site clearance, produced two main foci for disposal, comprising the shallow valley in the centre of the settlement, and the large ditch in the western extremity of the excavated area. Together, the deposits from these two areas provided the densest concentrations of artefacts recovered from the occupation sequence, together with large quantities of animal bone. Considerable differences are evident, however, between the components of the central dumps and the fills of the ditch, especially in relation to the character of the artefacts and craft-working debris recovered (Loveluck and Atkinson, Volume 1, Chapter 5). At the same time, the condition of the different artefact and biological constituents of the deposits also provided indications of the extent to which the material within them can be regarded as broadly contemporaneous with Period 4, or residual from earlier phases in the settlement's history.

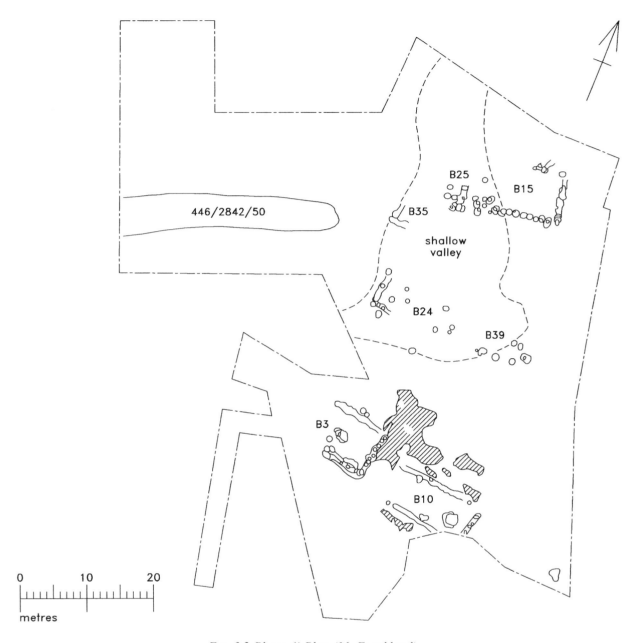

Fig. 3.2 Phase 4i Plan (M. Frankland).

Within the large central refuse dumps, particularly deposits 3758 and 5503, there is (superficially) a significant level of contradiction between finds which might be interpreted as reflecting extensive deposit disturbance, and those which could indicate relatively undisturbed refuse deposits contemporary with the phase, representing activities predominantly of the early to mid ninth century. The pottery evidence included an undoubtedly residual sherd of the seventh-century Walberberg pottery jar (vessel 13), but, significantly, sherds of a new pottery type – Early Lincolnshire Fine-shelled ware – were also present; this pottery appears to have been produced from sometime in the first half of the

ninth century (Young, Volume 2, Chapter 12). At the same time, three imported silver coins (*sceattas*, minted during the early decades of the eighth century) represent residual artefact elements in addition to the pottery sherd – and hence reflect a degree of deposit re-working (Loveluck and Atkinson, Volume 1, Chapter 5). Yet, significantly, the forms of evidence more prone to fragmentation on extensive refuse re-organisation and dispersal, i.e. the large number of clay loom-weights – indicate that the major components of these deposits were probably broadly contemporaneous with their phase of deposition, between the early and middle decades of the ninth century.

Penelope Walton Rogers has noted, for example, that Phase 4ii saw the deposition of the largest number of loom-weights within the Flixborough sequence, with over 200 weights represented from dumps 3758 and 6885 alone, and weighing over 13 kg. These loom-weights were also smaller and lighter than those from earlier or later periods (their deposition starts in late phase 3b deposits and continues into phase 5a), and they are suggested to represent the production of a finer quality cloth, possibly for export, at this time (Walton Rogers, Volume 2, Chapter 9 and Volume 4, Chapter 6; see also Chapter 7 this volume). The large size of the loom-weight fragments and the relatively complete nature of a significant number, especially from the central dumps 3758 and 6885, was also apparent. At the same time, Alan Vince has demonstrated that they were un-fired and probably manufactured from local clays (see ADS archive). If the whole of the dump deposits had been comprised of extensively re-worked constituents, a greater degree of fragmentation would have been expected amongst the un-fired loom-weights, and the occurrence of such a large concentration of weights of a similar character would be highly unlikely. Similarly, the animal bones from these dump deposits do not reflect characteristics which one would associate with extensively re-worked material, such as a high degree of fragmentation, abrasion, etc. The sediment matrix of the dumps, composed largely of ash with charcoal fragments, was also of key importance in providing excellent preservation conditions for animal bones (Canti 1992, 18; Canti, Volume 1, Chapter 2).

In summary, therefore, the loom-weights, and the sheer number of other textile-manufacturing artefacts from the central deposits, suggest discard relatively contemporaneous with use or consumption, during the early and mid ninth century. Consequently, when the large numbers of these finds are compared with the much smaller, demonstrably residual artefact component, it can be concluded that dumps such as 5503 and 3758 were not primarily composed of residual material. Furthermore, the distinctive and more extensive ash and charcoal components of their sediment matrices, relative to other sampled dumps, may also indicate the limited extent of re-working and mixing with other deposits.

The more often-used indicators of deposit formation and character – pottery and coinage – provided the smaller element of re-worked, identifiably residual material, although not all the imported material need have been residual. Most of the glass vessel fragments recovered from the central dumps could have been contemporaneous with the weaving refuse, as could the four fragments of the imported white ware vessel DR345, thought to originate from northern France, and found only in dump 3758 (Vince, Volume 2, Chapter 12). The weaving and spinning debris were also accompanied by a wide range of other craft-working tools, a considerable number of dress pins, fragments of window glass, a silver

stylus, and contemporaneous pottery – Early Lincolnshire Fine-shelled ware, Ipswich ware, and possibly late Maxey wares (Loveluck and Atkinson, Volume 1, Chapter 5).

The material dumped in the ditch, and filling the feature during Phase 4ii, was significantly different from the central refuse deposits in a number of respects. This may well reflect derivation of the material from a different part of the settlement, outside the excavated area. Thus, for example, although the number of vessels represented is small, the ditch deposits contained a significantly larger number of Ipswich ware sherds, compared with the one sherd of this ware from the dumps. Similarly, a larger number of imported continental vessels, including grey-burnished ware vessels 56 and 58, and a possible red-burnished ware sherd, were present in the ditch – and they are the first occurrences of these vessels, also suggesting a derivation from another part of the settlement. Sherds of Early Lincolnshire Fine-shelled ware were also recovered from the ditch, again suggesting deposits of the early to mid ninth century. Amongst the dress accessories encountered, smaller numbers of pins were recovered than from the central dumps, whilst strap-ends, hooked tags and buckles were only found in the ditch.

A similar exclusivity to the ditch deposits is also displayed in the occurrence of fibre-processing spikes, potentially relating to flax preparation, and imported Eifel quern fragments. Unfortunately, because many of the ditch deposits were machine-excavated, it is not possible to say whether flax preparation was carried out in the vicinity of the ditch, or whether the spikes were imported into this part of the site with the other components of the deposits. Nevertheless clearly zoned discard of textile-manufacturing debris is evident, with processing debris all but absent from the central dumps, and loom-weights absent from the ditch deposits (Loveluck and Atkinson, Volume 1, Chapter 5; Walton Rogers, Volume 2, Chapter 9). The character of the artefact material from the ditch deposits is certainly significantly different from that in the contemporaneous central dumps, to the extent that the importation of much of the material from outside the excavated area is likely (Loveluck and Atkinson, Volume 1, Chapter 5). In this sense, the analysis of the large vertebrate assemblage also recovered from the ditch fills offers an interesting comparison with that from the central dumps, as the material may well have been derived from different parts of the settlement (PLATE 2.2).

The filling in of this boundary feature over a relatively short period, during the early and middle decades of the ninth century, is suggested by the recovery of diag-nostically datable artefacts from all its major fills. These included strap-ends with early to mid ninth-century Trewiddle zoomorphic decoration from its lower fills, alongside Ipswich ware (Thomas, Volume 2, Chapter 1; Blinkhorn, Volume 2, Chapter 12). Two silver pennies of Aethelberht, King of Wessex, minted between AD 858 and 865, together with Ipswich and Early Lincolnshire

Fine-shelled wares were recovered from its uppermost fills (Archibald, Volume 2, Chapter 13). Hence, the feature had been completely filled in sometime after AD 865.

In relation to the deposits from Period 4, therefore, it is appropriate to conclude that the vast quantities of material recovered probably reflect the overall nature and range of activities undertaken on the settlement, during the early and mid ninth century. The extent of artefact discard, the nature of the deposits, and the potentially contemporaneous demolition of the buildings are suggestive of the levelling and clearance of the excavated area over a short period, during the middle decades of the ninth century.

The re-organisation of the settlement within the excavated area between the depositional Phase 4ii and the structural Phase 5a could reflect activities over a matter of weeks (FIG. 2.8). Yet, there are both significant similarities and differences in the composition of the deposits, to be set alongside the major change in the structural character of the settlement. The pottery from the dumps around the paths and from the oven area provides indications of the re-working of material, which had long been current in the excavated part of the settlement. Several dumps had sherds of greensand vessel 21, pieces of which had first appeared in broken form during the mid eighth century, and further sherds of vessel 21 and Walberberg vessel 13 were also recovered from the fill of post-hole 10336, possibly from a structure screening the ovens (Loveluck and Atkinson, Volume 1, Chapter 6). At the same time, the occurrence of an Iron Age pottery sherd, and two Iron Age fired-clay sling-shots (Wastling, Volume 2, Chapter 14), may constitute elements imported into the excavated area, deposited alongside Maxey wares, Early Lincolnshire Fine-shelled ware and Ipswich ware.

It is not possible to identify any newly imported Continental luxuries which were necessarily contemporaneous and not residual in this phase. Two Frisian type E 'porcupine' *sceattas* were certainly residual, having been minted during the early decades of the eighth century, and a series of glass vessel fragments could date from the seventh, eighth or ninth centuries. The remainder of the finds from the dumps consisted primarily of animal bones, again chemically protected by wood-ash, and debris related to all aspects of textile production, though without the zonation in deposition seen in the preceding period. In comparison with Period 4, the quantity of textile-manufacturing remains was small, and they could be residual from earlier in the ninth century, since the character of the material deposited – such as the smaller loom-weights – was identical. Overall, the central deposits dumped around the gravel paths during the mid to late ninth century probably reflect the use of the area as a communal refuse area. A significant proportion of the material was derived from activities within the excavated area, or its immediate vicinity. This is

suggested by the continued residual movement of sherds of pottery vessels 13 and 21, and is also shown by the direct relationship of dump 3711 with oven 6488, the former appearing to comprise ash sweepings from this oven (Loveluck and Atkinson, Volume 1, Chapter 6; see also FIG. 2.8 this volume). Nevertheless, the anomalous Iron Age finds, and further early Romano-British pottery, also suggest the continued importation of refuse from parts of the Anglo-Saxon settlement which had disturbed Iron Age and earlier Roman deposits (unlike the excavated area, which saw late fourth century pottery in its early phases).

Refuse strategies during Phase 5b represented a change from those practised for much of the previous century at Flixborough, in the sense that the former northern building plot recently used as an oven zone, and the central southern building plot in the vicinity of building 29, were used for refuse dumping. As in Phase 5a, the material deposited between the late decades of the ninth and the early decades of the tenth century had a demonstrably residual component, in the form of a range of seventh-, eighth- and ninth-century artefacts, including an inscribed lead plaque (Loveluck and Atkinson, Volume 1, Chapter 6; Brown and Okasha, Volume 2, Chapter 3). Yet new pottery wares were certainly imported into the settlement at this time, in small quantities: for example, Torksey ware, wares from Lincoln, and Late Saxon local wares (Young, Volume 2, Chapter 12). Other innovations included the adoption of a new heavier loom-weight for the production of a coarse (probably woollen) textile, on a small scale (Walton Rogers, Volume 2, Chapter 9). However, in comparison with the periods with large central refuse dumps, created either during or at the end of particular stages in the occupation sequence, the discard of animal bones in Phase 5b was very limited.

Of the nine large contexts from Period 4 with preservation records for vertebrate remains, material from three was described as fair and six as variable. Burnt fragments formed less than 10% of the assemblage in five contexts, whilst material from Context 3758 (a dump) included a number of scorched fragments. The scorch marks were very discrete, possibly formed by hot ash/cinders being placed on top of unburnt bone after deposition (this is significant, since context 3758 was one of the main deposits rich in wood-ash). This major dump deposit overlay the former sites of buildings 24 and 39 from Phase 4i, and Phase 3bv deposits 5653 and 5617; the latter formed the contemporaneous living surface during the early to mid ninth century. Sherds of vessel 13 found in 3758, and several eighth-century *sceattas* from the same deposit (and Context 5503) indicate an element of re-worked material within these deposits. A small proportion (10% or less) of the bone fragments were eroded, which corroborates this observation. This was also the case for Context 5503 (another large dump deposit), although the overall proportion of poorly-preserved fragments was less than in Context 3758. This better state of preservation in 5503 is also reflected in the recovery of more complete composite bone artefacts, such as comb RF 6139 (Volume 1, FIG. 5.12*), which contrasts with the much smaller comb fragments from 3758 (Loveluck and Atkinson, Volume 1, Chapter 6). Overall, the quantity of possibly re-worked vertebrate remains was considered to be generally low in proportion to the amount that appeared to be relatively undisturbed. This concurs with evidence provided by the unfired clay loom-weights (from Context 3785), which were remarkably intact, a phenomenon unlikely to have occurred if extensive re-working of the deposits was prevalent.

Two contexts (3085 and 3531) displayed particularly poor overall preservation of vertebrate remains, including eroded and bleached fragments, indicating a higher degree of fragmentation probably as a result of trample damage along the route of path 3085. Evidence of later intrusion into the deposits was provided by rabbit bones in several contexts (800, 2859, 3107, 3531, 11461, and 11603) and five partial skeletons were recorded, including two juvenile individuals from Context 3531.

Animal bones from Phase 5a exhibited variability of preservation, angularity and colour, which was noted throughout the recorded assemblages from this phase group. The degree of fragmentation was average and showed similarities to that observed in Phase 4ii assemblages, whilst evidence of dog gnawing and burning were minimal. The presence of residual pottery in Contexts 5139 and 5193 once again suggests a small proportion of re-worked material within these deposits, reflected in the bone assemblage by a component of much-eroded fragments. However, the proportion of possibly re-worked to undisturbed material appeared to be small. Similarly, probably re-worked bone fragments were noted in contexts 17, 72, 275, 503, 2610 and 12057; whilst additionally, material from Contexts 49 and 2611 was much more poorly preserved overall and may have contained a higher proportion of redeposited material. In contrast, material from Contexts 195, 1707, 5849 and 5864 was better and more uniformly preserved.

As well as showing evidence of residuality, Context 49 contained several well-preserved rabbit bones. The latter were also present in Contexts 67, 195, 207, 230, 273, 277, 297, 300, 440, 461, 480, 677, 2611, 2858 and 4920. Whole and part skeletons (Contexts 230 and 297) and juvenile bones (Contexts 207, 273, 300, 677 and 4920) were recorded.

Preservation of vertebrate remains from Phase 5b was mostly noted as variable, although material from three contexts (out of a total of nine) was recorded as poorly preserved. Angularity and the colour of the fragments were similarly varied. The degree of fragmentation was similar to that found in Phase 5a material, with over half the fragments in all contexts being between 5 and 20 cm in their largest dimension, and over 10% in seven contexts being smaller. The amount of dog gnawing and

burning observed was less than 10% but fewer contexts were affected than in Phase 5a. Evidence of butchery was noted on up to 20% of the bones in all contexts and fresh breakage was particularly evident, with over 10% of fragments in all nine contexts affected.

Overall, Phase 5b deposits contained residual Romano-British pottery and seventh-, eighth- and early ninth-century artefacts, but they also contained contemporaneous pottery and other finds, suggesting that both re-worked and primary material was present. The vertebrate remains from Contexts 1728, 2562 and 3216 (all dumps) indicated a high proportion of re-worked/residual material, whilst dump 5553 contained a smaller amount. Other contexts containing small quantities of probable residual bone were 5659, 6036, 8153, 8237 and 12076.

Phase 6 (10th century)

By the early to mid tenth century, much of the excavated area of the site was used for new, large buildings, probably reflecting part of the residential focus of the settlement, and contemporaneous refuse deposits, for example dump 1680 (FIGS 2.10 & 2.11), seem to have been limited to the area south and west of buildings 7 and 34. The refuse material from this period reflects the continued importation of contemporary, regionally produced commodities in small quantities, such as Torksey, Torksey-type and Lincoln pottery wares. Following the demolition of building 7, vast quantities of well-preserved animal bones were deposited over the former building area, in dumps 3891 and 3610, which also contained Torksey and Lincoln pottery wares (Loveluck and Atkinson, Volume 1, Chapter 7; Young, Volume 2, Chapter 12). There were certainly re-worked elements from earlier deposits within these dumps: for example, a fragment of the imported seventh- to ninth-century grey-burnished ware vessel 56, first seen in the ditch refuse deposits, could have been derived from within the excavated area or from outside it. Further sherds of second- and third-century Romano-British pottery also suggest continued importation of material from other parts of the settlement. However, the largest residual pottery element consisted of sherds of Maxey wares. Deposit disturbance and re-working is also reflected in the occurrence of an imported silver penny of Alfred the Great, minted between AD 871 and 875, within dump 3255.

Nevertheless, numbers of fragments of the new, heavier 'bun-shaped' loom-weights were also recovered from dumps 3610, 3891, 6797, and others, alongside previously unseen lead weights related to bullion exchange transactions (Walton Rogers, Volume 2, Chapter 9; Wastling, Volume 2, Chapter 11; Kruse 1992, 67–95). These artefacts were found in association with the vast animal bone deposits, together with the largest collection of iron-working debris from the entire occupation sequence, and fragments of Torksey and Lincoln Kiln-type pottery wares (Loveluck and Atkinson, Volume

1, Chapter 7). The iron-working evidence is particularly notable for the first significant presence of smelting debris, alongside smithing detritus; moreover, these industrial residues were found in large fragments, suggesting limited post-depositional re-working or fragmentation (Starley, Volume 2, Chapter 10). As with deposit 3758, from the mid ninth century, if the material from the massive dumps 3891 and 3610 had all been re-worked, a greater degree of fragmentation of the large, un-fired clay loom-weight pieces and iron-working waste might have been expected, alongside a much more abraded and fragmented animal bone assemblage. Since a high degree of fragmentation was not evident, a greater proportion of material from the dumps of 6ii is likely to have been a product of the early to mid tenth century, than of earlier periods. In addition, the material deposited during the period between the early to mid tenth century seems to have resulted from activities taking place both within and beyond the excavated area, since the sheer quantity of animal bones alone probably reflects organised, communal disposal.

Overall, preservation and angularity of the animal bone from Phase 6 was variable, with almost all contexts containing a mixture of spiky, battered and rounded fragments. Colour was similarly variable throughout: two contexts contained only brown fragments, the rest a mixture of fawn and brown. The degree of fragmentation was similar to that observed in Phase 5 material. Over half the fragments in all contexts were between 50mm and 200mm in largest dimension, eight contexts contained less than 10% smaller fragments, the rest up to 20%. However, unlike those of Phase 5, many contexts contained up to 10% of larger fragments. Dog-gnawed and burnt fragments formed up to 10% of the assemblage, and fragments with butchery marks formed up to 20% of the assemblage in all contexts. Fresh breakage was also evident on up to 20% of the fragments in most contexts.

The finds and pottery give a mixed impression of the residuality of the Phase 6 deposits and evidence from bone preservation suggests that some contexts contained more residual material than others. Contexts with both eroded bones and residual finds included 1672, 2488, 3417, 3610, 3891 and 6490, although the amount of residual material in the major dumps (Context 3891) was much less in proportion to the total volume of bone than in the other contexts, suggesting that the vast majority of remains were from primary or at least contemporaneous deposits. However, vertebrate remains from Context 3610 (dump) were particularly poorly preserved overall, suggesting a high degree of weathering or surface attrition. Contexts 1680, 3255, 3730, 4195, 5871, 5930 and 5988 all contained a small proportion of possibly re-worked bones but no residual finds. Intrusive rabbit bones were noted in Contexts 78, 533, 3417, 3236, 6961, 7077, 7078, 7090, 7506, 10296. Two partial skeletons were noted in Contexts 3417 and 7077 and juvenile bones in Contexts 3236, 7090 and 10296.

Phase 6iii (late 10th–early 11th century)

During the second half of the tenth century, indications of the importation of material into the excavated area from a habitation zone, probably located to the east, around a possible Late Saxon pre-cursor to All Saints' Church, demonstrate the use of the former occupation area as a communal refuse zone (Loveluck and Atkinson, Volume 1, Chapter 7; Loveluck, Volume 4, Chapter 2). At the same time, there is also evidence for the further disturbance and re-organisation of remains from earlier refuse deposits. Furthermore, zonation, in terms of where the latest datable Anglo-Saxon material was deposited, is also evident amongst the refuse material from this depositional phase (FIG. 2.12), in contrast to the occurrence of predominantly residual finds.

The latest Anglo-Saxon finds tended to be located in the south of the site, and along its eastern margins. For example, the discrete dump 6300 accumulated along the eastern edge of the site; in its abundant textile manu-facturing, iron-working debris and animal bones, it was very similar to deposits 3610 and 3891 from Phase 6ii. Torksey-type ware predominated amongst the later Saxon pottery wares, together with Late Saxon local ware, although the number of residual Maxey-type, Ipswich and Early Lincolnshire Fine-shelled ware sherds outnumbered the later types. Later Saxon 'bun-shaped' loom-weights also predominated, as did wool-comb teeth, and heavier pin-beaters, for producing the heavier woollen cloth of the tenth century at Flixborough (Walton Rogers, Volume 2, Chapter 9). Both residual and intrusive coinage was also present, in the form of a penny of Aethelwulf of Wessex, minted between AD 855 and 858, and a thirteenth-century penny of Henry III.

Further south, the 'dark soil' refuse deposits contained small numbers of late tenth- to early eleventh-century pottery sherds, amongst residual finds. They also contained occasional twelfth- to fourteenth-century pottery sherds, from the upper excavation 'spits' of deposits, reflecting their character as the High Medieval activity surface, associated with an oven and other features (Loveluck and Atkinson, Volume 1, Chapter 7). Consequently, the diagnostically datable Anglo-Saxon finds enable some tentative suggestions to be made as to the nature of certain aspects of life on the settlement in its latest Anglo-Saxon phase, although caution has to be exercised due to the intrusion of later material.

The two areas of dark soils (dated to Phase 6iii) showed differences in their finds profiles, suggesting that the deposits in the north-west area were derived from re-worked earlier material to a much greater degree than those to the south-east. This observation is, however, not borne out by the evidence from bone preservation, as almost all contexts appeared to contain weathered or worn bone material – most fragments being described as slightly battered. In fact, the proportion of poorly preserved, eroded fragments was higher in contexts 1286,

1449, 1454, 1459 and 1479 (south-east area), than in Contexts 1831, 1832, 1833, 1836 and 1837 (north-west area).

The nature of the poorly preserved bone was also different between the areas: the south-east contexts contained eroded and rounded fragments similar to those in all previous phases; whilst the north-west deposits contained bleached and weathered bones, suggesting that they had lain in a surface midden. Contexts other than dark soils, where a few eroded and rounded fragments indicated a degree of re-working, included 636, 1812, 3451, 6300, 6489, 6498 and 6499. The eroded, and possibly also weathered, vertebrate remains here may be the result of the use of the dark soils as the medieval activity surface, rather than re-working of earlier material. The preservation of material in Contexts 1461 and 7817 was much better than other contexts in this phase and no residual material was noted.

Intrusive medieval pottery and finds were noted from Contexts 636, 6300, 6489, 6499 and some of the bones from Context 6499 were distinctly differently (and better) preserved than the rest, possibly indicating that these, too, may have been intrusive. The twelfth- to fourteenth-century pottery was probably worked into the surface of the 'dark soils' when they formed the activity surface around the large oven and pits of Period 7. Other intrusive evidence in the form of rabbit bones was noted from Contexts 555, 779, 1282, 1835, 1836, 1840, 1982, 2008, 2016, 2021, 2024, 2177, 2182, 2183, 3413 and 6300. Context 555 contained an incomplete rabbit skeleton and Contexts 2177, 2182 and 6300 contained juvenile rabbit bones.

Summary

On the basis of the archaeological data outlined above, it is abundantly clear that, although some material was re-worked and/or re-deposited, the greatest part of the finds assemblage from Flixborough can be readily assigned to a specific period or phase. By association, therefore, the bulk of the animal bone assemblage can similarly be broadly attributed with confidence to the major chronological periods. Where secondary evidence for the presence of residual material was evident (in the form of the preservation and fragmentation of the animal bones themselves), this corroborated in most cases the conclusions drawn from the other finds assemblages.

The finds profiles, therefore, indicate that most of the bones are certainly representative of the settlement as a whole between the mid eighth and the mid to late tenth centuries AD. As a result, further detailed exploration of a range of themes relating to aspects of life on the settlement can now be undertaken through the detailed analysis of the vertebrate remains (see following chapters). Their value as components of the integrated analysis of all the forms of archaeological data from Flixborough, for examining site-specific questions, and also the wider importance of the results for early medieval

settlement studies in England are also discussed in Volume 4.

3.4 Aspects of taphonomy and preservation
by James Barrett, Keith Dobney, Deborah Jaques, John Carrott, Allan Hall, Amanda Bretman and Susan Haynes

Taphonomic pathways and the wet-sieved fish bone assemblage

Although recovery is unlikely to be a significant bias at Flixborough – a result of the systematic and large-scale sieving and sampling programme carried out at the site – fish bone is known to be susceptible to a variety of taphonomic processes. Moreover, different species and elements exhibit varying resistance to decay (Nicholson 1992; Lernau and Ben-Harris 1994; Nicholson 1996). It is thus essential to assess any intra-site variability in preservation prior to further analysis of the assemblage.

TABLES 3.1 and 3.2 show bone completeness (fragment-ation) and texture data for the sieved fish assemblage subdivided by phase and context type respectively. The two measures are correlated, if only weakly so (Spearman's rho = 0.240, p = <0.001),[1] as one might expect given that they characterise slightly different aspects of bone survival. Both suggest a relatively good level of preservation in all phases and context types. Between 22% and 47% of the diagnostic elements were over 80% complete and never more than 22% exhibited a poor (flaky or powdery) texture.

Despite this general observation, preservation was not constant across time and space. Kruskal-Wallis tests of the data summarised in TABLES 3.1 and 3.2 indicate significant differences in fragmentation and bone texture between phases and context types (% completeness by phase: chi-square = 26.12, df = 5, p = <0.001; texture by phase: chi-square = 59.44, df = 5, p = <0.001; % completeness by context type: chi-square = 25.67, df = 10, p = 0.004; texture by context type: chi-Square = 46.20, df = 10, p = <0.001).

The least fragmented and most solid fish bones appear to derive from Phases 3b, 4–5b and 6, with the most fragmented and fragile specimens being from Phases 1 and 2–3a. Fish bones from Phase 6iii occupy the middle ground. The clearest pattern is thus an improvement in preservation (and thus representation) of fish bones from Phase 2–3a to Phase 3b. Limiting consideration to the six most abundant context types, dumps appear to have contained the least fragmented and most solid fish bones, whilst, conversely, soakaways yielded the most frag-mented and brittle specimens. The preservation of material from other context types was somewhat more variable.

The incidence of other bone damage, in the form of crushing, partial digestion, carnivore tooth impressions,

	1	2–3a	3b	4–5b	6	6iii	Unphased[1]	Total
% Complete								
≤20	6	47	25	20	5	0	2	105
21–40	9	65	35	31	11	2	2	155
41–60	9	68	43	41	7	2	3	173
61–80	12	83	71	73	26	6	4	275
81–100	10	104	112	105	32	4	9	376
Total	46	367	286	270	81	14	20	1084
Texture								
1 (Excellent)	2	36	32	30	5	0	2	107
2 (Good)	7	122	158	130	39	5	5	466
3 (Fair)	27	176	86	97	31	9	9	435
4 (poor)	10	33	10	11	6	0	2	72
Total	46	367	286	268	81	14	18	1080

[1]Statistical tests discussed in the text exclude the unphased data.

%	1	2–3a	3b	4–5b	6	6iii	Total
% Complete							
≤20	13.0	12.8	8.7	7.4	6.2	0.0	9.7
21–40	19.6	17.7	12.2	11.5	13.6	14.3	14.3
41–60	19.6	18.5	15.0	15.2	8.6	14.3	16.0
61–80	26.1	22.6	24.8	27.0	32.1	42.9	25.4
81–100	21.7	28.3	39.2	38.9	39.5	28.6	34.7
Total	100	100	100	100	100	100	100
Texture							
1 (Excellent)	4.3	9.8	11.2	11.2	6.2	0.0	9.9
2 (Good)	15.2	33.2	55.2	48.5	48.1	35.7	43.1
3 (Fair)	58.7	48.0	30.1	36.2	38.3	64.3	40.3
4 (Poor)	21.7	9.0	3.5	4.1	7.4	0.0	6.7
Total	100	100	100	100	100	100	100

TABLE 3.1 Preservation of fish remains recovered from bulk-sieved samples by phase (NISP).

and burning, is summarised by phase and principal context type in TABLES 3.3 and 3.4. In these cases, both identified and unidentified specimens are considered. The number of modified bones is small for all four variables, with 141 crushed (1.3%), 111 burned (1.0%), 13 partly digested (0.1%), and one (<0.1%) gnawed specimens. Although the paucity of gnawed and partly-digested fish bones is consistent with the generally good state of preservation, the incidence of at least some crushed bones and the presence of at least some partly-digested specimens does imply a low level of carnivore modification or the presence of human faecal material

within the deposits (Wheeler and Jones 1989, 73–75).

The small samples of digested and gnawed specimens make intra-site patterning difficult to interpret. In the case of crushed bones, however, chi-square tests suggest no significant differences across time and space (crushed versus uncrushed specimens by phase: chi-square = 4.77, df = 5, p = 0.445; by context type: chi-square = 5.25, df = 5, p = 0.386). Conversely, burned bones do show some temporal and spatial patterning (burned versus unburned specimens by phase: chi-square = 66.73, df = 5, p = <0.001; by context type: chi-square = 45.05, df = 5, p = <0.001). They are over-represented in Phase 4–5b and

NISP	DUMP	PH	SOAK	OCC	PIT	DKSL	TCH	UNKN	DCH	SLOT	OVEN	Total
% Complete												
<20	41	13	26	14	4	0	1	6	0	0	0	105
21–40	61	24	30	18	2	5	4	7	1	2	1	155
41–60	68	22	41	15	9	2	4	11	1	0	0	173
61–80	128	34	42	27	17	11	7	7	1	0	1	275
81–100	176	46	58	30	28	7	15	11	4	1	0	376
Total	474	139	197	104	60	25	31	42	7	3	2	1084
Texture												
1 (Excellent)	52	15	15	10	5	1	3	4	2	0	0	107
2 (Good)	246	41	61	41	26	10	11	25	2	1	2	466
3 (Fair)	149	68	103	46	28	13	13	12	1	2	0	435
4 (Poor)	26	15	18	6	1	1	4	1	0	0	0	72
Total	473	139	197	103	60	25	31	42	5	3	2	1080

%	DUMP	PH	SOAK	OCC	PIT	DKSL	TCH	UNKN	DCH	SLOT	OVEN	Total
% Complete												
<20	8.6	9.4	13.2	13.5	6.7	0.0	3.2	14.3	0.0	0.0	0.0	9.7
21–40	12.9	17.3	15.2	17.3	3.3	20.0	12.9	16.7	14.3	66.7	50.0	14.3
41–60	14.3	15.8	20.8	14.4	15.0	8.0	12.9	26.2	14.3	0.0	0.0	16.0
61–80	27.0	24.5	21.3	26.0	28.3	44.0	22.6	16.7	14.3	0.0	50.0	25.4
81–100	37.1	33.1	29.4	28.8	46.7	28.0	48.4	26.2	57.1	33.3	0.0	34.7
Total	100	100	100	100	100	100	100	100	100	100	100	100
Texture												
1 (Excellent)	11.0	10.8	7.6	9.7	8.3	4.0	9.7	9.5	40.0	0.0	0.0	9.9
2 (Good)	52.0	29.5	31.0	39.8	43.3	40.0	35.5	59.5	40.0	33.3	100.0	43.1
3 (Fair)	31.5	48.9	52.3	44.7	46.7	52.0	41.9	28.6	20.0	66.7	0.0	40.3
4 (poor)	5.5	10.8	9.1	5.8	1.7	4.0	12.9	2.4	0.0	0.0	0.0	6.7
Total	100	100	100	100	100	100	100	100	100	100	100	100

TABLE 3.2 Preservation of fish remains recovered from bulk-sieved samples by context type (NISP). See Appendix 3 for key to context types.

pits, under-represented in Phase 2–3a and soakaways. These results contrast with the bone fragmentation and texture data. Soakaways, for example, contained the lowest representation of burned bone but among the highest levels of fragmentation and the poorest texture scores. Similarly, Phase 4–5b yielded relatively complete and solid bones despite having a high level of burned specimens and Phase 2–3a exhibited more fragmented and fragile bones despite producing few burnt specimens. One explanation for these patterns may lie in the reduced strength of bone which has been heated but not fully calcined (Nicholson 1992; 1996). In deposits showing poor preservation, a higher proportion of burnt specimens may well have been rendered unrecoverable by various additional taphonomic processes.

Histological studies of geese bones from Flixborough: an attempt to predict aDNA preservation

During the analysis of the Flixborough animal bone assemblage, an attempt was made to identify the various species of geese that may have been present, using recently-developed biomolecular techniques (principally through the extraction and sequencing of ancient

Modification	Common Name	Element	1[1]	2–3a[1]	3b[1]	4–5b[1]	6[1]	6iii[1]	Unphased	Total
Carnivore Gnawing	Pike	Dentary		1						1
Partial Digestion	Salmon & Trout Family	Caudal Vertebra						2		2
		Penultimate Vertebra						1		1
	Smelt	Caudal Vertebra							1	1
	Eel	Caudal Vertebra			1					1
		Ceratohyal				1				1
	Pike	Abdominal Vertebra						2		2
	Unidentified	Abdominal Vertebra				2		2	1	5
	Total Partly Digested		0	0	1	3	0	7	2	13
	Undigested		392	2723	2421	3200	1275	261	298	10570
	% Partly Digested		0.0	0.0	0.0	0.1	0.0	2.6	0.7	0.1
Crushing	Salmon & Trout Family	Abdominal Vertebra		1						1
		Caudal Vertebra					2			2
		Vertebra		1						1
	Smelt	Abdominal Vertebra		3	7	6	1			17
		Caudal Vertebra				1				1
	Eel	Abdominal Vertebra	4	7	13	22	8	3	1	58
		Caudal Vertebra	2	5	6	14	3		1	31
	Halibut Family	Abdominal Vertebra			2					2
		Caudal Vertebra		2	1		1			5
	Pike	Abdominal Vertebra	2	3	2	1				7
		Basioccipital	1							1
	Perch	Caudal Vertebra		5	2	2	1			9
	Unidentified	Caudal Vertebra		2		1	2			3

TABLE 3.3 *Bone modification of fish remains recovered from bulk-sieved samples by phase (continued opposite).*

Modification	Common Name	Element	1¹	2–3a¹	3b¹	4–5b¹	6¹	6iii¹	Unphased	Total
		Total Crushed¹	9	29	33	47	18	3	2	141
		Uncrushed¹	383	2694	2389	3156	1257	265	298	10442
		% Crushed	2.3	1.1	1.4	1.5	1.4	1.1	0.7	1.3
Burning	Salmon & Trout Family	Abdominal Vertebra				1				1
		Caudal Vertebra				1				1
		Vertebra				1				1
	Smelt	Abdominal Vertebra		1	1	3				5
		Caudal Vertebra					1			1
	Eel	Abdominal Vertebra		1	3	20	2	3		29
		Basioccipital				2				2
		Caudal Vertebra		3	4	22	2			31
	Halibut Family	Abdominal Vertebra				1				1
		Caudal Vertebra				4	1			5
	Pike	Abdominal Vertebra		1						1
		Caudal Vertebra				1				1
	Carp Family	Abdominal Vertebra			1	2	2			5
		Caudal Vertebra		1	1	4				6
	Unidentified			2	6	10	1	2		21
		Total Burnt¹	0	9	16	72	9	5	0	111
		Unburnt¹	392	2714	2406	3131	1266	263	300	10472
		% Burnt	0.0	0.3	0.7	2.2	0.7	1.9	0.0	1.0

¹Variables used for chi-square analyses, see discussion in text

TABLE 3.3 continued.

Modification	DUMP[1]	PH[1]	SOAK[1]	OCC[1]	PIT[1]	DKSL[1]
Total Carnivore Gnawing				1		
Total Partly Digested	3			1		7
Undigested	4855	1479	1366	1155	642	380
% Partly Digested	0.1	0.0	0.0	0.1	0.0	1.8
Total Crushed[1]	65	21	20	12	14	3
Uncrushed[1]	4793	1458	1346	1144	628	384
% Crushed	1.3	1.4	1.5	1.0	2.2	0.8
Total Burnt[1]	42	15	1	16	20	7
Unburnt[1]	4816	1464	1365	1140	622	380
% Burnt	0.9	1.0	0.1	1.4	3.1	1.8
Total NISP of Context Type	4858	1479	1366	1156	642	387

[1]Variables used for chi-square analyses, see discussion in text

TABLE *3.4 Bone modification of fish remains recovered from bulk-sieved samples by context type. See Appendix 3 for key to context types.*

mitochondrial DNA). In advance of these attempts, research was instigated into the histology of bone, which attempted to predict aDNA preservation. Although the full results are published elsewhere (Haynes *et al.* 2002), the following account summarises the results as they pertain to the Flixborough avian assemblage.

In a preliminary study (Barnes 1998), it was found that goose bones from Flixborough that yielded DNA also displayed excellent histological preservation. This finding was in agreement with previous studies that had highlighted the possible link between DNA preservation and histological preservation (Hagelberg *et al.* 1991; Colson *et al.* 1997a and b), and suggested that, on the basis of this relationship, bone histology could be used as a potential screening method for predicting samples that were most likely to yield DNA. Technical difficulties associated with ancient DNA research, principally degraded templates, low yields of DNA, and very low success rates (19% in the preliminary study), meant that anything which served to increase the likelihood of recovering DNA would save time and money later. An index which could be used to classify levels of histological preservation was devised by Hedges *et al.* (1995) for mammalian bone and it was proposed that this index be used as the basis for the classification of the goose bones from Flixborough prior to selection of bones for DNA extraction. Modifications to this index were made as a result of the differences in structure between mammalian and avian bone (Haynes *et al.* 2002).

Interestingly, the results obtained in this study for avian bone histology show a marked difference from those obtained for mammalian bone (Hedges *et al.* 1995).

Whereas in mammalian bone, if diagenetic alteration occurred it usually proceeded to completion, this was not true of the avian bone examined. Instead of seeing either very good or very bad preservation, there was a far more even distribution of bones throughout the categories, with the majority of bones falling into the intermediate category. This observation is unlikely to be the result of differences in structure between avian and mammalian bone, since a parallel study of mammalian bone by Colson *et al.* (1997a) also identified a similar distribution with respect to bone histology. The effect is perhaps more likely to be the result of differences in burial environments between different archaeological sites.

A feature that was not quantified in this study was the pattern of histological destruction. This also appears to differ between avian and mammalian bones. In avian bone, destruction appears to proceed from the inner surface (as opposed to the outer surface in mammalian bone). This may be a unique feature of avian bone or may be a site-specific observation. Further work on avian material from other sites (and non-avian material from this site) would be required to investigate this.

While it should be noted that there were nearly four times as many bones in the 'dump' deposit category, the observation that bones in 'dumps' were better preserved than bones in 'non-dump' deposits supports the expectation that burial environment (as opposed to age) is a critical factor for preservation. As previously mentioned, the exceptional preservation at this site has been attributed to the unusual burial environment: 'the sand has a calcareous component which, combined with its constant accretion, has meant that some of the underlying ash and occupation horizons have never suffered acid leaching' (Canti 1992).

Screening methods for DNA

Haynes *et al.* (2002) also observed a positive relationship between histological preservation and DNA survival in the goose humeri studied from Flixborough. However, the extreme correlation that was observed in the study by Colson *et al.* (1997a), in which the best category had 100% success and the lowest category 0% (with respect to DNA amplification), was not apparent for the Flixborough material. The best-preserved samples had a success rate of only 42%, but even those samples displaying the worst preservation had a success rate of 13%. Whilst screening samples on the basis of histological preservation can identify those samples with the best chances of DNA recovery, in the case of the geese bones from Flixborough, at least, samples with poor preservation could not be entirely excluded without the risk of possibly losing valuable data. If only samples with good histological preservation (i.e. classes 4 and 5) had been used, up to 44% of the sequence data (i.e. 24 DNA sequences – discussed in more detail in Chapter 7) would not have been available for interpretation.

DNA survival

It has been suggested (e.g. Hagelberg *et al.* 1991; Millard 1993) that burial environment is a critical factor for the preservation of biomolecules in archaeological remains. Whilst this appears to be the case for histological preservation, the relationship between environment and DNA survival was not found to be significant at Flixborough. The reasons for this are not clear, but again the need for a better understanding of the factors that influence DNA survival is apparent. The lack of a significant relationship between the age of a sample and the ability to recover DNA was expected, as it has previously been demonstrated that age does not influence DNA preservation (Pääbo 1989).

The preliminary study of ancient geese DNA mentioned previously (Barnes *et al.* 1998) postulated a possible correlation between the minimum shaft diameter of goose bone and DNA recovery. Our lack of any correlation in this respect, is encouraging, since it indicates that the extraction (and subsequent identification) of DNA from the bones of smaller geese species (e.g. barnacle and brent) remains possible.

In summary, the results obtained from an investigation of the geese bones from Flixborough into the use of histology as a screening method for DNA survival highlight the lack of understanding of the mechanisms of DNA preservation. Further research into this area may improve the potential for the application of screening methods and will also help in the development of DNA extraction protocols.

Preservation of the archaeobotanical remains

Since the very small assemblage of plant remains were for the most part preserved by charring, and came from well-drained sands, the presence of uncharred plant remains in a few contexts suggests these may be intrusive and of recent origin. There is also a distinct possibility of re-working of the charred material, especially as the deposits were potentially so mobile. However, some of the charred remains, such as the fine vegetative fragments and the pods of sea plantain (PLATE 3.1a–c), are surely too delicate to have survived re-working unless bodies of existing occupation material were moved *en bloc* (which, on the basis of stratigraphic evidence, appears not to have been likely in this instance).

Recent taphonomic pathways of the hand-collected molluscan assemblage

An unexpected aspect of the hand-collected shell assemblage was that, although Hall and Milles (1993) in an initial assessment exercise stated that 'most of the shell was in good condition (and likely to remain so)', when the remains were examined again for main phase recording (in 1999) this was no longer the case. Fragmentation and erosion scores for most contexts were recorded as either 2 or 3 (i.e. moderate or high); almost all of the bags of shell contained very many mm-size flakes of shell, and many also contained larger fragments which had separated post-excavation (and presumably post-assessment). The reason for this post-excavation deterioration of the shell is unknown but a possible explanation would be that the shell became damp during storage (which would account for the softening and subsequent erosion of the extremities of the valves). If it were then subject to fluctuations in temperature within a few degrees of freezing this might account for the larger flakes – perhaps caused by a process akin to 'freeze-thaw action' separating the shell along the plane of growth layers. Subsequent movement of the assemblage would certainly reduce many of the fragile larger shell flakes to mm-scale fragments.

Thus, although of little relevance to our understanding of the Saxon settlement, these findings highlight the crucial importance of correct post-excavation treatment and storage facilities, and throw into question our often complacent assumptions about the permanence of at least some parts of the physical archive.

Note

1   Completeness and texture values were recoded prior to analysis such that a positive coefficient indicates a positive correlation.

4 The Nature of the Bioarchaeological Assemblages

Deborah Jaques, Keith Dobney, James Barrett, Cluny Johnstone, John Carrott and Allan Hall

4.1 Introduction

The decision to present and discuss the bioarchaeological evidence from Flixborough under a series of broad thematic headings obviously provides a sound framework within which a range of diverse issues can be more readily explored (see Chapter 1). However, this structure allows little scope for a detailed discussion of the overall nature and character of the various categories of evidence. This chapter, therefore, provides the only conventional synthesis of the main characteristics and major components of the bioarchaeological assemblages.

All of these remains have played a major role in significantly advancing our understanding of a crucial period of English history. The sheer size of the Flixborough vertebrate assemblage (over 200,000 fragments) makes it one of the largest ever recovered of Middle or Late Saxon date in this country. The unique stratigraphic sequence at the site, linked with the presence of associated large assemblages of pottery, and other small-finds, has meant that the bioarchaeological remains can be extremely tightly dated. As a result, a detailed chronological picture can be drawn of many aspects of the nature and character of the settlement, which places the evidence in a local, regional, national and even international framework.

4.2 Recovery

The windblown sand deposits, which made up most of the sediment matrix at the site, meant that recovery of all finds categories was made somewhat easier than is often the case, both in terms of overall visibility within the excavated matrix and the ease by which material could be retrieved through various recovery techniques. A large-scale on-site dry-sieving programme was instigated which resulted in very large finds assemblages that included animal bones and marine shells. Although systematic, the on-site recovery programme unwittingly introduced several biases which had to be accounted for during subsequent detailed quantitative analysis (see Appendix 2 for details).

By far the most prevalent remains were those of non-human vertebrates (primarily mammals, birds and fish – see below). In addition, systematic sampling (>1,500 separate samples), wet-sieving and flotation of all context types provided representative assemblages of smaller vertebrates (primarily fish – the largest, most systematically recovered, Saxon fish bone assemblage from Britain to date), charred plant remains, and terrestrial and freshwater molluscs.

4.3 Vertebrates

A range of domestic and wild mammals was represented in the huge assemblage from Flixborough (TABLE 4.1), together with a vast collection of bird bones. The latter were mainly domestic, but included a quantity of wildfowl, game birds and scavengers. In total, 41,664 mammal and bird bones were recorded principally from the hand-collected and coarse-sieved assemblage. Fish bone also formed a significant part of the assemblage (TABLE 4.2). 6,232 identified and 4,332 of other specimens, were recovered by comprehensive sorting of the >2mm sample fraction from wet-sieved residues. 1,022 identified and 1,502 of other specimens, included additional hand-collected material and some bone recovered by sieving on site using 10 mm mesh.

4.4 Molluscs

Shell remains were rather sparse in the deposits. In total, fourteen boxes (each of approximately 16 litres) of hand-collected shell (primarily fragments of oyster, *Ostrea*

Species		Phase 1	Phase 2–3a	Phase 3b	Phase 4–5b	Phase 6	Phase 6iii	Total
Talpa europaea	mole	-	-	-	4	-	-	4
Oryctolagus cuniculus	rabbit	3	33	1	127	69	28	261
cf. *O. cuniculus*	?rabbit	-	-	1	2	1	-	4
Lepus sp.	hare	-	3	18	8	4	1	34
Clethrionomys glareolus	bank vole	-	-	1	-	-	-	1
Microtus agrestis	field vole	-	-	1	-	-	-	1
Microtine	vole species	-	-	1	-	-	-	1
Apodemus sylvaticus/A. flavicollis	wood/yellow-necked mouse	-	-	-	1	-	-	1
Mus musculus	house mouse	-	1	-	-	-	-	1
Murine	mouse species	-	1	3	-	-	-	4
Rattus sp.	rat	-	-	-	-	1	-	1
Cetacean	unidentified cetacean	-	1	4	-	6	4	15
Balaenoptera acutorostrata	minke whale	-	-	-	1	-	2	3
cf. *B. acutorostrata*	?minke whale	-	-	-	1	2	-	3
Tursiops truncatus	bottlenose dolphin	-	7	22	14	55	17	115
cf. *T. truncatus*	?bottlenose dolphin	-	4	17	14	12	3	50
Globicephala melas/Orcinus orca	pilot whale/killer whale	-	-	-	-	1	-	1
Canid	canid	-	-	2	1	3	2	8
cf. *Vulpes vulpes*	?fox	-	1	1	1	6	-	9
Canis f. domestic	dog	-	-	-	1	-	1	2
cf. *Martes martes*	?pine marten	-	-	5	-	1	-	6
Felis f. domestic	cat	-	-	12	23	17	11	63
Equus f. domestic	horse	1	82	316	431	514	157	1501
Sus scrofa	boar	-	-	2	-	2	1	5
Sus f. domestic	pig	36	716	1582	2559	1702	574	7169
Cervus elaphus	red deer	-	-	-	2	2	-	4
cf. *C. elaphus*	?red deer	-	-	-	3	-	-	3
Capreolus capreolus	roe deer	-	13	28	36	35	9	121
cf. *C. capreolus*	?roe deer	-	-	-	-	1	-	1
Bos f. domestic	cattle	52	1104	2939	2557	2567	1042	10261

TABLE 4.1 *Hand-collected vertebrate remains, by phase (continued overleaf).*

Deborah Jaques et al.

Species		Phase 1	Phase 2–3a	Phase 3b	Phase 4–5b	Phase 6	Phase 6iii	Total
Capra f. domestic	goat	-	7	35	16	26	3	87
cf. *Capra* f. domestic	?goat	-	1	8	4	8	2	23
Ovis f. domestic	sheep	24	258	525	990	546	179	2522
Caprovid	sheep/goat	55	614	1641	2450	1731	771	7262
Homo sapiens	human	-	11	1	6	2	29	49
Rana temporaria	frog	-	-	-	2	-	-	2
Bufo bufo	toad	-	1	-	-	1	-	2
Amphibian	amphibian	-	-	2	3	-	-	5
Subtotal		*171*	*2858*	*7168*	*9257*	*7315*	*2836*	*29605*
Cygnus sp.	swan	-	-	1	-	1	-	2
cf. *Ardea cinerea*	?grey heron	-	2	-	-	-	-	2
Anser brachyrhynchus	pink-footed goose	-	-	-	2	-	-	2
cf. *A. brachyrhynchus*	?pink-footed goose	-	-	1	-	-	-	1
Anser sp.	goose	31	489	985	1348	751	94	3698
cf. *Anser* sp.	?goose	-	-	-	1	-	-	1
cf. *Branta leucopsis*	?barnacle goose	7	191	351	107	185	5	846
cf. *Branta bernicla*	?brent goose	-	-	3	3	3	-	9
Anas cf. *platyrhynchos*	?Mallard	-	-	-	9	-	-	9
Anas crecca	teal	-	-	7	2	2	1	12
cf. *Anas crecca*	?teal	-	-	1	1	-	-	2
Anas sp.	duck	5	42	60	116	64	19	306
cf. *Anas* sp.	?duck	-	-	3	1	1	1	6
Raptor	raptor	-	-	-	2	-	-	2
cf. *Milvus milvus*	?red kite	-	-	19	-	1	-	20
cf. *Circus aeruginosus*	?marsh harrier	-	-	1	-	1	-	2
cf. *Buteo buteo*	?buzzard	-	-	20	4	1	-	25
Lyrurus tetrix	black grouse	-	7	17	-	9	-	33
cf. *L. tetrix*	?black grouse	-	-	-	2	-	-	2
Gallus f. domestic	chicken	38	846	1596	1817	1192	202	5691

TABLE 4.1 continued.

Species		Phase 1	Phase 2–3a	Phase 3b	Phase 4–5b	Phase 6	Phase 6iii	Total
cf. *Gallus* f. domestic	?chicken	1	3	2	5	1	1	13
cf. *Phasianus colchicus*	?pheasant	-	-	-	1	-	-	1
Grus sp.	crane	2	26	115	13	72	-	228
cf. *Grus* sp.	?crane	-	-	-	-	1	-	1
wader sp.	wader	-	12	11	6	6	-	35
?wader	?wader	-	-	1	1	-	-	2
cf. *Vanellus vanellus*	?lapwing	-	1	1	1	-	-	3
cf. *Pluvialis* sp.	?plover	2	173	76	16	31	3	301
Numenius arquata	curlew	-	7	1	3	9	-	20
cf. *N. arquata*	?curlew	-	6	1	1	1	-	9
cf. *Scolopax rusticola*	?woodcock	-	2	1	-	2	-	5
Laridae	gull family	-	3	2	-	2	-	7
cf. *Larus fuscus*	?lesser black-back gull	-	1	-	-	-	-	1
Columbidae	dove/pigeon family	3	29	75	29	35	2	173
cf. Columbidae	?dove/pigeon family	-	-	-	-	-	1	1
Tyto alba	barn owl	-	-	-	1	-	-	1
cf. *T. alba*	?barn owl	-	-	-	1	-	-	1
Strix aluco	tawny owl	-	-	-	2	1	-	3
Turdidae	blackbird family	-	1	-	-	1	-	2
cf. Turdidae	?blackbird family	-	-	3	-	-	-	3
Garrulus glandarius/Pica pica	jay/magpie	-	-	-	-	2	-	2
Corvus monedula	jackdaw	-	1	-	-	-	-	1
C. frugilegus	rook	-	-	-	1	-	-	1
C. corone/C. frugilegus	crow/rook	2	8	46	37	18	1	112
C. corax	raven	-	-	-	-	4	-	4
Subtotal		*91*	*1850*	*3400*	*3533*	*2397*	*330*	*11601*
Total		**262**	**4708**	**10568**	**12790**	**9712**	**3166**	**41206**

Table 4.1 continued.

Species	Common Name	Hand-collected	Sieved
Marine			
Clupea harengus	atlantic herring	-	11
Conger conger	conger eel	7	1
Gadus morhua	cod	12	2
Melanogrammus aeglefinus	haddock	5	2
Pollachius virens	saith	2	-
Molva molva	ling	1	-
Scomber scombrus	atlantic mackerel	1	-
Aspitrigla cuculus	red gurnard	1	-
Soleidae	sole family	2	-
Solea solea	sole	1	-
Subtotal		*32*	*16*
Migratory			
Acipenser sturio	sturgeon	9	2
Alosa alosa/A. fallax	allis shad/twaite shad	-	7
A. fallax	twaite shad	1	-
Salmonidae	salmon and trout family	258	157
Osmerus eperlanus	smelt	11	910
Anguilla anguilla	eel	119	3097
Dicentrarchus labra	european seabass	1	-
Platichthys flesus /Pleuronectes platessa	flounder/plaice	5	145
Subtotal		*404*	*4318*
Fresh Water			
Esox lucius	pike	338	588
Cyprinidae	carp family	57	319
cf. *Barbus barbus*	barbel?	-	1
Tinca tinca	tench	1	2
cf. *Blicca bjoerkna*	silver bream?	1	-
Scardinius erythrophthalmus	rudd	1	-
cf. *S. erythrophthalmus*	rudd?	-	1
Rutilus rutilus	roach	9	6
cf. *R. rutilus*	roach?	-	1
Leuciscus cephalus	chub	-	5
L. leuciscus	dace	1	7
Leuciscus sp.	chub/dace	-	9
Cobitidae	loach family	-	1
Lota lota	burbot	-	11
Perca fluviatilis	perch	68	290
Gymnocephalus cernua	ruffe	1	
Subtotal		*477*	*1241*

TABLE *4.2 Total number of fish remains by recovery technique (continued opposite).*

edulis) were recovered, representing material from 309 deposits (TABLE 4.3). The bulk sediment samples (processed either on site or later in the laboratory), produced some small assemblages of a somewhat restricted range of snail taxa (TABLE 4.4).

4.5 Plant remains

Like molluscs, plant remains were sparse in the deposits at Flixborough and almost always preserved by charring. There were a few uncharred remains which are suspected to be intrusive (found together with a few apparently modern insect remains). Otherwise, there were a small number of remains preserved as 'silica skeletons' – a

Species	Common Name	Hand-collected	Sieved
Other			
Clupeidae	herring family	1	3
Gadidae	cod family	2	5
Gasterosteidae	stickleback family	-	14
Pleuronectidae	halibut family	106	635
Subtotal		*109*	*657*
Total Identified		**1022**	**6232**
Other (Pleuronectidae 1st anal pterygiophores)		12	19
Unidentified		1483	4332
Total		**2517**	**10583**

TABLE 4.2 continued.

Context type (group)	Phase group 1	2–3a	3b	4–5b	6	6iii	Total
DEP	-	1	-	-	-	-	1
DKSL	-	-	-	-	17	18	35
DUMP	-	2	13	35	9	2	61
GULLY (FILL)	-	-	-	-	2	-	2
GRAVE (FILL)	-	1	-	-	-	-	1
HARD	-	-	1	-	-	-	1
HRTH	-	1	1	1	-	-	3
OCC	1	12	15	9	6	-	43
OVEN	-	-	-	2	-	-	2
PATH	-	-	-	6	-	-	6
PH	2	16	19	37	1	-	75
PIT	-	2	7	16	8	-	33
PPIPE	-	3	-	-	-	-	3
SLOT	-	1	-	3	1	-	5
SOAK	-	2	2	-	-	-	4
TCH	-	1	9	8	13	-	31
UNKN	-	1	-	2	-	-	3
Total	**3**	**43**	**67**	**119**	**57**	**20**	**309**

Key: DCH – Ditch fill; DEP– Depression fill; DKSL – Dark soil; DUMP - Dump; GLY – Gully fill; GRAVE – Grave fill; HARD – Hard standing/post pad; HRTH – Deposits associated with hearths; OCC – Occupation deposit; OVEN– Deposits associated with ovens; PATH – Path; PH - Post hole fills; PIT – Deposits associated with pits (e.g. fills, linings); PPIPE – Post pipe fills; SLOT – Slot fill; SOAK– Soakaway fill; TCH – Trench fill; UNKN – Unknown.

TABLE 4.3 Number of contexts from which shell was recovered by hand collection by phase group and context type.

special form of charred preservation. The range of taxa recorded was small (TABLE 4.5), represented by fruits, seeds and wood charcoal, and also by some (mostly unidentified) vegetative fragments. The last of these are infrequently reported in archaeological deposits and their frequency at this site in part reflects the ease with which they could be extracted from the deposits. As the list of 'other components' at the end of TABLE 4.5 shows, a wide variety of other materials were recorded incidentally to the plant remains.

Species	Common name
Littorina littorea	periwinkle
Buccinum undatum	whelk
Neptunea antiqua	red whelk
Mytilus edulis	mussel
Ostrea edulis	oyster
Cerastoderma edule	cockle
Hydrobia ?ventrosa	
H. ulvae	
H. ?ulvae	
?Hydrobia sp.	
Carychium minimum	
C. ?minimum	
Carychium tridentatum	
C. ?tridentatum	
Carychium sp.	
Planorbidae sp.	
Succineidae sp.	
Cochlicopa lubrica	
C. ?lubrica	
Cochlicopa lubricella	
C. ?lubricella	
Cochlicopa sp.	
Vertigo pygmaea	
V. ?pygmaea	
Vertigo sp.	
Pupilla muscorum	
Vallonia ?costata	
Vallonia excentrica	
V. ?excentrica	
Discus rotundatus	
Vitrea crystallina	
Aegopinella nitidula	
A. ?nitidula	
?Aegopinella sp.	
?Oxychilus sp.	
Cecilioides acicula	
Trichia ?hispida	
Trichia sp.	
?Trichia sp.	
Cepaea sp.	
Cepaea or *Arianta* sp.	
Helix sp.	

TABLE *4.4 List of marine mollusc and snail taxa recovered.*

4.6 The chronological framework (see also Chapter 3)

Six broad periods of settlement activity dating between the early 7th and the early 11th centuries AD, were identified, and these were further divided into numerous sub-phases (TABLE 4.6). Initially, on the basis of consultation with the project manager, 62 contexts, with 100 or more fragments of animal bone, were amalgamated into 16 phase groups, which it was felt best represented the structural sequence. These groups, with some slight modifications, were then applied to all recorded contexts. Later, in the light of substantial work on the stratigraphic sequence, and feedback from the pottery specialists, these phase groups were re-classified into six broader categories (see Chapter 3). Material from some contexts was included or excluded according to the application of different phase groups, usually on the basis of information received from the post-excavation team. Although in most cases, more broadly dated material was generally excluded from further detailed analysis, certain exceptions were made. Thus, deposits from the fills of ditch 446/50, which were artefactually extremely rich, could only be assigned to the broad phase group 2i–4ii. However, assemblages from these fills were recorded and analysed in some detail for the purpose of illuminating our understanding of its depositional and taphonomic history.

4.7 The hand-collected and dry-sieved assemblages

Material from almost 2982 contexts was recorded from the site, and 1045 of these contexts produced bones. For the hand-collected and dry-sieved assemblage, material from 797 deposits was eventually recorded, of which only 62 contexts produced 100 or more fragments of bone. Vertebrate remains from these 62 deposits amounted to 32,035 identified fragments, i.e. 75% of the whole identified bone assemblage. For ease of interpretation and comprehension, the following account of the hand-collected vertebrate and shell assemblages is discussed by broad phase group as discussed in Chapter 3 and outlined in TABLE 4.6.

Phase 1 – mid–late 7th century

Very few bioarchaeological remains were recovered from Phase 1 deposits, amounting to only 262 identified bird and mammal fragments. Of the 31 bone producing contexts, 25 represented post-hole fills and material from these deposits formed the bulk of the assemblage (178 identified fragments). Bones were also recovered from four occupation layers (75 fragments) and two pit fills (9 fragments).

As can be seen from TABLE 4.1, approximately 33% of the Phase 1 assemblage were the remains of sheep/goat,[1] although cattle fragments were also fairly numerous. Roughly equivalent numbers of pig, chicken and geese bones were identified, suggesting that these species also provided a significant input into the diet during this time. Other species present were relatively insignificant in terms of actual numbers of fragments, although two crane bones were identified. Three rabbit bones from Contexts 3323, 3668 and 4493 were almost certainly intrusive and suggested some later, post-twelfth-century disturbance of

GYMNOSPERMAE

Coniferae (conifer): charcoal fragments, *wood fragments	1

ANGIOSPERMAE

cf. *Salix* sp(p). (?willow): charcoal fragments	5
Salix/Populus sp(p). (willow/poplar/aspen): charcoal fragments	19 (5%)
Betula sp(p). (birch): *fruits	1
cf. *Betula* sp(p). (?birch): charcoal fragments	2
Alnus sp(p). (alder): charcoal fragments	6
Alnus/Corylus (birch/hazel): charcoal fragments	3
Corylus avellana L. (hazel): charcoal fragments	27 (7%)
charred nuts and/or nutshell fragments	12
Quercus sp(p). (oak): charcoal fragments	80 (21%)
large charred wood fragments	2
cf. *Quercus* sp(p). (?oaks): charred bud and/or bud scales	1
Cannabis sativa L. (hemp): charred achenes	1
Urtica urens L. (annual nettle): *uncharred achenes	3
Polygonum aviculare agg. (knotgrass): charred fruits	1
*uncharred fruits	4
P. persicaria L. (persicaria/red shank): charred fruits	2
Bilderdykia convolvulus (L.) Dumort. (black bindweed): charred fruits or fruit fragments	3[1]
*uncharred fruits	4
Rumex acetosella agg. (sheep's sorrel): charred fruits	1
Rumex sp(p). (docks): charred	8
*uncharred fruits	1
Chenopodium album L. (fat hen): charred seeds	6[1]
*uncharred seeds	12[1]
Atriplex sp(p). (oraches): charred seeds	6[1]
*uncharred seeds	3
Suaeda maritima (L.) Dumort. (annual seablite): charred seeds	1
Chenopodiaceae (goosefoot family): charred seeds	4
Stellaria media (L.) Vill. (chickweed): charred seeds	1
Spergula arvensis L. (corn spurrey): *uncharred seeds	1
[*Agrostemma githago* L. (corncockle): charred seeds	1]
Silene vulgaris (Moench) Garcke (bladder campion): *uncharred seeds	3
S. vulgaris/S. alba (Miller) Krause in Sturm (bladder/white campion): charred seeds	2[1]
Ranunculus sardous Crantz (hairy buttercup): charred achenes	4
Raphanus raphanistrum L. (wild radish): charred pod segments and/or fragments	2[1]
Rubus fruticosus agg. (blackberry/bramble): charred seeds	1
*uncharred seeds	1
Rubus sp(p). (blackberries, etc.): charred seeds	1
Potentilla anserina L. (silverweed): charred achenes	1
cf. Pomoideae (?*Crataegus/Malus/Pyrus/Sorbus*): charcoal fragments	1
Prunus domestica ssp. *insititia* (L.) C. K. Schneider (plums, etc.): charred fruitstones	3
Vicia faba L. (field bean): charred cotyledons or seeds	2
cf. *Vicia* sp(p). (?vetches, etc.): charred seeds	1
cf. *Pisum sativum* L. (?garden/field pea): charred cotyledons or seeds	3[1]
Medicago lupulina L. (black medick): charred pods and/or pod fragments	1

TABLE *4.5 Complete list of plant taxa (and other components) recorded from samples at Flixborough (continued overleaf).*

cf. *Trifolium* sp(p). (?clovers, etc.): charred seeds	3
Leguminosae (pea family): charred pods and/or pod fragments	1
charred seeds	6[1]
Linum usitatissimum L. (cultivated flax): charred seeds	3
cf. *Acer* sp(p). (?maple, etc.): charcoal fragments	2
Viola sp(p). (violets/pansies, etc.): *uncharred seeds	2
cf. Umbelliferae (?carrot family): charred mericarps	1
cf. *Calluna vulgaris* (L.) Hull (?heather, ling): charred root and/or basal twig fragments	1
Fraxinus excelsior L. (ash): charcoal fragments	6
Galium aparine L. (goosegrass, cleavers): charred fruits	3[1]
Galium sp(p). (bedstraws, etc.): charred fruits	1
Boraginaceae (borage family): mineralised nutlets	2
*uncharred nutlets	2
[*Galeopsis* sp(p). (hemp nettles): charred nutlets	1]
Hyoscyamus niger L. (henbane): seeds	1
Rhinanthus sp(p). (yellow rattles): charred seeds	1
Plantago maritima L. (sea plantain): charred capsules	7
charred seeds	4
P. cf. *lanceolata* L. (?ribwort plantain): charred seeds	1
Sambucus nigra L. (elder): *seeds or seed fragments	5
[*Valerianella dentata* (L.) Pollich (narrow fruited cornsalad): charred fruits	1]
[*Anthemis cotula* L. (stinking mayweed): charred achenes	1]
Carduus/Cirsium sp(p). (thistles): achenes	1
[*Centaurea* sp(p). (knapweeds, etc.): charred achenes	1]
Lapsana communis L. (nipplewort): charred achenes	2[1]
Juncus sp(p). (rushes): charred capsules	18 (5%)
charred seeds	1
Gramineae (grasses): charred caryopses	13[1]
charred culm nodes	5
*uncharred caryopses	2
Gramineae/'Cerealia' (grasses/cereals): charred caryopses	1
charred culm nodes	5[1]
'Cerealia' indet. (cereals): charred caryopses	21 (5%)[2]
[charred coleoptiles	1]
charred culm fragments	1
charred culm nodes	1
Puccinellia maritima (Hudson) Parl. (common salt-marsh grass): charred culm fragments	5
cf. *Puccinellia* sp(p). (?salt-marsh grasses): charred caryopses	1
Bromus sp(p). (bromes, etc.): charred caryopses	4
cf. *Bromus* sp(p). (?bromes, etc.): charred caryopses	5
Triticum 'aestivo-compactum' (bread/club wheat): charred caryopses	9[1]
T. cf. *"aestivo compactum"* (?bread/club wheat): charred caryopses	1
Triticum sp(p). (wheats): charred caryopses	5[1]
cf. *Triticum* sp(p). (?wheats): charred caryopses	2
Secale cereale L. (rye): charred caryopses	2[1]
cf. *S. cereale* (?rye): charred caryopses	1
Hordeum sp(p). (barley): charred caryopses	15
charred caryopses, incl. hulled/sprouting	1
charred rachis fragments	1
cf. *Hordeum* sp(p). (?barley): charred caryopses	8
Avena sp(p). (oats): charred caryopses, some or all sprouting	1
cf. *Avena* sp(p). (?oats): charred caryopses	5

TABLE 4.5 continued.

S. maritimus/S. lacustris s.l. (sea club rush/bulrush): charred nutlets	1
S. lacustris s.l. (bulrush): charred nutlets	2
Eleocharis palustris s.l. (common spike rush): charred nutlets	7
silicified exocarp	1
Carex sp(p). (sedges): charred nutlets	10[1]
*uncharred nutlets	1

Other components of the samples

amphibian bone	28 (7%)
ash	10+?2
ash concretions §	30 (8%)
baked clay/daub	60 (16%)
bark fgts (ch)	2
barnacle shell fgts	1
beetles*	3
beetles (contaminant)*	1
bird bone	66 (17%)
bird tracheal ring	5
bone fgts	216 (56%)
brick/tile	2+?4
burnt bone fgts	72 (19%)
burnt clay	5
burnt fish bone	1
?burnt soil	1
burnt stone	17
Cecilioides acicula	47 (12%)
'Cenococcum' (sclerotia)	2+?1
chalk	1
'char'§	2
charcoal	300 (78%)
charred ?arthropod	1
?charred bread §	2
charred buds	1
charred herbaceous detritus §	27 (7%)
charred seaweed §	4+?2
charred seeds	1
coal	2
coarse sand	7
cockle shell fgts	1
concreted sediment §	14
concretions §	3+?3
crab shell fgts	1
daub	2+?37 (10%)
?dog coprolite	1
earthworm egg caps*	6+?1
earthworm egg caps (contaminant)*	5
earthworm egg caps (min)	2
eggshell fgts	21 (5%)
?faecal concretions	2
Fe nail(s)	1
Fe object(s)	1+?3

TABLE 4.5 continued.

fish bone	107 (28%)
fish scale	13
Flint	18 (5%)
fly puparia*	4
glass	2+?1
glassy slag	29 (8%)
gravel	69 (18%)
grit	38 (10%)
gritstone	1
Helix aspersa	1
herbaceous detritus*	1
Heterodera (cysts)*	6+?1
insects*	15
iron rich concretions	1
iron rich slag	2
land snails	4
?lava quern fgts	1
'lime' concretions§	71 (18%)
lime/tufa	4
limestone	113 (29%)
mammal bone	13
marine mollusc shell fgts	2
metallic slag	12
mortar	1+?1
mussel shell fgts	1
ostracods	1
oyster shell fgts	28 (7%)
?peat fgts	1
pebbles	8
percid scale	1
'pinched' stems (ch)§	34 (9%)
planorbid snails	1
plant fuel ash§	39 (10%)
pottery	6
reptile bone	1
root bark/epidermis fgts (modern)*	1
?root moulds	1
root moulds (min)	4
root/rhizome fgts (ch)§	6
root/rootlet fgts*	24 (6%)
root/rootlet fgts (?modern)*	2
root/rootlet fgts (modern)*	121 (31%)
sand	153 (40%)
sandstone	1
silicified herbaceous detritus§	1
slag	7+?4
small mammal bone	24 (6%)
snails	109 (28%)
snails (ch)	1
snails (contaminant)*	1
?spirorbids	1
stone	6
stones	38 (10%)
teeth	16

Table 4.5 continued.

tufa	7+?6
twig fgts	1
twig fgts (ch)	2
unwashed clay sediment	3
unwashed sediment	1
winkle shells/fgts	1
wood fgts	1
wood fgts (min)	3
woody root fgts (?modern)*	1
woody root fgts (modern)*	8

Complete list of plant taxa (and other components) recorded from samples at Flixborough. Items marked * were neither charred, silicified, nor mineralised, and are presumed to have been of recent origin. Numbers of contexts in which the remains were recorded (out of a total of 386 examined for plant remains in some way) are also given, with percentage frequency in the few cases where a value of 5% or more was achieved. Taxa in square brackets were only recorded from Phase 7 (medieval); number in square brackets are numbers of records from Phase 7 deposits for taxa which were also recorded in earlier phases. Nomenclature and order follow Tutin *et al.* (1964–90).

TABLE *4.5 continued.*

Phase	Included sub-phases	Date
1	1a, 1b	mid–late 7th century
2–3a	2, 2–3a, 3a and 3a–3bi	late 7th–mid 8th century
3b	3bi, 3bi–3bii, 3bi–3bv, 3bi–4i, 3bii, 3bii–3biii, 3bii–3bv, 3biii, 3biii–3bv, 3biv, 3biv–3bv, 3biv–4i, 3bv and 3bv–4i.	mid 8th–early 9th century
4–5b	4i–4ii, 4ii, 4ii–5a, 5a, 5a–5b, 5a–5b?, 5b and 5b–6i	9th century
6	6i, 6i–ii, 6ii and 6ii–6iii	10th century
6iii	6iii and 6iii–7	late 10th–early 11th century

TABLE *4.6 Phase groups used in the analysis of the vertebrate remains, the sub-phases that are included within each phase and the date range that each phase represents.*

the deposits. In fact rabbit remains were found in larger quantities from deposits from Phases 4–5b, 6 and 6iii, but not from Phases 2–3a and 3b. Whilst many of these remains appeared different in colour and preservation to other mammal and bird remains from similar associated deposits, and sometimes clearly represented articulated elements from single individuals, a number of rabbit bones could not so easily be dismissed as being later and intrusive using these criteria. Only direct dating of these bones could resolve the question as to whether a pre-Norman occurrence of rabbit is represented at Flixborough. This was not, however, undertaken as part of the funded post-excavation analysis and thus remains to be addressed. So, in the absence of direct evidence to the contrary, it has been assumed that all rabbit bones at Flixborough most likely represent later intrusive material not contemporaneous with the Saxon occupation.

Only three of the Phase 1 contexts yielded any hand-collected oyster shell (two left valves and some fragments,

total weight 40 g); all of the remains were poorly preserved (average erosion: 3.0; average fragmentation: 2.7). The two left valves showed characteristic evidence of having been opened using a knife or similar implement, indicating that humans had consumed them.

Phase 2–3a – late 7th–mid 8th century

The vertebrate assemblage recovered from deposits of this date amounted to 4738 identified fragments. Although post-hole fills formed 47% of the 126 contexts producing bone, much of the assemblage (83% of the fragments) was recovered from just 10 deposits; the latter included four occupation layers, two dump deposits, two fills from soakaway 3967 and two fills from pit 5389.

Numbers of identified specimens (NISP) for the major domesticates (including chicken and geese) suggested that cattle remains were prevalent in this period, forming 27% of the total assemblage (TABLE 4.7). This shows an increase of 5% in the relative frequency of cattle from

Species %	2–3a	3b	4–5b	6	6iii
Cattle	27	32	22	30	36
Caprine	22	24	29	27	33
Pig	18	17	22	20	20
Chicken	21	17	16	14	7
Goose	12	10	12	9	3

TABLE 4.7 Relative frequency of major domesticates using NISP counts.

Phase 1, with a considerable decrease in the caprine remains (34% in Phase 1 to 22% in Phase 2–3a). However, the limited number of fragments from Phase 1 renders any comparisons problematic. Chicken bones (at 21%) from this phase were almost as numerous as caprine remains, with pig (18%) and geese (13%) making smaller contributions.

Although the economy was, as one might expect, based on the main domestic animals and birds, exploitation of wild resources, especially birds, was also significant during this period. Whereas wild mammals formed less than 2% of the identified mammal remains, 28% (512 fragments) of the bird bones were assigned to wild species. Two deposits, Contexts 4963 (occupation) and 5314 (dump), produced large quantities of plover and wild geese bones. When fragment counts for selected groups of wild bird species are combined for this phase (TABLE 4.8), it can be seen that waders (including curlew, plover, woodcock, and 'unidentified wader') constitute 40% of the wild bird assemblage. The remains of wild geese (?barnacle geese mainly – see Appendix 1 for an outline of identification criteria) were quite numerous at 38% of the assemblage, whilst bones identified as duck, probable wood pigeon, black grouse and crane were also present. These fragments, along with the presence of roe deer and hare, indicated that the Phase 2–3a inhabitants of Flixborough were supplementing their diet with additional species that were procured from a variety of habitats (fenland, woodland and more open country) through wild fowling and hunting (see Chapters 5 and 8 for more details of the environment and procurement strategies).

In addition, approximately 42 cetacean (whale, dolphin) fragments were recovered from five deposits assigned to this phase group. The remains were present in a range of context types including dumps, occupation deposits and a soakaway fill. Most of the bones were identified as bottlenose dolphin and mainly comprised skull, mandible, rib, and vertebrae fragments.

Forty-three contexts produced hand-collected shell with a total weight of 2554g. With the exceptions of two mussel (*Mytilus edulis*) valves, a common whelk (*Buccinum undatum*), and a single fragment of whelk (not identifiable to species), all of the remains were of poorly preserved (average erosion: 2.4; average fragment-

ation: 2.1) oyster shell. Four of the valves showed damage from burrowing polychaete worms, but no other evidence of damage from marine biota was noted. A little under half (44%) of the valves showed distinctive evidence of having been opened, and thus presumably eaten, by humans.

Phase 3b – mid 8th–early 9th century

This rather broad phase was somewhat complex, with many sub-phases related to activities in and around a number of buildings occupied during this time period. Large dump deposits mainly occupied the 'central depression' during this period, gradually covering the remains of building 13. A number of occupation/yard deposits associated with building 13 were also located in this area during the early part of this phase. Although a total of 10,679 identified fragments (TABLE 4.1) was recovered from 116 deposits, the most important contexts for the recovery of bone were the fourteen dump deposits which yielded the bulk (72% – 7,538 identifiable fragments) of the material from this phase. The greatest concentrations of bone (6,272 fragments) derived from Contexts 5617, 5983 and 6235.

As with the previous phase, post-hole fills were the most numerous bone-bearing contexts, but very few of these deposits produced more than 20 fragments. The next largest bone assemblage (1349 identified fragments) originated from twelve pit fills. However, most of the remains (1093 fragments) were recovered from a single context, 6710, the fill of pit 6709. Much of the rest of the material (1036 fragments) from this phase came from 24 occupation deposits, including yard and floor layers. Trench and soakaway fills provided a further 161 fragments.

In this phase, bird bones were slightly less abundant in relation to mammal bones, with wild birds forming 25% of the avian assemblage. Domestic mammals once again predominated, and even fewer bones (<1% of the assemblage) than in Phase 2–3a represented wild species. However, material from these 3b deposits exhibited the greatest diversity of species compared with all other phases.

Overall, little difference was observed between the frequency of the major domesticates from Phases 2–3a and 3b (TABLE 4.7). Proportions of cattle remains slightly increased to form 31% of the assemblage, with a corresponding decrease in chickens, whilst the proportions of pig and geese remains were almost identical to those from Phase 2–3a.

As was the case for the previous phase, caprine remains from phase 3b included a small number of fragments identified as goat; most were horncores, mainly recovered from dump deposits (Contexts 5617, 5983 and 6235). Minor domestic species were represented by several cat bones, mainly identified from Context 6235 – a dump deposit. Additionally, several canid bones were recorded from this phase. Unfortunately, it was not possible to

Species	1	%	2–3a	%	3b	%	4–5b	%	6	%	6iii	%
Black grouse	0	0	7	1	17	2	2	1	9	2	0	0
Columbidae	3	14	29	6	75	10	29	8	35	8	3	9
Corvid	2	10	9	2	46	6	38	11	24	5	1	3
Crane	2	10	26	5	115	15	13	4	73	16	0	0
Duck	5	24	42	8	71	9	129	37	67	15	21	64
Wader	2	10	201	40	91	12	28	8	49	11	3	9
Wild geese	7	33	191	38	355	46	112	32	188	42	5	15

TABLE *4.8 Number and frequency of wild bird groups using NISP counts.*

determine whether these fragments represented dog or fox. A tibia from Context 6441 was similar both in morphology and in size to fox, whilst a radius fragment from Context 6235 was consistent in size with fox but lacked morphologically distinctive features. The third fragment, from Context 968, was recognisable as a canid tibia, but erosion of the bone surface prevented a more secure identification.

As already noted for the assemblages from earlier phases, wild mammals were not numerous. However, those of some economic importance included roe deer (28 fragments), hare (18) and wild boar (2). With the exception of a single fragment, all the roe deer remains from Phase 3b were recovered from dump deposits (Contexts 4322, 5617, 5983, 6028 and 6235). Skeletal element representation suggested that whole carcasses were present on site and that the cervid remains represented butchery and consumption refuse rather than waste from direct provisioning of joints or craft activities. The refuse middens produced a canine and mandible identified as wild boar and most of the hare remains. Metapodials and tibia fragments were the most numerous elements for hare, some of the metatarsals representing a single individual. Other mammal remains included five bones (from Contexts 6040 and 6136) tentatively identified as pine marten, in addition to a small number of mice and vole fragments.

Large quantities of bird remains were recovered, particularly from three dump deposits (Contexts 5617, 5983 and 6235); they made up 36% to 41% of the total assemblage from these contexts, the overall frequency of birds for the entire 3b assemblage being 32%. Domestic birds such as chicken and geese obviously formed the most economically important component of the bird assemblage, but evidence from the bones for wild taxa suggested that wildfowling and hunting still provided a significant input of wild species into the diet of the inhabitants during the mid-late eighth century. Wild geese, waders (mostly plovers), ducks (including teal), wood pigeon, black grouse and crane were all identified from this assemblage. Looking at the frequencies of the wild species (TABLE 4.8), it can be seen that wild geese make up 46% of the wild birds, whilst crane remains (the most numerous from any phase) have a frequency of 15%,

and waders 12%. Dump deposits (mainly Context 6235) contained a significant collection of raptor bones. A single bone was tentatively identified as marsh harrier, although erosion of the fragment prevented confirmation of this identification. The other species present were ?buzzard (19 fragments) and ?red kite (20 fragments).

Also worthy of note were 154 fragments identified as cetacean. Generally, these remains were present within dump deposits and were once again mostly identified as bottlenose dolphin. Some fragments, however, could not be determined conclusively and could represent other species of similar size, e.g. Risso's dolphin (*Grampus griseus*) or white-beaked dolphin (*Lagenorhyncus albirostris*).

Phase 3b also yielded the largest quantity of hand-collected shell totalling 18,033g from 67 contexts, most of this (10,892g, 24% of the assemblage from the whole site) being concentrated in the 13 dump contexts from this phase and, in particular, in Contexts 5617 (4371g), 6235 (3929g), and 5983 (1274g). Preservation of the remains was once again poor (average erosion: 2.7; average fragmentation: 2.5). Two contexts (2722 and 6040) contained fragments of whelk shell (not identifiable to species), Context 4322 gave two fragments of unidentified marine shell, and Contexts 11699 and 11766 yielded a few fragments of land snail shell (*Cepaea/Arianta* sp.). Other than the remains noted above, most of the recovered shell was identified as oyster. Thirty-six percent of the oyster valves showed damage indicative of having been opened by humans and a small number (6%) showed damage from other marine biota (mostly burrowing by polychaete worms, with a single valve having some barnacle encrustation).

Phase 4–5b – 9th century

Early in this phase, buildings were constructed in the central area over the Phase 3b dumps, but, by the mid 9th century, these were again replaced by large accumulations of refuse, representing deliberate dumping episodes. The 265 deposits from this phase produced 12,878 fragments of identified bone, of which 9230 (72%) were recovered from 49 dump deposits. Almost half (48%) of the overall number of fragments from the dump deposits was recovered from Contexts 3758 and 5503. Post-hole fills were the most numerous (114) and contained approximately 8% (1033 fragments) of the vertebrate assemblage, as did the 26 occupation deposits (1054 fragments). Material from pit fills (27) amounted to 482 fragments, with a further 594 fragments deriving from 16 trench fill deposits.

Observing the range of species present (TABLE 4.1), it is evident that domestic and wild birds and mammals are all represented in the assemblage. Overall, the vast majority (72%) of the remains were mammal, with 2% of that total representing wild species. Bird remains represented 28% (NISP) of the total assemblage – wild birds this time representing only 10% of the avian assemblage, a decrease of 14% from the previous phase.

When comparing the relative abundance of the three main domesticates (cattle, caprine and pig) in more detail, it is apparent that cattle no longer predominate (TABLE 4.9), in contrast to the pattern for preceding phases – and the most numerous bones are now those of caprine (40%). A higher proportion of pig remains was also identified, their frequency increasing from 23% to 30%. More detailed analysis indicated that in sub-phase 4ii the highest frequency of pig remains (36%) occurred, with dump deposits (Contexts 3758 and 5503) yielding most of the material from this sub-phase. Caprine remains, on the other hand, gradually rose in number throughout Phase 4–5b, with the exception of sub-phase 5a–5b. The assemblage from the latter, largely influenced by material from Context 12057 (a dump deposit), showed a high proportion of cattle remains.

Bones of chickens and geese, when compared with the other main species (cattle, caprine and pig), showed similar proportions to earlier phases (approximately 16% and 11% respectively). Horse remains were few, amounting to 431 fragments or approximately 5% of the mammal assemblage. Caprine remains included a number of goat horncores, together with several fore-limb bones and a pelvis fragment. These were mostly recovered from dump deposits 5503 and 12057. Bones of other species were fairly infrequent, but included over 100 rabbit fragments, almost certainly intrusive and representing some contamination of deposits by later material. Twenty-three cat bones were also identified, mostly from the dump deposits, with a group of bones from Context 5139 representing the part-skeleton of a single individual. This phase also included one of only two fragments from the site (the other from Phase 6ii) confidently identified as dog. Additionally, an ulna was tentatively identified as fox on the basis of its size and morphology.

Other wild mammals were mainly represented by cervid remains, of which most (36 fragments) were identified as roe deer. These included a range of skeletal elements, with over half representing major meat-bearing bones. Although dump deposits produced most of the fragments, no obvious patterns of refuse disposal for different parts of the body were identified. Additionally, red deer phalanges and possible antler fragments were

Species	2–3a	3b	4–5b	6	6iii
Cattle	41	44	30	39	41
Caprine	33	33	40	35	37
Pig	26	23	30	26	22

TABLE *4.9 Relative frequency of major domestic animals using NISP counts.*

recovered from Contexts 2610, 5139, 6490 and 12057. The remains of hare were also noted from a number of the dump deposits and a single trench fill.

As already noted above, the frequency of wild birds drops significantly in this phase, with an evident decrease in wild geese (TABLE 4.8). The bones of crane were also far less frequent than in the previous phase. However, it was noticeable that the proportion of duck substantially increased from 9% (of the wild bird species) in Phase 3b to 37% in Phase 4–5b. This high frequency is maintained throughout the period until sub-phases 5a–5b where numbers appear to fall. Duck remains have been included in the wild bird counts for all phases but unfortunately, morphologically and biometrically, it was not possible (as with the large geese bones) to determine whether the duck bones represented wild or domestic individuals or a combination of the two.

Cetacean remains from this phase amounted to 118 fragments, the bulk of which were recovered from dump and occupation deposits. Most fragments were again identified as bottlenose dolphin or possibly taxa of an equivalent size. One bone was definitely identified as minke whale, whilst four other fragments possibly represented the same species. All were from juvenile individuals.

Phase 4–5b also gave the greatest number of shell-bearing contexts (119) with a total weight of shell of 7472 g, most of them once again being oyster. Only twelve contexts gave small amounts of shell other than of oyster; these other species included common whelk (*Buccinum undatum*), red whelk (*Neptunea antiqua*) periwinkle (*Littorina littorea*) and mussel valve. The shell was mostly poorly preserved, and a few of the oyster valves showed damage by other marine biota (17 valves showed polychaete worm burrowing and three had evidence of encrustation by barnacles). Forty-five percent of the oyster valves showed damage characteristic of having been opened by humans.

Phase 6 – 10th century

A total of 9925 identified fragments (24% of the overall assemblage recovered from the whole site), was recovered from 90 contexts. Bones came from a wide range of context types and, as with previous phases, dump deposits yielded the largest numbers of fragments (71% of the identified assemblage). This phase included dump deposit 3891, which produced 5680 identified fragments, the largest accumulation of vertebrate remains from a single deposit, forming almost 60% of the total identified assemblage from the phase. Dark soils and trench fills, 27% and 20% (respectively) of the total number of deposits, were also fairly productive, but, between them, only contributed 20% of the vertebrate material from this phase. Small accumulations of bone were recovered from occupation deposits and pit fills.

Basic frequencies of mammal (75%) and bird (25%) bones remained similar in this phase to those from Phase 4–5b. Wild mammals were again rather sparsely represented, forming less than 2% of the mammal bones; however, wild bird species increased in relative frequency to 17% of the identified bird assemblage. When comparing proportions of the five main domesticates, it is apparent that cattle increased in frequency, accounting for 30% of the assemblage (TABLE 4.7). This represented a marked shift from the previous phase when caprine remains were prevalent. Caprine and pig were less abundant in Phase 6, decreasing slightly to 27% and 20% respectively. The proportions of domestic bird (chicken and goose), were also reduced, but still formed a significant part of the assemblage.

Deposits from Phase 6 produced the largest number of horse bones (514) from any phase for the site, with dump deposits producing most of these remains (and 80% being recovered from Context 3891, alone). Fragments associated with the head, such as maxillae, mandibles and isolated teeth predominated throughout. Remains of goats were identified, and were again mostly represented by horncones. Whilst the latter were mainly recovered from Context 3891, a collection of other goat elements was identified from pit fill 78. Additional domestic species present included cat (17 fragments), which was also most commonly recovered from dump deposits. A single burnt cat humerus from Context 3891 may have been chopped through the distal articulation. This was difficult to verify because of the damaged nature of the bone.

Dark soil deposits (Contexts 1834 and 1836) contained several poorly preserved fragments tentatively identified as fox. A number of metapodials was also recovered from these deposits, but these were recorded only as canid. Additional possible fox remains were recovered from a number of pit fills (Contexts 78 and 923) and an occupation layer (Context 3413). A single calcaneus from dark soil 7054 was tentatively identified as dog, but again this could not be conclusively determined.

The 37 bones of deer represent the next most numerous wild mammal taxa in this phase. With the exception of two, all were identified as roe deer. Many (23) of these were recovered from the same large dump deposit as the horse bones mentioned above (Context 3891), whilst a range of other deposits (dark soils, trench, pit and posthole fills) produced the remaining 12 fragments. A mix of skeletal elements, representing both meat-bearing and non-meat-bearing bones, were present, with mandibles (9) and fore-limbs (scapulae, humeri and radii) being the

most abundant. A single calcaneus and a second phalanx – both non-meat-bearing elements – were identified as red deer.

A large Muridae femur, recovered from a pit fill (Context 923) dated to sub-phase 6ii, was identified as a black rat (*Rattus rattus*).[2] The possible significance of the presence of this non-indigenous species is discussed in more detail in Chapter 9.

Rabbit was the most frequently represented wild species from this phase (69 fragments). As discussed for previous phases, it is highly unlikely that these are contemporaenous with the other bones from these deposits. Interestingly, although dump deposits yielded the largest amounts of bone, only a single rabbit fragment was recovered from this context type. Perhaps not surprisingly, dark soil deposits produced 40 rabbit fragments, whilst 22 came from five pit fills.

Wild bird species were more abundant in Phase 6, with wild geese remains forming the largest component (42% of the wild bird assemblage). Amongst the copious geese bones were three possible brent goose scapulae. The frequency of crane bones increased to 16% from 4% in the previous phase (4–5b). This value is similar to that of Phase 3b. Indeed, frequencies for the main groups of wild species (TABLE 4.8) from this phase show an almost identical pattern to those seen in Phase 3b for the same groups. The presence of ducks (although not necessarily all wild), waders and wood pigeons, along with the geese and crane remains, suggests the rise in importance once again of local wild resources.

The largest quantity of cetacean remains, amounting to 289 fragments, was recovered from Phase 6 deposits – dump 3891 in particular. Besides the remains identified as bottlenose dolphin, which again dominated this component of the assemblage, several fragments were tentatively identified as minke whale, possibly representing juvenile individuals. Five fragments were also identified as possibly representing either pilot or a killer whale.

Phase 6 contexts (57 in total) gave the second highest total weight of shell (11,126g) which was, again, poorly preserved. Similar to Phase 3b, the shell was mostly recovered from dump deposits (9 contexts, total of 8,262g) and in particular from Context 3891 (7,270g). Nine contexts gave marine shell remains other than oyster which included: common whelk, red whelk and mussel. Three contexts (1837, 2127, and 6471) yielded a small land snail assemblage – all identified as ?*Cepaea/Arianta* sp. Once again, a small number of oyster valves showed damage from other marine biota; nineteen had been burrowed into by polychaete worms and four had been slightly encrusted by barnacles. Evidence of opening, and presumably consumption, by humans was recorded from 45% of the oyster valves.

Phase 6iii – late 10th–early 11th

Phase 6iii had almost the same number of bone-bearing contexts (84) as the previous phase, but only a third of the quantity of identified fragments (3182) was recovered. This phase was characterised by dark soil deposits which formed 93% of the context types and were the most prolific bone-bearing contexts (providing 74% of the identified assemblage). Of these, only four (636, 1459, 2180 and 3451) produced more than 100 fragments. Three dumps contributed 25% of the remaining identified assemblage, most of which (697 fragments) was recovered from Context 6300. Other context types were scarce and produced very little bone.

The relative abundance of the five main species showed a considerable difference from previous phases (Table 4.7). Cattle were the most frequently occurring species (38% of the assemblage), followed closely by caprines (35%). Pig remains stayed fairly constant, forming 21% of the assemblage, but the most prominent change was the substantial decrease in the frequency of chicken and goose remains to just 3%. However, the smaller size of the assemblage in relation to the number of fragments from the other phases, and the predominance of a different context type from which the bone was recovered, may perhaps be significant factors in these potential differences.

Wild mammals were somewhat scant, but nine fragments were identified as roe deer. Many of the bones were either humeri or radii suggesting they represent waste from consumption and may even reflect provisioning of select joints. Rabbit bones were also present (28 fragments) but, as in previous phases, are likely to be intrusive. A single tibia was identified as possibly representing wild boar. Wild bird species were somewhat fewer in number than from earlier deposits and were represented by just 34 fragments, most of which were identified as duck.

Cetacean remains amounted to 42 fragments, of which most were again identified as bottlenose dolphin, with a few fragments which could have represented another delphinid of a similar size. Several minke whale fragments, from juvenile individuals, were also present, together with a few fragments which could only be identified as cetacean.

The twenty contexts from this phase yielded a total of 2121g of hand-collected shell. Preservation was very poor (average erosion: 3.0; average fragmentation: 2.9), and once again they were almost exclusively oyster shell.

4.8 The wet-sieved assemblages

As previously mentioned, an extensive sampling strategy was undertaken during excavation which resulted in 1759 sediment samples being taken, 1563 of which were from Anglo-Saxon deposits. These were processed, mainly on site, and the flots and residues were subsequently examined for biological and artefactual remains.

A total of 790 sample residues, representing all the broad phase groups and a range of context types, were sorted for mammal, bird, fish, small mammals, amphibian, reptile and eggshell fragments. Vertebrate material was recovered from all but 27 of the samples, with mammal and fish bone being well represented, i.e. present in over 96% and 79% of the samples, respectively (Table 4.10). Microfauna (60%), bird (54%), amphibian (29%) and eggshell (12%) remains were less common. Large fragments of charcoal and mollusc shells were recovered from less than a quarter of the samples, whilst botanical material other than charcoal was rarely encountered. In addition to the 'environmental remains', a wide variety of artefactual material was recovered from these samples, including slag, various iron objects, glass fragments and several pieces of worked bone.

The aims of the analyses of the material from the samples were manifold, but principally involved the recovery and identification of the remains of specific taxa (e.g. small mammals, amphibians and, in particular, fish) which would have been subject to bias in retrieval as a result of hand-collection and dry-sieving. Likewise, for the larger mammals (cattle, caprines and pigs), a selected suite of small and juvenile elements (incisors, deciduous 4th premolars and phalanges) was recorded to identify their possible under-representation in the hand-collected assemblage. Additionally, material from 104 samples (representing 95 contexts) was recorded for the purpose of making preservation and fragmentation records; only mammal remains were utilised for this analysis (see Chapter 3 for discussion on preservation).

The fish bone assemblage

Not surprisingly, the bulk of the fish remains were recovered from the wet-sieved samples. Although approximately 28 freshwater, migratory and marine taxa were identified at Flixborough, the assemblage was dominated by just seven, all of which were freshwater or migratory. Based on the sieved assemblage, these were: eel (3097 fragments, 49.7%), smelt (910, 14.6%), flounder or plaice (approx. 780, 12.5%), pike (588, 9.4%), cyprinid (351, 5.6%), perch (290, 4.7%) and salmonid (157, 2.5%) (Tables 4.11 and 4.12). This suite of taxa was relatively uniform throughout the assemblage.

As can be seen from Tables 4.11–4.13, fish remains were recovered from all of the major phase groups, but the latter were not all represented within each feature type. Phase 1 was represented by post-holes and dumps, whilst Phase 2–3a was dominated by soakaways. Conversely, Phases 3b, 4–5b and 6 were represented largely by dumps and Phase 6iii predominantly by dark soils. Analysis revealed that there were differences in the relative abundance of the seven dominant taxa between context types.

When analysis was limited to the five major context types (dumps, post-holes, soakaways, occupation deposits and dark soils), the ratio of migratory to freshwater taxa

Context type	Overall Total	Mam Total	Mam %	Fish Total	Fish %	Bird Total	Bird %	Mf Total	Mf %	Amp Total	Amp %	Egg Total	Egg %
Dark soil	89	85	96	49	55	34	38	46	52	27	30	3	3
Dark soil/occupation	6	6	100	6	100	5	83	6	100	2	33	0	0
Ditch fill	75	67	89	36	48	15	20	25	33	13	17	0	0
Dump	128	125	98	127	99	116	91	109	85	58	45	23	18
Occupation deposit	107	106	99	88	82	57	53	63	59	39	36	9	8
Pit fill	108	98	91	84	78	50	46	61	56	26	24	9	8
Post-hole fill	222	213	96	176	79	110	50	119	54	48	22	34	15
Slot fill	22	22	100	21	95	14	64	14	64	5	23	6	27
Soakaway fill	13	13	100	12	92	10	77	11	85	5	38	9	69
Subsidence	5	5	100	5	100	4	80	4	80	1	20	1	20
Trench fill	10	10	100	10	100	4	40	8	80	6	60	2	20
Slot/foundation trench/beam slot fill	11	11	100	11	100	9	82	9	82	4	36	1	9
Total	**796**	**761**	**96**	**625**	**79**	**428**	**54**	**475**	**60**	**234**	**29**	**97**	**12**

TABLE 4.10 *The total number and percentage (%) of samples from which mammal (Mam), fish, bird, microfauna (Mf), amphibian (Amp) and eggshell (Egg) were recovered.*

increased through the sequence from Phases 1 to 3b. It continued to increase in Phase 4–5b in dumps and occupation deposits, but decreased for post-holes. In Phase 6, there was a negative correlation between occupation deposits (for which the sample size was very small) and dumps. Migratory taxa continued to be common in the former (and were common in dark soils, which first appear in this phase), but decreased in frequency dramatically in the latter. In Phase 6iii, the ratio of migratory to freshwater taxa increased in dumps, but the sample size once again was very small. This phase was represented predominantly by dark soils, where the ratio decreased slightly from that noted in Phase 6.

Attempts to discern spatial patterns in the Flixborough fish assemblage are made difficult by the same factors which complicate the interpretation of temporal trends (see Chapter 8 for details). There are statistically significant differences in the distribution of fish taxa across the principal features of the site (TABLE 4.13). Given the variable representation of each context type between phases, however, it is difficult to control for time. Insofar as the two variables can be divided, FIGS 4.1–4.6 indicate that the broad trends of species abundance are relatively consistent between features. The main departure from this rule is the anomalous abundance of pike and perch in the soakaways of Phase 2–3a. Although a unique characteristic of these deposits, even this pattern is partly related to temporal trends. The soakaways of Phase 3b have few pike and no perch, reflecting the general shift in emphasis from freshwater to migratory taxa at the site in the mid eighth to early ninth centuries (see Chapter 8 for more details).

Small mammal and amphibian remains

TABLE 4.14 shows the range of mammal species (excluding the main domesticates) recovered from the selected samples. As already noted, small mammal remains were recovered from 60% of the bulk-sieved samples and were recorded in all the represented periods. The greatest number of fragments was from Phase 4–5b deposits, although the species and families represented were fairly similar throughout.

Many of the fragments could not be identified to species but were recorded as 'mouse/vole', 'vole species' or 'mouse species'. Those vole fragments which could be identified further included the remains of bank and field vole, the latter being more prevalent. The presence of numerous field voles is suggestive of an immediate environment of rough ungrazed open grassland, whilst bank voles show a preference for thicker more closed vegetation in either woodland or grassland habitats. Mice were also present, the identified remains including wood/yellow-necked mouse, house mouse, and several fragments tentatively attributed to harvest mouse. Shrew bones were recorded in small quantities from most phases; these creatures are ubiquitous and found in most environments/habitats providing that there is some low vegetation available.

Common Name	NISP 1	2–3a	3b	4–5b	6	6iii	Unphased	Total
Marine								
atlantic herring				8		2	1	11
conger eel						1		1
cod			1	1				2
haddock				2				2
Subtotal	*0*	*0*	*1*	*11*	*0*	*3*	*1*	*16*
Migratory								
sturgeon[1]				2	p			2
allis shad/twaite shad		1	1	3	1	1		7
salmon & trout family	5	25	53	49	18	5	2	157
smelt	29	228	263	290	52	13	35	910
eel	76	485	613	1230	451	128	114	3097
halibut family	11	79	236	205	73	19	12	635
plaice/flounder	1	14	78	36	10	2	4	145
Subtotal	*122*	*832*	*1244*	*1815*	*605*	*168*	*167*	*4953*
Fresh Water								
pike	60	294	95	69	56	9	5	588
carp family	22	108	71	62	41	5	10	319
barbel?				1				1
tench		2						2
rudd?		1						1
roach		1	3	1	1			6
roach?		1						1
chub/dace		5	2	2				9
chub			3	2				5
dace		1	3	1	2			7
loach family			1					1
burbot		4	2	5				11
perch	22	138	56	16	52	4	2	290
Subtotal	*104*	*555*	*236*	*159*	*152*	*18*	*17*	*1241*
Other								
herring family		1		1			1	3
cod family		3	1				1	5
stickleback family[1]	p	9	4	1	p	p	p	14
Subtotal	*0*	*13*	*5*	*2*	*0*	*0*	*2*	*22*

TABLE 4.11 Number of sieved fish remains by phase using NISP counts (continued opposite).

Common Name	NISP 1	2–3a	3b	4–5b	6	6iii	Unphased	Total
Total identified	**226**	**1400**	**1486**	**1987**	**757**	**189**	**187**	**6232**
Other (Pleuronectidae 1st anal pterygiophores)		2	11	2	4			19
Unidentified	166	1321	925	1214	514	79	113	4332
Total	**392**	**2723**	**2422**	**3203**	**1275**	**268**	**300**	**10583**

TABLE 4.11 continued.

Some of the amphibian/reptile bones, found in 29% of the selected samples, could be identified to species.[3] Most fragments represented frogs and toads, although several bones of newt were recorded, and lizard was also tentatively identified. Not surprisingly, many of the amphibian remains were from deposits such as ditch, pit and post-hole fills which probably acted as pitfall traps. Most of the newt bones were recovered from dump deposits. Although newts need pools, ponds or ditches with standing water in them for breeding in the spring, they spend the rest of the year on land inhabiting a range of environments such as open woodland or scrub, or marshy areas.

Notes

1 Although a few goat elements were positively identified in the Flixborough animal bone assemblage, the vast majority of the caprine bones that could be identified to species were assigned to sheep. It is, therefore, assumed that most caprine remains are those of sheep *not* goats.

2 Identification of the black rat femur was kindly confirmed by Dr Anton Ervynck of the I.A.P., Belgium.

3 Identification of amphibian bones was kindly confirmed by Dr Chris Gleed-Owen of the Herpetological Conservation Trust.

Common Name	% 1	2–3a	3b	4–5b	6	6iii	Total
Marine							
atlantic herring				0.4		1.1	0.2
conger eel						0.5	
cod			0.1	0.1			
haddock				0.1			
Subtotal	*0.0*	*0.0*	*0.1*	*0.6*	*0.0*	*1.6*	*0.3*
Migratory							
sturgeon				0.1			
allis shad/twaite shad		0.1	0.1	0.2	0.1	0.5	0.1
salmon & trout family	2.2	1.8	3.6	2.5	2.4	2.6	2.5
smelt	12.8	16.3	17.7	14.6	6.9	6.9	14.6
eel	33.6	34.6	41.3	61.9	59.6	67.7	49.7
halibut family	4.9	5.6	15.9	10.3	9.6	10.1	10.2
plaice/flouder	0.4	1.0	5.2	1.8	1.3	1.1	2.3
Subtotal	*54.0*	*59.4*	*83.7*	*91.3*	*79.9*	*88.9*	*79.4*
Fresh Water							
pike	26.5	21.0	6.4	3.5	7.4	4.8	9.4
carp family	9.7	7.7	4.8	3.1	5.4	2.6	5.1
barbel?				0.1			
tench		0.1					
rudd?		0.1					
roach		0.1	0.2	0.1	0.1		0.1
roach?		0.1					
chub/dace		0.4	0.1	0.1			0.1
chub			0.2	0.1			0.1
dace		0.1	0.2	0.1	0.3		0.1
loach family			0.1				
burbot		0.3	0.1	0.3			0.2
perch	9.7	9.9	3.8	0.8	6.9	2.1	4.7
Subtotal	*46.0*	*39.6*	*15.9*	*8.0*	*20.1*	*9.5*	*19.9*
Other							
herring family		0.1		0.1			
cod family		0.2	0.1				0.1
stickleback family		0.6	0.3	0.1			0.2
Subtotal	*0.0*	*0.9*	*0.3*	*0.1*	*0.0*	*0.0*	*0.3*
Total Identified	**100.0**	**100.0**	**100.0**	**100.0**	**100.0**	**100.0**	**100.0**

TABLE 4.12 Relative frequency of sieved fish remains by phase using NISP counts.

Common Name	DUMP	PH	SOAK	OCC	PIT	DKSL	Total
Salmon & Trout Family	96	27	10	10	4	6	153
Smelt	483	102	99	79	62	14	839
Eel	1332	518	171	367	253	179	2820
Total Halibut Family	512	69	29	60	40	42	752
Pike	185	90	213	60	15	10	573
Total Carp Family	142	57	61	51	12	9	332
Perch	119	26	119	14	5	4	287
Total	2869	889	702	641	391	264	5756

Key: DKSL – Dark soil; DUMP – Dump; OCC – Occupation deposit; PH – Post hole fills; PIT – Deposits asssociated with pits (e.g. fills, linings); SOAK – Soakaway fill.

TABLE 4.13 Number of sieved fish remains by context type using NISP counts. See Appendix 3 for key to context types.

FIG. 4.1 Dumps
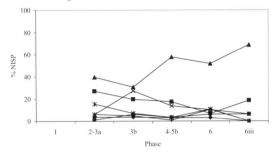

FIG. 4.4 Occupation
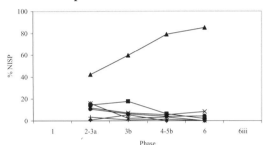

FIG. 4.2 Postholes
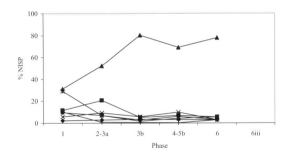

FIG. 4.5 Pits
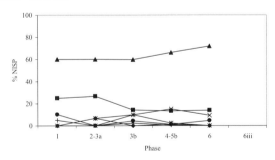

FIG. 4.3 Soakaways
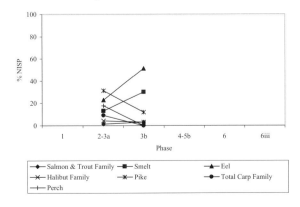

FIG. 4.6 Dark soils
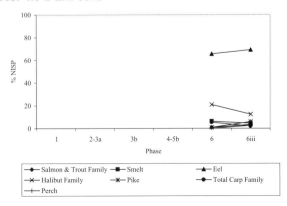

FIGS 4.1–4.6 Flixborough sieved fish: % NISP by context type, phase and taxon.

Species		1	2–3a	3b	4–5b	6	6iii	Total
Talpa europaea	mole	-	-	1	1	2	1	**5**
Sorex araneus	common shrew	-	-	2	7	-	1	**10**
S. minutus	pygmy shrew	-	-	1	2	1	5	**9**
cf. *S. minutus*	?pygmy shrew	-	-	-	1	-	-	**1**
Sorex sp.	shrew species	-	1	4	8	4	2	**19**
Neomys fodiens	water shrew	-	-	-	-	-	2	**2**
Oryctolagus cuniculus	rabbit	-	1	1	5	69	1	**77**
Lepus sp.	hare	-	1	2	-	-	-	**3**
Microtine/murine	vole/mouse	1	6	15	34	6	7	**69**
Microtine	vole species	2	8	10	37	11	13	**81**
Clethrionomys glareolus	bank vole	-	-	5	19	5	4	**33**
Microtus agrestis	field vole	4	8	20	85	14	14	**145**
Murine	mouse species	1	28	26	77	22	18	**172**
Apodemus spp.	wood/yellow-necked mouse	-	1	8	19	8	2	**38**
cf. *Micromys minutus*	?harvest mouse	-	-	-	1	1	-	**2**
Mus musculus	house mouse	1	9	9	10	1	-	**30**
Mustelid	mustelid	-	-	1	1	-	-	**2**
Mustela nivalis	weasel	-	-	-	1	-	-	**1**
Felis f. domestic	cat	-	1	4	2	-	-	**7**
cf. *Felis f. domestic*	?cat	-	-	1	-	-	-	**1**
Amphibian	amphibian	11	48	90	245	161	35	**590**
reptile	?lizard	-	-	1	3	-	1	**5**
Total		**20**	**112**	**201**	**558**	**305**	**106**	**1302**

TABLE 4.14 *Vertebrate remains recovered from selected bulk-sieved samples, by phase.*

5   Landscape and Environment

David Slater, Keith Dobney, Deborah Jaques, James Barrett,
Cluny Johnstone, John Carrott and Allan Hall

5.1 Introduction

No site of former human occupation existed in isolation
from its environment. The first Anglo-Saxon inhabitants
at Flixborough found a landscape moulded by natural
forces acting over geological time, with climate a major
determinant in shaping areas such as the Humber estuary
and its surroundings over the past 10,000 years (Long *et
al.* 1998). It can also be assumed that other major changes
had been generated by humans through centuries, if not
millennia, of previous human interaction with the land.
In the millennium subsequent to the life of the Saxon
settlement, industrial development, river management
and agriculture have created an environment on the
Lower Trent that must be quite different from what was
present a thousand years ago. The area is within perhaps
one of the most heavily managed agricultural regions of
Britain, with the result that extensive marshlands have
been drained, riverbanks have been artificially embanked,
and now the chemical industry has a significance presence
on the old floodplain. However, limited areas do survive
locally that are thought to resemble ancient habitats.

5.2 Palaeohabitats of the Lower Trent:
a modern ecological perspective

In general terms, the modern countryside of the local
region surrounding Flixborough can be divided into three
main zones (for detailed geological and edaphic information for the region see Gaunt 1997 and Ellis 1998). All
place names quoted below can be found in FIG. 5.1.

1   The Humber estuary and its associated fringe of
    wetland habitats dominate the area north of the site
    of Flixborough. The estuary itself has, for many
    reasons, undergone fundamental change over the last
    hundred years (Pethick 1990), evidence of which is
    discussed below.

2   The zones west and south of the site have been
    described by Peterken and Game (1984) as one of the
    most intensively cultivated regions of Britain. Most
    hedges have been removed, there is very little
    unimproved pasture, and most watercourses are
    reduced to scoured canals and ditches.

3   Finally, the area east of the site comprises the
    remnants of a sandy heathland, and relatively
    elevated land in an area of very low-lying ground
    along the rivers, most of which has been lost to
    major urban and industrial development (Eversham
    1991).

Wetlands around the Lower Trent

The river and wetland system around the confluence of
the Trent and the Humber has undergone fundamental
change in the last 10,000 years and continues to be
dynamic (Long *et al.* 1998). It is widely acknowledged
that, following the draining of Lake Humber at the end of
the Pleistocene, the area around the Humberhead Levels
was a large, continuous expanse of complex wetland,
comprising inundated river floodplains, meres, carrs, fens
and, more recently (since peat became extensive),
floodplain mires, until intensive farming began
(Buckland and Dinnin 1994). Repeated drainage schemes
over the last few centuries have destroyed most of the
once more extensive wildfowl habitats within 20 miles of
the estuary (Wildfowl and Wetland Trust 1963). The
numerous islands in the upper Humber are still crucial
roosting sites for many wildfowl that feed on the available
surrounding food sources such as winter-sown crops. In
the 1960s, this area was the most important arrival point
for wintering pink-footed geese in Northern Europe.
Although some of these wetland habitats still persist,
they are now very irregular and discontinuous.

Saltmarsh exists in the western half of the estuary at

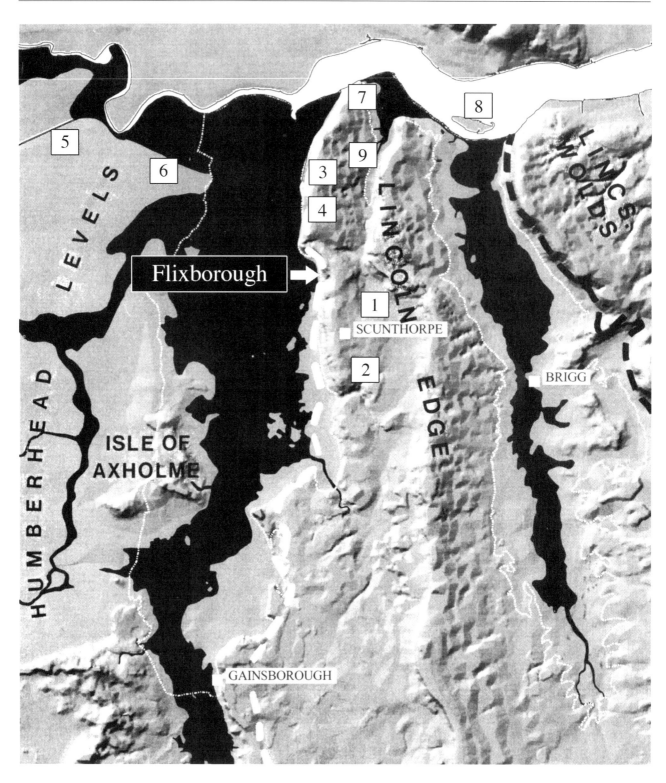

FIG. 5.1 Present-day habitats of the Lower Trent Valley mentioned in the text.

the mouth of the Trent at Blacktoft Sands, where it forms fringes on large inter-tidal mudflats. Salinity is hugely important here for habitat creation. The lower salinity of this area, compared with the outer estuary, today encourages club-rush and reeds to colonise the higher marsh, while *Agropyron* species dominate the saltmarsh on the seaward side (Fuller 1982). The tidal reedbeds at Blacktoft Sands are the second largest in Britain and today the reserve attracts thousands of wintering waterbirds every year, including wigeon, pink-footed geese, mallard, teal and golden plover. Despite these large numbers, there are fewer species than would be expected in a similar-sized freshwater marsh through the effects of brackish tides (LTNC 1998).

Some studies have shown that ecosystem changes in saltmarshes can occur over decades as a result of sea-level variation (Orson *et al.* 1998). In order to make predictions about the nature of wetlands around the Humber, and then to project these into the past, it is important to understand how the whole system functions and what factors might have affected it.

One major factor in understanding the past environment of the area around Flixborough is sea-level change. Sea-level has varied enormously since the end of last glacial maximum. Various lines of evidence indicate that sea-level rose through the Neolithic and Bronze Age, fell during the Iron Age, and then rose rapidly again during the Roman period, resulting in the flooding of many coastal wetlands. This was followed by a short-lived decrease in sea-level until late Anglo-Saxon/early medieval times when, after about AD 1250 sea-level has steadily risen until the present day (Rackham 1986). Wetland habitats, formed over the centuries would have been hugely variable, complicated by the effects of storm surge activity and human-driven processes such as deforestation. In simple terms, when wetlands were high

relative to the sea, freshwater marshes with silt and mud deposits formed. However, when they were low, saltmarshes formed (Rackham 1986). Late Holocene evidence for these changes have recently been reported from the region, where a palynological study carried out on deposits of early Roman (2040 ± 40 BP) and Anglo-Saxon (1080 ± 40 BP) date at Barrow Haven in the middle Humber, indicated the formation of saltmarsh. Study of mid-late Roman deposits from the site produced pollen suggesting the presence of freshwater sedge fen and reedswamp environments (Long *et al.* 1998).

During the rise in sea-level 8000 years ago, peat formed in the Humberhead levels, and as more peat accumulated, drainage became poorer thus inhibiting the percolation of water down through the sediments. These areas gradually became independent of surrounding water levels and became steadily elevated above the surrounding lands producing so-called 'raised mires'. Fragments of what were, until very recently, a large complex of raised mires in the region can still be seen today at Thorne and Hatfield moors (Eversham 1991; see also Fig. 5.2). Palaeo-environmental evidence suggests that an extensive patchwork of mires spread south-east from the Ouse in the area of the town of Goole (Buckland and Dinnin

Fig. 5.2 Thorne and Hatfield moors. Reproduced from Buckland and Dinnin 1997.

1997), through which flowed nutrient-rich fresh water, supporting rich fen communities confined between the Went, Ouse, Don and the Trent.

This extensive system of mires and fens has been reduced to the Thorne and Hatfield remnants as a result of human activity over the last few hundred years. Throughout Britain, this once extensive habitat has been destroyed at a dramatic rate (FIG. 5.2), as a result of drainage, warping and peat-cutting. Although evidence for these activities in the region may extend perhaps back to Roman times, it is widely acknowledged that the majority of damage has occurred since 1626 when Vermuyden (a Dutch engineer) began major drainage works (Buckland and Dinnin 1997). He was also responsible for the redirecting of the river Don from its original course into the lower reaches of the Trent, which must have had considerable influence on the wetland dynamics of the region by introducing freshwater to otherwise poor fen communities (Gaunt 1975).

'Wet-warping' was used in Humberhead Levels around Thorne Moors in the mid-seventeenth century to reclaim the land for agriculture and involved the intentional flooding of the fields via a sluice gate from the Humber at high tide. This process, followed by a period of livestock grazing, yielded some of the most productive arable fields in Britain. 'Dry warping', carried out at Hatfield, involved the excavation and carting of mineral soils over the peat to improve nutrient richness.

Peat-cutting or 'winning' has occurred extensively in the region over the last two hundred years, and was (until the later twentieth century), done by hand, enabling many of the original peatland plants and animals to survive (Limbert 1986) However, a resurgence in demand for peat since the 1960s and mechanised peat extraction techniques, have dramatically changed this. Until only a few years ago, 2000 acres of intact mire (the largest uncut lowland mire in England) survived. Today, however, only remnants of this habitat still occur at Hatfield Moor, and none of the original uncut vegetation can be found at Thorne Moor (Eversham 1991).

The vertebrate fauna of the two moors today is more diverse than one would expect. Peat moorland is only one habitat of many; pond/scrub, reedbed, open/cut-over mire, scrub, mire woodland and carr woodland also occur, and peat moorland itself varies according to human activity, type, and age (Bain 1992). The mature and less recently worked areas hold the highest diversity (Limbert 1994).

The freshwater fens and carrs that surround the moors, survive today in isolated pockets. Reedbeds and riverbank habitats have been drastically altered by river management as well as drainage in the last three hundred years. Today, the river Trent is a large canalised river that has been graded, widened, straightened and artificially embanked. This process has involved the felling of large areas of riparian woodland, clearing of marginal reed swamps, and the elimination of sandbanks (Smith 1975). The draining of surrounding farmland has led to the drying and shrinkage of the peat, leaving the surrounding agricultural land several metres lower than the river itself. The effect upon local vertebrate fauna of this type of river management has not been widely studied, but there have been some obvious consequences. Draining results in the loss of pools and shallows reducing fish breeding areas, subsequently affecting species such as herons and cormorants. Cliff nesters, such as sand martins and kingfishers, and those birds that use the steep sand banks for cover (e.g. water rails and green sandpipers), are also disadvantaged by the remodelling and removal of the river banks. The lack of river-edge vegetation can be detrimental to perching riverine bird species, whilst shelter for animals on windy days can be limited (Smith 1975; Fuller 1982). In addition, the Lower Trent has been heavily influenced by industrial pollution, reducing invertebrate numbers. Despite these changes, many species of piscivorous birds (such as mergansers, herons, cormorants and sawbills) continue to over-winter on the Lower Trent, (Whitton and Lucas 1997). Where the river is still able to flood further upstream (such as at Besthorpe, Nottinghamshire), mallard, teal and wigeon have all over-wintered in large numbers during the twentieth century, and where marginal reed-beds are still available, hundreds of dabbling and diving ducks can be found out of the breeding season (Wildfowl and Wetland Trust 1963).

Almost all of the natural pools and marshy patches in the heathland around Scunthorpe have been reclaimed. Thus only artificially created water habitats (in the form of ornamental lakes, flooded gravel pits or brick pits) exist to attract waterfowl out of the breeding season. In a recent survey by the Lincolnshire Trust for Nature Conservation, the brick pit at Burton-upon-Stather, close to the River Trent (not far from the site of Flixborough) was found to be rich in birdlife and was a significant stopover for transient wildfowl in the winter (LTNC 1998).

An unusual isolated inland wetland remnant does exist in the form of a small area of saltmarsh just west of Thorne Moors at Bell's Pond. This could have originated from early warping, followed by the rapid colonisation of saltmarsh plants, and is maintained today only by the pumping of brackish water from Thorne colliery. Its origins are by no means clear, but the species present indicate a history long before the Humber estuary was embanked and industrialised (Eversham 1991).

Local woodland

Although today most of the woodland occurs on the east side of the River Trent, limited palynological information indicates that pine and oak forest once existed over the peatlands to the west of Flixborough. This is thought to have been cleared through burning long before Anglo-Saxon times and to have subsequently been prevented from returning by grazing livestock (Eversham 1991).

Many trees have been planted in the last century, but Lincolnshire still has pockets of ancient (pre-AD 1600) woodland (Harding and Peterken 1975). These pockets are surrounded by heavily cultivated land and have been treated as islands, protected from invading species (Peterken and Game 1984). Previous research into the woodlands of Lincolnshire suggests that 'ancient' woodland here is a mixture of primary and ancient secondary woodland in varying proportions, and with little evidence of previous cultivation (Peterken 1975). This, together with historical evidence, has led to the conclusion that most of the ancient woodland remaining in Lincolnshire contains at least a core of primary woodland.

Much of the woodland in the county, however, is of more recent origin. Burton Wood, closest to the site of Flixborough, (replanted in the 1920s and 1930s [LTNC 1998]) did not exist for many years before that, as is demonstrated by the 1805 map of the region. Coleby Wood, just to the north of Burton Wood, is present on the 1805 map, but is believed to have been planted after AD 1600 (LTNC 1998). Although native trees such as ash, oak and elder are present in this wood, the presence of some introduced species – larch and sycamore, both thought to have been introduced in the 17th century – suggests that Coleby wood bears little resemblance to the woodland of Anglo-Saxon times. Perhaps the nearest probable ancient woodland to the site of Flixborough is at Broughton, east of Scunthorpe (A. Pyke pers. comm.), much of it probably primary, although its origins are uncertain and need further investigation.

It is not thought that mature woodland was much more widespread in the Saxon period than it is today. Much of the deforestation in England is thought to have occurred during the Roman era (Rackham 1980; Parker 1988), and it is likely that the pattern of woodland remained similar from Roman through to post-Norman times, although the pollen record does indicate some immediate post-Roman re-afforestation (Lillie 1998). The Domesday evidence shows a very patchy cover of underwood in the region at that time, with most of the mature wood occurring in the south of the county (Darby 1952). Coppicing has been well documented in Anglo Saxon times, and it seems that the woodland would have been very similar in its vegetation make-up to contemporaneous ancient deciduous woodland, i.e. a mixture of primary denizens, inefficient colonisers and other plants that colonise more readily.

Periglacial sands, heathland and the Wolds

The River Trent effectively forms the boundary between two very different geomorphological regions (Gaunt 1997). The site of Flixborough itself is situated on a sandy spur, which rises up a steep escarpment to the east. On top of this escarpment are the Lincolnshire Wolds, an area of (comparative) 'upland' (comprising a dissected chalk plateau) some 72km (45 miles) long and 8–13km (5–8 miles) wide, which reaches a maximum height of 169m (548 feet). Wind-blown periglacial sands support some of the most ancient habitats in Lincolnshire, present

long before the peat formed to the west of the Trent. In some more open areas, unusual woodland has developed, with sallow, birch, rowan and oak predominating. This could be unusual only because of lack of livestock grazing in those areas. It seems that much of north Lincolnshire would have been covered with sandy heathland from about 4000 years ago, where grazing pressure prevented woodland development (Buckland and Dinnin 1997).

However, almost all the sandy heaths and warrens in the region have been lost to urban development and afforestation, at least where peat did not form (Eversham 1991). Until recently, one of the last significant sites of sandy heath was Atkinson's Warren, very close to the site of Flixborough. Although reportedly destroyed in the late 1980s, it has recently been surveyed by the LTNC and is now listed as a very important and typical lowland heathland (LTNC 1998). Heathland is a habitat that was hugely extended in Britain by agriculture and heaths vary according to their wetness. The 'dry' heaths on well-drained soils such as periglacial sands are dominated by ling and bell heather (Fuller 1982). Without burning or grazing, such heaths are quickly invaded by woodland species such as birch; they are thus extremely suitable areas for afforestation by humans. Vertebrate communities in these heaths vary enormously, depending on numerous factors, including competition with other vertebrate species such as rabbits. In modern communities, bird breeding habitats are also altered in heathland by the presence of numerous rabbits (Fuller 1982).

5.3 Evidence from the bioarchaeological remains

The preceding text provides a broad picture of the range of habitats present in the immediate and general vicinity of the site of Flixborough today and likely to have existed there in the recent and more distant past. We can now turn to the range of bioarchaeological remains recovered from excavations at the site to provide contemporaneous information as to the nature of the local environment during middle and late Saxon times. With the recovery of such a vast quantity of vertebrate remains, in addition to other, more limited, archaeobotanical and molluscan evidence, it could be expected that a detailed picture of the surrounding (and perhaps wider) environment of the site could be reconstructed. Of course, in order to achieve this, a number of basic assumptions have been made:

1   *that all the resources brought to the site and consumed were procured locally or in the nearby region.* If, however, animals or their commodities, were being shipped large distances (i.e. in the case of those which were rare or highly prized), they will *not* reflect local or even regional environmental preferences at all;

2   *that all remains recovered represent all (or at least most) that were procured.* If, however, remains of

common organisms are under-represented or not represented at all in the assemblage (e.g. as a result of poor recovery, other taphonomic factors, or by the distinct possibility that humans were not indiscriminative about which animals they exploited), evidence for common environmental conditions or habitats will also be overlooked;

3 *that the present day or recent habitat preferences of the organisms have changed little or not at all in the intervening 1000 or so years.* Assumptions based on the behaviour and preferences of those organisms, which can be viewed and studied today, often form the basis of our palaeobiological reconstructions of the past (on the principle of uniformitarianism). However, evidence suggests that these factors remain far from static over thousands or hundreds of years, or sometimes even decades, meaning that all interpretation should be treated with caution.

In the case of vertebrate remains, previous authors (e.g. Robinson 1985; Parker 1988) have stated that they can be useful in helping to reconstruct past habitats, if they satisfy various criteria which may be summarised as follows:

1 a species is known to be habitat-specific; i.e. a species is much more abundant in one kind of habitat than others;

2 the habitat preferences of the species for ancient habitats can be reliably assessed;

3 the size of the assemblage is large enough to allow credible conclusions to be drawn.

Birds as palaeoecological indicators

The diversity of bird species and the sheer size of the avian assemblage recovered from Flixborough (see Chapter 4; TABLE 4.1) provide an important opportunity to explore the range of habitats exploited by the inhabitants. TABLE 5.1 gives information for selected 'wild' bird species (identified from the Flixborough assemblage) with regard to how habitat-specific each species is at the present day. These figures are based on the 'register of ornithological sites', the British Trust for Ornithology's extensive survey of 4000 sites in the British Isles (Fuller 1982). The frequency of occurrence of each taxon between individual 'habitats' has been calculated rather than its abundance. At face value, the data appear to indicate that certain avian species are more habitat-specific than others, and thus potentially more useful for past habitat reconstruction.

However, as previously mentioned, it is extremely important to view these apparent habitat preferences in a modern context. For example, a species that today appears to be very habitat-specific could, in fact, reflect current pressures of human persecution. This must certainly be the case for the black grouse, in modern times an upland bird, but one that historically has been recorded in a wide range of habitats, especially heathland and wetland. Limbert (1992) cites evidence that black grouse were once common on the moors around Thorne and Hatfield. They are, however, easily exterminated from lowland areas and their modern distribution must represent a 'refugium' from human activities. Changes in land use have also deprived the black grouse of much of its lowland habitat, and at the same time has improved conditions for other indigenous and introduced game-birds such as partridges, quail and pheasants (Hudson and Rands 1988).

Red kite and buzzard could also be viewed in a similar light, both having been persecuted by humans (in the case of the red kite to extinction from England). Both species used to be seen in the North Lincolnshire region even during the twentieth century (Snow 1971), and the bones of red kite have frequently been identified from urban sites of Roman and medieval date, leading to the suggestion that these birds once filled an important urban scavenger niche and were common sights within medieval towns (Mulkeen and O'Connor 1997). At Flixborough, their usefulness as palaeoecological indicators is also perhaps tempered by their interpretation as birds used for falconry, and thus possibly brought from elsewhere (see Chapter 10).

Perhaps one of the most interesting avian groups in the Flixborough assemblage are the geese. The problems of species identification, and the separation of wild and domestic forms using skeletal morphology alone have been outlined elsewhere (see Chapter 7). However, through the combined application of aDNA and biometrical data, we can now be certain that pink-footed geese, brent geese and barnacle geese are all present in different frequencies in the Flixborough assemblage (see also Chapter 7). Of the thousands of modern sites included in the BTO's survey, these three species of wild geese were only found wintering on saltmarsh. Since it is likely that most wildfowling in the past was carried out during the winter months (Allison 1985), it is possible that the inhabitants at Flixborough were extensively exploiting the saltmarsh zones, which, most probably, were located further to the east of the site (i.e. on the Humber rather, than around the mouth of the Trent).

Although there is no doubt that the saltmarshes of the region were being exploited (see other vertebrate, molluscan and botanical evidence detailed in Chapter 8), the very low levels of brent geese remains in the assemblage may indicate that most of the wildfowling for geese was actually undertaken on arable and unimproved pasture nearer to the site (see Chapter 8 for details). Recent studies of the distribution of geese in Britain (Owen 1976) suggest that brent geese do not seem to adapt well to long-term inland feeding and prefer to feed on coastal mudflats.

In general, ducks are much more aquatic in their feeding behaviour [than geese?] and the only duck that utilises terrestrial habitats in this respect is the wigeon (Vonkanel 1981). This species is an exception because it

	Habitat types	Wintering on rich-fens	Open swamps and high marshes	Breeding on rich-fens	Breeding on raised mires	Wintering on rivers	Breeding on rivers	Breeding on lakes	Breeding on lowland heaths	Breeding on chalk downland	Wintering on coastal grazing marshes	Breeding on floodmeadow	Wintering on floodmeadow	Breeding on coastal grazing marshes	Wintering in woodland	Breeding in woodland	Wintering on rocky coasts	Breeding on rocky coasts	Breeding on machair	Breeding on sand dunes	Wintering on salt-marshes	Breeding on salt-marshes
Ardea cinerea	grey heron	85.7				72		1			100	92.3	92.3			38.2	23.5				92.9	
Cygnus sp.	swan					25.6	24.9	53			87.5	60.7	76.9	53.8					66.7		50	
Anser brachyrhynchus	pink-footed goose																				46.4	
Branta leucopsis	barnacle goose																				14.3	
Branta bernicla	brent goose																				42.9	
Tadorna tadorna	shelduck							7	4.3		75	7.1	100	61.5			23.5	21.8	91.7	66.7	89.3	64.2
cf. *Anas platyrhynchos*	mallard?	85.7	79.5	79.5	90	71.6	77.9	90	30.4		87.5	89.3	84.6	84.6			35.3	21.8	91.7	55.5	96.4	50.9
A. crecca	teal	57.1	79.5			19.7	6.8	23	8.6		100	17.9		30.8					58.3	11.1	82.1	9.4
A. penelope	wigeon							8			87.5		61.5				29.4		25		85.7	
A. clypeata	shoveller							15			75	7.1	50	30.8					58.3	11.1	57.1	7.5
Milvus milvus	red kite															20						
Buteo buteo	buzzard															33.1						
Lyrurus tetrix	black grouse															35						
Grus sp.	crane																					
Vanellus vanellus	lapwing	52.4			50			34	65.2		100	78.6	88.5	92.3					100	50	92.9	58.5
Pluvialis squatarola	grey plover																23.5				82.1	
P. apricaria	golden plover																				67.9	
Numenius arquata	curlew				80				47.8			28.6					58.8			16.7	100	
Scolopax rusticola	woodcock															47.1					14.3	

TABLE 5.1 Habitat preference data (after Fuller 1982) (continued overleaf).

David Slater et al.

	Habitat types	Breeding on salt-marshes	Wintering on salt-marshes	Breeding on sand dunes	Breeding on machair	Breeding on rocky coasts	Wintering on rocky coasts	Breeding in woodland	Wintering in woodland	Breeding on coastal grazing marshes	Wintering on floodmeadow	Breeding on floodmeadow	Wintering on coastal grazing marshes	Breeding on chalk downland	Breeding on lowland heaths	Breeding on lakes	Breeding on rivers	Wintering on rivers	Breeding on raised mires	Breeding on rich-fens	Open swamps and high marshes	Wintering on rich-fens
Laridae sp.	gull	34	96.4	22.2	66.7	92.7	94.1			15.4	88.5	3.6	100									95.2
cf. *Columba palambus*	wood pigeon?		39.3			14.5		47.8			100		100	95.8					70	71.8		
Tyto alba	barn owl							45.8														
Strix aluco	tawny owl							47.7											50			52.4
Garrulus glandarius	jay							50.2	38.75										50			61.9
Corvus corax	raven							32.5														
Corvus corone /Corvus frugilegus	crow/rook		64.3			30.9	58.8		39.1		92.3		100						60			85.7

TABLE 5.1 continued.

is a grazer and, although it does feed in large groups on inter-tidal flats, and is usually restricted to saltmarsh in the winter, it will also readily feed on dry grassland and flooded pasture. Unfortunately, as for the geese, the identification of the bones of many duck species on the basis of morphological criteria alone is fraught with problems, and to date the application of aDNA techniques (in order, for example, to confirm the presence of wigeon) has not been applied to the Flixborough duck assemblage. Problems with the identification of duck species are further complicated by the impossibility of distinguishing wild and domestic individuals. The other duck species positively identified in the assemblage (i.e. mallard and teal), are both generalists, occurring in large numbers in a wide range of habitats in the British Isles. Some of the largest populations of teal and mallard winter in the Humber today (Prater 1981), and there is no reason why large numbers should not also have been present during Saxon times. Interestingly, the remains of duck are not common in the Flixborough assemblage (certainly when compared with geese), although they appear to increase in importance during the ninth century (Phase 4–5b).

The bones of crane, however, occur in significant numbers in the Flixborough assemblage. On the basis of preliminary aDNA results, it is almost certain that the remains are from the common crane, *Grus grus* (Panithanarak 2004). More extensive analysis of bio-metrical data has allowed us to postulate that they may even have been a resident subspecies separate from and larger than those from continental Europe, a race now extinct in the British Isles (Dobney *et al.* in prep.).

Common crane, which still occur in continental Europe, occupy all types of freshwater habitat, especially shallow open ponds. In winter, they compete with livestock for acorns, and feed on earthworms (Diaz *et al.* 1996). Whether they can be used as good indicators for palaeo-habitats is debatable. They do favour wetland habitats in the summer, but are frequently found on pastures in the winter (Diaz *et al.* op. cit.). Their presence at Flixborough is more likely to reflect the exploitation of locally-caught birds which were almost certainly breeding in the Lincolnshire Fens to the south and west of the site.

Mammals as palaeoecological indicators

Wild mammals

Although not as numerous and diverse as the birds, the wild mammalian fauna identified from Flixborough provides some additional clues for local habitat recon-struction during the Saxon period. The only wild mammal species to appear frequently in the Flixborough assemblage is the roe deer. Unlike red deer, the roe is currently neither an exclusively woodland nor a wholly upland animal and, in fact, has been recorded throughout history in fenlands, such as in Cambridgeshire and south-east Yorkshire (Rackham 1986). Their current distribu-tion is believed to result from extensive hunting in the lowlands in the medieval period and, perhaps, through more recent introductions. Nowadays, they survive well in the mosaic of fragmented arable and pastureland where 'woodland islands' provide some cover during the day. Their presence throughout the Flixborough occupation sequence may suggest that a similar fragmented landscape also existed during Saxon times.

Several bones were identified as pine marten, a species which occurs in a wide range of habitats, although wooded areas are their preferred environment. Currently, their distribution is quite limited and it is believed that in England today only remnant populations exist in North Yorkshire and Northumberland (Corbet and Harris 1991). Documentary evidence (Thompson 2001) suggests that until the nineteenth century pine martens were found throughout Britain and it seems that persecution by humans for its fur is the likely cause of its more recent scarcity. Pine marten foot bones (showing fine cut marks) have been recovered from eighth-ninth century deposits at Fishergate in York (O'Connor 1991). These were interpreted as evidence for pelts and may or may not have been locally procured, since O'Connor (1991, 259) has suggested that local populations of pine marten could have existed in pine woodland which may have grown on areas of Devensian coversands near to York. The absence of knife marks on the bones from Flixborough and the presence of skeletal elements representing major limb bones strongly support the hypothesis that habitats

Year	Extent of permanent grassland	Extent of meadow	Extent of unimproved pasture
1938	230,679	41,187	189,576
1965	116,958	4856	112,102*
1995	49,000	142	48,860**
%loss	78.60%	99.70%	74%

*semi-improved

**older than 5 years

TABLE 5.2 Habitat loss in Lincolnshire since 1938.

suitable for pine martens were reasonably close and that these animals were in fact trapped locally.

Domestic mammals

As a result of their ubiquitous presence in archaeological assemblages, domestic animal remains are somewhat overlooked in their use as habitat indicators. However, the importance of certain domestic livestock over others at particular sites or geographical locations must reflect the presence of favourable, perhaps even, directly manipulated habitats (if it can be assumed the bones arrived inside animals being farmed locally). Thus, a large, well-dated assemblage of domestic livestock remains can actually contribute valuable information in reconstructing the broad agricultural landscape of the period. In the case of Flixborough, the sheer quantity of remains representing the most common farmyard animals (cattle, sheep, and pig) indicates the availability of sufficient pasture and woodland in the region. These areas sustained the large flocks of sheep and herds of cattle and pigs indicated by the vast dumps of bones (for more detailed discussion of the exploitation of the agricultural landscape see Chapter 8).

Fish as indicators of pollution

Attempts have been made by, for example, O'Connor (1989, 198) to assess changes in water quality during the Saxon period based on the abundance of pollution-sensitive fish taxa such as shad, grayling and burbot. Although there is no doubt that the relative abundance of these taxa today may indicate changes in water quality, the rarity or absence of these taxa at Flixborough is also mirrored at early historic sites throughout Britain and North-western Europe (e.g. Enghoff 1999; 2000). Rather than indicating early contamination of a river as large as the Trent, it seems more likely that these species were naturally rare, difficult to catch or excluded from the cultural repertoire of desirable taxa.

Plants as palaeoecological indicators

Insofar as the charcoal recorded at Flixborough can be taken as representative of the environs (this assumes no long-distance transport of wood or timber), by far the greatest proportion of the charcoal recovered was oak, *Quercus*. It was recorded from 21% of contexts and most of the larger fragments of charcoal proved to be this species. Where *Quercus* charcoal fragments were measured, they were mostly in the size range 10–30 mm but there was one case where at least one fragment exceeded 100 mm (Sample 4705) and one sample with a fragment as large as 160 mm (Sample 2404).

The other taxa identified as charcoal were hazel (*Corylus*, in 7% of contexts) and willow/poplar/aspen (*Salix/Populus* 5%), with <5% each of ash (*Fraxinus*), alder (*Alnus*), ?birch (*Betula*) and ?Pomoideae (which includes apple, pear, rowan, and hawthorn). There was a single record (from Context 4920) for charred coniferous wood, probably pine (*Pinus*), though the fragments had an appearance like cinders, with strong vitrification and distortion of the wood structure, and it was not possible to make a closer identification. A modest range of taxa is thus indicated, reflecting a rather limited range of sources, with most of the charred wood probably representing structural timber (oak). That woods of different kinds grew in the environs of Flixborough is not perhaps surprising given the diversity of soils types reflecting, in turn, a diversity of drift and solid geologies within a small area.

Plant remains (and at least one mollusc taxon) likely to have originated in saltmarsh were regularly recorded in the assemblages from Flixborough, cf. data in Hall (2000, table 9). An assemblage from Context 5983 (Sample 10220/BS) perhaps provides one of the best examples of a group largely, if not wholly, originating in saltmarsh. Together with tentatively identified culm of the saltmarsh grass *Puccinellia maritima,* and capsules of sea plantain, *Plantago maritima*, there were traces of several plants which could easily have grown in saltmarsh, though they are certainly not indicators of it, by themselves – silverweed (*Potentilla anserina*), black medick (*Medicago lupulina*), hairy buttercup (*Ranunculus sardous*) and spike-rush (*Eleocharis palustris*). Also present in the sample were moderate amounts of both 'pinched' stems (see p. 263 for an explanation) and charred herbaceous detritus, of ash, concretions, and 'glassy slag', and traces of charred rush (*Juncus*) capsules.

Evidence for site environment and living conditions

All of the recovered snail assemblages were small and only a few taxa were represented (see Chapter 4; TABLE 4.4). The overall character of the assemblages (other than the small number indicative of saltmarsh) was consistent through the deposits, both spatially and temporally. These all indicated a local environment of dry, probably short-turfed, grassland with damper (or perhaps merely more shaded) conditions (indicated by, for example, *Carychium* spp. and *Vitrea crystallina*) present within cut features. There were also hints of denser cover, such as nearby woodland/scrub, given by the presence of *Discus rotundatus* in contexts from Phases 1 through to 6.

Perhaps one of the most surprising aspects of this site is that occupation was, apparently, continuous over a long period and with many phases of building and rebuilding on deposits consisting of unconsolidated sand. It seems inconceivable that this sand was not largely vegetated (or in some other way protected from the elements) or mass-movement under the influence of wind and rain must surely have been a regular occurrence. The likelihood that a cover of turf would be detectable through plant macrofossil remains is small, given the rapidity with which uncharred remains would decay, unless some kind of seed bank became established, but the lighting of bonfires on areas of turf might, one supposes, produce some charred remains which would find their way into the occupation deposits, dispersed from their original concentration in a burnt surface. As previously discussed, however, the land snail assemblage appears to suggest a cover of short grassland over the site throughout its occupation. In fact, deposits identified during excavation as turf lines were recorded in four cases for the pre-Saxon period (Phase 0) and once for Phase 7 and later (post-Saxon). Samples from two of the Phase 0 'turf line' contexts were examined and one of these produced modest numbers of sclerotia (resting bodies) of a soil fungus, probably *Cenococcum*, consistent with the formation of a soil but offering no further information about the nature of vegetation on it.

Conclusions

Today, the modern North Lincolnshire countryside is dominated by arable land (heavily treated with fertilizers and pesticides), and largely lacking hedgerows or other landscape features. Although this is a product of several thousand years of manipulation by humans, its present-day appearance is the result of very recent agricultural practices instigated after the Second World War. Land use maps of the twentieth century indicate substantial grassland areas around the Lower Trent which gradually gave way to cereals and other crops through time (Ordnance Survey 1966). Thus, over the last sixty or so years it would seem that there has been dramatic and wholesale loss of permanent grassland, meadow and unimproved pasture through an intensification of arable cultivation. Some of these grasslands were very important to fauna and flora such as orchids and breeding birds.

Prior to the 1930s, there is patchy historical information about the changes in these habitat types. Evidence from the pollen profiles for the recent history of the Trent valley are also far from complete, a result of the removal of the uppermost peat deposits through peat extraction, destruction by agricultural practices, or desiccation. In addition, the surrounding sandy areas are poor preservers of palaeoenvironmental information (Lillie 1998, who reviews in detail what palynological evidence does exist from the late Holocene).

From the limited range of bioarchaeological and historical information which exists for the region, a general picture of the environment of the area surrounding the site of Flixborough during middle to late Saxon times can be constructed. This is of a very large and diverse wetland habitat stretching away from the site to the west and north. Large well-established reed beds would have been plentiful along the Trent, edged with some riverine woodland. The area nearer to Flixborough would probably have been rich fenland (under the influence of the freshwater from the Trent, and the Don on its old course), which was probably interspersed with intact raised mires. The areas south and east of Flixborough are likely to have been rich lowland heath and unimproved pasture, and areas of woodland would have been deciduous, patchy and coppiced, not unlike those seen today. Lower sea-level at the time would also imply an absence of saltmarsh on the Trent (unlike today), with the highest saline influences being found much further downstream. This has possible implications for the distance travelled in procuring the saltmarsh materials represented by the halophile plant and mollusc remains recovered from the site (see Chapter 8).

These are broad conclusions, which, on the evidence that exists are far from definitive; however, they do provide a broad interpretative framework which can be tested when more data become available.

6 Patterns of Disposal and Processing

Keith Dobney, Deborah Jaques, James Barrett, Cluny Johnstone, John Carrott and Allan Hall

6.1 Introduction

Human occupation of the site of Flixborough over several centuries has created a complex record of stratigraphy and material culture which serves as a rich source of information with which to investigate in some detail a variety of human economic and cultural activities. In the following chapter, the bioarchaeological data are used to explore further the patterns of disposal of animal and plant waste material at the site. The principal themes addressed relate to possible changes through time (or between deposit classes) of the types of material disposed of, and how these materials might have been processed prior to disposal.

6.2 The disposal of vertebrate remains

In general, it can be assumed that high-status settlements are most likely to be conspicuous consumers in terms of both the quantity and quality of the available food resources. They may also in turn be centres of redistribution of certain animal foodstuffs and products, as well as foci for specialised economic or industrial production involving animal products. All these diverse human activities inevitably produce large quantities of waste which must be disposed of. Thus the complex relationship between elements of production, consumption and redistribution at any site can be explored in the study of this refuse or garbage, in which the bones of animals are often the most commonly preserved component. For example, changes in the relative frequency of vertebrate species, or their respective limb, head and axial elements, through time, and their patterns of distribution across the site, provide both direct and indirect evidence of a wide range of past human activities.

As previously mentioned, we are extremely fortunate that the area of the site – threatened by sand quarrying

(and subsequently excavated) – comprised a large hollow on the periphery of the main settlement which was almost continuously used as the main dumping area for much of the waste produced by the inhabitants. The huge 'bone-rich' dumps (also containing a range of artefacts) proved to be a rich source of information. Although these dumps produced most of the vertebrate remains, bone was also recovered in smaller quantities from a wide range of other context types across the site (TABLE 6.1). The following account provides a detailed examination of the composition of these major context types (in respect of the range of animal bones recovered from them) in order to explore patterns relating to aspects of human activity.

Before any detailed conclusions regarding differences in possible disposal patterns across the site can be made, it must be pointed out that a variety of biasing factors can occur with respect to the relative frequency of different context types within and between periods. FIG. 6.1 shows the relative frequency of bone-bearing contexts by phase at the site. Initial impressions indicate that the greatest proportion (39%) these date to Phase 4–5b, with values from the remaining periods all much the same (12–19%). However, this pattern is not followed when the frequency of bone by major phase is considered (FIG. 6.2). In this case, although the highest frequencies of bone are still found in contexts from Phase 4–5b (30%), values from Phases 3b and 6 are nearly as high (reaching 26 and 24% respectively). Thus in Phases 3b and 6, larger quantities of bone are found in fewer contexts overall.

Focussing in more detail on context type also indicates more obvious discrepancies within and between phases. FIG. 6.3 shows the relative frequency of major bone-bearing context types present in each main phase of occupation at Flixborough. What is immediately apparent is the rather high frequency of post-holes in the early to middle phases, the low frequency of dumps in the earliest

	2–3a	3b	4–5b	6	6iii	
Dump	2	14	49	12	3	80
Occupation	25	24	26	13	1	89
Post-hole	59	47	114	7	0	227
Pit	9	12	27	13	1	62
Trench	6	12	16	18	0	52
Dark soil	0	0	0	24	78	102
Soakaway	11	4	0	0	0	15
Total	**112**	**113**	**232**	**87**	**83**	**627**

TABLE *6.1 Number of bone-bearing deposits classified by context type and phase.*

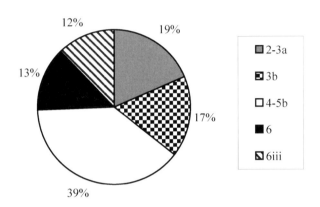

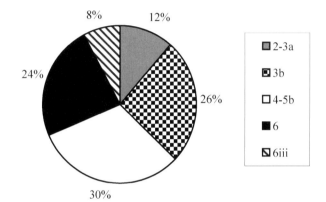

FIG. *6.1 Relative frequency of bone-bearing contexts by phase.*

FIG. *6.2 Relative frequency of bone (NISP) by phase.*

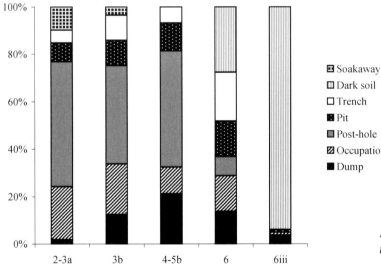

FIG. *6.3 Relative frequency of the major context types by phase.*

and latest, and the high frequency of so-called dark-soils in the two latest phases. The relative frequencies of occupation and pit type contexts remain fairly constant throughout (with the exception of Phase 6iii, where a very limited range of contexts types is represented). If we consider comparisons with individual context types across the major phases (FIG. 6.4), a broadly similar pattern is apparent.

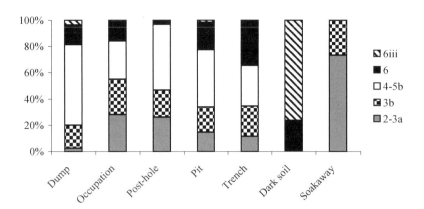

FIG. 6.4 Relative frequency of individual context types by phase.

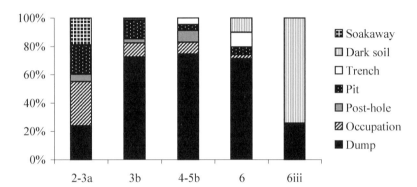

FIG. 6.5 Relative frequency of NISP from major context types by phase.

Relative bone frequency by context type

When bone frequency is considered, a very different picture emerges. FIG. 6.5 shows the relative frequency of identified bone fragments (NISP) by major phase and context type. By far the largest concentrations of bones from Phases 3b–6 are, not suprisingly, from contexts described as 'dumps'. Occupation deposits, pits and features described as soakaways contained a substantial quantity of the bone from Phase 2–3a, whilst post-holes, despite being the most numerous context type encountered in Phases 2–3a, 3b and 4–5b, not surprisingly contained small amounts. Pit-type contexts were also important in terms of relative abundance of bone in Phase 3b, whilst significant quantities of bone were recovered from contexts described as 'Trench' only ascribed to Phase 6. The strong bias towards dark soil deposits in Phase 6iii is reflected in the high concentrations of bone recovered from this context type.

Thus, from this initial appraisal of the range of contexts and quantity of bone recovered, it is already apparent that there are major differences (and, in some cases, similarities) through time in the distribution of the vertebrate remains at the site of Flixborough. If the evidence for limited re-working of material, discussed in Chapter 3, is to be believed, then these differences must

represent diachronic aspects of changing waste disposal at the site. A more detailed study of the composition of these major context types follows, in an attempt to provide an interpretative framework for understanding aspects of disposal.

Comparison of the frequency of birds and mammals between context types

Factors contributing to the preparation, consumption and ultimate disposal of the remains of different vertebrate taxa can be many and varied, e.g. sometimes related to the overall size of the animals, the products required from each, their specific culinary role, or their socio-economic status. Birds and fish were (and still are) often treated differently from mammals in this respect. Thus, a simple classification of the hand-collected vertebrate records from Flixborough into broad taxonomic categories was undertaken in order to shed further light on differences within the site and over time.

FIG. 6.6 shows the relative proportions of birds and mammals by major context type and through time (fish are excluded since these are comparisons of hand-collected and coarse dry-sieved data – for statistics relating to bulk-sieved fish remains, see below). It is interesting that there appears to be a similar pattern of

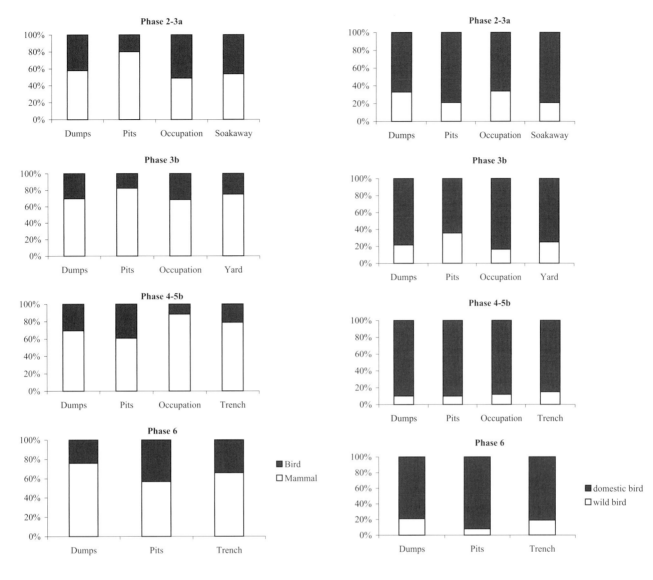

FIG. 6.6 *Relative frequency of mammal and bird bones by phase and context type.*

FIG. 6.7 *Relative frequency of domestic and wild bird bones by phase and context type.*

distribution of these two major vertebrate groups in Phases 2–3a through to 3b, with pit-fills containing the highest proportion of mammals and higher proportions of birds being present in dumps and occupation deposits. The contents of one pit fill, Context 6710, stood out from other deposits in Phase 3b. A great many of the crane fragments (24 fragments) from this phase were identified from this deposit and, whilst the crane remains from the large dump deposits included a range of skeletal elements, Context 6710 was overwhelmingly dominated by humeri (17 from a total of 24 identified fragments). Distinctive cat gnawing was evident on these bones. When the species representation in this pit fill (and, to a certain extent, in pit fill 6440) was compared with the overall frequencies of the main taxa from this phase, several apparent anomalies emerged. A greater proportion of the vertebrate remains were cattle than in the dump deposits (49 and

45% in contrast to 27, 28 and 33%), and goose and fowl frequencies were less than half of those of dumps. Context 6710 also yielded fewer bird species, but the proportion of the main species, fowl and goose, were considerably lower because of the presence of the high proportion of crane bones.

In Phase 4–5b, on the other hand, increased proportions of birds were found within pit-fills, with an increase in mammal remains evident from so-called "occupation" deposits. The pattern of higher frequencies of bird remains in pits also continued into Phase 6, and here birds were less frequent in the dump deposits. From these simple statistics it is apparent that a change in the composition of some of the major context types (i.e. pits and occupation deposits) occurs at the beginning of the ninth century, where more bird remains were deposited in pits and more mammal remains were deposited in

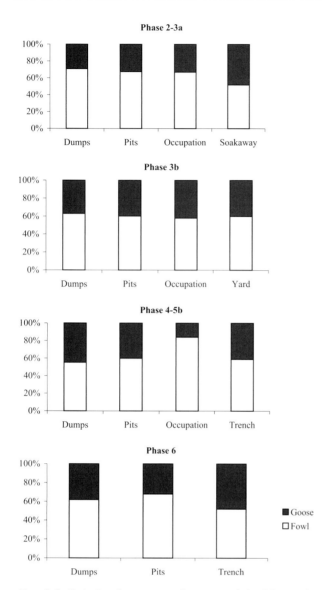

Fig. 6.8 Relative frequency of geese and fowl bones by phase and context type.

occupation deposits. The composition of the dumps, however, remains essentially similar throughout, although a gradual decrease in the frequency of bird bones is perhaps apparent.

If we consider the bird data in isolation, some further interesting observations can be made. Fig. 6.7 shows the relative frequency of wild and domestic birds, once again by each major phase and context type. Here, little difference can be seen between the two bird groups, with domestic birds (i.e. chicken and large goose) always significantly more frequent than wild specimens. However, once again, contexts from Phase 4–5b stand out in their generally suppressed levels of wild birds, consistent in all major context types. In this case, there are genuinely far fewer wild bird taxa present in all contexts assigned to this period, which makes it hardly suprising that they are statistically reduced in all major

context types compared with other periods. However, what is really interesting is the fact that wild birds stay at a very low frequency in pits from Phase 6, a period where the number and diversity of wild bird remains is on a par with those for Phases 2–3a and 3b. When considering the relative frequency only of domestic birds (large goose and fowl), very little difference appears to exist across the phases and context types (Fig. 6.8). The exception once again appears to be Phase 4–5b, where higher frequencies of fowl are present in occupation deposits

Birds generally have a much smaller body size than their counterparts in the mammal world, of course, particularly when comparing them with the most commonly recovered economically important mammals from the site (i.e. cattle, sheep and pig). As a result, their bones are more likely to be represented in kitchen/table waste (i.e. the remains of food directly consumed at the table) than butchers' or craft waste (i.e. elements or parts of the body removed during primary butchery). In addition, the generally smaller size and lighter nature of bird bones render them perhaps more tolerable around habitation and perhaps their higher frequencies in occupation deposits from Phases 2–3a and 3b supports this view. It could be argued, that there is an emphasis on table refuse in the occupation deposits from Phases 2–3a and 3b, and that this emphasis shifts to pits in Phase 4–5b. This obvious reversal of roles of pits and occupation deposits in Phase 4–5b is difficult to explain, although it would appear that a change in disposal practices has occurred.

Comparison of the frequency of fish between context types

Like birds, the remains of fish will often be associated directly with consumption refuse rather than with preparation or butchery. Except for the largest specimens, and where specialist curing or preservation are involved (e.g. removal of head for stockfish production or splitting of the carcase for smoking, brining, etc.), most of the bones of fish will be discarded after consumption. Thus, it might be expected that a generally similar pattern of distribution by phase and context type to that already outlined for birds should also be present in the fish remains from Flixborough. Interestingly, this appears not to be the case. Fig. 6.9 shows the frequency of fish bones recovered from the sieved samples by phase and major context type. From this, it is evident that the distribution of fish bones is very similar throughout all phases and context types, with the exception of Phase 2–3a. Dumps contained by far the greatest quantities of fish remains (in all cases >60%), whilst post-holes, occupation deposits, trenches and pits contained far fewer. Remains from Phase 2–3a are obviously different, with very much the largest proportion (51%) deriving from a single soakaway deposit, whilst 27% and 16% were recovered from occupation and post-hole deposits respectively.

A tentative link between the differential disposal of birds and fish (compared with mammals) cannot, there-

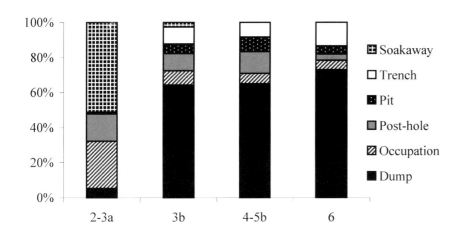

FIG. 6.9 Relative frequency of fish bones from wet-sieved samples from major context types by phase.

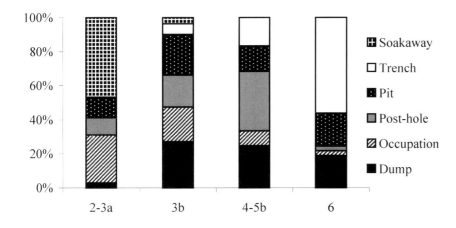

FIG. 6.10 Relative frequency of bird bones from major context types by phase.

fore, be postulated, since it would appear that most fish bones from Phases 3b–6 found their way into the large communal refuse dumps and not into more localised pit and occupation deposits. In contrast to the evidence from the fish remains, higher frequencies of bird remains were distributed throughout the range of context types (FIG. 6.10); this was particularly noticeable for material from Phases 3b, 4–5b and 6. Interestingly, however, a comparison of the bird bones from Phase 2–3a deposits with the fish bone data from the same phase showed there to be remarkable similarities between the two patterns [of disposal].

6.3 The disposal and deposition of plants and molluscs

There was no particular pattern with regard to the location of the larger assemblages of plant remains, except inasmuch as they tended to be in the ash- and bone-rich dumps (notably Context 3758 in sub-phase 4ii and Context 5983 in sub-phase 3biv), and in the fills of pits and post-holes (it should be noted that these were all amongst the top five most frequently recorded context types at this site). There was also considerable spatial

variation within layers for which more than one sample was examined (compare the lists for material from samples from Context 5983 in table 3 of Hall's (2000) report, for example). The sample type also affected the results: GBA (*sensu* Dobney *et al.* 1992) subsamples, not surprisingly, tended to yield very much less plant material in absolute terms than bulk-sieved samples from the same contexts and, for this particular site, were of very limited value as a route to recovery of plant remains, though they offered an opportunity to examine the finer (0.3–1.0 mm) fraction which had been lost during bulk-sieving. No particular pattern was discernible in terms of distribution of plant remains through time.

Hand-collected shell was present in contexts from all phases of the site (mostly from Phase 3b [39% of assemblage by weight] and Phase 6 [24%]). Phase 4–5b contained the most shell-bearing contexts (119) but only 16% of the assemblage by weight. Shell was recovered from a range of context types but mostly from dumps (66 contexts, 57%) with the largest concentrations within Phase 3b (13 dump contexts, 24%) and Phase 6 (9 dump contexts, 18%).

The disposal of shellfish remains appears to have been fairly systematic throughout the occupation of the site –

Context type	Phase group 1	2–3a	3b	4–5b	6	6iii	Total
DEP		16					16
DKSL					1,055	507	1,562
DUMP		833	10,892	4,652	8,262	1,614	26,253
GLY					87		87
GRAVE CUT		12					12
HARD			305				305
HRTH		26	3	1			30
OCC	14	549	742	335	365		2,005
OVEN				67			67
PATH				150			150
PH	26	690	2,395	1,371	54		4,536
PIT		53	1,219	467	212		1,951
PPIPE		72					72
SLOT		18		37	53		108
SOAK		265	25				290
TCH		18	2,452	377	1,038		3,885
Total	**40**	**2552**	**18,033**	**7457**	**11,126**	**2121**	**41,329**

Key: DCH – Ditch fill; DEP – Depression fill; DKSL – Dark soil; DUMP – Dump; GLY – Gully fill; GRAVE – Grave cut; HARD – Hard standing/post pad; HRTH – Deposits associated with hearths; OCC – Occupation deposit; OVEN – Deposits associated with ovens; PATH – Path; PH – Post hole fills; PIT – Deposits associated with pits (e.g. fills, linings); PPIPE – Post pipe fills; SLOT – Slot fill; SOAK – Soakaway fill; TCH – Trench fill; UNKN – Unknown.

TABLE 6.2 *Total shell weight (gms) recovered by hand collection by phase group and context type.*

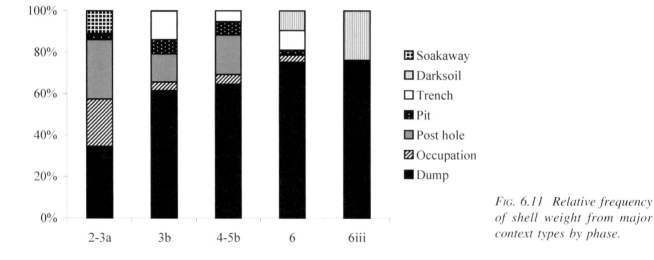

FIG. 6.11 *Relative frequency of shell weight from major context types by phase.*

most of the remains were concentrated in 'dump' deposits – with some other dumping or accumulation in cut features (e.g. pits, post-holes. See TABLE 6.2 and FIG. 6.11). Very few remains were recovered from non-cut features (e.g. hard standing, paths). Though this may simply reflect the fact that remains, casually discarded onto surfaces where they would be subject to trampling and other destructive processes, have consequently not survived (see Chapter 8 for full discussion of shellfish exploitation).

6.4 Carcase preparation and disposal

With the exception of growing crops, the acquisition and production of meat and other primary and secondary animal products for consumption is perhaps the single most important pastime of many human groups in the past. Direct evidence for many of these procurement activities can be found in the animal bones discarded on and around many archaeological sites. Each animal carcase comprises a range of body parts of different utilitarian value (depending on the product required). Thus, carcases can be dismembered into smaller meat units which often contain bones. Some units are discarded directly, some consumed immediately, some further processed and transported short distances to other parts of the site or long distances away from the site altogether. Others are utilised further in industrial or craft activities.

In simple terms, a preponderance of the major meat-bearing bones, such as scapulae, humeri, pelves, femora, thoracic and lumbar vertebrae, and ribs, may indicate the presence of domestic or household waste, since these elements usually remain with the meat when being cooked, although they may sometimes be 'boned out' prior to cooking. Minor meat-bearing elements such as radii, ulnae, tibiae and cervical vertebrae, are also associated with household refuse, although these are usually considered to come from cuts of lower quality and hence, usually (but not always) of less value.

The presence of large numbers of terminal limb elements (i.e. tarsals, carpals, metapodials, and phalanges), in association with a high proportion of material from heads (i.e. skull fragments, horns, and teeth), may be indicative of waste from primary butchery. An assemblage dominated by such elements indicates both slaughter and initial carcase preparation, since these are the parts usually removed once the animal has been slaughtered, bled and hung.

Products other than meat were also utilised. For example, horns were chopped or sawn from the skull, or broken off when the skull was smashed for access to the brain, and the valuable keratinous hornsheath removed for horn-working. Similarly, fresh hides were removed from the carcase to be cured and tanned into leather. Terminal limb elements such as metapodials (particularly of sheep and smaller mammals) and their associated phalanges were often left attached to the hides, thus a preponderance of metapodials and phalanges in an assemblage may also be an indication of the presence of tanners' waste.

These are obviously very simplistic models, and the real picture at any site is likely to have been far more complex. The possible multiple routes by which bone could be deposited within a site are diverse, and liable to be confused by combinations of all these. As a result, it would be unusual in most instances to be able to define with certainty all the activities represented by an assemblage. However, some patterns are observable at Flixborough.

Skeletal element distribution

FIGS 6.12–6.16 show the relative frequency of main skeletal elements of the major domestic mammals (cattle, sheep and pig) by broad phase, based on the minimum number of individual (MNI) counts for each element and presented as simple bar charts. The values have been calculated by comparing each element with the most frequently occurring ones (i.e. the element represented by 100% in each graph. See TABLES 6.3–6.7). The data presented show a series of distinctive patterns.

Although there are minor differences in the distribution of cattle elements between Phases 2–3a and 3b, the overall pattern for both periods is very similar. Here, mandibles are the most commonly encountered bone fragment, whilst the remaining teeth and post-cranial elements are represented in similar but much lower frequencies. This pattern also appears to be reflected in the distribution of both sheep and pig elements. These data are in complete contrast to those from Phase 4–5b where a much more varied (and in general higher) proportion of post-cranial elements are represented. Once again the pattern also appears to be repeated for sheep and pigs. Data from Phase 6 appear to represent a return to the pattern seen in the Phases 2–3a and 3b (for cattle and sheep), although the relative proportion of certain post-cranial elements is increased. The pattern for pigs in Phase 6 does not, however, follow that of cattle and sheep, instead remaining almost identical to that shown in Phase 4–5b. Finally, and once again in complete contrast to the previous phase, data from Phase 6iii show a much lower frequency of mandible fragments and an increased relative importance of selected post-cranial elements (somewhat exaggerated in the profile for pig). Aside from the reduced frequency of mandibles, the pattern from Phase 6iii is very similar to that presented in Phase 4–5b.

Skeletal element representation for domestic fowl showed that most parts of the body were present. This is unsurprising, given that carcase preparation of birds would have been minimal, and most skeletal elements should be expected to have been discarded together. FIG. 6.17 shows the MNI of all identified skeletal elements expressed as a proportion of the most frequent element. Taking into account the smaller numbers of bones from Phase 1, only slight differences between phases are apparent. All phases (excluding Phase 1) show a preponderance of humeri, ulnae, femora and tibiotarsi – the major meat-bearing elements.

Bones from the pectoral girdle (scapula and coracoid) are less numerous, whilst those found towards the tip of the wing (carpometacarpi and digits) are noticeably under-represented. The latter may have been discarded/chopped off prior to cooking, depending on the personal preference of the cook. Similarly, the lack of tarsometatarsi suggests that the lower legs were removed during carcase preparation. Counts for 'unidentified' elements showed that chicken cranium fragments and phalanges were present, but were not particularly numerous, with other parts of the body such as radii and sterna being well represented. Records of bone from the wet-sieved samples (representing 134 contexts) do not show the presence of many additional carpometacarpals (25) or phalanges/digits (1). Absence or under-representation of the skull and terminal limb elements suggests that these may have been removed elsewhere. The fact

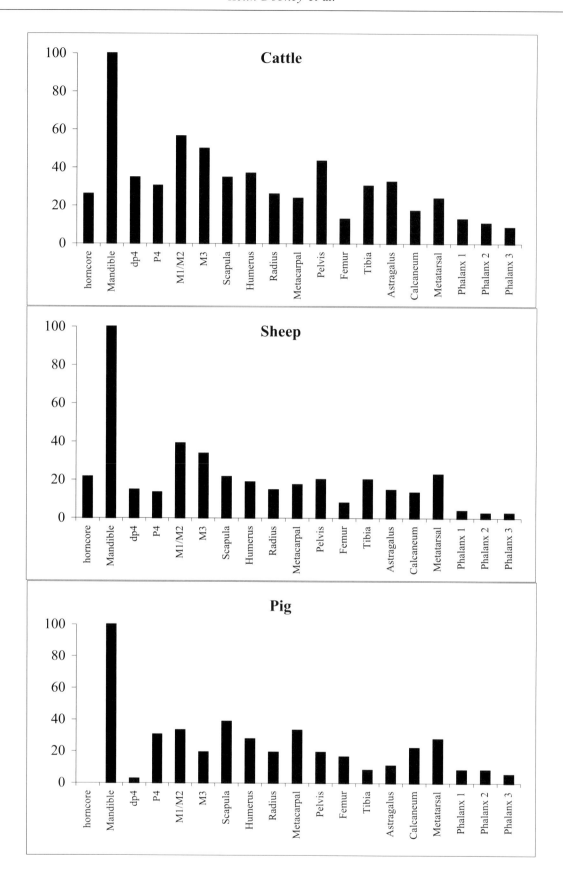

Fɪɢ. *6.12 Skeletal element representation (MNI) – Phase 2–3a.*

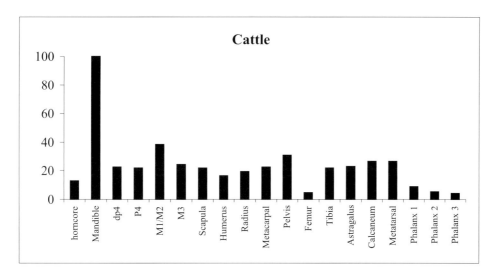

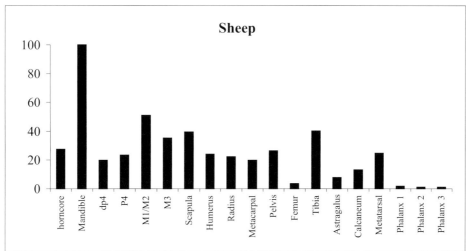

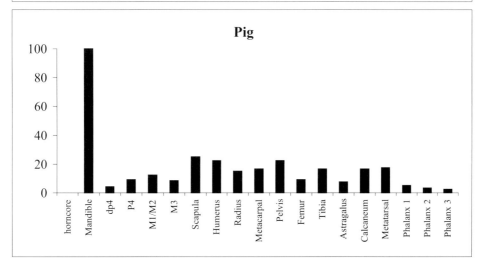

FIG. *6.13 Skeletal element representation (MNI) – Phase 3b.*

Keith Dobney et al.

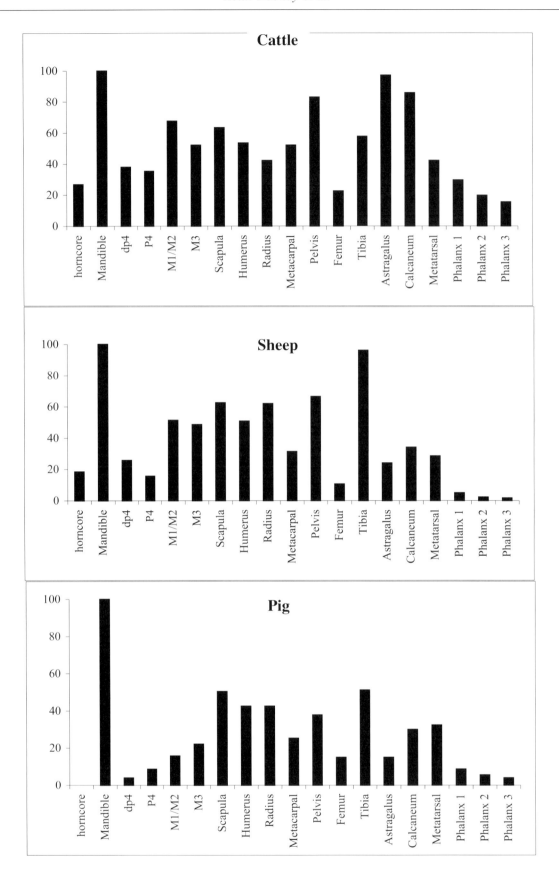

Fig. 6.14 Skeletal element representation (MNI) – Phase 4–5b.

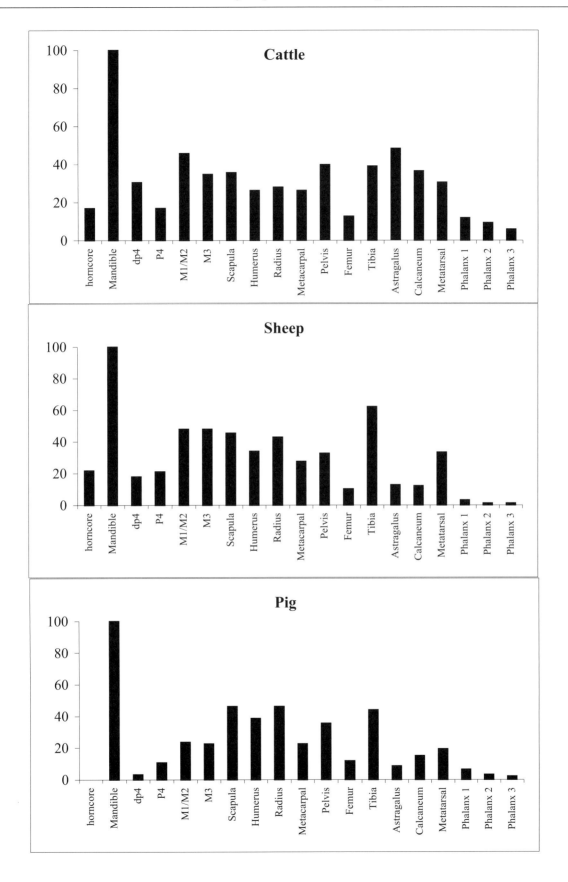

FIG. 6.15 Skeletal element representation (MNI) – Phase 6.

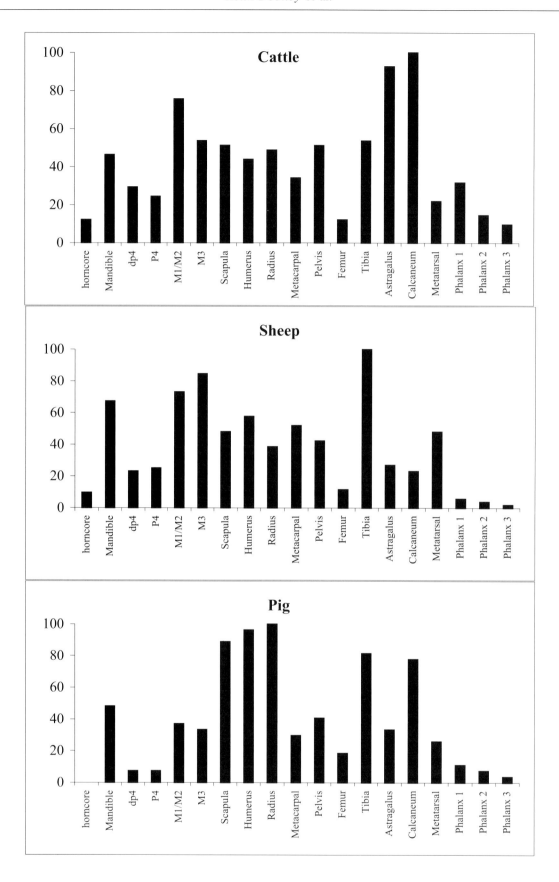

Fig. 6.16 Skeletal element representation (MNI) – Phase 6iii.

Element	Cattle	Sheep	Pig
horncore	12	16	n/a
Mandible	46	74	36
dp4	16	11	1
P4	14	10	11
M1/M2	26	29	12
M3	23	25	7
Scapula	16	16	14
Humerus	17	14	10
Radius	12	11	7
Metacarpal	11	13	12
Pelvis	20	15	7
Femur	6	6	6
Tibia	14	15	3
Astragalus	15	11	4
Calcaneum	8	10	8
Metatarsal	11	17	10
Phalanx 1	6	3	3
Phalanx 2	5	2	3
Phalanx 3	4	2	2
Total	**282**	**300**	**156**

TABLE 6.3 MNI by skeletal element for the three main domestic mammals – Phase 2–3a.

Element	Cattle	Sheep	Pig
horncore	22	46	n/a
Mandible	169	167	120
dp4	38	33	5
P4	37	39	11
M1/M2	65	85	15
M3	41	59	10
Scapula	37	66	30
Humerus	28	40	27
Radius	33	37	18
Metacarpal	38	33	20
Pelvis	52	44	27
Femur	8	6	11
Tibia	37	67	20
Astragalus	39	13	9
Calcaneum	45	22	20
Metatarsal	45	41	21
Phalanx 1	15	3	6
Phalanx 2	9	2	4
Phalanx 3	7	2	3
Total	765	805	377

TABLE 6.4 MNI by skeletal element for the three main domestic mammals – Phase 3b.

Element	Cattle	Sheep	Pig
Horncore	19	33	n/a
Mandible	71	179	127
dp4	27	46	5
P4	25	28	11
M1/M2	48	92	20
M3	37	87	28
Scapula	45	112	64
Humerus	38	91	54
Radius	30	111	54
Metacarpal	37	56	32
Pelvis	59	119	48
Femur	16	19	19
Tibia	41	172	65
Astragalus	69	43	19
Calcaneum	61	61	38
Metatarsal	30	51	41
Phalanx 1	21	9	11
Phalanx 2	14	4	7
Phalanx 3	11	3	5
Total	**699**	**1316**	**648**

TABLE 6.5 MNI by skeletal element for the three main domestic mammals – Phase 4–5b.

Element	Cattle	Sheep	Pig
horncore	20	34	n/a
Mandible	118	156	93
dp4	36	28	3
P4	20	33	10
M1/M2	54	75	22
M3	41	75	21
Scapula	42	71	43
Humerus	31	53	36
Radius	33	67	43
Metacarpal	31	43	21
Pelvis	47	51	33
Femur	15	16	11
Tibia	46	97	41
Astragalus	57	20	8
Calcaneum	43	19	14
Metatarsal	36	52	18
Phalanx 1	14	5	6
Phalanx 2	11	2	3
Phalanx 3	7	2	2
Total	**702**	**899**	**428**

TABLE 6.6 MNI by skeletal element for the three main domestic mammals – Phase 6.

Element	Cattle	Sheep	Pig
horncore	5	5	n/a
Mandible	19	35	13
dp4	12	12	2
P4	10	13	2
M1/M2	31	38	10
M3	22	44	9
Scapula	21	25	24
Humerus	18	30	26
Radius	20	20	27
Metacarpal	14	27	8
Pelvis	21	22	11
Femur	5	6	5
Tibia	22	52	22
Astragalus	38	14	9
Calcaneum	41	12	21
Metatarsal	9	25	7
Phalanx 1	13	3	3
Phalanx 2	6	2	2
Phalanx 3	4	1	1
Total	**331**	**386**	**202**

TABLE *6.7 MNI by skeletal element for the three main domestic mammals – Phase 6iii.*

that the sieved material does not include significant numbers of bones that are small and easily missed during hand-collection reinforces this hypothesis.

FIG. 6.18 show the percentage of different chicken elements within selected context types. Since no significant differences in the frequency of elements can be seen across context type through time, it would appear that chicken remains were uniformly discarded across the site. The vast majority of the bones probably represent consumption refuse from pre-prepared chickens, i.e. carcase preparation occurred elsewhere.

The use of multivariate statistics (in this case correspondence analysis) also indicates that there are major differences in the relative importance of skeletal elements of the major domestic mammals between the broad phases. FIG. 6.19 show the results of correspondence analysis on MNI values for sheep skeletal elements by phase. Each point on the plot represents a single context and only those deposits containing >100 identifiable fragments have been included. Data for several phases tend to cluster into groups. For example, with the exception of a few points, very little overlap exists between the data for Phases 2–3a, 3b and 4–5a. Assemblages from Phase 2–3a tend to be characterised by unusually high numbers of head fragments (mandibles and horncores), whilst those from Phase 3b are characterised primarily by heads and lower limb elements (metapodials). Both are located to the right of the central axis. Conversely, assemblages from deposits dated to

Phase 4–5b tend to cluster to the left of the central axis and are thus more strongly influenced by the frequency of other post-cranial elements, which are primarily more heavily meat-bearing bones.

For cattle, the picture is somewhat similar (FIG. 6.20), although there are some notable differences from the pattern observed for sheep. Once again, assemblages from Phase 4–5b cluster (in the main) to the left of the central axis, as do those from Phase 6. In contrast to the data for sheep, material from Phase 3b shows no patterning, the values being scattered randomly around both axes, whilst those from Phase 6iii cluster to the left of the central axis.

For pigs, it is clear (with a few notable exceptions) that assemblages from Phases 2–3a and 4–5b are distinctly grouped (FIG. 6.21). Whilst assemblages from Phase 2–3a are primarily dominated by heads and feet (usually interpreted as primary butchery waste in the form of initial carcase preparation), those from Phase 4–5a are dominated by major meat-bearing elements, strongly indicative of secondary butchery or consumption waste.

Thus, using simple and multivariate statistics to compare the patterns of skeletal element representation for the major domesticates between broad phases, it would appear that several major shifts in carcase disposal occurred at the site over time. More specifically, data for sheep indicate that Phases 2–3a, 3b and 6 are somewhat similar, whilst a major change in skeletal element representation occurs in Phases 4–5b and 6iii. For cattle and pig, it is also clear that Phase 4–5b stands out from the rest.

Although these patterns appear to indicate major changes in human behaviour with regard to consumption and disposal, there are a number of considerations that must be taken into account before proceeding with further interpretation. Many factors can influence the relative frequency of bones within an archaeological assemblage that have nothing to do with past human behaviour. Basic taphonomic processes such as differential preservation and fragmentation of certain elements, excavation and recovery techniques, ease of identification – to name but a few – may all contribute to patterns in the data. Since here we are comparing a range of elements of different size-classes and levels of robusticity, it is obvious that certain bones will always and inevitably be over- or under-represented in any assemblage. For example, since teeth are covered with enamel (the hardest calcified tissue in the body, which almost always survives better than bone), it could be expected that higher proportions of tooth crowns would be always be present in any assemblage which has suffered at least some degree of adverse preservation conditions. However, their small size (in comparison with other skeletal elements) invariably means that they are actually under-represented as a result of recovery bias, which favours larger fragments.

Since the data presented for each general phase represent an amalgamation of material from a range of

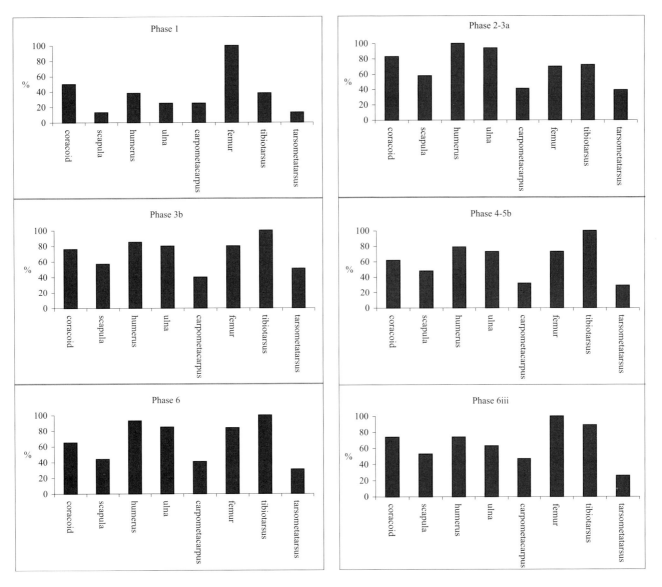

FIG. 6.17 *Domestic fowl skeletal element representation (MNI) by phase.*

diverse context types, it could be argued that such an obvious change in apparent disposal practices, as suggested for Phase 4–5b, might simply be an artefact of the changing frequency of varying context types between phases. For example, an overwhelmingly high frequency of pits from one period may be contrasted with a high number of dumps or floor surfaces from another. Thus variations between phases could merely reflect the differential use of certain features in refuse disposal, and *not* differences between the use of similar context types.

As has already been shown (TABLE 6.1), there is certainly a large discrepancy between the number of bone-bearing context types represented in each phase. The early phases of the site (2–3a, 3b and 4–5b) show broadly similar frequencies of post-holes, occupation deposits and pits, whilst Phases 6 and 6iii appear very different from these and from each other. However, once the frequency of bone fragments per context type is considered, it is

apparent that the material from Phases 3b, 4–5a and 6 is primarily from dumps, whilst that from 2–3a represents a much wider range of context types, and that from Phase 6iii is primarily from dark soil deposits.

Whilst the variation in skeletal element representation for Phases 6iii and even 2–3a may perhaps reflect different context types, the pattern established for Phase 4–5b cannot be explained so readily. The overwhelming preponderance of bone found in the large so-called 'dumps' of Phases 3b, 4–5a and 6 suggest that the differences in skeletal element representation noted in Phase 4–5b must be explained by a fundamental change in human consumption and disposal practices occurring in the ninth century. If we consider individual 'larger' assemblages from contexts, i.e. those containing >100 identified fragments, these are almost all exclusively from dumps. When the different subphases are compared within the broad phasing groups, the pattern of skeletal

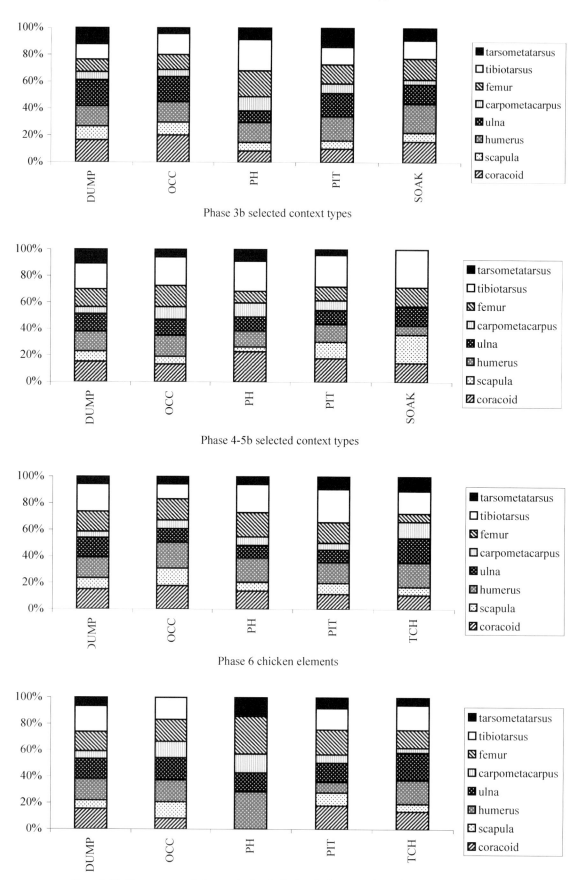

FIG. 6.18 Frequency of domestic fowl skeletal elements by selected context type.

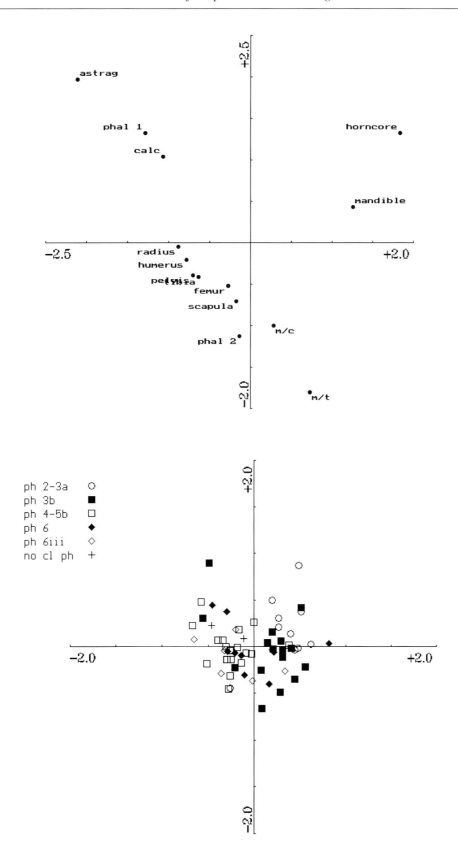

Fɪɢ. *6.19 Correspondence analysis of sheep skeletal elements by phase.*

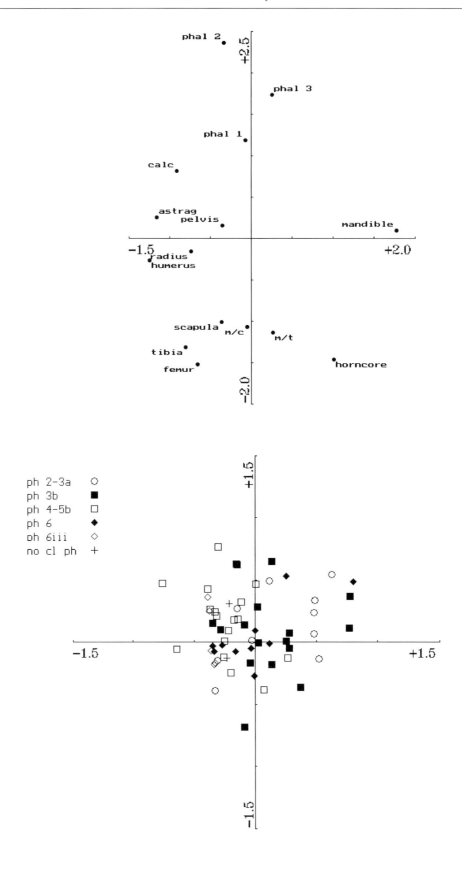

FIG. 6.20 Correspondence analysis of cattle skeletal elements by phase.

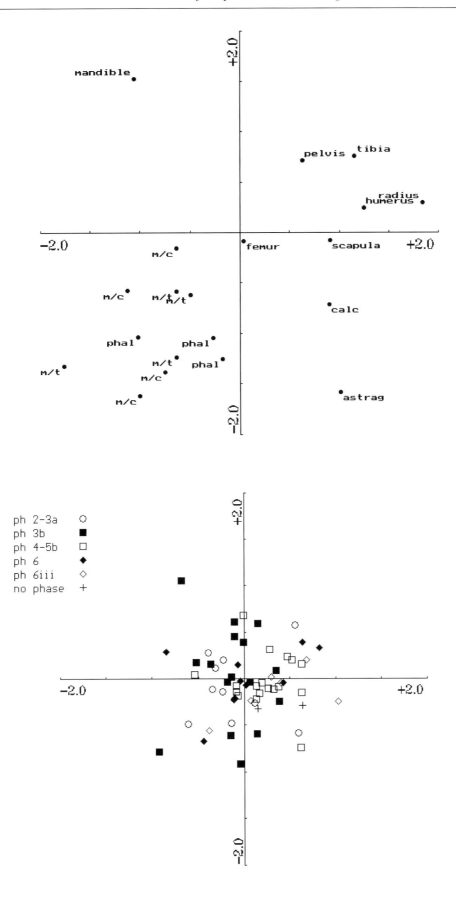

F IG. *6.21 Correspondence analysis of pig skeletal elements by phase.*

element representation outlined previously is still maintained (TABLES 6.8–6.17 & FIGS 6.22–6.31). In fact it would appear that the change in Phase 4–5b can in fact be seen to occur at the very beginning of the ninth century (i.e. in sub-phase 4ii), and changes to the pattern previously seen in Phase 6 perhaps occur at the end of the ninth century (i.e. in sub-phase 5b).

FIGS 6.32–6.34 plot the results of correspondence analysis carried out on the MNI values for individual skeletal elements for sheep, cattle and pig by context type, using only deposits containing >100 identifiable fragments. Although for caprine elements the data points are scattered randomly around the central axes, this is not the case for cattle and pig remains. In fact it would appear that there is a somewhat more consistent pattern of skeletal element distribution in cattle and pig bones from occupation deposits, which is primarily influenced by the presence of terminal limb elements. In addition, if only skeletal element data for dump deposits are plotted by phase for all the major domesticates, there appears to be little or no overlap between assemblages from Phases 3b and 4–5b (FIGS 6.35–6.37), with material from Phase 4–5b dominated primarily by meat-bearing elements.

It is occasionally possible to differentiate the waste from fish processing and consumption (e.g. Barrett 1997), or to recognise the preparation of storable (and tradable) products such as salted herring (Enghoff 1996). Fish processing methods vary by species and cultural context (e.g. Zohar and Cooke 1997). At the most basic level, however, cranial elements are more likely to be found at processing sites whereas a predominance of appendicular bones (which lie immediately behind the skull) and vertebrae are most consistent with consumption sites.

Appendix 4 provides the element distributions for all taxa from the sieved assemblage by phase and context type. These data indicate that some whole fish were brought to the site – all parts of the skeleton are represented for all the common taxa. No cranial elements of cod or herring were identified, but given the tiny number of specimens representing these species it would be unwise to interpret this evidence alone as indicative of processing and transport (see below). Even for the more abundant taxa, the sample sizes are too small to identify patterning in the relative abundance of particular skeletal elements. To discern whether specific bones (and thus parts of fish) were over- or under-represented in different contexts it is necessary to group the data into numbers of cranial elements and vertebrae.

When this is done for the seven most abundant taxa (TABLE 6.18), chi-square analyses reveal no significant differences (at p = 0.05) in the abundance of cranial elements and vertebrae between context types (statistics not shown). There is no identifiable intra-site spatial patterning in the distribution of fish elements. Either fish waste was uniformly discarded across the site or some

deposits simply contain residual dump material.

Conversely, there are some significant patterns in the relative abundance of cranial elements and vertebrae between phases. These differences exist for cyprinids, eel, flatfish (mostly flounder) and smelt (TABLE 6.19). They can be illustrated by plotting the ratio of cranial elements to vertebrae by phase (FIG. 6.38). It is impossible to calculate an 'expected' ratio (assuming whole fish) for grouped categories such as cyprinids or flatfish given inter-species differences in the number of vertebrae. For eels and smelt, however, whole fish would produce ideal ratios of approx 0.23 and approx. 0.56 respectively given the identification protocol used for the Flixborough assemblage, data from Maitland and Campbell (1992) and no recovery and taphonomic biases.

There is no simple interpretation of these results given the potentially confounding factors and the radically different sample sizes and context types represented in each phase. Nevertheless, Phase 1 does stand out as a period when many fish may have been transported to the site after decapitation. Conversely, the ratio of cranial to caudal elements would imply that whole fish are best represented in Phase 2–3a for eels, smelt and cyprinids. This ratio of cranial to caudal elements also increases from Phase 1 to 2–3a for flatfish, but peaks in Phase 3b for this taxon. After Phase 2–3a (for eels, smelt and cyprinids) and Phase 3b (for flatfish) there is a general trend of decreasing ratios – possibly implying that greater numbers of decapitated fish were being transported to the site once again.

On the whole, these patterns are not closely associated with other temporal trends in the assemblage. The peak in the ratio of cranial to caudal elements for flatfish does, however, correspond with the increasing abundance of this taxon already noted for Phase 3b. It is thus possible that the latter pattern is partly the result of a shift from 'off-site' to 'on-site' processing of flatfish.

Overall, the element representation data imply that some migratory and freshwater fish were transported to Flixborough after processing. This practice was least common in Phases 2–3a and 3b, with slight differences between taxa. It is worth noting, however, that the relevant species are not those commonly cured for long-range trade. Moreover, they would all have been locally abundant (see Chapter 8). These patterns may thus relate to local trade, taxation or tithe (see Chapter 10). Alternatively, they could represent off-site butchery and transport by a satellite community or the inhabitants of Flixborough itself.

Evidence for butchery

Evidence for the butchery of animal carcases was seen on the remains of the main domestic mammal species (cattle, sheep and pig) from all phases at Flixborough (FIGS 6.39–6.42).

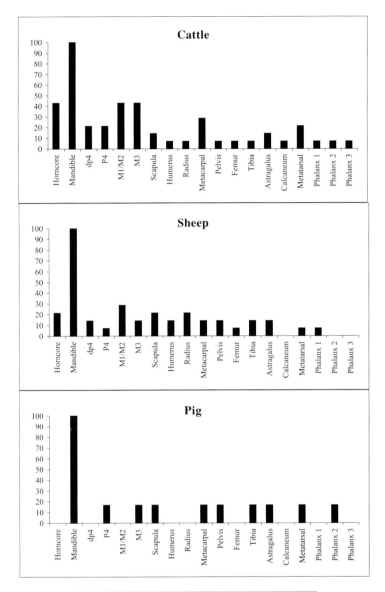

FIG. *6.22 Skeletal element representation (MNI) (Dump context 5369) Phase 2–3a.*

Element	Cattle	Sheep	Pig
Horncore	6	3	n/a
Mandible	14	14	6
dp4	3	2	0
P4	3	1	1
M1/M2	6	4	0
M3	6	2	1
Scapula	2	3	1
Humerus	1	2	0
Radius	1	3	0
Metacarpal	4	2	1
Pelvis	1	2	1
Femur	1	1	0
Tibia	1	2	1
Astragalus	2	2	1
Calcaneum	1	0	0
Metatarsal	3	1	1
Phalanx 1	1	1	0
Phalanx 2	1	0	1
Phalanx 3	1	0	0
Total	**58**	**45**	**15**

TABLE *6.8 MNI by skeletal element for the three main domestic mammals – (Dump context 5369) Phase 2–3a.*

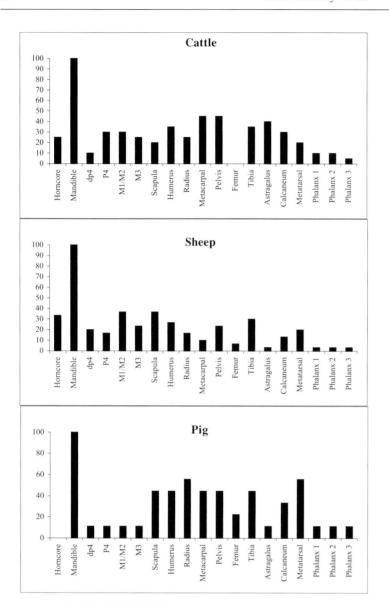

Fig. 6.23 Skeletal element representation (MNI) (Dump context 5983) subphase 3biv.

Element	Cattle	Sheep	Pig
Horncore	5	10	n/a
Mandible	20	30	9
dp4	2	6	1
P4	6	5	1
M1/M2	6	11	1
M3	5	7	1
Scapula	4	11	4
Humerus	7	8	4
Radius	5	5	5
Metacarpal	9	3	4
Pelvis	9	7	4
Femur	0	2	2
Tibia	7	9	4
Astragalus	8	1	1
Calcaneum	6	4	3
Metatarsal	4	6	5
Phalanx 1	2	1	1
Phalanx 2	2	1	1
Phalanx 3	1	1	1
Total	**108**	**128**	**52**

Table 6.9 MNI by skeletal element for the three main domestic mammals – (Dump context 5983) subphase 3biv.

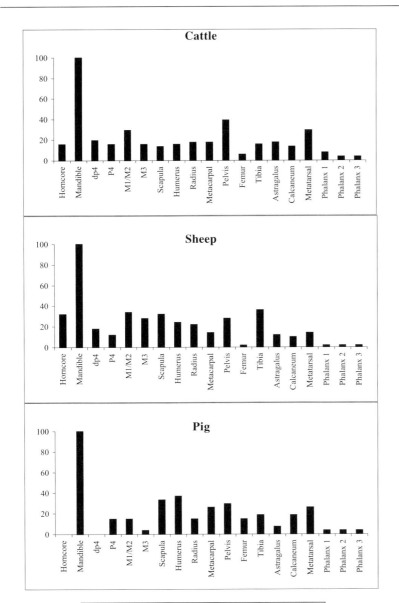

FIG. 6.24 Skeletal element representation (MNI) (Dump context 6235) subphase 3bv.

Element	Cattle	Sheep	Pig
Horncore	8	16	n/a
Mandible	51	50	27
dp4	10	9	0
P4	8	6	4
M1/M2	15	17	4
M3	8	14	1
Scapula	7	16	9
Humerus	8	12	10
Radius	9	11	4
Metacarpal	9	7	7
Pelvis	20	14	8
Femur	3	1	4
Tibia	8	18	5
Astragalus	9	6	2
Calcaneum	7	5	5
Metatarsal	15	7	7
Phalanx 1	4	1	1
Phalanx 2	2	1	1
Phalanx 3	2	1	1
Total	**203**	**212**	**100**

TABLE 6.10 MNI by skeletal element for the three main domestic mammals – (Dump context 6235) subphase 3bv.

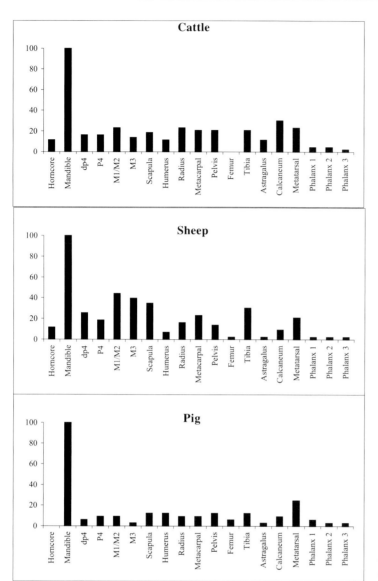

FIG. *6.25 Skeletal element representation (MNI) (Dump context 5617) subphase 3bv.*

Element	Cattle	Sheep	Pig
Horncore	5	5	n/a
Mandible	43	43	32
dp4	7	11	2
P4	7	8	3
M1/M2	10	19	3
M3	6	17	1
Scapula	8	15	4
Humerus	5	3	4
Radius	10	7	3
Metacarpal	9	10	3
Pelvis	9	6	4
Femur	0	1	2
Tibia	9	13	4
Astragalus	5	1	1
Calcaneum	13	4	3
Metatarsal	10	9	8
Phalanx 1	2	1	2
Phalanx 2	2	1	1
Phalanx 3	1	1	1
Total	**161**	**175**	**81**

TABLE *6.11 MNI by skeletal element for the three main domestic mammals – (Dump context 5617) subphase 3bv.*

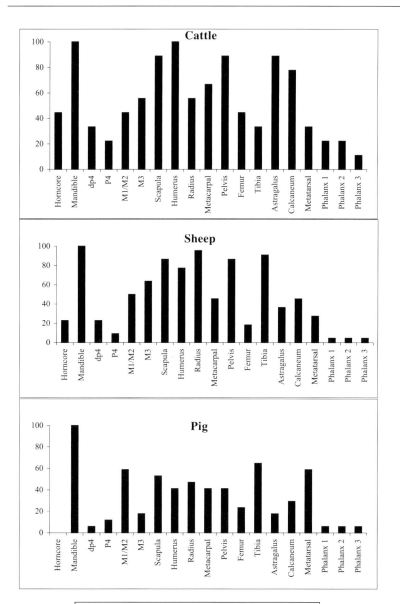

Fig. 6.26 Skeletal element representation (MNI) (Dump context 3758) subphase 4ii.

Element	Cattle	Sheep	Pig
Horncore	4	5	n/a
Mandible	9	22	17
dp4	3	5	1
P4	2	2	2
M1/M2	4	11	10
M3	5	14	3
Scapula	8	19	9
Humerus	9	17	7
Radius	5	21	8
Metacarpal	6	10	7
Pelvis	8	19	7
Femur	4	4	4
Tibia	3	20	11
Astragalus	8	8	3
Calcaneum	7	10	5
Metatarsal	3	6	10
Phalanx 1	2	1	1
Phalanx 2	2	1	1
Phalanx 3	1	1	1
Total	**93**	**196**	**107**

Table 6.12 MNI by skeletal element for the three main domestic mammals – (Dump context 3758) subphase 4ii.

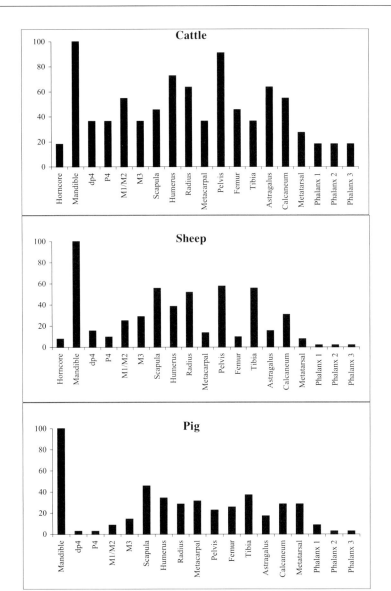

FIG. 6.27 Skeletal element representation (MNI) (Dump context 5503) subphase 4ii.

Element	Cattle	Sheep	Pig
Horncore	2	4	n/a
Mandible	11	52	35
dp4	4	8	1
P4	4	5	1
M1/M2	6	13	3
M3	4	15	5
Scapula	5	29	16
Humerus	8	20	12
Radius	7	27	10
Metacarpal	4	7	11
Pelvis	10	30	8
Femur	5	5	9
Tibia	4	29	13
Astragalus	7	8	6
Calcaneum	6	16	10
Metatarsal	3	4	10
Phalanx 1	2	1	3
Phalanx 2	2	1	1
Phalanx 3	2	1	1
Total	**96**	**275**	**155**

TABLE 6.13 MNI by skeletal element for the three main domestic mammals – (Dump context 5503) subphase 4ii.

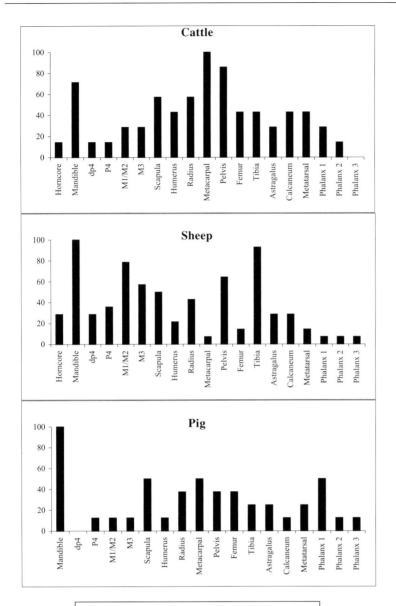

FIG. *6.28 Skeletal element representation (MNI) (Dump context 5193) subphase 4ii–5a.*

Element	Cattle	Sheep	Pig
Horncore	1	4	n/a
Mandible	5	14	8
dp4	1	4	0
P4	1	5	1
M1/M2	2	11	1
M3	2	8	1
Scapula	4	7	4
Humerus	3	3	1
Radius	4	6	3
Metacarpal	7	1	4
Pelvis	6	9	3
Femur	3	2	3
Tibia	3	13	2
Astragalus	2	4	2
Calcaneum	3	4	1
Metatarsal	3	2	2
Phalanx 1	2	1	4
Phalanx 2	1	1	1
Phalanx 3	0	1	1
Total	**53**	**100**	**42**

TABLE *6.14 MNI by skeletal element for the three main domestic mammals – (Dump context 5193) subphase 4ii–5a.*

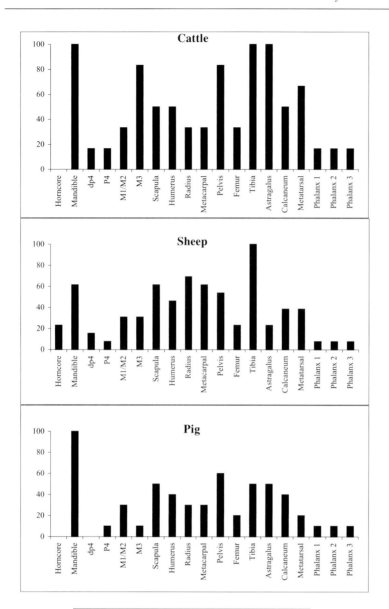

Fig. 6.29 Skeletal element representation (MNI) (Dump context 5139) subphase 5a.

Element	Cattle	Sheep	Pig
Horncore	0	3	n/a
Mandible	6	8	10
dp4	1	2	0
P4	1	1	1
M1/M2	2	4	3
M3	5	4	1
Scapula	3	8	5
Humerus	3	6	4
Radius	2	9	3
Metacarpal	2	8	3
Pelvis	5	7	6
Femur	2	3	2
Tibia	6	13	5
Astragalus	6	3	5
Calcaneum	3	5	4
Metatarsal	4	5	2
Phalanx 1	1	1	1
Phalanx 2	1	1	1
Phalanx 3	1	1	1
Total	**54**	**89**	**57**

Table 6.15 MNI by skeletal element for the three main domestic mammals – (Dump context 5139) subphase 5a.

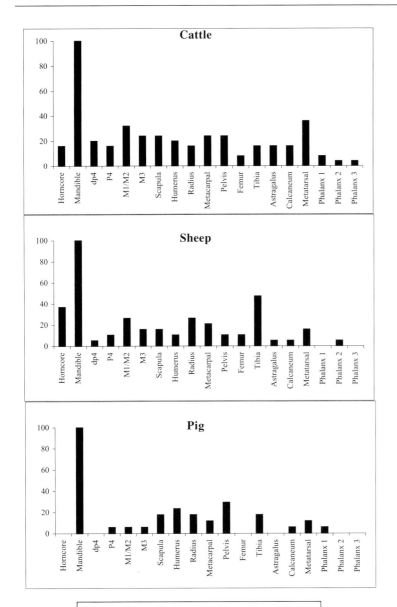

Fig. 6.30 Skeletal element representation (MNI) (Dump context 12057) subphase 5a–b.

Element	Cattle	Sheep	Pig
Horncore	4	7	n/a
Mandible	25	19	17
dp4	5	1	0
P4	4	2	1
M1/M2	8	5	1
M3	6	3	1
Scapula	6	3	3
Humerus	5	2	4
Radius	4	5	3
Metacarpal	6	4	2
Pelvis	6	2	5
Femur	2	2	0
Tibia	4	9	3
Astragalus	4	1	0
Calcaneum	4	1	1
Metatarsal	9	3	2
Phalanx 1	2	0	1
Phalanx 2	1	1	0
Phalanx 3	1	0	0
Total	**106**	**70**	**44**

TABLE 6.16 MNI by skeletal element for the three main domestic mammals – (Dump context 12057) subphase 5a–b.

Keith Dobney et al.

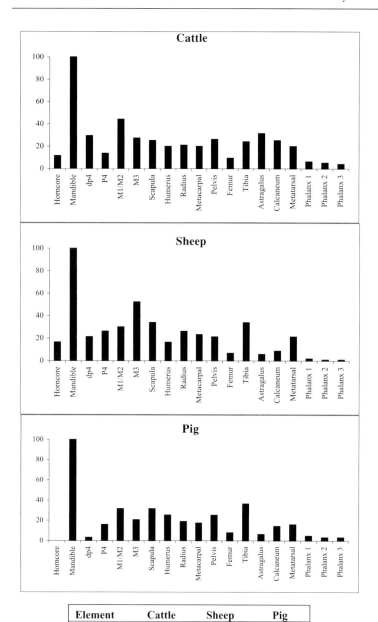

Fig. 6.31 Skeletal element representation (MNI) (Dump context 3891) subphase 6ii.

Element	Cattle	Sheep	Pig
Horncore	11	17	n/a
Mandible	95	103	63
dp4	28	22	2
P4	13	27	10
M1/M2	42	31	20
M3	26	54	13
Scapula	24	35	20
Humerus	19	17	16
Radius	20	27	12
Metacarpal	19	24	11
Pelvis	25	22	16
Femur	9	7	5
Tibia	23	35	23
Astragalus	30	6	4
Calcaneum	24	9	9
Metatarsal	19	22	10
Phalanx 1	6	2	3
Phalanx 2	5	1	2
Phalanx 3	4	1	2
Total	**442**	**462**	**241**

TABLE 6.17 MNI by skeletal element for the three main domestic mammals – (Dump context 3891) subphase 6ii.

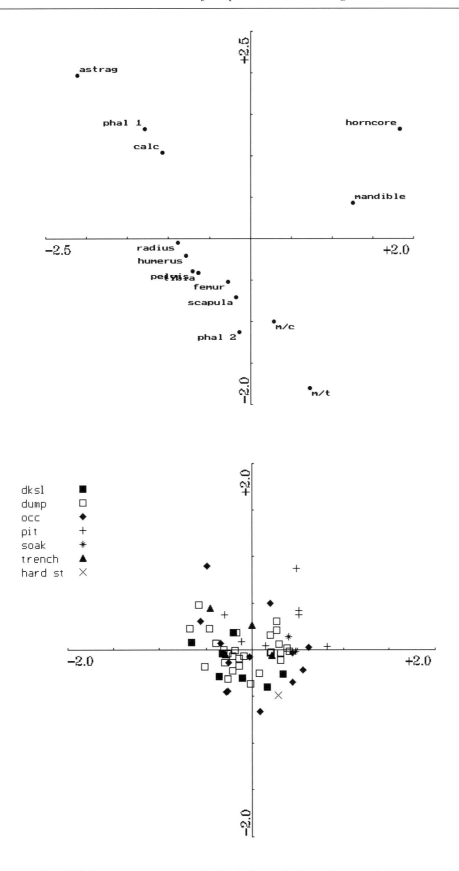

Fig. 6.32 Correspondence analysis of sheep skeletal elements by context type.

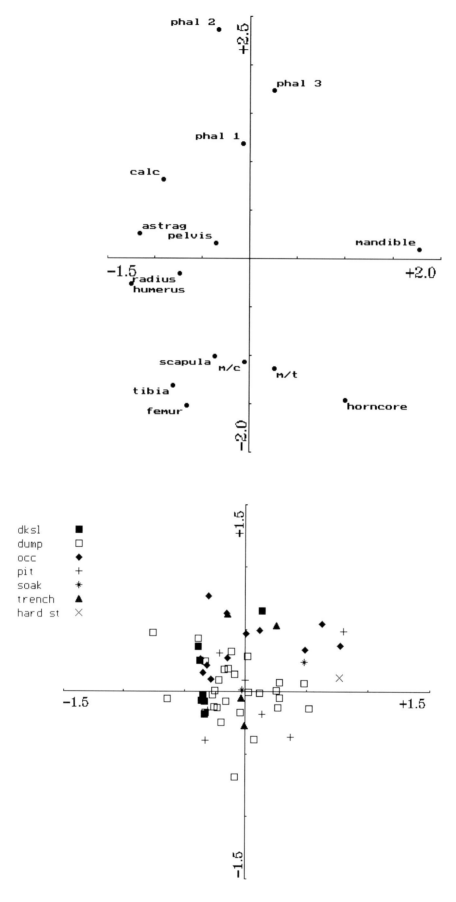

FIG. 6.33 Correspondence analysis of cattle skeletal elements by context type.

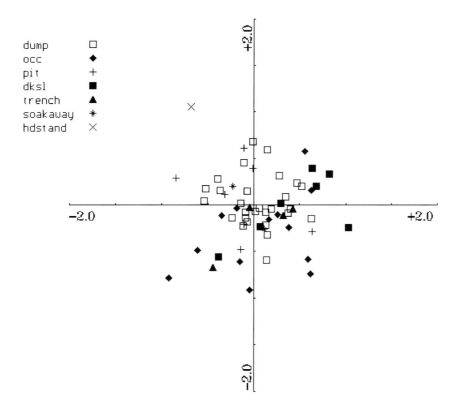

FIG. 6.34 Correspondence analysis of pig skeletal elements by context type.

For cattle, the overall frequency of butchery evidence noted from the bones was quite low and butchery practices appeared to be consistent throughout the occupation sequence (FIG. 6.39). It would appear that most marks were the result of chopping, almost certainly occurring during the primary butchery of carcases and subsequent jointing. There is, in fact, very little evidence in this vast assemblage for knife-marks on the bones, indicating that filleting of meat from the bones was not common. This type of butchery, however, may have left few traces on the bones themselves. Longitudinal splitting of long bones appeared to have been relatively common, and was particularly evident on metapodials from Phases 2–3a–6, but was less apparent on material from Phase 6iii. There appeared to have been limited butchery of the mandibles, which were mostly chopped either horizontally or vertically through the ascending ramus, probably in order to remove the jaw from skull and perhaps to provide ease of access to the tongue.

Moderate numbers of sheep bones showing butchery were noted, although the frequency of butchery overall was lower than for cattle (FIG. 6.40). Unusually, there appeared to be more chop than knife-marks on the sheep bones, perhaps the result of the overall generally eroded appearance of much of the bone surface, which may have prevented knife-marks being readily observed. Rather interestingly, the longitudinal splitting of long bones, previously mentioned with respect to cattle, was also

observed in the sheep remains, once again mainly involving the metapodials. If this evidence is taken to reflect specific activities such as marrow extraction in general (see Dobney *et. al.* 1996 and Dobney 2001), it would seem a major investment for a limited return, given the small size of sheep metapodials. Relatively high numbers of horncores were recovered from Phases 2–3a and 3b deposits. These had been removed from the skull by chopping through the base and may possibly represent evidence for one of the few craft or industrial activities at the site which utilised skeletal raw materials, i.e. horn-working.

As with sheep, pig bones showed moderately high frequencies of butchery, with once again more chop than knife-marks represented (FIG. 6.41). Also, like cattle and sheep, butchered pig bones were less frequently recorded from Phase 6iii than from all other phases. Pig mandibles showed the highest frequency of butchery-marks and, in this case, the butchery was quite specific. It appeared that the mandibles had been chopped through the region of the mandibular symphysis (or thereabouts), with additional evidence for either a horizontal or vertical chop through the ascending ramus (13–20% of mandibles showed this butchery pattern, but it was not present in material from Phase 6iii).

Perhaps the most interesting evidence for butchery was that found on the remains of horses (FIG. 6.42). Compared with cattle, sheep and pigs, the bones of horses were far less numerous in the Flixborough assemblage

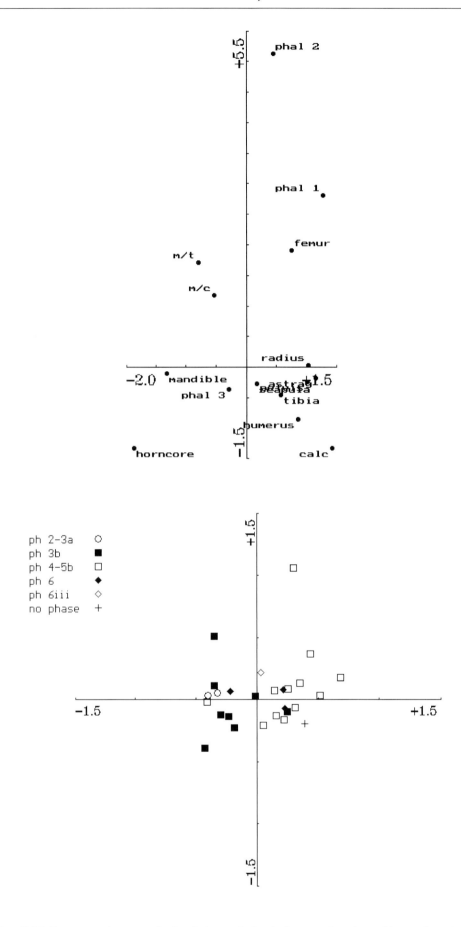

Fig. 6.35 Correspondence analysis of sheep skeletal elements by phase (dump deposits only).

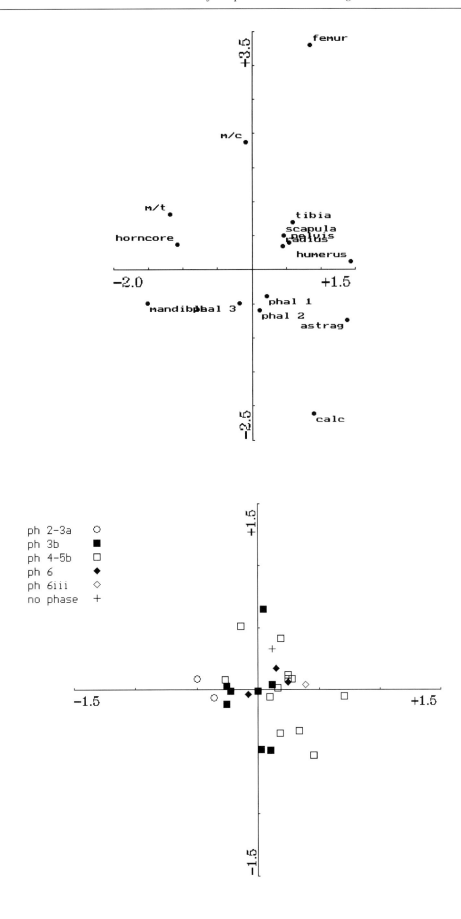

FIG. 6.36 Correspondence analysis of cattle skeletal elements by phase (dump deposits only).

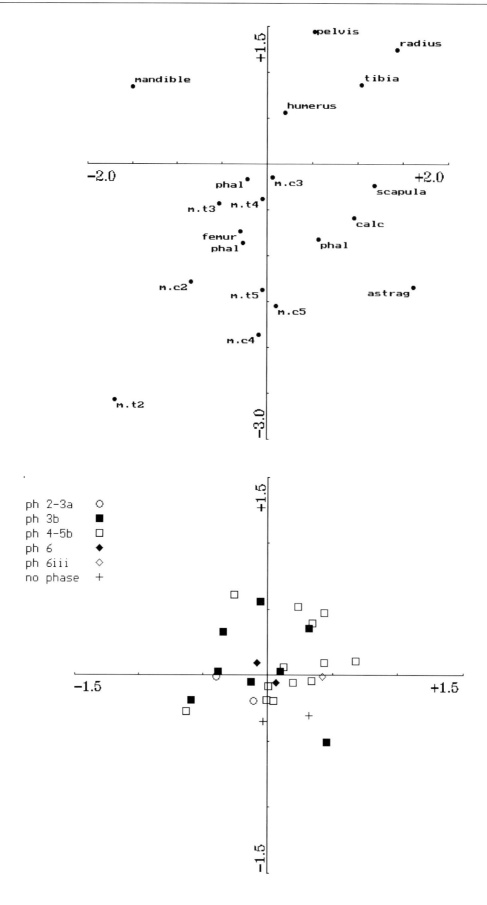

FIG. 6.37 Correspondence analysis of pig skeletal elements by phase (dump deposits only).

Common Name	Elements	DUMP[1]	PH[1]	SOAK[1]	OCC[1]	PIT[1]	DKSL[1]
Salmon & Trout Family	Appendicular	1					
	Cranial[1]	5	1		1		
	Vertebrae[1]	90	26	10	9	4	6
	Cranial:Vertebrae	0.06	0.04	0.00	0.11	0.00	0.00
Smelt	Appendicular	11	2	4			
	Cranial[1]	106	29	33	21	15	2
	Vertebrae[1]	366	71	62	58	47	12
	Cranial:Vertebrae	0.29	0.41	0.53	0.36	0.32	0.17
Eel	Appendicular	22	7	2	5	3	1
	Cranial[1]	104	36	18	30	21	11
	Vertebrae[1]	1206	475	151	332	229	167
	Cranial:Vertebrae	0.09	0.08	0.12	0.09	0.09	0.07
Total Halibut Family	Appendicular	15	2	3	2	1	1
	Cranial[1]	94	13	2	10	14	7
	Vertebrae[1]	403	54	24	48	25	34
	Cranial:Vertebrae	0.23	0.24	0.08	0.21	0.56	0.21
Pike	Appendicular	7	6	12	4	1	
	Cranial[1]	40	21	58	11	2	2
	Vertebrae[1]	138	63	143	45	12	8
	Cranial:Vertebrae	0.29	0.33	0.41	0.24	0.17	0.25
Total Carp Family	Appendicular	4	2	3	4		
	Cranial[1]	37	10	13	16	1	
	Vertebrae[1]	101	45	45	31	11	9
	Cranial:Vertebrae	0.37	0.22	0.29	0.52	0.09	0.00
Perch	Appendicular		3	10			
	Cranial[1]	25	7	37	1	2	1
	Vertebrae[1]	94	16	72	13	3	3
	Cranial:Vertebrae	0.27	0.44	0.51	0.08	0.67	0.33

[1]Variables used for chi-square analyses - no significant differences at p = 0.05.
See discussion in text.

TABLE 6.18 Sieved fish: element distribution summary by context type. See Appendix 3 for key to context types.

(constituting 5% of the domestic mammal fauna). However, butchery-marks were apparent on a much higher proportion of horse bones than those of other species, many of them deriving from deposits of Phase 6 date. Most horse butchery seems to have been concentrated on pelves and mandibles. Mandibles mostly appear to have been chopped across the diastema, with some cut through the ascending ramus, suggesting tongue removal. Those marks noted on the pelves were concentrated around the acetabulum, indicating the 'boning out' of the upper hind limb. This type of butchery of the pelvis could represent either carcase dismemberment for ease of disposal or the production of prime meat joints. A number of other horse elements were also chopped; this could again be consistent with either carcase disposal, or jointing for meat. In addition to chop-marks, numerous knife-marks were also recorded on some horse astragali, possibly suggesting skinning, whilst several metapodials appear to have been split longitudinally, perhaps to allow access to the marrow.

Common Name	Elements	1[1]	2-3a[1]	3b[1]	4-5b[1]	6[1]	6iii[1]	Unphased	Total	Chi-square	DF	P
Salmon & Trout Family	Appendicular			1					1			
	Cranial[1]		1		5	1			7			
	Vertebrae[1]	5	24	52	44	17	5	2	149	6.63	5	NA[2]
	Cranial:Vertebrae	0.00	0.04	0.00	0.11	0.06	0.00	0.00	0.05			
Smelt	Appendicular		7	4	7				18			
	Cranial[1]	8	84	63	56	9		8	228			
	Vertebrae[1]	21	137	196	227	43	13	27	664	29.46	5	<0.001
	Cranial:Vertebrae	0.38	0.61	0.32	0.25	0.21	0.00	0.30	0.34			
Eel	Appendicular	2	9	7	21	8			47			
	Cranial[1]	1	50	67	91	25	8	5	247			
	Vertebrae[1]	73	426	539	1118	418	120	109	2803	19.66	5	0.001
	Cranial:Vertebrae	0.01	0.12	0.12	0.08	0.06	0.07	0.05	0.09			
Total Halibut Family	Appendicular		7	13	2	3			25			
	Cranial[1]	1	10	74	43	9	3	5	145			
	Vertebrae[1]	11	76	227	196	71	18	11	610	13.64	5	0.018
	Cranial:Vertebrae	0.09	0.13	0.33	0.22	0.13	0.17	0.45	0.24			
Pike	Appendicular	4	21	3	2	2			32			
	Cranial[1]	17	76	20	12	10	2	1	138			
	Vertebrae[1]	39	197	72	55	44	7	4	418	5.61	5	0.346
	Cranial:Vertebrae	0.44	0.39	0.28	0.22	0.23	0.29	0.25	0.33			
Total Carp Family	Appendicular	7	7	2	4	1			14			

TABLE 6.19 *Summary of element distribution of fish remains from sieved samples by phase (continued opposite). See Appendix 3 for definitions of terminology.*

Common Name	Elements	1[1]	2–3a[1]	3b[1]	4–5b[1]	6[1]	6iii[1]	Unphased	Total	Chi-square	DF	P
	Cranial[1]	2	37	20	19	6		1	85			
	Vertebrae[1]	20	75	60	46	37	5	9	252	11.62	5	0.04
	Cranial:Vertebrae	0.10	0.49	0.33	0.41	0.16	0.00	0.11	0.34			
Perch	Appendicular	3	10						13			
	Cranial[1]	8	40	11	6	7	1		73			
	Vertebrae[1]	11	88	45	10	45	3	2	204	10.74	5	0.057
	Cranial:Vertebrae	0.73	0.45	0.24	0.60	0.16	0.33	0.00	0.36			

[1]Variables used for chi-square analyses – see discussion in text.

[2]Too many cells have low counts.

TABLE 6.19 continued.

For the analysis of cut-marks recorded on the fish bone assemblage from Flixborough, the sieved and hand-collected assemblages are considered together (TABLE 6.20). This decision is based partly on their rarity and partly on the assumption that the presence and absence of butchery-marks will be less biased by recovery factors than the relative abundance of different elements or species. The marks were identified based on the presence of clear V-shaped cross-sections using a binocular microscope at magnifications between 6.3 and 50 times (see Blumenschine *et al.* 1996; Barrett 1997).

Overall, there were 16 definite (and one probable) marks made by butchery. Excluding the latter (on a cyprinid abdominal vertebra), they occur on bones of the following taxa: cod (two), conger eel (two), eel (one), flatfish (probably flounder, one), pike (three), salmon (five) and unidentified (two). Together, these marks fall into four or five broad groups based on their location and probable interpretation. Cuts on the jaw bones of pike are almost certainly related to hook removal. Marks on the ceratohyal and epihyal of conger eel could have been made during gutting or attempts to remove flesh from the head. A cut first anal pterygiophore, probably from a flounder, was also indicative of gutting. Butchery-marks in the transverse plane on cleithra and anterior vertebrae probably indicate decapitation. These occurred on cod, eel, pike and salmon bones. Finally, transverse cuts on cod and salmon caudal vertebrae indicated either that the fish were cut into steaks or that the vertebral column was severed in order to remove its anterior part (leaving the posterior caudal vertebrae in the butchered product).

This last cut-mark on cod deserves special consideration. In this species, removal of anterior vertebrae can be associated with preservation in the form of stockfish (dried without salt) or klipfisk (dried with salt) which were widely traded later in the Middle Ages (Barrett 1997). It is thus conceivable that a few cured cod were 'imported' by Flixborough's inhabitants. If so, however, the numbers involved must have been nominal. Only two cod bones were recovered from the entire sieved assemblage and only 12 came from the hand-collected material. Moreover, it would be unwise to reconstruct long-range trade patterns on the basis of a single cut-mark which might also have resulted from processing of a local catch (see also Chapter 8).

In broad terms, therefore, butchery evidence from Flixborough was present in relatively modest frequencies and appeared to change very little through time. The exception for mammal bones appeared to be represented in the material from Phase 6iii, which seems to show proportionately less butchery than the earlier phases. This may simply reflect the fact that most of the animal bones from Phase 6iii were from deposits described as 'dark soils', not from large communal 'dumps' characteristic of the earlier phases, the result of a shift in focus of the early eleventh-century settlement. Overall, this 'low intensity' butchery of mammals is very different from

Common Name	Cut Marks	Element	1	2–3a	3b	4–5b	6	6iii	Unphased	Total
Conger Eel	Knife Mark	Ceratohyal					1			1
	Chop Mark	Epihyal				1				1
Cod	Knife Mark, Transverse	Abdominal Vertebra Group 1					1			1
	Chop Mark, Transverse	Caudal Vertebra Group 1		1						1
Salmon & Trout Family	Chop Mark, Transverse	Abdominal Vertebra					2			2
	Knife Mark, Transverse	Abdominal Vertebra					1			1
	Chop Mark, Transverse	Caudal Vertebra			1	1				2
Eel	Knife Mark, Transverse	Cleithrum		1						1
Flounder/Plaice	Chop Mark, Transverse	First Anal Pterygiophore				1				1
Pike	Knife Mark, Transverse	Cleithrum		1						1
	Knife Mark, Transverse	Dentary				1				1
	Chop Mark, Transverse	Maxilla	1							1
Carp Family	Knife Mark?	Abdominal Vertebra				1				1
Unidentified	Chop Mark				2					2
Total			1	3	3	5	5	0	0	17

TABLE 6.20 *Sieved and hand collected fish: cut marks by phase. See Appendix 3 for definitions of terminology.*

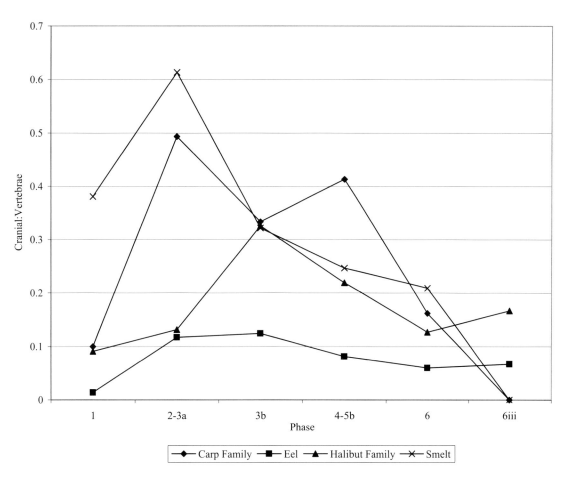

FIG. *6.38 Flixborough sieved fish: ratio of cranial to caudal elements by phase and taxon.*

that seen in earlier, Roman, so-called 'soup-kitchen' deposits (von Mensch 1974) and, apart from limited evidence for some marrow extraction (from split long bones) and possible horn-working (chopped horncores), was primarily butchering for joints of meat. No 'standard' butchery practice appears to have been utilised at Flixborough, other than chopping where it was easiest to separate joints.

The butchery evident on horse bones could well indicate the consumption of horse flesh by the inhabitants. This is potentially interesting in the context of the origin of the taboo against horseflesh avoidance, particularly for Britain. It is generally accepted that the coming of Christianity to Britain saw the beginnings of the gradual decline and eventual prohibition in horse sacrifice and

consumption as a way of separating pagans from Christians (see Simoons 1994, 187–88, for detailed discussion). The famous papal decree of Pope Gregory III to St Boniface (*circa* AD 732) forbidding the eating of horseflesh by Christians, although not implemented by all immediately, appeared to have provided the main impetus for the apparent complete avoidance of horseflesh in Britain which has lasted until the present day. The evidence for horse butchery at Flixborough in all occupation phases, along with evidence for Christianity, perhaps suggests that the papal decree was still not adhered to several centuries after it was issued and that consumption of horse meat was still a significant part of the cultural landscape of late Anglo-Saxon England, at least amongst high-status and even royal households.

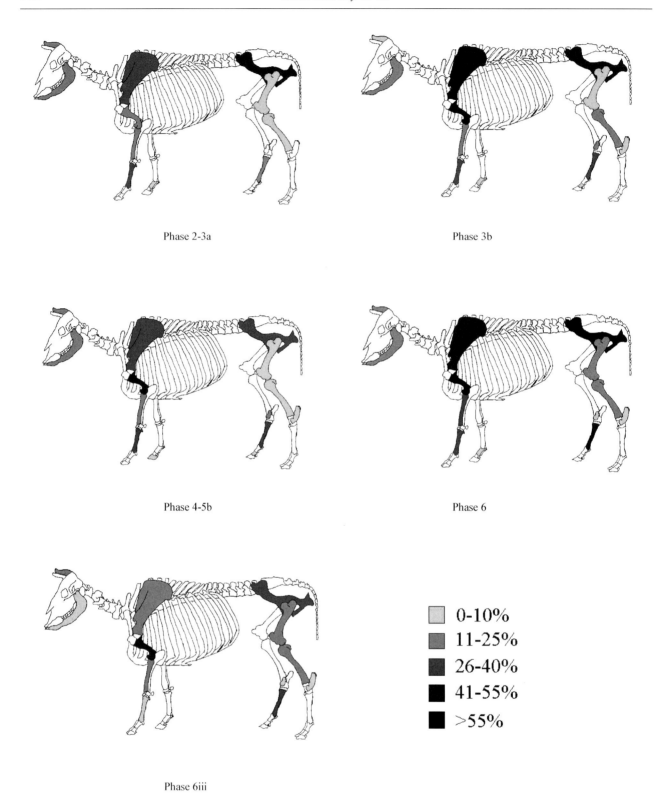

Phase 2-3a

Phase 3b

Phase 4-5b

Phase 6

Phase 6iii

☐ 0-10%
▨ 11-25%
▰ 26-40%
■ 41-55%
■ >55%

FIG. 6.39 Relative frequency of butchery marks on major cattle bones by phase.

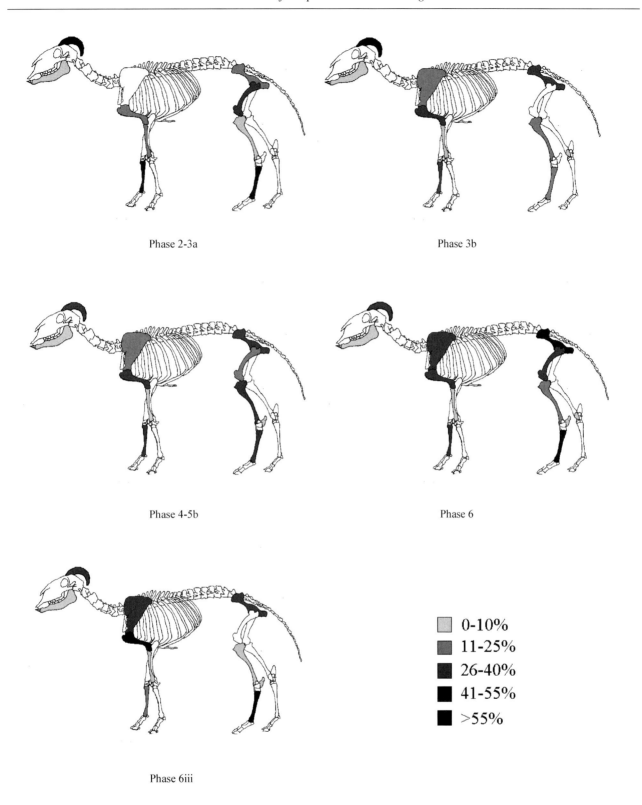

Phase 2-3a

Phase 3b

Phase 4-5b

Phase 6

Phase 6iii

▨	0-10%
▨	11-25%
▨	26-40%
■	41-55%
■	>55%

FIG. 6.40 Relative frequency of butchery marks on major sheep bones by phase.

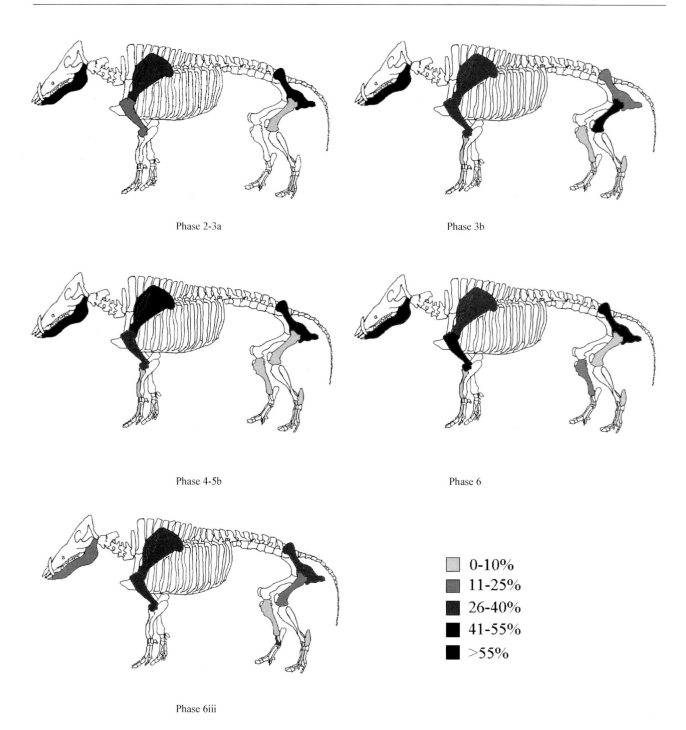

Phase 2-3a

Phase 3b

Phase 4-5b

Phase 6

Phase 6iii

☐ 0-10%

▨ 11-25%

▨ 26-40%

■ 41-55%

■ >55%

Fig. 6.41 Relative frequency of butchery marks on major pig bones by phase.

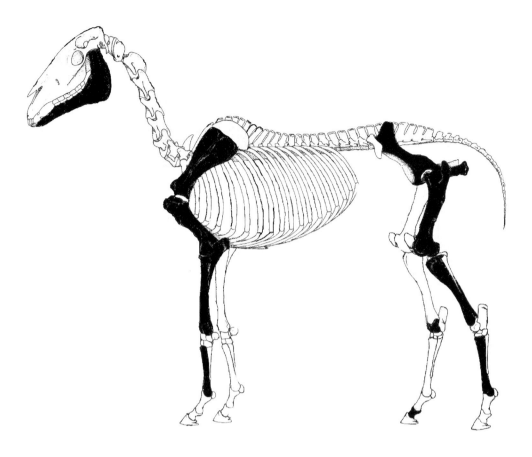

FIG. 6.42 Relative frequency of butchery marks on major horse bones (all phases).

7   The Agricultural Economy

Keith Dobney, Deborah Jaques, Cluny Johnstone, Allan Hall, Beverley La Ferla and Susan Haynes

7.1 Introduction

Study of the remains of domestic animals and plants can provide detailed insight into many aspects of the agricultural economy of an archaeological site. At Flixborough, this opportunity is perhaps unique as a result of the overall quantity and quality of data which have been recorded. However, although detailed information has been recovered, it is still biased in its coverage as a result of the imbalance of zooarchaeological and archaeobotanical data. In the case of the former, a vast dataset exists from all major phases of occupation at the site, whereas for plant remains, the preservation of identifiable charred seeds, stem fragments and charcoal has been much more limited. Thus, despite the existence of some limited evidence for the arable economy (see below), the following account is primarily focussed upon the evidence for the livestock economy.

7.2 The evidence for arable crops

As previously mentioned, evidence for crop plants at Flixborough was extraordinarily sparse and the single sample relatively rich in cereal crop weeds (together with modest concentrations of poorly preserved cereal grains) was of post-Saxon date (pit fill Context 1410). The cereal taxa recorded from the Saxon deposits at the site (in descending order of frequency) were barley (*Hordeum*), wheat (some tentatively identified bread/club wheat, *Triticum 'aestivo-compactum'*, with other material not identified beyond genus), rye (*Secale cereale*) and oats (*Avena*). A high proportion of the determinations were tentative and remains were often rather poorly preserved. The only cereal chaff recorded was a trace of barley rachis (ear stalk) from a single sample from Context 3911, a Phase 3a post-pipe fill associated with Building 1a.

It may be suspected that such low concentrations and poor preservation indicate re-working, but whatever their origins, these few remains do not stand as good evidence for the processing of the crops in the vicinity, nor for the widespread use of cereals at the site. No pattern in occurrence of cereals through the sequence could be discerned. The only other crop plants recorded were seeds of the legumes field bean (*Vicia faba* var. *minor*) and ?pea (cf. *Pisum sativum*), and seeds of flax (linseed, *Linum usitatissimum*) and hemp (*Cannabis sativa*), all recorded in very small amounts from very few contexts, scattered through the sequence.

The remains indicate that chaff and crop processing by-products were not being burnt at the site, not necessarily that cereals were not being used. It could have been the case that the by-products of crop processing were important as animal fodder or sold on. If dung was going straight out onto the fields for manuring purposes, and there was an in-field out-field system, then very few charred remains of cereals and crop processing waste would be expected at the site itself. It is also possible that the grain was bought in (already cleaned or ground) as food rents in keeping with other 'high status' indicators at the site (see Chapter 10) and is thus invisible in the archaeological record. Alternatively, drying of grain prior to milling and other final processing activities could have taken place in the vicinity of the mills rather than at the site itself.

7.3 Patterns of production and consumption

The frequency data for the domestic livestock remains outlined in Chapters 4 and 6 above points to the importance of these animals to the inhabitants at Flixborough, and show that significant changes in the frequency of the major domestic mammals and birds occurred through time. Obviously, the assemblage of vertebrate remains recovered from excavations at Flixborough must reflect the disposal of vast quantities of waste from a variety of possible activities occurring both on the site and away from it.

Livestock are kept for their primary products, which can obviously only be obtained once the animal is dead. Thus the animals are reared and fattened until the primary products are required, and then they are slaughtered. Slaughter can occur throughout a range of developmental ages, depending on the type of product required, thus 'age-at-death' profiles reconstructed from the excavated bones and teeth can provide detailed information regarding these husbandry activities. For example, if animals are being raised for prime meat, it is most efficient to slaughter the animals once full carcase size has been achieved, i.e. when the animal reaches 'late sub-adult' stage. However, if young tender meat is required (something often linked with the diet of higher-status groups and individuals), then animals will be slaughtered at a very young age, i.e. when 'juvenile'.

Livestock can, of course, also provide a range of important secondary products, which can be directly consumed as part of the diet (e.g. offspring, eggs, milk and processed dairy products) or which have other non-dietary uses (e.g. wool for textile production). Live animals are usually slaughtered once their usefulness for producing these secondary products has ended and their primary products can then be utilised.

Deadstock, on the other hand, obviously produce a range of primary dietary products, the most important being meat, offal and fat. A range of non-dietary products such as marrow fat, sinews and skins, which can have both domestic and industrial uses (e.g. marrow fat for lubrication, cosmetics and lamp fuel, hides for tanning, horns and bone for working into objects) are also provided.

These products from livestock and deadstock are usually part of a broader, more complex, agricultural economy, and evidence for a whole range of economic activities for different domestic species can be bound together in the waste that is eventually disposed of. For example, dairy herds are comprised primarily of adult female animals that produce milk. In order to do this, they must be regularly in calf (or lamb) to stimulate lactation; this would have been even more crucial in the past where more primitive breeds would not have produced as much milk (or for as long) as modern 'improved' dairy breeds. Thus young male calves/lambs would be viewed as an essential by-product, effectively in competition with humans for the valuable milk. The most efficient means to deal with this problem is to cull these surplus animals very early in their lives. These animals were, therefore, either discarded wholesale as unnecessary waste, or alternatively, were consumed as very young tender meat. If the latter was the case, the animals had to be reared for a little while after birth, which involved a higher investment of labour. The European taste for veal (which has Roman origins) provides ample evidence of the dairy and high cost/status meat industry going hand-in-hand.

Evidence for a range of activities involving both livestock and deadstock can be recovered from the animal bones themselves in a variety of ways. Thus, in order to understand the various facets of the agricultural economy as reflected by the bones of domestic livestock at Flixborough, detailed analysis of the zooarchaeological data is required.

The importance of major domesticates

A variety of simple techniques has been used to attempt to establish the relative importance of the major domestic animals[1] in each phase. This involved the use of 1) numbers of identifiable specimens (NISP), 2) total weight of identifiable specimens, and 3) counts of minimum number of individuals (MNI). FIGS 7.1 and 7.2 show the relative frequencies of the three major domestic mammals ('major mammal') and two domestic bird species ('major bird'). Calculations using NISP (FIG. 7.1) indicate that most (67–90%) of the identifiable bone fragments for all periods were from the three major mammal taxa, whilst 10–33% of fragments derived from domestic fowl and goose. There is apparently little change in these proportions over time, although between Phases 6 and 6iii the proportion of identifiable specimens of domestic bird decreases somewhat. When calculating minimum numbers of individuals, a slightly different pattern emerges (FIG. 7.2). Although domestic mammals outnumber domestic birds in all phases, differences in frequency are less marked in several. Values from Phases 2–3a and 4–5b are remarkably similar, with domestic fowl and geese accounting for over 40% of the total number of individuals present (as calculated using MNI counts for skeletal elements).

Previous discussions (see Chapter 6) have outlined the possible reasons for differences between certain phases based on a bias in the frequency of different context types encountered. Thus, for example, the lack of large dump deposits, and over-representation of features described as 'soakaways' may provide plausible non-economic explanations for differences in Phases 2–3a and 6iii. However, as also previously discussed, the same cannot hold true for differences between Phases 3b, 4–5b and 6 where large dump deposits are a common feature. The higher frequency of domestic birds in Phase 4–5b seems likely to indicate that increasing numbers of these were consumed during the ninth century (in fact during sub-phase 4ii – the early ninth century) compared with the late eighth and tenth centuries (as represented by Phases 3b and 6 respectively). Of course, it is obvious that, in terms of quantities of meat, domestic chickens and even large domestic geese contributed much less than the major domestic mammal taxa.

If we now turn to the five major domestic animals individually, further interesting observations can be made. FIGS 7.3 and 7.4 show the relative frequency of major domestic animals, again using NISP and MNI counts. In both figures, the relative frequencies of cattle, sheep and

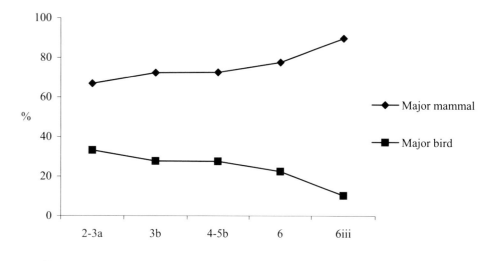

FIG. 7.1 Relative frequency of major domestic mammals and bird using NISP counts.

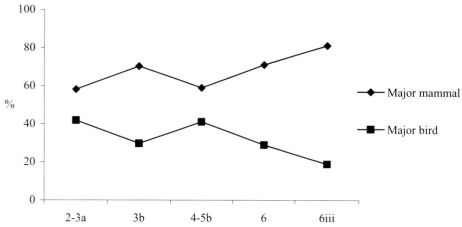

FIG. 7.2 Relative frequency of major domestic mammals and bird using MNI counts.

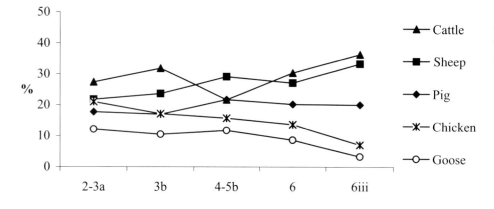

FIG. 7.3 Relative frequency of major domestic animals using NISP counts.

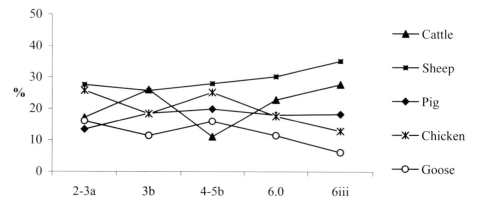

FIG. 7.4 Relative frequency of major domestic animals using MNI counts.

pigs change markedly through time and, whilst Phase 4–5b is once again somewhat unusual, these data also indicate how similar Phases 3b and 6 are to one another.

Leaving aside the differences seen in the relative frequencies for cattle, sheep and pigs (this is dealt with in more detail below), NISP counts for all six phases show that the remains of chicken form the largest component of the avian assemblages (ranging from 43% in Phase 1 to 62% in Phase 6iii). Some caution must be exercised, however, when considering information for Phases 1 and 6iii, as both have somewhat limited datasets (TABLE 7.1). MNI counts (TABLE 7.2) reinforce the pattern for chickens outlined above, with frequencies ranging from 37 to 51% and Phases 4–5b and 6iii showing the highest frequencies.

In comparison with the other major domestic species (cattle, sheep, pig and goose), chicken remains formed a considerable proportion (between 14 and 21%) of the identified assemblages (once again based on NISP counts), with Phase 6iii material showing a considerable decrease in the frequency of remains to 3% (FIG. 7.3). However, it is also interesting to note that MNI counts for chicken and goose are higher than the values for cattle (and, in the case of chicken, even pigs) in Phase 4–5b (FIG. 7.4). In terms of numbers of individuals present, chicken and goose are very important, particularly in Phase 4–5b.

The importance of the major domestic mammals (cattle, sheep and pig)

As previously noted, there do appear to be some quite major changes in the relative importance of the three major domestic mammals at Flixborough over the roughly two-and-a-half centuries encompassed by Phases 2–3a to 6iii. These changes can be explored by further analyses of the data.

Taxa	Phase 1	Phase 2–3a	Phase 3b	Phase 4–5b	Phase 6	Phase 6iii
Black grouse	0	7	17	2	9	0
Chicken	39	849	1598	1822	1193	203
Columbidae	3	29	75	29	35	3
Corvid	2	9	46	38	24	1
Crane	2	26	115	13	73	0
Duck	5	42	71	129	67	21
Goose	31	489	985	1349	751	94
Laridae	0	4	2	0	2	0
Owl	0	0	0	4	1	0
Raptor	0	0	40	6	3	0
Swan	0	0	1	0	1	0
Turdidae	0	1	3	0	1	0
Wader	2	201	91	28	49	3
Wild goose	7	191	355	112	188	5

TABLE 7.1 Bird NISP counts.

Taxa	Phase 1	Phase 2–3a	Phase 3b	Phase 4–5b	Phase 6	Phase 6iii
Black grouse	0	2	4	1	2	0
Chicken	8	69	119	161	91	19
Columbidae	1	6	11	7	4	1
Corvid	1	2	7	5	5	1
Crane	1	3	12	3	7	0
Duck	1	5	9	16	12	5
Goose	4	43	74	102	59	9
Laridae	0	1	1	0	1	0
Owl	0	0	0	1	1	0
Raptor	0	0	5	2	2	0
Swan	0	0	1	0	1	0
Turdidae	0	1	1	0	1	0
Wader	0	30	10	6	7	1
Wild goose	2	23	42	14	18	1

TABLE 7.2 Bird MNI counts.

FIGS 7.5 and 7.6 show the total number and weight of identified specimens (NISP) for cattle, sheep and pig, whilst FIGS 7.7 and 7.8 show the relative frequencies of each. For NISP counts, the sizeable assemblages (mostly dump contexts) from Phases 3b, 4–5b and 6 show a large increase in the numbers of sheep and pig bones between Phases 3b and 4–5b and a similar decrease in Phase 6. For identifiable cattle bones, the opposite is the case. When relative frequencies are presented, cattle are the most commonly identified species of the three in Phase 3b (reaching their highest value for all phases), followed by sheep and pig. However, in Phase 4–5b, pig and sheep

remains become more common at the expense of cattle, which this time reaches its lowest value for all phases. In Phase 6, the relative frequency of cattle bones increases to once again attain values higher than those for sheep and pig. However, they do not dominate the assemblage as they had previously in Phase 3b.

This increase in sheep and pig and decrease in cattle during Phase 4–5b could be seen as perhaps an artefact of the selected recording protocol which includes only certain identifiable skeletal elements and ignores others (see protocol Appendix 1). The latter were classified more broadly as 'large', 'medium' and 'small' mammal. FIG.

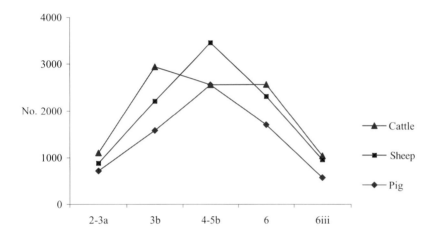

FIG. 7.5 Major domestic mammals (NISP).

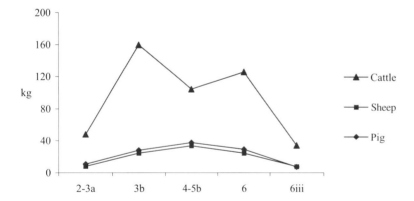

FIG. 7.6 Major domestic mammals – weight of identified specimens (kg).

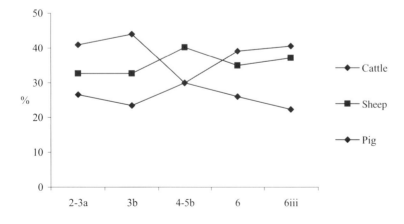

FIG. 7.7 Relative frequency of major domestic mammals (NISP).

7.9 shows the relative frequency of large versus medium-sized mammal fragments. Interestingly, these data also exhibit a decrease in large mammal (considered to be mostly cattle) bones and a rise in the numbers of medium mammal (assumed to be the remains of mostly sheep and pig) during the ninth century (Phase 4–5b), confirming the pattern set by the 'identifiable' elements.

Using MNI counts, and calculating their relative frequencies, provides much the same pattern as the other methods (FIGS 7.10 and 7.11). In this case, however, the actual and relative frequency differences between Phases 3b, 4–5b and 6 are more exaggerated. As a result, cattle

remains are never as frequent as those of sheep in any phase, whilst the relative frequency of sheep and pig MNI counts are as much as 25% and 15% (respectively), more common than cattle in Phase 4–5b.

The relative frequencies of the major domestic mammals (cattle, sheep and pig) have also been calculated using a simple taxonomic ratio (after O'Connor 1991). In this case, pig is used as the baseline against which cattle and sheep are compared, i.e. cattle and sheep values expressed as a ratio of both NISP and MNI counts for pig (FIGS 7.12 and 7.13). Once again, these data show similar patterns to those already discussed, in particular

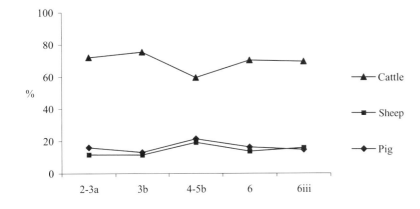

FIG. 7.8 Relative frequency of major domestic mammals (weight of NISP).

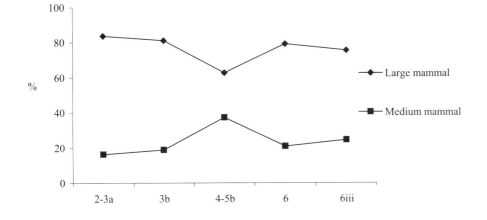

FIG. 7.9 Relative frequency of "Large" versus "Medium-sized" mammal fragments (selected contexts).

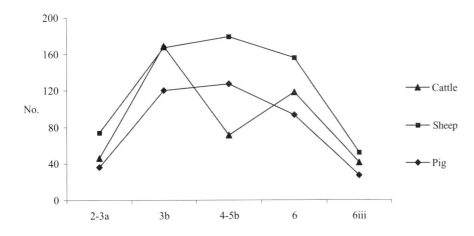

FIG. 7.10 Major domestic mammals (MNI).

the marked reduction of cattle remains in the ninth century (Phase 4–5b). Ratios using MNI counts (Fig. 7.13) also show more clearly than other analyses the steady rise in the importance of sheep (compared to pig) through time, particularly noticeable between Phases 4–5b and 6iii.

In summary, broadly similar changes in the frequency of the main domesticates occur, regardless of the method of quantification used. Cattle provided an overwhelming component of the protein diet throughout all the major phases (usually 60–80%), with pigs and sheep contributing a much smaller proportion (usually 10–20%). However, during Phase 4–5b, there appeared to be a decrease in the importance of beef and a related increase in the consumption of pork and mutton. In this same period (Phase 4–5b), more domestic bird remains were present.

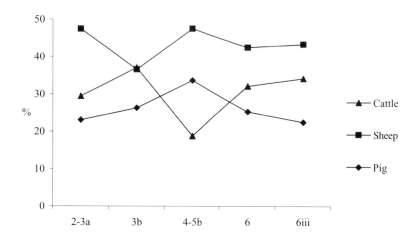

Fig. 7.11 Relative frequency of major domestic mammals (MNI).

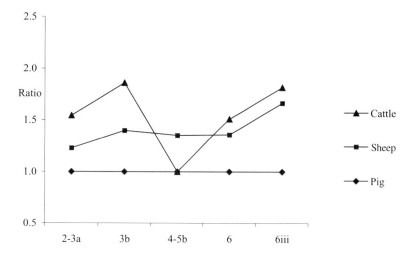

Fig. 7.12 Relative frequency of main domestic mammals (using 'pig equivalents' on NISP counts).

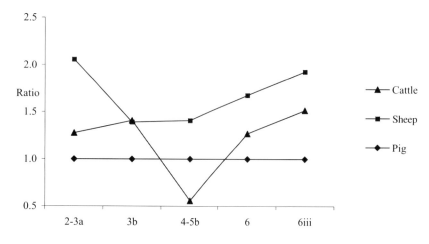

Fig. 7.13 Frequency of main domestic mammals (using 'pig equivalents' on MNI counts).

Proportions of meat in the diet

In order to appreciate the role of farmed meat in the diet of the Flixborough inhabitants, calculations of the amount of meat available from each major domestic mammal taxon can be made.

Body size (and hence carcase weight) is an important consideration when assessing the true economic importance of the various domestic species. The carcases of large animals will obviously provide more meat and other consumable products than those of smaller ones. Comparisons of the relative numbers of different species (based on simple fragment counts or minimum numbers of individuals) can, therefore, be misleading when trying to interpret their economic significance.

Relative proportions of carcase or meat weights for the three major domestic mammal taxa can be roughly calculated by applying estimates of average body weight established from modern animals or extrapolated for ancient counterparts. Although potentially useful, variations in the size, sex, and nutritional status of different breeds/varieties of domestic stock, render the application of this technique to archaeological material somewhat questionable. However, as long as it is borne in mind that absolute values are not attainable, this technique can be used as an additional means of assessing the *relative* importance of each species.

Other studies (e.g. Bourdillon and Coy 1980 and O'Connor 1991) have used the data published from the study of the vertebrate remains from Manching (Boessneck *et al.* 1971, 9; O'Connor *op. cit.*). Taking the mid-points in the suggested ranges (i.e. cattle live weight @ 275kg, sheep @ 37.5kg and pig @ 85kg), it can be calculated that 7.3 sheep would provide as much meat as a single cow and 2.3 sheep should be equivalent to a single pig. These same ratios have been used to calculate body weights for cattle, sheep and pig from the Flixborough assemblage.

Before considering the present data, however, it must be remembered that this method is based on two assumptions: that the same percentage conversion can be applied from live body weight to dead carcase weight, and that these conversion rates are consistent between the three species. These assumptions are obviously somewhat problematic, since the proportion of meat from a pig carcase, relative to its live weight, is likely to be significantly higher than that for sheep.

Figs 7.14 and 7.15 show the total postulated meat weights that cattle, sheep and pigs made to the diet of the Flixborough inhabitants in each major phase. These figures are arrived at by simply multiplying the live weight ratios (outlined above) by the NISP and MNI counts for each taxon. Figs 7.16 and 7.17 show the relative proportions for each. From these data it can be seen that cattle contributed a significant component of the protein diet throughout all the major phases (usually between 60–80%), with pigs and sheep contributing a much smaller proportion (usually between 10–20%). What is still apparent, however, is the decrease in importance of beef and the related increase in the consumption of pork and mutton during Phase 4–5b.

One further interesting observation is the discrepancy in meat weight values produced using NISP and MNI counts. Meat weight values based on NISP counts indicate a much lower overall meat consumption at the site than those based on MNI counts. Thus the values in Fig. 7.14 range from 9000 to 28,000 kilos of meat consumed, whilst those from Fig. 7.15 range from 16,000 to 62,000 kilos of meat. In addition, values based on NISP counts show a similarity in values for the major dumping phases (i.e. Phases 3b, 4–5b and 6) of around 30,000 kilos, whereas values based on MNI counts show a much wider variation between the same major dump phases.

The exaggerated differences between comparisons of all calculations based on NISP and MNI counts have

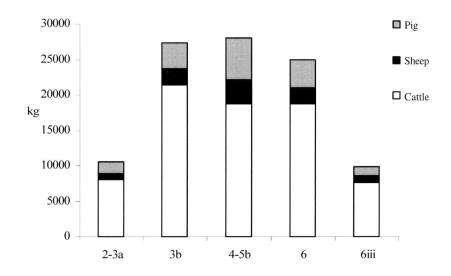

Fig. 7.14 Postulated meat weights based on NISP (kg).

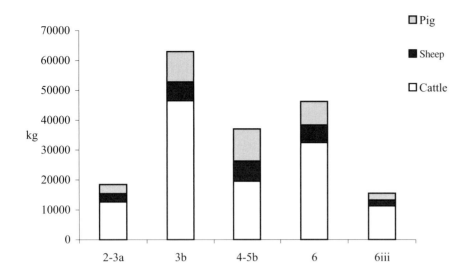

FIG. 7.15 Postulated meat weights based on MNI (kg).

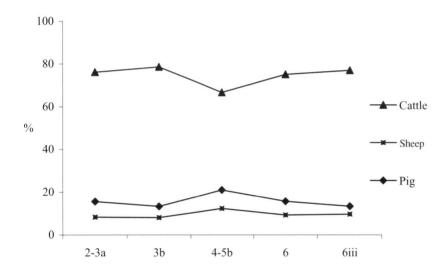

FIG. 7.16 Relative frequency of major domestic mammals from reconstructed meat weight values (using NISP).

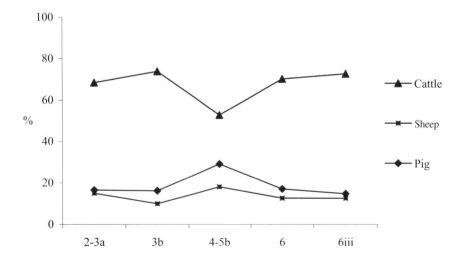

FIG. 7.17 Relative frequency of major domestic mammals from reconstructed meat weight values (using MNI).

already been noted, and much has been written about the merits and drawbacks of each technique (for review see Gautier 1984). The discrepancies noted here serve as a reminder that the presentation of absolute values for meat weights (and other similar kinds of analyses) should be regarded with caution. In this case, however, the relative frequencies from both methods do present a more consistent pattern, which indicates a major change in meat consumption during the ninth century (Phase 4–5b). The pattern seen in these data also complements that seen in the absolute and relative frequency bone counts.

Agricultural and economic practices as shown by age-at-death

The reconstruction of age-at-death data for domestic livestock at Flixborough has provided a range of information about some of the agricultural and economic practices which occurred at and around the site through the late eighth to the tenth centuries AD. As was the case for establishing the relative importance of the major domesticates, a number of different techniques has been used in order to reconstruct age-at-death profiles for the major domestic animals in order to control for the many problems and assumptions inherent in the various analyses. These have involved the use of tooth eruption and wear, supplemented by long-bone development and epiphysial fusion (see Appendix 1 for details of methodology involved).

Tooth wear

The assemblage from Flixborough has provided a very large dataset of jaws and teeth. Data were available for each major phase, which has meant that statistically meaningful comparisons of age-at-death over time can be made. Using data from tooth eruption and occlusal wear, Figs 7.18–7.20 show changes in the relative frequencies of broad age categories for the major domestic mammals in each phase (for cattle and pig after O'Connor 1988 and for sheep after Payne 1973; 1987).

For cattle (Fig. 7.18), although a wide range of ages are represented in the assemblage for all phases (i.e. from neonatal to elderly individuals), the emphasis is on adult and elderly individuals throughout. What is striking about these patterns is their similarity throughout the occupation of the site. For example, the survivorship curve barely changes its profile in any period; it shows a steady kill-off of individuals until late adult/elderly stage (over 5 years of age). The only minor variation in this pattern is a slight rise in the number of neonatal animals, together with an increase in elderly animals (approximately 8 years or older), in the ninth century (Phase 4–5b). There are no specific peaks of killing, indicating animals being selectively culled at a particular age and, as a result, this profile is difficult to interpret.

A broadly similar pattern – of little change through time – can be seen when reconstructing kill-off patterns

for sheep teeth and jaws (Fig. 7.19). All age categories (except category A) are represented for each major phase, with an emphasis on sub-adult and early adult animals (Payne's stages E–G: 2–6 years). There is a gradual kill-off of younger animals (stages B–D: 2–24 months), after which most individuals are killed. If there is any noticeable change at all, it is that there is a slight shift in the peak age for killing sheep towards slightly younger animals (i.e. from stage G – 4–6 years – in Phases 2–3a and 3b to stage F – 3–4 years – in Phases 4–5b and 6). In Phase 6iii, the profile appears to return to that shown in Phases 2–3a and 3b, with a peak of killing at stage G (although the sample size for jaws is much smaller here than for all the other phases).

For pigs, the pattern is once again one of little or no change through time (Fig. 7.20). However, unlike the case for cattle and sheep, there are, indeed, specific age categories of pigs that were selectively slaughtered (i.e. sub-adult 2 and Adult 2). These two groups represent animals approximately 12–18 months and just over 2 years of age. If we assume that all these animals were born at roughly the same time of year (i.e. spring) – and detailed study of dental enamel defects on the pigs from Flixborough would support this assumption (see this chapter and Dobney *et al.* 2002) – these profiles indicate the seasonal killing of pigs, probably in winter.

The construction of broad age categories on the basis of tooth eruption and wear has shown that, although there are differences in the patterns of exploitation of some of the domestic livestock, there is apparently little change in management and exploitation of each individual species through the main phases of occupation. This is very interesting since it has already been shown that there are major differences in the frequency of individual species through time.

Mandible wear stages

However, broad age categories are just that, and they may mask subtle and specific changes involving more closely related age groups. In an attempt to study age categories in greater detail, the method of analysing tooth wear data developed by Grant (1982) was employed on the remains of the major domestic mammals. Simply described, individual tooth wear records for selected cheek teeth within jaws are given a numerical score (missing teeth can be assigned scores/values on the basis of the patterns of related wear from teeth in the same jaw and other jaws). This is obviously easier to perform for large assemblages like those from Flixborough, where the variations in wear combination can be more obviously recognised through very large sample size. These numerical values are then summed for each individual tooth row and a single value (known as the mandible wear stage value or MWS) is produced. From these data, histograms can be produced showing the number or frequency of individual wear stage values present within an assemblage. Where sufficient data exist, over fifty

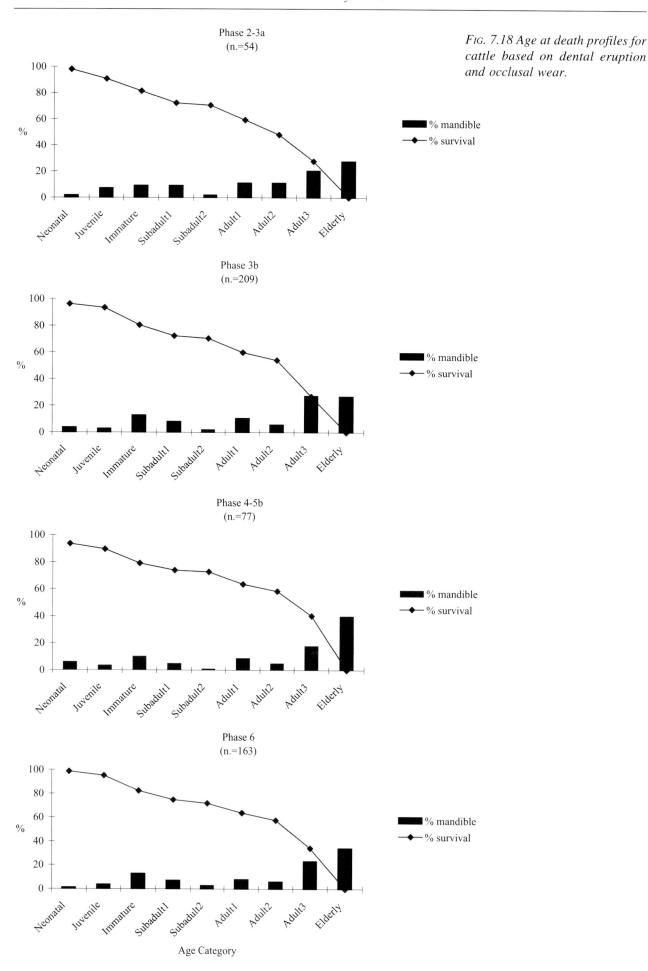

FIG. 7.18 Age at death profiles for cattle based on dental eruption and occlusal wear.

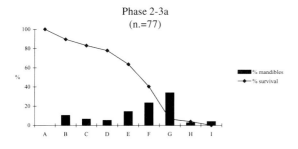

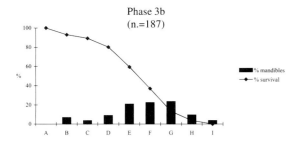

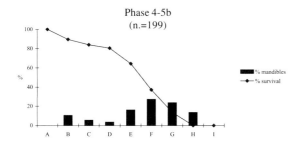

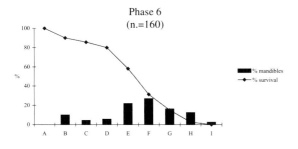

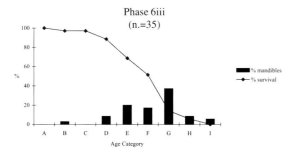

Fig. 7.19 Age at death profiles for sheep based upon dental eruption and occlusal wear.

categories or stages can be plotted, in sharp contrast to the 9–10 broad age categories previously outlined.

Although ostensibly a more refined method of portraying age-at-death data, several fundamental caveats must be considered when interpreting these data. The first is the impression given by the histograms that all wear stages last an equal amount of time. This is quite patently not the case; some individual wear stages (e.g. G) persist for long periods, whereas others (e.g. A–D) are transient, lasting in some cases for just a few weeks. Thus, subtle changes in the wear stage value histograms may, in reality, reflect this anomaly rather than differences in the timing of age-at-death.

An attempt to address this methodological question was undertaken on the large assemblage of pig mandibles from Flixborough (Tams 2002). In this study, the actual crown heights of molars were correlated with the Grant wear stages in an attempt to show the range of variation of crown height values between individual wear stages. This study showed significant correlation between crown height measurements and tooth wear stages. A second problem with mandible wear stage analysis stems from the fact that different combinations of wear stage scores can produce the same wear stage values for individual mandibles. These problems aside, mandible wear stage analysis has been used to good effect by many researchers, a number of whom have produced some very intriguing results (see Ervynck 2004 for detailed discussion). Used in conjunction with the other techniques for age-at-death estimation, it can thus still be a very useful additional technique.

Fig. 7.21 shows the data relating to mandible wear stage values for cattle. The previous observation, regarding a range of broader age categories for Flixborough cattle, is confirmed by the general pattern for all phases (thus all values from 1–53 are represented to some degree). There do, however, appear to be a number of discrete peaks in the histogram profiles that warrant further attention. From ninth century contexts (Phase 4–5b), there appears to be a higher proportion of very young animals (MWS values 2–4, i.e. animals of only a few months old) compared with all other phases (see Chapter 10 for discussion of possible vellum production). Data from Phase 2–3a show what appear to be two discrete age groups of animals, one juvenile (at around MWS value 6–8), the other sub-adult (around MWS values 20–22). A similar, more distinct, early peak is present in the assemblage from tenth century deposits (Phase 6), although this seems to occur slightly later (MWS values 8–10) than that seen in Phase 2–3a. The profile for older animals from both phases is very similar, with a broad peak of killing around MWS values 45–49, and a whole group of other values spread out from 32–44. Thus, the profiles for Phases 2–3a, and 6 are very similar (with the exception of the sub-adult peak present in Phase 2–3a).

Apart from the small peak of very low MWS values present in Phase 4–5b, similarities in profile also occur

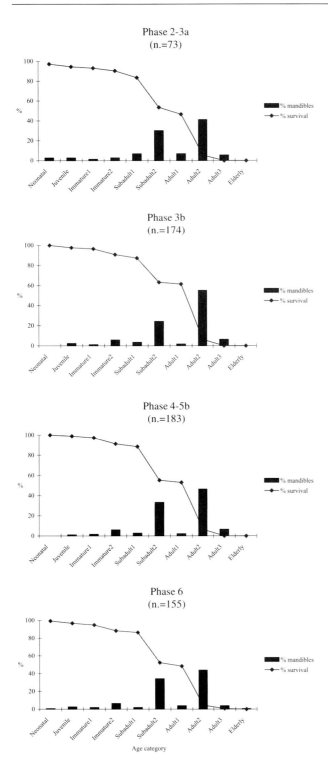

Fig. 7.20 Age at death profiles for pig based upon dental eruption and occlusal wear.

between Phases 3b and 4–5b. A somewhat early peak (MWS values of 13–16) and a later one (MWS values 31–34) are shared by both phases. However, the broad peak of older animals seen in Phase 3b (MWS values 42–47) appears to be slightly earlier than the peak for adult and elderly animals that the other phases appear to share (i.e. MWS values 45–49). However, in Phase 4–5b, this peak of 'older' individuals appears to be clustered within a narrower band of MWS values.

The pattern for sheep is somewhat different to that for cattle (Fig. 7.22). In this case, patterns of MWS values for almost every major phase appear (with a few minor exceptions) to be very similar indeed (as was the case when viewing the broad age category data shown by Fig. 7.19). In all cases, several killing peaks can be observed involving young animals (i.e. the first between MWS values 11 and 16, the second between 17 and 25). Two later, more substantial, peaks can be seen between MWS values 28–37 and 38–44, and appear to represent the age when the most animals were killed. A smaller peak of older animals (MWS values 38–44) can be seen in Phase 6. This observation fits well with that proposed using the broad age categories outlined previously (Fig. 7.19), where a shift to slightly younger animals (i.e. from adult to sub-adult) through time was also postulated.

For pig, the pattern is dramatically different to that seen for cattle, but somewhat similar to that for sheep. Fig. 7.23 shows the MWS values for pig by major phases of occupation. Analysis reveals that several discrete periods of slaughter are represented, particularly for the major dumping phases where sample size is substantial (i.e. upwards of 200 mandibles for each phase). Although a small number of animals were killed at an age represented by MWS values 7–14 (approximately 7–10 months old), the vast majority were killed at >18 months (MWS values 20–42). Within this latter group, two peaks are visible representing two separate cohorts of animals being killed (i.e. those with less worn teeth and those with more advanced wear). Since the degree of occlusal wear is broadly related to age, these should represent animals of different age groups. However, although these two groups are visible, their composition is by no means the same for each phase. Once again, data for Phases 3b and 6 appear remarkably similar, the profiles created by the histograms mirroring each other's peaks and troughs. Data from these phases indicate a separation of the so-called 'younger' and 'older' slaughtered majority either side of MWS values 25–27. In both cases, the 'younger' group is smaller and comprised of individuals with a more limited range of MWS values (i.e. from 19–24), whilst the larger 'older' group include animals with a broader range of MWS values (i.e. from 28–45).

Data for Phase 4–5b show a somewhat different pattern to that described from Phases 3b and 6. As previously mentioned, most of the animals fall in one of two discrete age groups in the histogram. However, in contrast to Phases 3b and 6, the 'younger' group now appears to

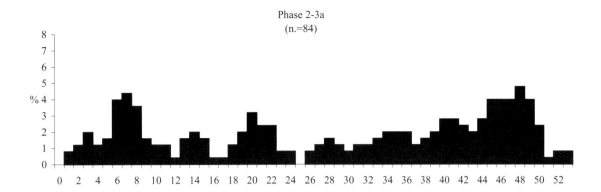

Phase 2-3a
(n.=84)

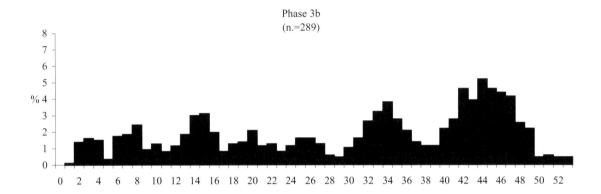

Phase 3b
(n.=289)

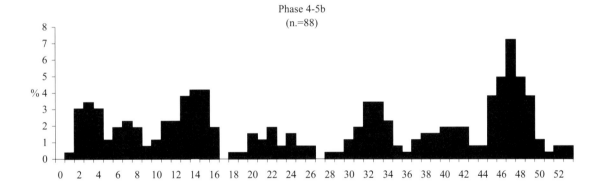

Phase 4-5b
(n.=88)

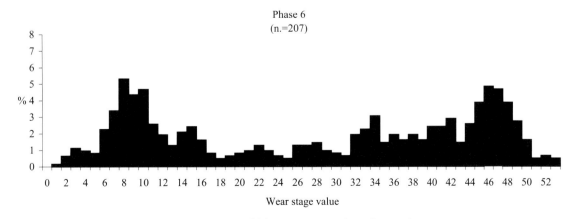

Phase 6
(n.=207)

Wear stage value

FIG. 7.21 Mandible wear stage data for cattle.

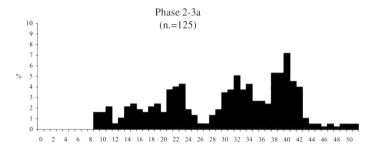

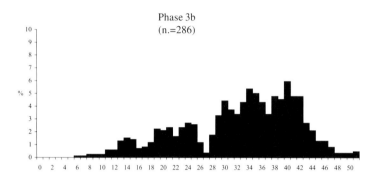

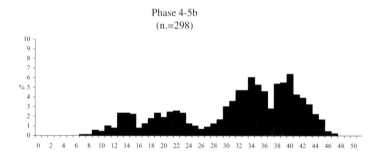

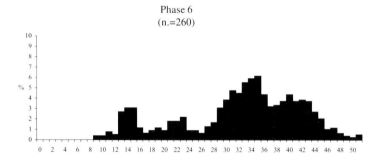

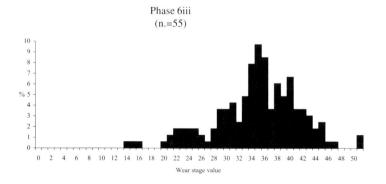

FIG. 7.22 Mandible wear stage data for sheep.

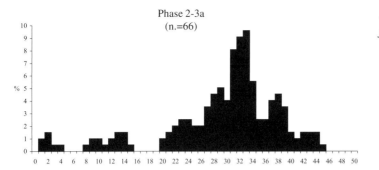

Phase 2-3a
(n.=66)

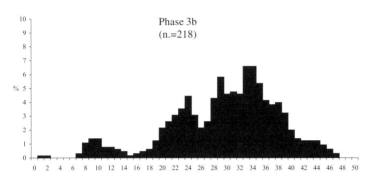

Phase 3b
(n.=218)

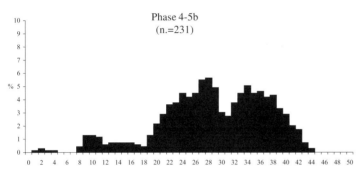

Phase 4-5b
(n.=231)

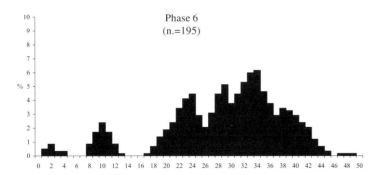

Phase 6
(n.=195)

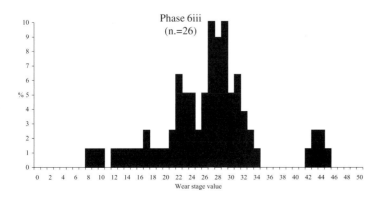

Phase 6iii
(n.=26)

Fɪɢ. *7.23 Mandible wear stage data for pig.*

dominate the picture, and with a wider range of MWS values (i.e. 19–29). Although slaughter appears to have begun with animals of a very similar age in all phases, economic decisions in Phase 4–5b seem to have favoured the inclusion of older animals, not represented in Phases 3b and 6. The 'older' and 'younger' groups appear to separate at MWS values 30–32, later than that seen in Phases 3b and 6. The 'younger' group, although present in all phases, appears also to be numerically less important during Phase 4–5b. One final pattern to emerge from the histograms that may be worthy of some note is the finding that, although young pigs are present in all phases, those represented by MWS values 13–16 are most noticeable in Phase 4–5b.

Data for the dental eruption and wear of pig teeth at Flixborough appear to indicate several peaks of slaughter, perhaps three distinct age cohorts, for all periods represented. However, although the pattern for Phase 4–5b is broadly similar to that for 3b and 6, it could be argued that a subtle change in the age at which some of the animals were slaughtered occurred during the ninth century. Do these observed differences between periods and phases, however, really reflect changes in the ages at which the animals are being slaughtered? As has already been mentioned, although tooth wear is age-related, it is also extremely dependent on changes in diet. So animals of a similar age, which have been fed a substantially coarser diet (i.e. one with a more abrasive effect on teeth), could appear to be 'older'. Thus, could the subtle changes in apparent age-at-death between pigs in Phases 4–5b and Phases 3b and 6 not be changes in the ages at slaughter at all, but a shift in the diet of animals between periods?

Various reasons have already been given for the rationale of grouping and analyzing the osteological data from Flixborough by major period, and one obvious reason for doing so is that sample sizes are greatly increased. The fact that the Flixborough assemblage is so large, however, allows us to view some of the data by the more discrete sub-phases in order to gain an even more detailed insight into the patterns observed by grouping them by major period. We can, therefore, explore in more detail whether the subtle changes in pig slaughtering ages seen in the histograms and described above, are only present in specific sub-phases.

FIG. 7.24 shows the MWS values for the Flixborough pigs broken down into the various sub-phases. Although not as large as those used previously, sample sizes for each phase are still substantial enough to allow some degree of comparison to be made. The patterns shown by data from the sub-phases making up Phase 4–5b (i.e. 4ii, 4ii–5a, 5a, 5a–5b and 5b) do indeed show a gradual decline in the numbers of the 'older' animals through time – and a shift towards 'younger' ones. The peak of animals with MWS values between 26–28 in all sub-phases representing 4–5b, and their lower frequencies in all sub-phases representing Phases 3b and 6, can also be

observed, as can the small peak of young animals with MWS values between 12–18 seen only in sub-phases representing Phase 4–5b.

The analysis of data from individual sub-phases making up Phase 4–5b appears to show a shift in age profile over time; this is more likely to be the result of changes in the age of slaughter than of differences in the abrasive quality of the diet in different periods. As already mentioned, MWS values represent a composite of information from several teeth, the same MWS values being achieved by different combinations of eruption and wear. Thus, subtle differences between age-at-death profiles created by this method run the risk of being an artefact of the method itself. One way of testing this is to compare the eruption and wear status of individual teeth.

Cross-tabulation of tooth eruption and wear scores of adjacent teeth (i.e. M1–M2 and M2–M3 –TABLES 7.3 and 7.4) helps address the "age versus diet" hypothesis by comparing eruption (independent of the abrasive qualities of the diet) with wear. Thus animals with a more abrasive diet will wear their teeth at a faster rate and as a result should show a shift towards more advanced wear scores in relation to the eruption of later teeth. The data shown in TABLES 7.3 and 7.4 show that there are few or no differences in the distribution of wear stages through all periods represented. There is certainly no evidence for an increase in the wear of 1st or 2nd molars compared with the eruption of 2nd and 3rd molars.

The implications from these ranges of data for tooth eruption and wear presented by a variety of different techniques appear to be somewhat contradictory. Whilst the use of Grant MWS values indicates a broad similarity of slaughter ages between periods, those from the sub-phases within Phase 4–5b strongly suggest change through time. Conversely, data from individual teeth show a remarkably similar pattern for all major periods. How can these apparently different profiles be interpreted? On balance, evidence from tooth eruption/wear, as well as associated crown heights (after Tams 2002) from the pigs at Flixborough lead us to conclude that, although there was an apparent seasonal pattern to the culling of pigs, there was little or no change in slaughter patterns through all periods of occupation. Pigs were an important seasonal resource in the past, being traditionally killed during the winter months, and the pattern for the data from Flixborough suggests this was also the case throughout the whole of the main occupation sequence, with animals being killed mainly during their second and third winters.

Epiphysial fusion

As well as tooth eruption and wear, evidence of age-at-death can be gleaned from the state of fusion of elements of the post-cranial skeleton. Since the epiphysial fusion plates calcify and fuse in a relatively ordered sequence (broadly understood for humans and most domestic mammals – see, for example, Silver 1970) they can be

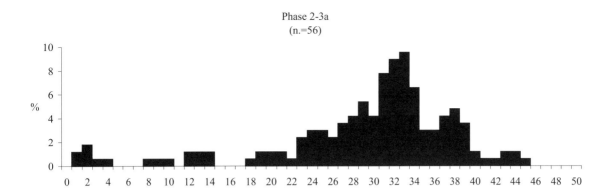

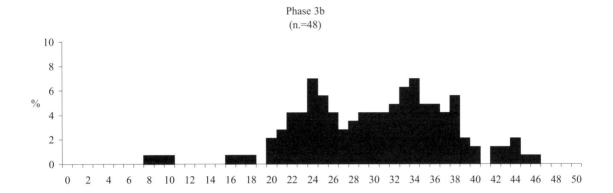

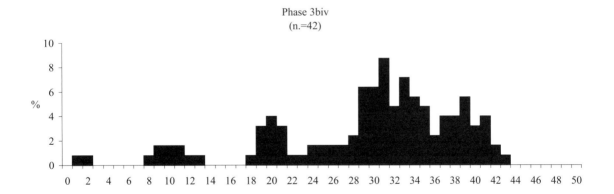

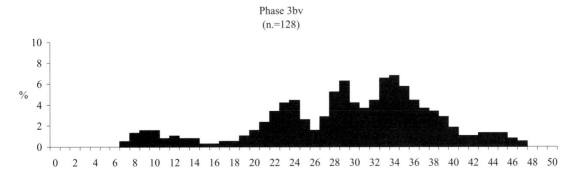

Fig. 7.24 Mandible wear stage data for pig (by sub-phase) (continued overleaf).

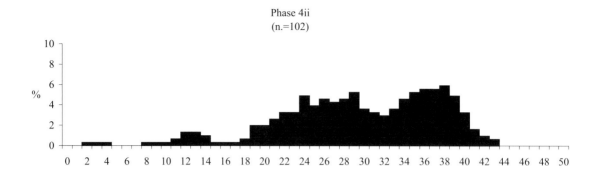

Phase 4ii
(n.=102)

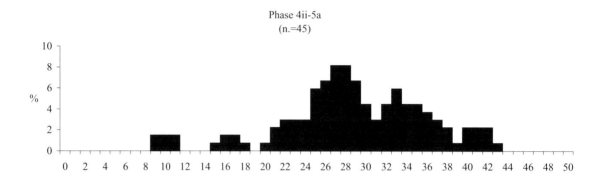

Phase 4ii-5a
(n.=45)

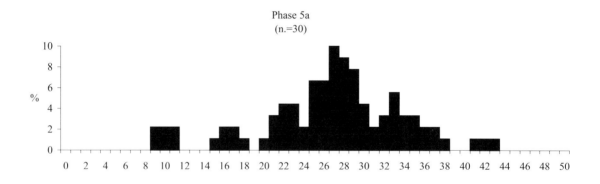

Phase 5a
(n.=30)

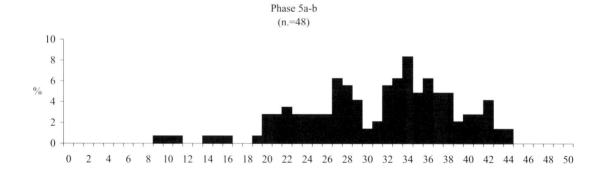

Phase 5a-b
(n.=48)

FIG. 7.24 continued.

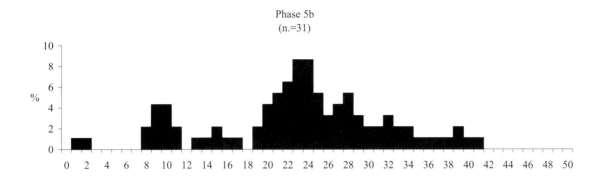

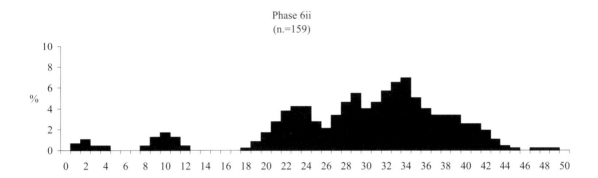

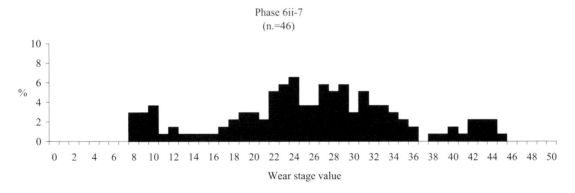

Fig. 7.24 continued.

used to assess age-at-death, albeit crudely. These data can then be compared with those established from analysis of teeth.

Figs 7.25–7.27 show the relative proportions of fused epiphyses for various categories of skeletal elements grouped into broad aged groups (after O'Connor 1989). For cattle (Fig. 7.25), it would appear that, for all phases, 5–15% of animals died or were killed by the time 'early' elements fused (i.e. around 12–18 months old), whilst a significant proportion (30–40%) were killed by the 'intermediate' stage (i.e. between 2–3 years old). Few animals were then killed between 'intermediate' and

'late' fusing stages (approximately 3–4 years) in Phases 3 and 6iii, whilst a further 10–12% were killed between these stages in Phases 4–5b and 6. Data from Phase 2–3a (although a smaller dataset) indicate a major cull of animals (a further 25%) aged between 3–4 years, indicating a major difference in slaughter patterns from the other later periods. Finally, a further slaughter of animals occurred by the 'final' stage (i.e. animals of around 7–9 years old), most obvious in Phases 3b and 6iii, and at this stage between 30–45% of individuals were still being kept into adulthood.

Although this general pattern for cattle confirms that

Phase 2-3a

M2 \ M1	C	V	E	H	U	a	b	c	d	e	f	g	h	i	j	k	l	m	n	Total
0	2		1																	3
C																				
V							1	1												2
E																				
H								2												2
U																				
a								1												1
b											1	1								2
c												1								1
d												4	3		1	2	4			14
e											1	3	1		2	5	4			16
f												2	3	1	2	2				10
g															1		5	2		8
h																	1			1
i																1	1	1		3
j																	1			1
k																		2		2
l																				
	2		1			1	2	2			2	11	7	1	6	10	15	6		66

Phase 3b

M2 \ M1	C	V	E	H	U	a	b	c	d	e	f	g	h	i	j	k	l	m	n	Total
0	1																			1
C																				
V						2	5	2												9
E							1	1												2
H							1	2												3
U																				
a								1	1	1	2									5
b										1	6	7	1							15
c									2	1	10	1	1							15
d											2	10	11	6	5	5	4	1		44
e											4	4	7	5	5	7	6			38
f												2	2	4	6	9	7	2		32
g													1	4	2	11	7			25
h															1	6	4			11
i															1	4	2			7
j																1	3			4
k																	4			4
l																	3			3
	1					2	6	4	4	4	15	33	22	17	20	25	39	26		218

TABLE 7.3 *Cross-tabulation of 1st (M1) and 2nd (M2) permanent molar wear stages (by phase) (continued opposite).*

Phase 4–5b

M2 \ M1	C	V	E	H	U	a	b	c	d	e	f	g	h	i	j	k	l	m	n	Total
0	1		1																	2
C																				
V							3	5												8
E							1		2	2										5
H																				
U																				
a								1	3	1	2									7
b									2	2	1	6	2							13
c										3	7	6	2	4	1					23
d											6	12	10	10	5	2	3			48
e											6	9	5	4	6	4	4	1		39
f												3	4	7	4	9	2			29
g													1	3	4	12	3			23
h															1	1	6	5		13
i																3	8	4		15
j																	2	4		6
k																				
l																				
	1		1				4	6	7	8	22	36	20	25	24	14	44	19		231

Phase 6

M2 \ M1	C	V	E	H	U	a	b	c	d	e	f	g	h	i	j	k	l	m	n	Total
0	3		2																	5
C																				
V							4	3												7
E						1	2	4	1											8
H																				
U																				
a										1	2	1								4
b										3	4	4	2							13
c											2	5	2	5						14
d										1	3	8	5	6		3	2	1		29
e											5	8	1	7	7	6	8			42
f												2	2	6	3	5	5	1		24
g													1	4		2	7	3		17
h															1	2	7	2		12
i																1	4	1		6
j																	6	4		10
k																	3			3
l																			1	1
	3		2			1	6	7	1	5	16	28	13	28	11	19	39	15	1	195

TABLE 7.3 *continued.*

Phase 2–3a

M3 \ M2	C	V	E	H	U	a	b	c	d	e	f	g	h	i	j	k	l	m	
0		2		2		1													5
C																			0
V							1	1	1										3
E							1		5										6
H											1								1
U									5	11	7								23
a									2	4	1								7
b									1	1		6		1					9
c											1	2	1	2		1			7
d															1	1			2
e																			0
f																			0
	0	2	0	2	0	1	2	1	14	16	10	8	1	3	1	2	0	0	63

Phase 3b

M3 \ M2	C	V	E	H	U	a	b	c	d	e	f	g	h	i	j	k	l	m	
0		9	2	3		2													16
C																			0
V						2	7	4	1										14
E						1	8	6	13	1									29
H								5	7	1									13
U									17	13	6	1							37
a									6	16	18	4	3						47
b										7	8	16	3						34
c												4	5	5		2	1		17
d														2	3	1			6
e																1	2		3
f															1				1
	0	9	2	3	0	5	15	15	44	38	32	25	11	7	4	4	3	0	217

TABLE 7.4 *Cross-tabulation of 2nd (M2) and 3rd (M3) permanent molar wear stages (by phase) (continued opposite).*

seen using the broad age categories for tooth wear, the differences seen in epiphysial fusion data for Phases 2–3a and 4–5b are not reflected by tooth eruption and wear data. The patterns for sheep and pig are, however, broadly similar to those already outlined for tooth eruption and wear data. Unlike the pattern in the data for cattle, very little difference exists between the profiles for all periods. For sheep (FIG. 7.26), there appears to be a single major culling event of animals between 'intermediate 2' and 'late fusion' categories (around 2–3.5 years). Except in Phase 2–3a, 40–45% of all animals appear to survive beyond into adulthood (i.e. older than 5 years).

For pigs (FIG. 7.27), a similar picture of little or no change between the phases is also apparent. Once again, however, data for Phase 2–3a suggest perhaps some divergence from the rest. The kill-off profile for pigs

indicates two major culling episodes early in the animals' lives – i.e. between 'early' and 'intermediate 1' – (1–2 years of age) where around 50% of animals are killed, and between 'intermediate 1 and 2' (2–3 years) where a further 25–30% are killed). Data from Phase 2–3a indicate that this latter cull was focused towards older animals. This profile is also reflected in both the broad and detailed tooth eruption and wear data previously outlined.

Unlike those of mammals, most bird long-bones do not have epiphyses that fuse to the ends of the shaft (diaphysis). Both proximal and distal articulations are composed of cartilage, except in the tibiotarsus and the tarsometatarsus. The rate of growth varies among different breeds/species of birds depending on whether they walk and swim soon after hatching or if they remain

Phase 4–5b

M3	C	V	E	H	U	a	b	c	d	e	f	g	h	i	j	k	l	m	
												M2							
0	8	5				3	2	1	2										21
C																			0
V						2	4	9	1										16
E						2	7	7	19	3	1								39
H								3	6	1									10
U								3	18	17	3								41
a									2	16	18	4	3	5					48
b										2	7	10	2	4	1				26
c												8	6	3	3				20
d												1	1	3	2				7
e													1						1
f																			0
	0	8	5	0	0	7	13	23	48	39	29	23	13	15	6	0	0	0	229

Phase 6

M3	C	V	E	H	U	a	b	c	d	e	f	g	h	i	j	k	l	m	
												M2							
0	7	8						1											16
C																			0
V						3	2	2	2		1								10
E						1	11	5	9	2									28
H								4	3										7
U								3	11	27	7		1						49
a									3	9	8	4	1		1				26
b										4	7	5	4	2	1				23
c											1	8	6	3	5	1			24
d														1	3	2			6
e																	1		1
f																			0
	7	8	0	0	0	4	13	15	28	42	24	17	12	6	10	3	1	0	190

TABLE *7.4 continued.*

inactive in the nest for a time (Starck 1994). Chickens belong to the first category (precocial), which grow more slowly than the second group (altricial birds); however, ossification occurs relatively quickly (Cohen and Serjeantson 1996) in comparison with mammals.

Excluding Phases 1 and 6iii, where fragment numbers are generally too small to be of interpretative value, data for domestic fowl from Flixborough show that over 85% of the major limb elements were assigned to the adult category. Although variations were noted for different elements and phases, these were very minor. The proximal articulation of the tarsometatarsus is the last epiphysis to fuse. Research into the maturation of modern breeds has suggested that this occurs in faster-growing modern varieties between three-and-a-half and four-and-a-half months (Church and Johnson 1964), and between five and seven months in the slower maturing breeds (Latimer 1927). The domestic fowl from Flixborough are probably most similar to the more primitive breeds that are kept today (e.g. Old English Game birds) and thus would probably have shown a rate of maturation similar to (or even slightly slower than) those individuals used in Latimer's research.

For geese, immature bones were almost completely absent from the record at Flixborough. Single examples (from a total of approximately 4500 goose fragments) were recorded from deposits from Phases 2–3a, 3b and 4–5a. In the medieval period, documentary evidence suggests that geese were culled as 'green geese', at an age of approximately 12–16 weeks and as 'stubble geese', which were older individuals slaughtered in autumn (Harvey 1993). Preliminary research into the development

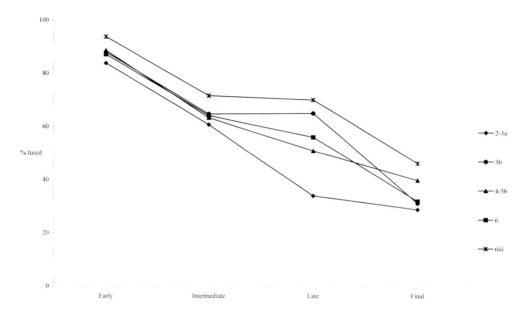

FIG. 7.25 *Cattle epiphysial fusion by phase.*

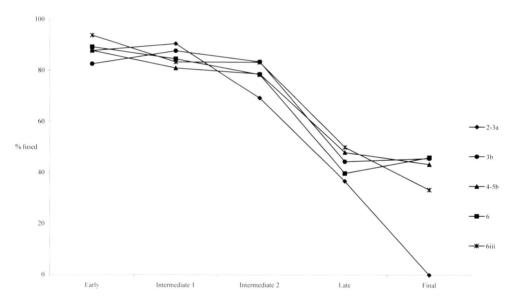

FIG. 7.26 *Sheep epiphysial fusion by phase.*

of the goose skeleton suggests that by 16 weeks goose bones would be fully fused and that it would not be possible to tell from the (archaeological) bones at what age a bird had been killed (Serjeantson 2002). Given these initial results regarding the establishment of age-at-death profiles for geese, it would seem that most of the geese from Flixborough would have been at least 16 weeks old; however, any further refinement of the age structure is, as yet, impossible. Whether these individuals were kept purely for meat (and killed at a younger age), or whether secondary products such as eggs and feathers (which would require the keeping of older individuals) were of more importance, cannot be confidently ascertained.

7.4 Slaughter patterns and Anglo-Saxon husbandry

What do the age-at-death data (gleaned from tooth eruption, wear and long bone fusion) for the main domestic animals at Flixborough tell us about agricultural practices during the Middle and Late Saxon periods?

Cattle

Bones of cattle assigned to the mature and elderly categories represent individuals well past the age when they would have produced prime beef; these would have been young males best killed as immature or young sub-

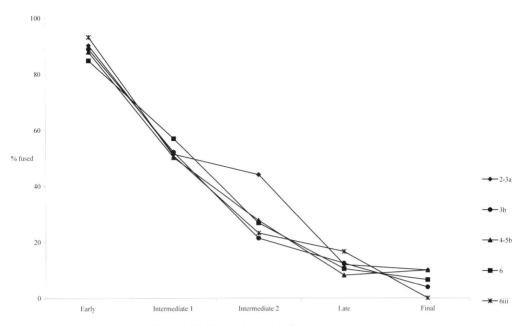

FIG. 7.27 Pig epiphysial fusion by phase.

adults. Therefore, the vast majority of cattle at Flixborough were, most likely, multi-purpose beasts, i.e. old dairy cows whose milk yields had begun to decline or who could no longer produce healthy calves, or oxen no longer fit to pull plough or cart. In short, although these animals were not bred specifically for beef, they were certainly eaten when their primary function was complete.

A high-status estate centre such as Flixborough would have been obtaining supplies from its numerous subordinate estates primarily as taxes or renders. What is, therefore, interesting about the cattle age-at-death data is that they appear to indicate that the consumption of prime beef or very young veal calves, categories of meat considered to be associated with conspicuous wealth and privilege, were not common fare for the inhabitants. Instead, the large quantities of beef consumed at the site derived from spent dairy cows and draught oxen. This appears to challenge not only preconceived ideas about what constitutes status and privilege in terms of diet, but also our current perception of the system of provisioning during Saxon times. Why were the aristocracy apparently settling for the old beasts whilst at the same time provisioning the *wics* with prime aged animals? Perhaps current models of Saxon provisioning systems are too simplistic and, in reality, this disparity reflects more a lack of choice offered by an under-developed market rather than a lack of control (O'Connor 2001). Since the rules of clientship and food rent ensured that the majority of deadstock provided to the elite would anyway have been re-distributed to others down the social hierarchy, there was little real need or incentive for the tenants of rural farmsteads to provide animals in their prime to their respective elite estate centres (Sykes pers. comm. April 2005).

When the data from Flixborough are compared with others within the region and beyond, it is clear that this pattern is by no means the norm. The patterns of cattle slaughter shown in two assemblages from York that are broadly contemporaneous with the earlier and later parts of the sequence at Flixborough, i.e. the Mid-Saxon material from 46–54 Fishergate – interpreted as a *wic* or emporium (O'Connor 1991 and 2001) – and the ninth-tenth century material from 16–22 Coppergate (O'Connor 1989), are very similar to one another (FIG. 7.28). As with Flixborough, in both cases, the most frequent remains are from adult animals. However, sub-adult animals are certainly more frequent at both the York sites, and elderly animals are a small component. With slowly-maturing cattle varieties, these sub-adult animals probably represent prime beef animals supplied to the trading emporium (or *wic*) of Fishergate during Mid-Saxon times and the Viking inhabitants of York during the later ninth and tenth centuries. However, if we examine the cattle age-at-death pattern produced by other Mid-Saxon *wic* assemblages, e.g. Ipswich and Hamwih, Southampton (Crabtree 1996 and Bourdillon and Coy 1980 – the latter data not presented here), we find that different slaughter patterns emerge. From Ipswich, the bulk of the assemblage consisted of the remains of mainly sub-adult cattle, few adults and moderate proportions of elderly stock (FIG. 7.28). This early *wic* and later high-status estate centre was obviously obtaining and consuming prime beef cattle and not older multi-purpose beasts (quite unlike the pattern for Flixborough and Coppergate). At Hamwih, a mortality profile for cattle very similar to that from Ipswich is also found (Bourdillon and Coy *op. cit.* 4, fig. 17).

The pattern of slaughter from Lincoln, another Saxon

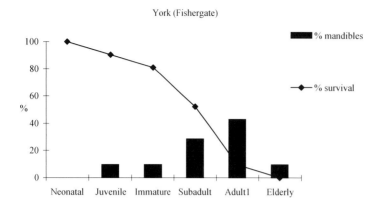

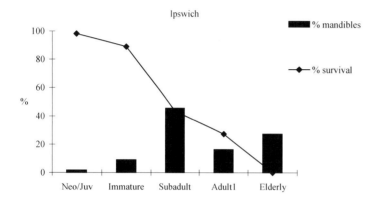

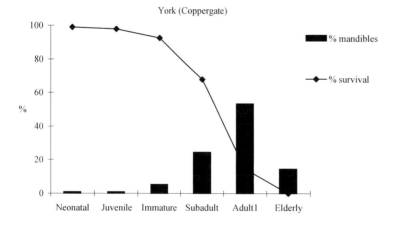

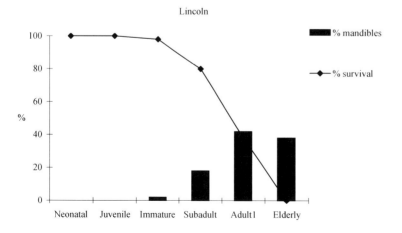

Fig. 7.28 Comparative age at death profiles for cattle.

settlement, which became an early Anglo-Scandinavian urban centre, is similar to that already described for York, i.e. with an emphasis on adult animals. However, there also appears to be a high number of elderly beasts (as was the case at Flixborough). A similar profile can be seen at the fifth-seventh century rural site of West Stow, Norfolk (Crabtree 1989, 76 and fig. 37). At the Mid-Saxon high-status estate centre of Wicken Bonhunt, Essex (Crabtree unpublished; 1996) the slaughter pattern for cattle appears to have been even more focussed towards old and elderly animals, with very few young, juvenile or even sub-adult animals represented at all (Fig. 7.29).

Although, there appears to be no 'typical' slaughter profile for cattle for particular time periods during Saxon and later Anglo-Scandinavian periods, or for types of site (e.g. estate centres, *wics*, or later urban centres like York and Lincoln), at most sites, older adult animals appear to be most frequently slaughtered. High-status estate centres, represented by sites such as Flixborough and Wicken Bonhunt, do not (as one might expect) show high proportions of juvenile and sub-adult animals associated with the conspicuous consumption of young and prime meat animals.

Comparisons of contemporaneous sites further afield show broad consistency with these findings. Wigh's (2001) comparisons of numerous Viking age assemblages from Swedish sites such as Birka (a trading emporium similar to and contemporaneous with the English *wic* sites), Pollista Övergran, and Lingnåre (both farmsteads), St Gertrud and Trädgårdmästaren in Sigtuna (urban

centre), and the German site of Haithabu (urban) show vertebrate assemblages primarily dominated by mature cattle remains (all cited in Wigh 2001). However, the trading emporia of Dorestadt in the Netherlands (Prummel 1983), Ribe in Denmark (Hatting 1991), and various early medieval sites from Ireland (McCormick 1987), have all produced assemblages similar to that from Ipswich, i.e. with higher proportions of younger prime meat-bearing animals represented. This emphasis on older animals at many of these sites (including Flixborough) surely indicates the importance of cattle as dairy producers and draught animals and that it was the meat of older animals that was commonly consumed.

Interestingly, historical evidence, in the form of [early medieval?] law texts from Ireland, suggests the year-round slaughter of cattle. An early Irish poem states that slaughter should not occur until the calf has reached the age of an ox (Ó Riain 1985, *Corpus genealogiarum Sanctorum Hiberniae*, 182.1 *ni horta-laeg ría n-áes daim*). Evidence for dairying is mentioned (though not commonly) in a variety of early Irish sources and later English ones. For example, Irish sources make reference to keeping calves away from their mothers in order to provide milk for human consumption (Kelly 1997, 39), whilst a tenth or eleventh century English document, estate memoranda, indicates that the cowherd is entitled to the milk of an old cow for seven days after she has newly calved (Swanton 1996, 29). In addition, an exchange between Ethelbert, king of Kent, and his thegn Wulflaf, concerning land at 'Wassingwell' and Mersham

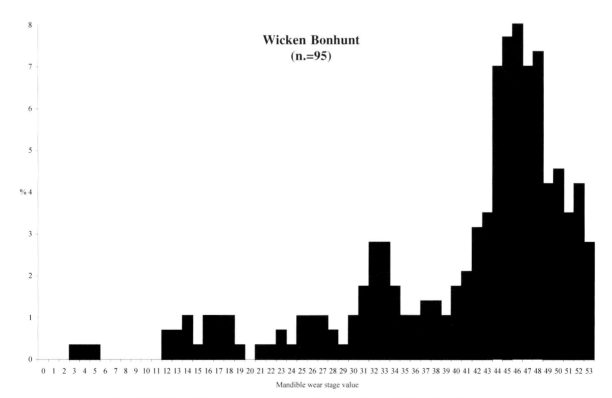

Fig. 7.29 Mandible wear stage data for cattle from Wicken Bonhunt.

(AD 858), mentions two dairy farms situated at Wye pasture from which a total of '40 weys' of cheese was to be paid as food rent (*EHD* 93).

Sheep

Husbandry practices for sheep appear to have changed very little throughout the occupation sequence at Flixborough, particularly with respect to slaughter patterns. Interestingly, texts of Old and Middle Irish make numerous references to sheep. A short legal passage on the proper quality of sheep makes no mention of their flesh, but is primarily concerned with the qualities of the fleece and skin (*CIH* ii 675.13–17; Kelly 1997, 68). This obviously reflects the principal importance of wool (and sheepskins). However, these same Irish law texts indicate that most of the male lambs would normally be slaughtered in their first summer or autumn as, in fact, happens today.

This is in complete contrast to the evidence from Flixborough where the kill-off patterns indicate an emphasis on older animals certainly not killed within their first year of life. However, the age profiles of all animals at Flixborough may not wholly represent the full range of economic activities that the animals were used for. As previously mentioned, this is because most of the animal resources at the site were probably sent there as food rent or renders paid to the lord in return for, for example, protection, favours, grants of land or of other animals. The presence (or indeed absence) of certain age groups in the assemblage does not necessarily reflect the true culling pattern. For example, the absence of very young sheep at Flixborough tends to argue in favour of an emphasis on wool, against the consumption of lamb by high-status individuals (although some lambs are present), and against the use of sheep for dairying purposes. However, as for cattle, the heavy emphasis on mature animals seen in the archaeological record may only reflect the proportion of the flock provided as food rent and could indeed include the remains of mature ewes surplus to the dairying flock.

Sheep's milk, like that of cows (see above), was obviously important in Anglo-Saxon England and is mentioned in the literature. The shepherd in *Ælfric's Colloquy* says '*In the early morning I drive my sheep to pasture and in the heat and cold, stand over them with dogs lest wolves devour them; and I lead them back to their folds and milk them twice a day... and in addition I make cheese and butter*' (Swanton 1996, 170). An estate memorandum, drawn up during the tenth or eleventh centuries, indicates the duties and perquisites of various estate workers. In the case of the shepherd, he was apparently entitled to '*12 nights dung at Xmas, one lamb from the year's young, one bellwether's fleece and the milk of his flock for 7 days after equinox*', whilst the goatherd was entitled to the '*milk of his herd after Martinmas and a one year old kid if he takes good care of his herd*' (Swanton 1996, 29).

Comparisons with evidence from several Mid-Saxon *wic* sites show similarities of possible economic strategies with Flixborough (FIG. 7.30). At Hamwih (Bourdillon and Coy 1980), around 60% of sheep were killed once they were older than 2 years of age (Payne stages greater than E). Similarly, at Fishergate, York (O'Connor 1991), most animals supplied to the site were killed between the ages of 2 and 4 years, suggesting that the animals were kept for wool and meat. However, at Ipswich (Crabtree 1996), a very different slaughter profile was encountered, one in which the economic emphasis was on immature and sub-adult animals (aged approximately 6 months to 2 years) – a slaughter pattern more obviously reflecting primary meat production and consumption.

Sheep culling patterns at urban sites such as Coppergate, York (O'Connor 1989) and Flaxengate, Lincoln (O'Connor 1982) again show similar patterns to those at Fishergate and Flixborough, indicating that the early urban markets of the tenth century were primarily supplied with the carcases of adult animals, originally kept for wool. The large assemblage from the Mid-Saxon estate centre of Wicken Bonhunt (Crabtree unpublished) also shows an emphasis on adult animals, with the vast majority of mandible wear stage values falling between 29 and 44 (FIG. 7.31). However, a small assemblage from the Late Saxon waterfront at Lincoln (Dobney *et al.* 1996) indicated the exploitation of exclusively immature and sub-adult individuals – animals of prime meat producing age (FIG. 7.30). In contrast, the pattern from the early Saxon (fifth–seventh century) rural settlement of West Stow (Crabtree 1989, 86 and fig. 46) showed the presence of animals killed between 6 months and 8 years of age, but with an emphasis (38%) on immature animals of between 6 months and 1 year. The latter figure indicates the slaughter and consumption of surplus males as prime meat providers, but also the use of older animals that would have produced numerous wool clips.

Further afield, in Sweden, two distinct age profiles appear in urban and rural assemblages and are interpreted as reflecting 'producer' and 'consumer' economies (Wigh 2001, 107 and fig. 71). The urban assemblages (from Sigtuna and Birka) contain mainly animals bred for meat (aged between 9 months and 2 years), the very age group that is poorly represented at the rural sites of Pollista Övergran and Ängdala. At Feddersen Wierde, northwestern Germany, over 60% of the sheep were >2 years of age (Reichstein 1972), whilst at the Danish site of Ribe (Hatting 1991), the vast majority of sheep were older than 4 years when culled, indicating a primary emphasis on animals originally used for wool, before being used to provision the eighth-century trading centre with mutton. No such obvious pattern exists for the Flixborough sheep or for most other contemporaneous Saxon sites. It would appear that, as for cattle, sheep were multipurpose beasts, principally bred for their secondary products of wool and dairying.

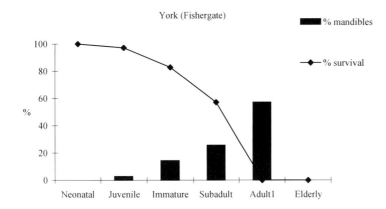

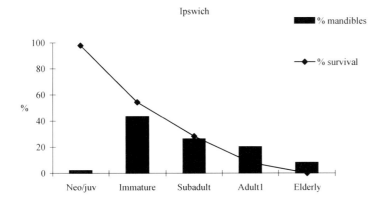

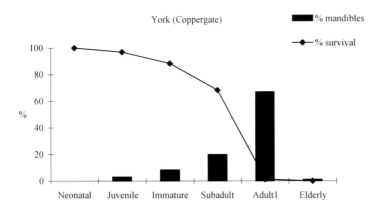

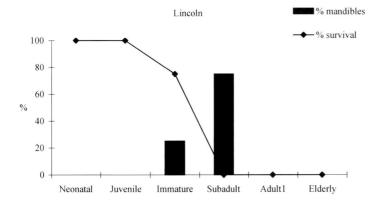

Fɪɢ. *7.30 Comparative age at death profiles for sheep.*

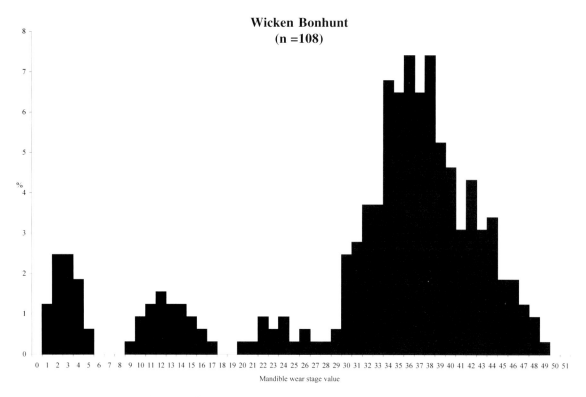

FIG. 7.31 Mandible wear stage data for sheep from Wicken Bonhunt.

Pigs

Detailed analysis of mandible wear stage data (previously outlined) indicates the seasonal culling of pigs. What is interesting about the slaughter pattern is that the vast majority of pigs killed at Flixborough were animals mostly past their optimal age for meat production. This pattern contrasts somewhat with those from the contemporaneous sites of Fishergate (admittedly a rather small assemblage), Ipswich, Coppergate and Flaxengate, where the emphasis is on sub-adult animals of around 2–3 years of age (FIG. 7.32).

Comparison of mandible wear stage data from Flixborough with the evidence from the huge pig assemblage from Mid-Saxon Wicken Bonhunt (Crabtree unpublished; 1996), shows an extremely similar pattern of slaughter to that from Flixborough (FIG. 7.33), and also shows evidence for seasonal killing. Although the subtleties of detailed mandible wear stage evaluation have been lost by combining mandible wear stage classes into broader groups in the original publication, data from rural (and earlier) West Stow (Crabtree 1989) show that there are higher proportions of juvenile and immature animals in this latter assemblage. Noddle (1980, 400) indicates that the vast majority of pigs from Middle and Late Saxon North Elmham, Norfolk, were mature (although the proportion changes from 50–85% for the Mid-Saxon period to 45–50% in late ninth to tenth century deposits). Similar culling profiles to those seen at Flixborough have been reported from Saxon Portchester Castle, where large numbers of pigs were killed between mandible wear stages 21–35 – i.e. during second and third years of life (Grant 1975; 1976), although the relative frequency of pigs at Portchester was much lower than found at Flixborough, Wicken Bonhunt and North Elmham.

In terms of the contemporaneous documentary evidence, a number of Irish law texts corroborate much of the Anglo-Saxon zooarchaeological evidence for seasonal killing, and the killing of pigs at a variety of ages, but with an emphasis on older animals. One Irish law text indicates that a female pig of 6–8 months was regularly killed at Martinmas, i.e. November 11th (Kelly 1997, 85, referring to the Julian Calendar). However, a number of other texts indicate that many were not slaughtered in their first autumn or winter, but more usually between their second autumn (16 months of age) and the following spring (at 2 years old). The law texts also show evidence of the killing of sows after they had produced 2–3 litters, and there are numerous references to the slaughter of older pigs (Kelly *op. cit.*), a practice which, on the face of the evidence outlined above, appears to have been widespread during Saxon times in England (see also Chapter 10).

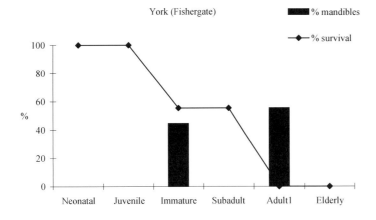

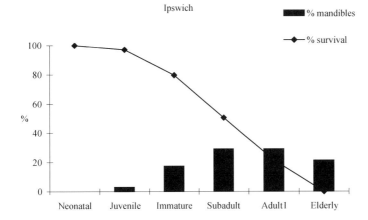

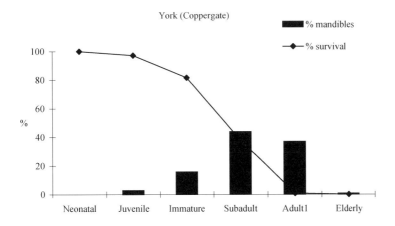

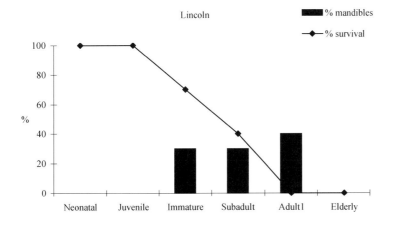

FIG. 7.32 Comparative age at death profiles for pig.

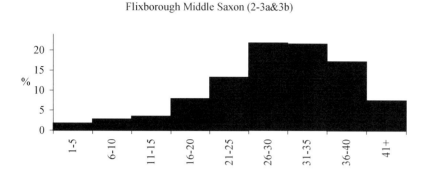

Flixborough Middle Saxon (2-3a&3b)

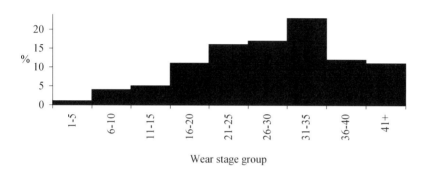

Wicken Bonhunt Middle Saxon

Wear stage group

Fig. 7.33 Mandible wear stage groups for pig from Wicken Bonhunt and contemporary phases from Flixborough.

The agricultural economy as reflected by the size and shape of livestock

Selected measurements of animal bones can provide detailed information on the agricultural economy through a variety of parameters. Differences in the size of domestic livestock, for example, can reflect variations in both the sex and (in certain circumstances) variety/breed of animals that are represented. This is obviously crucial to our understanding and interpretation of aspects of livestock husbandry, and the vast biometrical dataset from Flixborough has allowed some remarkably detailed analysis to be undertaken and some informed conclusions to be made. A variety of different statistical techniques has been used to analyse and present the data. These data and results are presented below for individual taxa, with regard to questions asked of the dataset as they pertain to different aspects of the agricultural economy. In the case of geese, biometrical data are presented and discussed in conjunction with the results of a recent biomolecular case-study carried out by Dr Susan Haynes.

Large cattle and the possible presence of oxen

A simple comparison of the mean values for various cattle bone measurements from each chronological phase at Flixborough shows a clear and consistent pattern. In almost all cases, the highest values were obtained from individuals from Phase 2–3a, whilst the lowest values were almost exclusively found in Phase 6iii (TABLE 7.5). These data, however, do not represent a gradual size

decrease in cattle from the mid eighth to the mid eleventh centuries. In fact, although the smallest and largest specimens are from the earliest and latest phases (i.e. Phases 2–3a and 6iii), those from the late eighth to the end of the tenth century (Phases 3b–6) remain remarkably similar. A similar pattern is evident when evaluating data showing mean reconstructed withers heights of cattle from each phase (TABLE 7.6, and FIGS 7.34 a and b).

An additional way of visually displaying these data is to calculate the percentage difference of the mean values for each measurement from a standard value. In the case of the Flixborough cattle, the 'standard' data against which all other values have been compared are those from Phase 3b. Thus in FIG. 7.35, values for Phase 3b are represented by a horizontal line at value 0. This figure shows that in most (but not all) cases the percentage difference values for a number of measurements are always highly positive for Phase 2–3a and mostly negative for Phase 6iii.

In order to establish whether any of these observed differences are statistically significant, Student t-tests were carried out on the datasets, and results of these are presented in TABLE 7.7. Here the most significant results confirm the pattern already shown by FIG. 7.35 (i.e. comparisons specifically of third molar, humerus, calcaneum, and metacarpal breadth measurements, astragalus length measurements, and withers height reconstruction), particularly between Phases 2–3a and 6iii.

3rd Molar (M3)						
LM3	**No**	**Min**	**Max**	**Mean**	**SD**	**V**
2–3a	64	31.17	39.97	35.62	1.75	4.91
3b	192	30.05	43.03	35.84	1.84	5.14
4–5b	101	30.87	41.00	35.72	1.87	5.24
6	182	29.80	42.96	35.96	1.99	5.52
6iii	35	32.32	39.78	35.23	1.98	5.61
BM3						
2–3a	65	11.65	17.10	14.86	1.18	7.93
3b	190	10.92	18.61	14.50	1.34	9.26
4–5b	100	11.74	18.56	14.95	1.38	9.22
6	181	11.00	18.36	14.40	1.62	11.22
6iii	35	12.09	16.80	14.67	1.11	7.53

Humerus						
BT	**No**	**Min**	**Max**	**Mean**	**SD**	**V**
2–3a	18	63.92	89.82	75.32	7.02	9.32
3b	25	64.03	81.59	69.87	5.30	7.58
4–5b	24	64.07	81.21	70.33	4.01	5.70
6	21	64.90	79.53	70.34	4.67	6.64
6iii	7	61.85	76.19	68.76	4.63	6.73
HTC						
2–3a	18	29.03	36.56	33.19	2.47	7.43
3b	25	28.90	36.90	31.67	2.30	7.26
4–5b	24	27.39	38.66	32.01	2.49	7.79
6	21	28.10	36.47	31.57	2.30	7.29
6iii	8	26.90	32.32	30.29	2.08	6.88
SD						
2–3a	7	27.42	41.85	35.77	5.37	15.01
3b	8	30.40	41.68	33.90	4.40	12.98
4–5b	7	30.40	38.91	33.19	2.88	8.67
6	4	30.70	36.28	34.05	2.56	7.52
6iii	2	27.01	29.86	28.44	2.02	7.09

Tibia						
Bd	**No**	**Min**	**Max**	**Mean**	**SD**	**V**
2–3a	13	54.16	67.13	59.80	4.94	8.26
3b	53	52.61	70.04	58.54	4.31	7.36
4–5b	18	20.63	28.79	58.52	4.87	8.32
6	29	20.9	30	58.62	5.16	8.80
6iii	29	50.2	68.1	57.27	5.04	8.80
Dd						
2–3a	13	40.34	53.82	45.87	3.90	8.50
3b	53	38.17	54.5	44.57	3.82	8.57
4–5b	47	50.13	67.56	44.31	3.94	8.89
6	57	50.5	72.1	44.67	3.68	8.24
6iii	26	37.0	52.7	43.26	4.24	9.80
SD						
2–3a	11	21.93	29.82	25.11	2.72	10.83
3b	28	21.15	31.15	24.50	2.45	10.00
4–5b	46	35.98	53.32	24.71	2.43	9.83
6	56	36.69	55.4	24.86	2.38	9.57
6iii	11	19.9	27.8	23.33	2.01	8.62

Table 7.5 Summary statistics for selected cattle measurements (by phase) (continued overleaf).

			Astragalus			
GLl	**No**	**Min**	**Max**	**Mean**	**SD**	**V**
2–3a	17	58.58	70.76	64.14	3.48	5.43
3b	56	52.56	69.39	62.58	3.53	5.64
4–5b	100	55.21	70.07	62.51	3.18	5.09
6	83	54.55	73.32	62.00	3.68	5.94
6iii	56	54.78	70.70	61.21	3.85	6.29
Bd						
2–3a	16	37.05	47.70	42.36	3.81	8.99
3b	56	32.75	46.15	40.09	2.90	7.23
4–5b	99	34.74	50.22	40.50	3.20	7.90
6	82	33.86	50.30	40.31	3.71	9.20
6iii	55	33.18	51.36	39.27	3.41	8.68
Dl						
2–3a	16	32.11	39.81	36.07	2.21	6.13
3b	55	28.20	39.72	34.99	2.20	6.29
4–5b	97	30.48	39.09	35.02	1.91	5.45
6	82	29.85	40.80	34.53	2.37	6.86
6iii	51	29.26	38.90	33.95	2.29	6.75

			Metacarpal			
GL	**No**	**Min**	**Max**	**Mean**	**SD**	**V**
2–3a	6	181.76	202.83	188.64	7.30	3.87
3b	31	175.44	205.12	187.34	8.19	4.37
4–5b	29	168.53	210.30	188.43	10.01	5.31
6.00	29	162.40	212.80	188.36	11.15	5.92
6iii	11	169.34	207.45	183.15	10.31	5.63
SD						
2–3a	6	25.57	36.51	29.15	3.84	13.17
3b	35	24.89	37.14	30.13	3.05	10.13
4–5b	33	25.41	37.87	31.02	3.58	11.54
6.00	34	24.70	38.60	29.81	3.74	12.54
6iii	13	24.79	37.56	28.20	3.22	11.41
Bp						
2–3a	8	49.97	61.99	52.72	3.95	7.48
3b	38	46.36	65.11	52.89	4.78	9.03
4–5b	34	46.43	66.27	54.52	5.14	9.42
6.00	36	43.39	63.40	53.02	5.20	9.81
6iii	14	44.90	64.70	48.53	4.63	9.55
BFd						
2–3a	6	51.01	62.41	54.61	4.10	7.50
3b	31	49.03	70.34	55.99	5.34	9.53
4–5b	32	48.32	66.83	57.44	5.65	9.84
6.00	33	47.90	67.20	56.39	5.94	10.54
6iii	13	49.11	65.54	51.27	4.69	9.15
Dd						
2–3a	6	28.47	34.39	30.11	2.15	7.15
3b	25	26.38	36.45	30.11	2.70	8.98
4–5b	31	27.01	36.67	31.49	2.64	8.39
6.00	30	26.77	36.26	30.90	2.76	8.94
6iii	10	27.14	32.88	28.21	1.73	6.12

Table 7.5 continued.

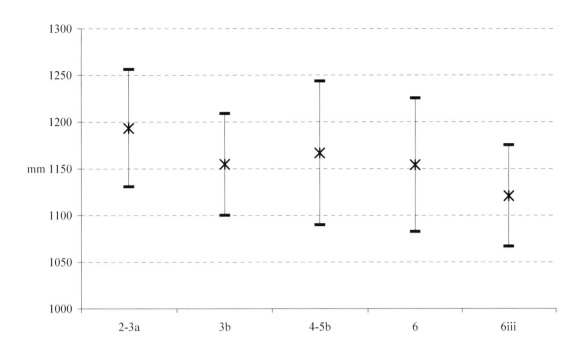

FIG. 7.34a *Reconstructed mean cattle withers height by phase.*

	2–3a	3b	4–5b	6	6iii
Mean	1193.4	1154.6	1166.6	1154.1	1120.9
SD	62.81	54.57	77.05	71.49	54.08

Table 7.6 Mean cattle withers height by phase.

Although an extremely valuable statistical tool, simple comparisons of population means tell us very little about the distribution of individual measurement values. These may mask more complex patterns of possible changes in the size and shape of the Flixborough cattle through time. Plots for the numerous tibia measurements appear to provide evidence for sexual dimorphism (see PLATE 7.1, FIGS 7.36 and 7.37). Histograms showing the number and range of tibia distal breadth values (Bd) show a bimodal distribution for all phases – except for Phase 4-5b (see FIG. 7.36). These plots show a higher number of less robust individuals to the left of the chart, and a lower number of more robust ones to the right. In Phase 4–5b, however, intermediate-sized animals (with values of between 61 and 63mm for this bone measurement) blur this apparent bimodality. Descriptive statistics (in this case a strongly negative kurtosis calculation of –0.986) indicate that the values for Phase 4–5b are much less strongly clustered than those for Phases 6 and 3b. This pattern can be similarly seen in FIG. 7.37, where both distal breadth (Bd) and distal depth (Dd) measurements

are plotted together. Here, two separate groups are visible, although, once again, a number of individuals of inter-mediate size from Phase 4–5b fill the void between larger, more robust, and smaller, more gracile, animals.

Possible sexual dimorphism is also apparent in other cattle measurements. For example, values for breadth and depth measurements for humeri indicate the presence of two separate groups of animals (FIG. 7.38), and once again this separation is perhaps less clear in those individuals from Phase 4–5b (FIG. 7.39). Cattle calcaneum measurements also indicate the presence of sexually dimorphic groups in the three major periods where sufficient data are present (FIG. 7.40), possibly separating around the greatest length value of 135mm. Closer inspection of these data also indicates the possible presence of perhaps three or even four distinct groups. However, since allometric growth of the calcaneum can be correlated with age, these additional groupings may represent a mixture of age- and sex-related size differ-ences.

By far the most markedly sexually dimorphic post-

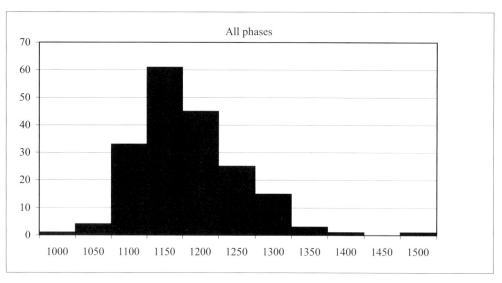

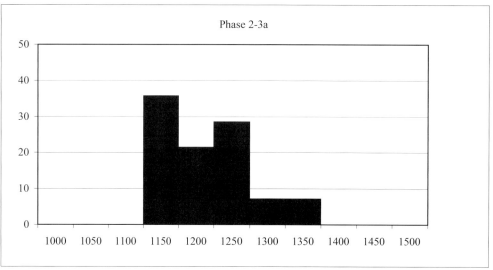

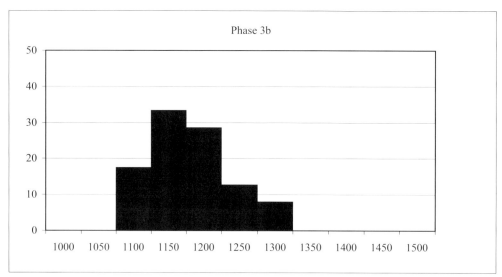

FIG. *7.34b Distribution of mean cattle withers height values (by phase) (continued opposite).*

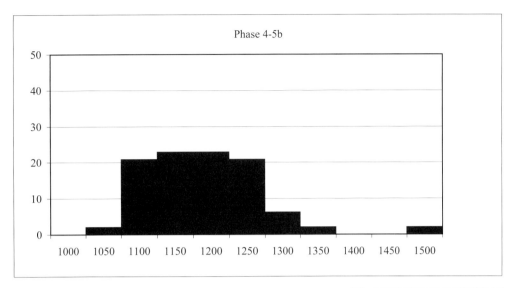

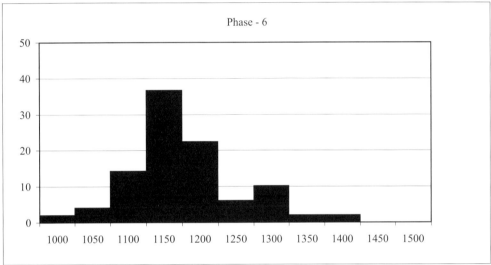

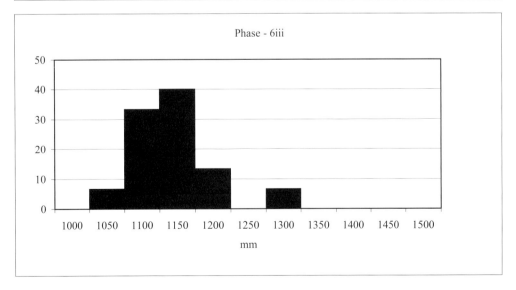

FIG. 7.34b *continued.*

Skeletal element	Measurement	Periods compared	Probability		
			Equal variance	Unequal variance	
M3	Breadth	2–3a and 3b	0.056	0.042	*
		2–3a and 4–5b	0.669	0.658	
		2–3a and 6	0.039	0.017	*
		2–3a and 6iii	0.445	0.437	
		3b and 4–5b	0.007	0.008	**
		4–5b and 6	0.005	0.003	**
Humerus	BT	2–3a and 3b	0.006	0.009	**
		2–3a and 4–5b	0.006	0.012	**
		2–3a and 6	0.012	0.016	*
		2–3a and 6iii	0.033	0.015	*
		3b and 4–5b	0.738	0.737	
		3b and 6	0.755	0.752	
		3b and 6iii	0.617	0.596	
		4–5b and 6	0.991	0.991	
		4–5b and 6iii	0.385	0.438	
		6 and 6iii	0.444	0.452	
Tibia	Bd	2–3a and 3b	0.363	0.278	
		2–3a and 6iii	0.139	0.141	
Calcaneum	C	2–3a and 3b	0.155	0.252	
		2–3a and 4–5b	0.056	0.142	*
		2–3a and 6	0.131	0.220	
		2–3a and 6iii	0.018	0.068	*
		3b and 6iii	0.122	0.099	
		6 and 6iii	0.172	0.139	
Astragalus	GLl	2–3a and 3b	0.112	0.117	
		2–3a and 6	0.030	0.031	*
		2–3a and 6iii	0.006	0.006	**
		3b and 6iii	0.051	0.051	*
Metacarpal	GLl	3b and 6iii	0.181	0.242	
		4–5b and 6iii	0.148	0.163	
	BFd	3b and 4–5b	0.300	0.300	
		4–5b and 6	0.470	0.469	
		4–5b and 6iii	0.056	0.043	*
Metatarsal	GLl	4–5b and 6	0.356	0.356	
	BFd	3b and 4–5b	0.318	0.356	

*Table 7.7 Results of Student t-tests carried out on cattle measurements between selected phases. Probability values marked ** indicate a highly significant difference (<1% probability that the difference is due to chance). Probability values marked with * indicate a highly significant difference (<5% probability that the difference is due to chance). Values showing no asterisk indicate no significant difference (>5% probability that the difference is due to chance).*

cranial elements in cows are the metapodials (see FIG. 7.2) – specifically the metacarpal, and from Flixborough we are fortunate in having a large dataset to study. Initial analysis shows that, in contrast to most of the other elements which show the largest mean values for Phase 2–3a (see above), the largest mean values for all breadth measurements taken on the metacarpal appear in Phase 4–5b (see TABLE 7.5). Bivariate plots (FIGS 7.41 and 7.42)

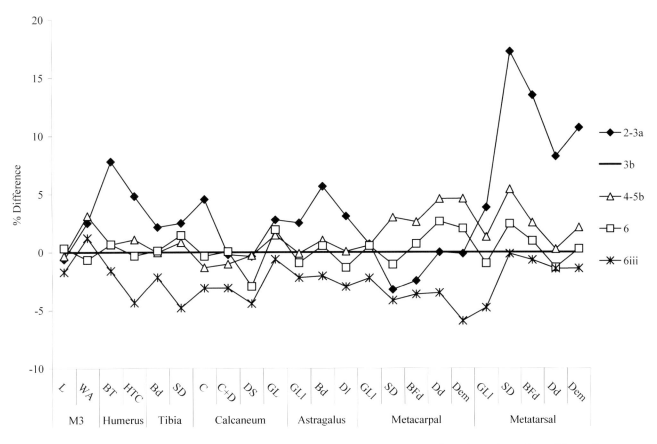

F*IG. 7.35 Percentage difference of various cattle bone measurement values from those from Phase 3b.*

show the distribution of values obtained for a range of length and breadth measurements for all phases combined. The patterns obtained make it very clear that several distinct groups are represented, but that the characteristics of each group are very different. When grouping all phases, it is apparent that the smaller group is a discrete entity, made up of individuals which, although varying greatly in length, do not significantly vary in breadth. The larger groups, however, appear far more diffuse and certainly less clustered, with a much broader range of breadth values represented.

How can this pattern be explained? At least two conclusions can be reached for such a pattern: that the groups represent sexual dimorphism in a single domestic cattle herd; and/or that there are two separate varieties of cattle at the site. The fact that a high degree of sexual dimorphism is present in cattle is no surprise, and the first hypothesis appears to be the most credible in terms of what is known about the conformation of the three different sexual groups (i.e. males, females and castrates).

Perhaps the most significant aspect here is the apparently diffuse nature of the group of larger individuals when compared with the smaller ones. It is very unlikely that these large animals all represent entire bulls used solely for breeding purposes, since there are far more than would be required. In a normal pastoral system based around meat production, a few males are

left entire in order to function as sires for the continuation of the breeding herd. Contemporaneous Irish law texts show widespread ownership of bulls even by those of low rank. The author of the *Críth Gablach* expects the lowest rank of *bóaire* to keep 7 cows and 1 bull, whilst the highest rank of *bóaire* has 20 cows, 6 oxen and 2 bulls (Kelly 1997, 48). However, in Ireland, these are proportions linked to a cattle husbandry regime focused primarily on dairying, which was probably not the case in Eastern England during the Anglo-Saxon period. Males surplus to these breeding requirements can be either killed immediately, or grown on. These animals are usually castrated, which makes them easier to handle (because they are less aggressive and less sexually active) and encourages increased muscle mass and prolonged development. The process of castration should be reflected in the skeleton in the form of more robust and longer-limbed individuals exhibiting greater variation.

The patterns which are present at Middle-Late Saxon Flixborough are, therefore, extremely significant in that they appear to indicate the presence of numerous small gracile cows, a more robust and longer limbed group of oxen (castrated males), and probably a few very robust and stocky bulls (entire males). Oxen were kept not only for their ability to increase the production of meat, but also for their use as traction animals. Animals used to pull ploughs or wagons were important sources of power,

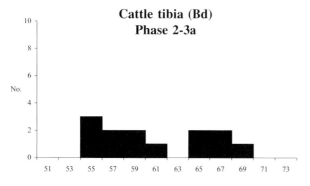

Cattle tibia (Bd)
Phase 2-3a

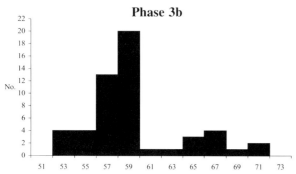

Phase 3b

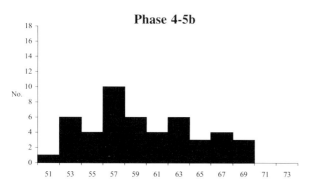

Phase 4-5b

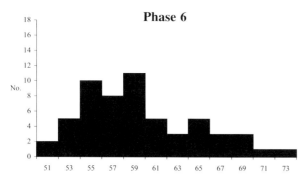

Phase 6

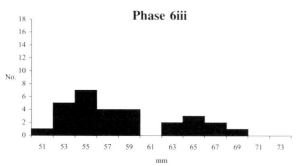

Phase 6iii

mm

Fig. 7.36 (left) Cattle tibia – distal breadth (Bd) measurements (by phase).

this function far outweighing their value in the diet. Since oxen used for traction would be kept alive well beyond their prime (in terms of efficient meat production), their presence at the site (along with breeding/dairy cows) corroborates the evidence for an emphasis on full adult and elderly animals in all periods as previously discussed.

When the data are considered by individual period, a slightly more complex picture emerges (Figs 7.43 and 7.44). For Phases 3b and 6, two very distinct groups are represented. However, although the distribution of the larger group in Phase 3b appears more diffuse than the smaller group in terms of breadth values, those from Phase 6 do not. The distribution for Phase 4–5b on the other hand appears far less discrete, with values for individual bones once again filling the gaps seen in the other periods. Perhaps one of the most interesting observations (seen also in the tibia measurements discussed previously) is the wider range of intermediate values seen in Phase 4–5b. If we assume that this indicates that more oxen are represented in this period, the fact that this period is the only time where elderly cattle outnumber all other age categories becomes extremely significant.

Simple values of length and breadth provide a good indication of changes in size but are not independent of it. In order to explore the variability of the shape of animals, indexes that are size-independent must therefore be used. Fig. 7.45 shows the distribution of metacarpal size index values for each phase, and the large, robust individuals occur above the index value of 34 on the *x*-axis in Phases 3b and 4–5b. In these periods there appears to be a continuous distribution of values which makes the separation of females and oxen difficult. However, in Phase 6 there is a more obvious separation of less robust and more robust animals, but no values beyond 34 on the *x*-axis. This perhaps indicates that those with index values between 30 and 34 are probably castrated oxen.

The fact that oxen should be present or even common at a high-status estate centre such as Flixborough should be no surprise. Their prime importance as draught animals (particularly used to pull the ploughshare) is reflected in the fact that (along with horses) they are one of the most common types of domestic animals mentioned in Anglo-Saxon charters and wills. A grant by Offa, King of Mercia, to the church of Worcester, of land at Westbury and Henbury, Gloucestershire (AD 793–796) mentions 7 oxen as part of tribute or food rent payable to the Royal estate, whilst an exchange between Ethelbert, King of Kent, and his thegn, Wulflaf (AD 858), of land at 'Wassingwell' and Mersham (*EHD* 93) allows Wulflaf to pasture four oxen with the King's oxen. The Old English lease of Beddington, Surrey, by Denewulf, bishop of

**Cattle tibia
Phase 2-3a**

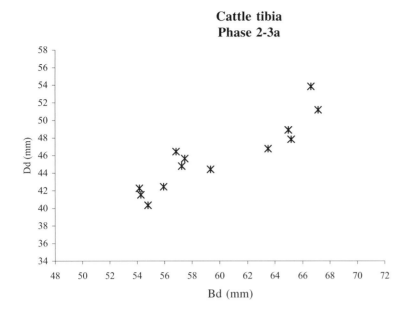

FIG. 7.37 Cattle tibia – distal breadth (Bd) and distal depth (Dd) measurements (by phase) (continued overleaf).

Phase 3b

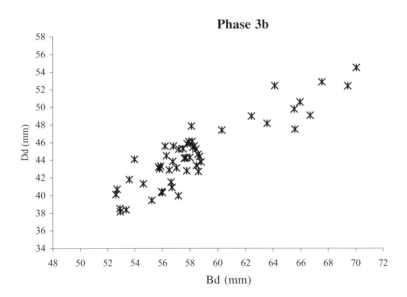

Phase 4-5b

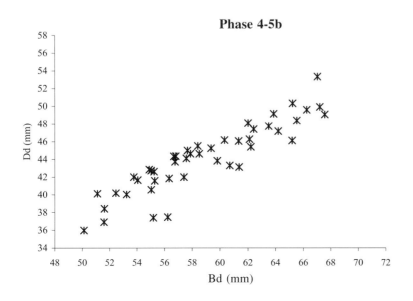

Phase 6   *Fig. 7.37 continued.*

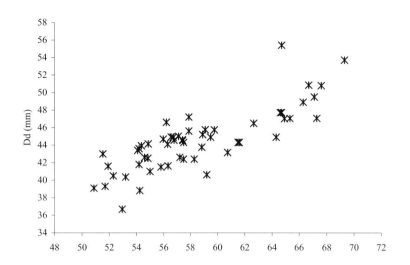

Phase 6iii

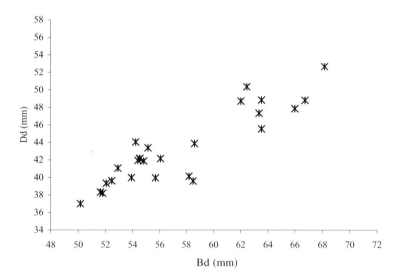

Winchester, to King Edward the Elder (AD 899–908) – of interest for its reference to havoc wrought by Viking raids – mentions 'cattle left after a severe winter', which included 9 oxen 114 pigs, 50 wethers, 110 full grown sheep, and pigs and sheep for herdsmen (20 of which are full grown) (*EHD* 101).

The Old English will of Bishop Ælfwold of Crediton (AD 997–1016) leaves a plough-team of oxen, as well as wild horses around his Ashburton estate in Devon (*EHD* 122), whilst that of Ælfric, Archbishop of Canterbury (AD 1002–1005) leaves 10 oxen (*EHD* 126). An Old English letter to King Edward the Elder explaining the history of an estate at Fonthill, Wiltshire (AD 899–924), mentions the theft of unattended oxen (*EHD* 102), whilst oxen also appear in an Old English record of establishment of free status (probably written in the second half of

the tenth century). In it, a serf's freedom is bought with eight oxen (*EHD* 147).

In one of the few surviving estate memoranda, a tract drawn up during the tenth or eleventh centuries, under the section entitled '*Concerning the Oxherd*', it states that... '*With his ealdorman's knowledge, the oxherd may pasture two or more oxen with the lord's herd on the common pasture – with that to earn shoes and gloves for himself. And his food-cow may go with the lord's oxen.*' (Swanton 1996, 29). Oxen even appear in literature. The ploughman in *Ælfric's Colloquy* states '*I go out at daybreak driving the oxen to the field, and yoke them to the plough... I have to fill the oxen bins with hay, and water them, and carry their muck outside.*' (Swanton 1996, 170). Anglo-Saxon place-names in England make numerous references to the all-important plough oxen,

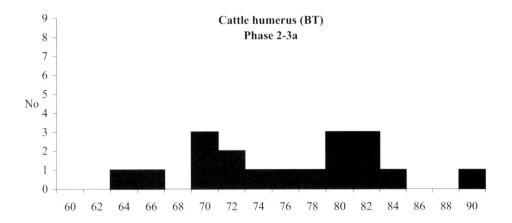

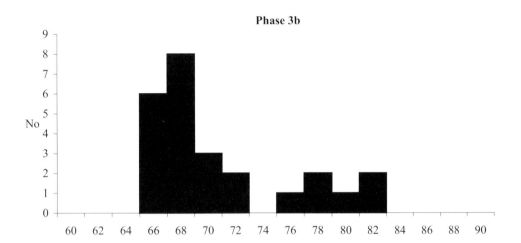

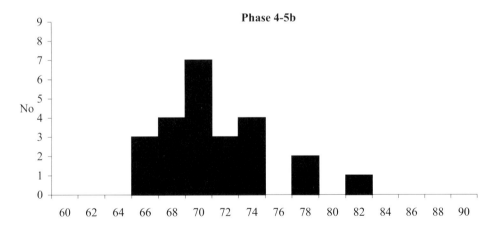

FIG. 7.38 Cattle humerus – distal breadth (BT) measurements (by phase) (continued overleaf).

e.g. Oxcombe, Oxenden, Oxenhall and Oxford, whilst the *Cotton Tiberius* calendar depicts four heavy oxen pulling a heavy plough at the beginning of the year (January). In the Frankish Law codes, the importance of cattle and oxen is also obvious, coming second only to pigs (and above horses, sheep, etc.) in the hierarchy of

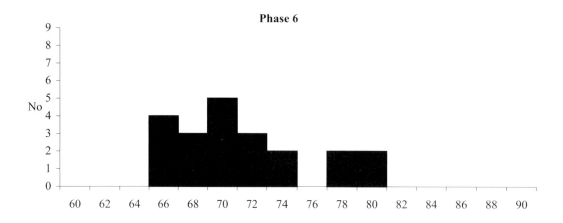

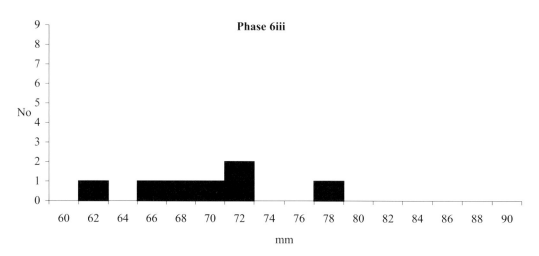

Fig. 7.38 continued.

importance of domestic animals as shown by the number of laws and amount of fines levied (Fischer Drew 1991, 49).

In terms of their management, the Irish law codes provide perhaps the most detailed insight into the management of oxen. According to these tracts, most castrated male cattle would be slaughtered in their first year. Some would be selected on the basis of their strength and docility as draught oxen – training probably started in their third year (Kelly 1997, 48). Trained oxen were certainly highly prized and, in a ninth-century gloss on *Bechbretha*, they are classed along with milch cows as 'noble dignitaries of livestock' (*CIH* iii 924.24 from Kelly, *op. cit.*). When fully grown they would be considerably larger than a milch cow – which is aptly illustrated by an old Irish legal passage on trees which indicates that more oak bark is needed to tan an oxhide than a cowhide (*CIH* I 202.20; 582.7 also from Kelly, *op. cit.*).

Evidence for the presence of 'improved' cattle

In terms of the domestic livestock, it is likely that the vast majority would have been procured locally or certainly from the broader region, most likely through the provision of food rents. However, biometrical analyses of the cattle bones from the site has provided some tantalising evidence for the possibility that, during the early-mid eighth century (Phase 2–3a), and even later, the cattle at Flixborough may have actually included individuals of a different variety or breed, possibly not of local origin (see also Chapter 10).

Fig. 7.46 shows calculated shoulder (withers) height values for a range of Saxon and Anglo-Scandinavian cattle remains from England (where data were available). In addition, Fig. 7.47 shows the comparison of astragalus length measurements for cattle from Flixborough and a number of contemporaneous sites in East Anglia and beyond.[2] What is striking about all these data is the fact that the values for all phases at Flixborough (with the exception of those for Phase 6iii) are some of the highest

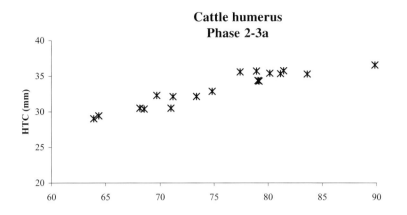

**Cattle humerus
Phase 2-3a**

FIG. 7.39 Cattle humerus – distal breadth (BT) and height of distal condyle (HTC) measurements (by phase).

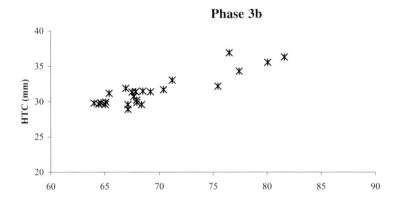

Phase 3b

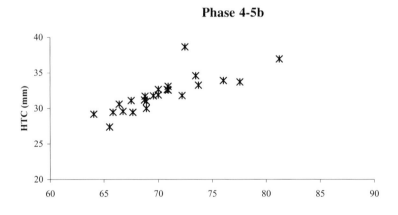

Phase 4-5b

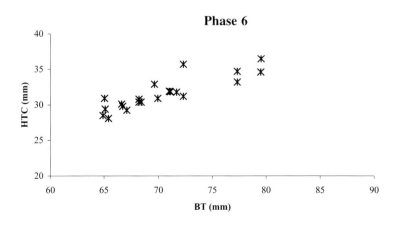

Phase 6

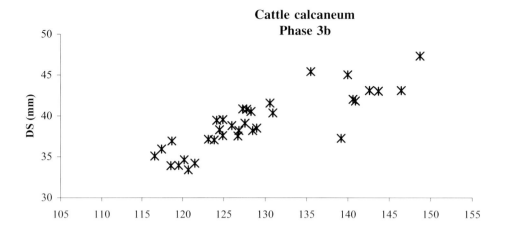

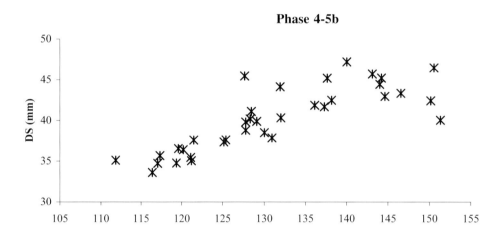

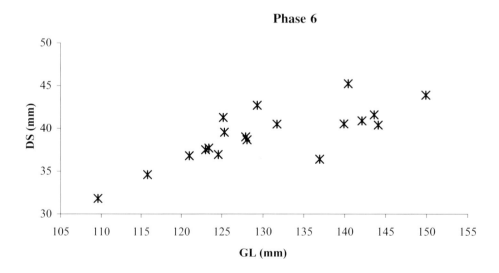

FIG. 7.40 *Cattle calcaneum – greatest length (GL) and depth of shaft (DS) measurements (by phase).*

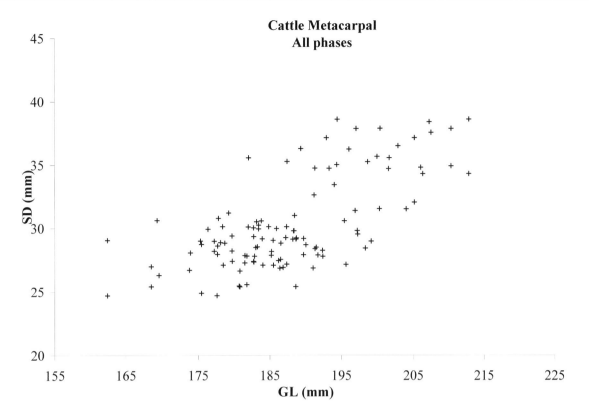

Fig. 7.41 Cattle metacarpal – greatest length (GL) and shaft diameter (SD) measurements (all phases).

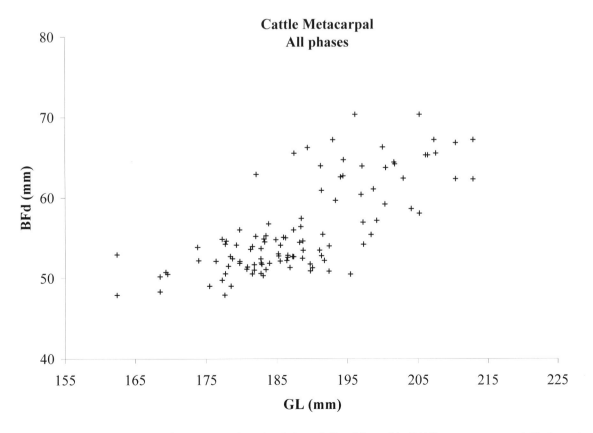

Fig. 7.42 Cattle metacarpal – greatest length (GL) and distal breadth (BFd) measurements (all phases).

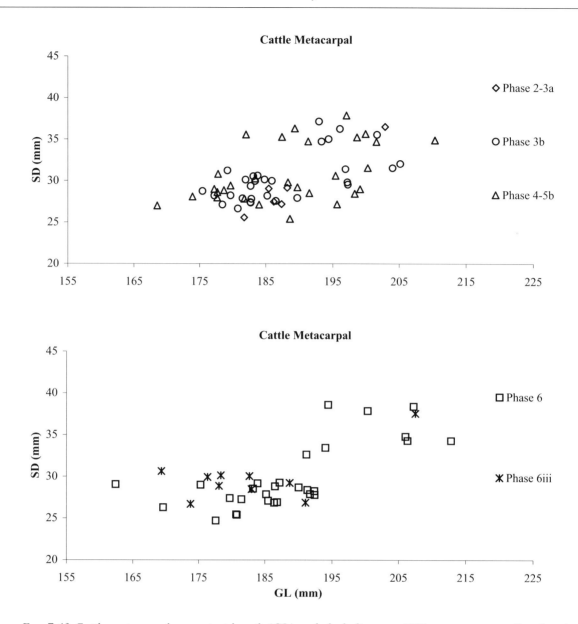

Fig. 7.43 Cattle metacarpal – greatest length (GL) and shaft diameter (SD) measurements (by phase).

recorded to date at any Saxon site in England and the near Continent; indeed those from Phase 2–3a at Flixborough are the highest of any site presented.

How can this observation be interpreted? The presence of unusually tall cattle could reflect differences in husbandry regimes between different site types (e.g. larger numbers of taller draught oxen or even large bulls present at selected sites such as Flixborough). There are, however, few reasons to suspect that there were relatively more oxen represented at Flixborough than at any other site. In fact although detailed biometrical analyses have explicitly shown the presence of oxen at Flixborough, the vast majority of remains are almost certainly from adult cows.

There is, therefore, a distinct possibility that these taller animals represent different varieties of cattle, i.e. animals that had been selectively bred for particular

characteristics. These may have been animals that were highly sought after, commanded high monetary or prestige value and, therefore, were more likely to have been transported long distances (see Chapters 9 & 10). McCormick (1987) noted that cattle bones from royal sites in Ireland tended to be larger than average, which he suggested might indicate competitive cattle breeding among the Irish aristocracy. He stated that '*large cattle require more food and are sometimes difficult to handle. They provide large carcases and may be regarded as status symbols by their owners.*' The size of cattle is also continually stressed in the early Irish literature (e.g. *TBC* LL 36.1323–6 from Kelly 1997).

Simple comparisons are not always easy to make. From within the region of Eastern and North Eastern England, there are a number of key assemblages of late Middle and

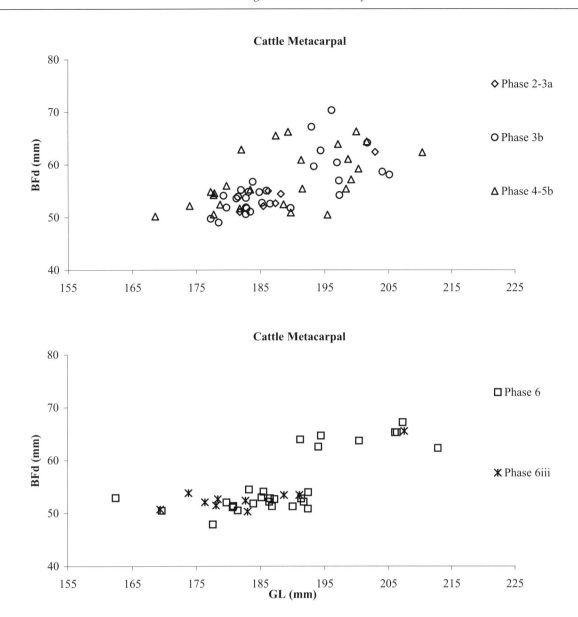

FIG. 7.44 *Cattle metacarpal – greatest length (GL) and distal breadth (BFd) measurements (by phase).*

Late Saxon date, all from what were emerging urban centres (e.g. York and Lincoln). As such, they may have been the foci of very different elements of society and activities that drew on resources very different from those at Flixborough. Nonetheless, these data show that, whatever the origin of these large cattle, they are primarily of Mid-Saxon date and few (if any) were present in the Mid-Saxon emporia or later Saxon/Anglo-Scandinavian markets of York or Lincoln.

Little or no information regarding differences in size, shape or even colour of cattle appears to be present in contemporaneous Anglo-Saxon laws, charters, wills or literature. Once again, we must turn to pictorial and written records from contemporary Irish society, which make clear that variations in colour, size, horn disposition, and hardiness were already established in the sixth to eighth

centuries (Kelly 1997). For example, legal references indicate seventh-eighth century Irish cattle included a range of colours, although most were black (e.g. eighth century law text *Bretha Nemed Toísech – CIH* vi 2216.7–8; cf. *CIH* iv 1299.10 from Kelly *op. cit.*). A very distinctive variety of white, red-eared cattle are mentioned in both mythological and more mundane law contexts, which Bergin (1946) suggests may actually be the same breed as the Chillingham cattle of Northumberland.

If the cattle from Flixborough do, indeed, represent a large variety/breed, they appear to have few parallels in the region, in the country or even on the continent. Those that come close are either from other *wic* sites (Hamwih, Ipswich and Dorestadt) or from another high-status estate centre (similar to Flixborough) in eastern England – Wicken Bonhunt (see also Chapter 10).

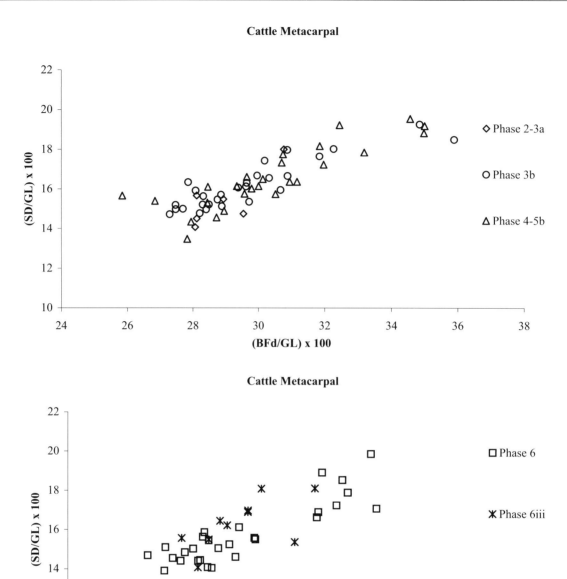

FIG. 7.45 *Cattle metacarpal size index plots (by phase).*

Sheep and the absence of wethers

In comparison with the data for cattle, biometrical evidence for sheep shows little or no change through time. Simple comparisons of mean values for a range of skeletal element measurements and reconstructed withers heights (FIG. 7.48) indicate a possible small size decrease by Phase 6iii, although this is only apparent for distal tibia breadth and metacarpal greatest length values. The

static nature of sheep size and shape through the major periods at Flixborough is more clearly seen in FIG. 7.49 which shows the percentage difference of the mean value for each measurement compared with that from Phase 3b. Unlike the pattern seen for cattle (see FIG. 7.35), where percentage difference values were often as much as 5–8%, those for sheep never exceed 4% and in most cases rarely exceed 2%. The distribution of measurement values also show similar patterns of distribution for all

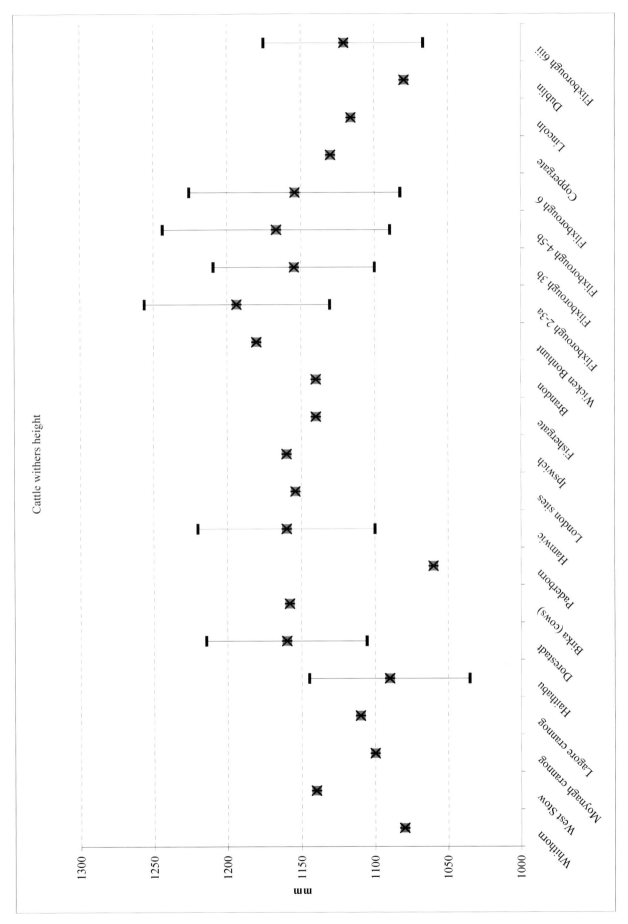

Cattle withers height

FIG. 7.46 *Mean cattle withers heights values from the various Flixborough phases and comparative sites from England and the Continent.*

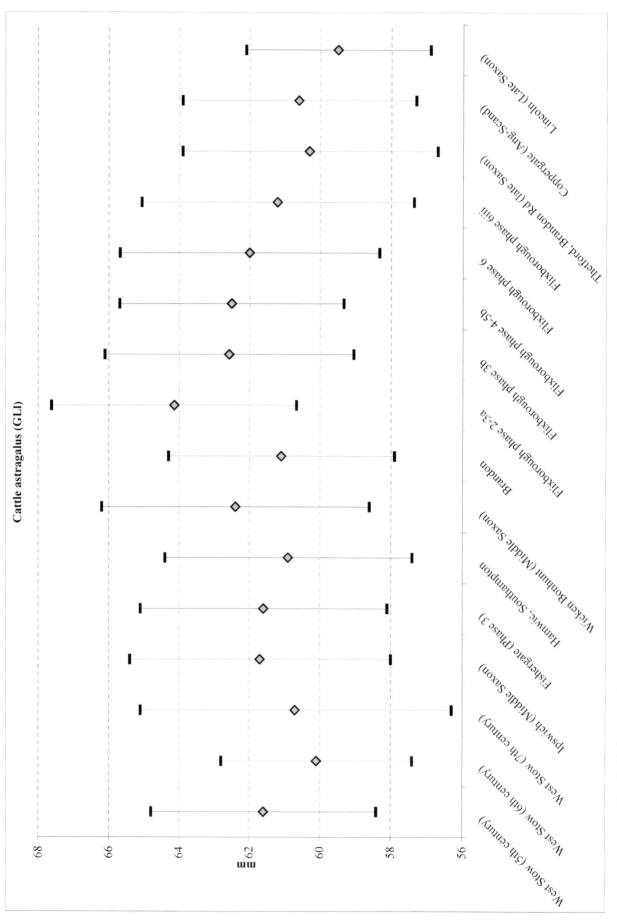

FIG. 7.47 *Mean cattle astragalus greatest length from the various Flixborough phases and comparative sites from England.*

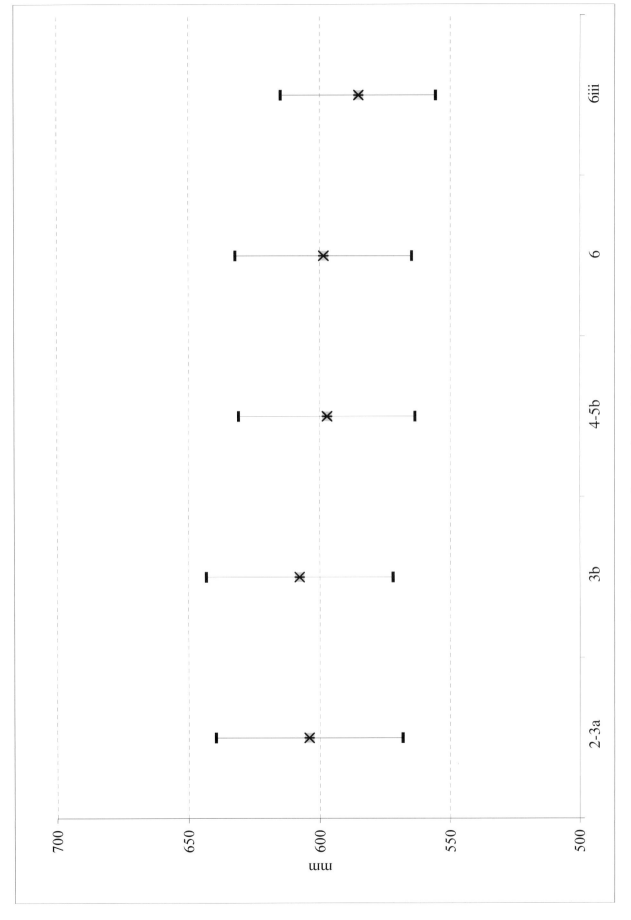

FIG. 7.48 *Reconstructed mean sheep withers height by phase.*

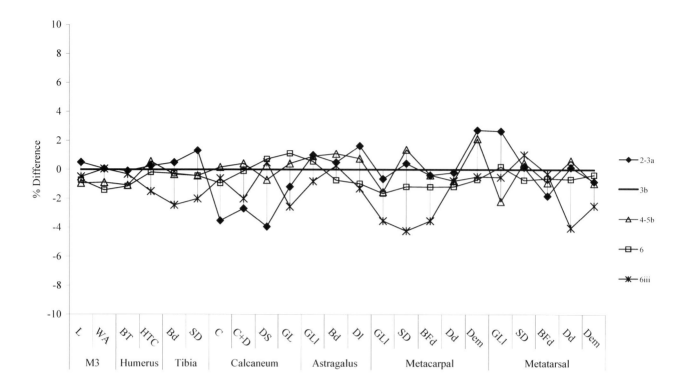

FIG. 7.49 Percentage difference of various sheep bone measurement values from those from Phase 3b.

phases. Unlike the trend seen for cattle, sheep distal tibia breadth measurement values show no bimodality in their distribution. Instead, a single homogeneous population is apparently represented for each phase.

However, bivariate plots for the large dataset of distal tibia measurements of breadth (BFd) and depth (Dd) show an interesting pattern for the ninth century (Phase 4–5b). Although in all periods the vast majority of values show a similar distribution, a group of outliers can be seen in Phase 4–5b (FIG. 7.50). These individuals appear to be a different shape from most of the animals from the ninth century, and also from those from other periods. Although values for breadth of the distal tibia are very similar, anterior-posterior depth values are lower. Such an apparently distinctive change in the conformation of part of the sheep population of the ninth century would be expected to be reflected by other elements of the skeleton. Interestingly, however, no such evidence can be observed in any other skeletal element.

A survey of the mean withers height for Anglo-Saxon sheep in the region and in England generally, appears to show that the Flixborough sheep were of similar height to the vast majority of others of broadly contemporaneous date, with only a few exceptions (FIG. 7.51). One interesting outlier is the value for the very small sheep at the high-status Mid-Saxon estate centre at Brandon, which has the lowest mean value for withers height from any in the survey. In contrast, the figures for sheep from the Continent (at both Haithabu and Dorestadt) – as for

the cattle from these sites – remain some of the largest yet reported.

However, unlike the data for cattle (see previous) and chickens (see further), there is no biometrical evidence for the presence of castrated individuals (wethers) at Flixborough. Scatterplots of size and shape indices for metapodials show little in the way of patterning into sexual groups.

Wethers do, however, figure prominently in Anglo-Saxon wills and charters and were obviously extremely important as wool producers. For example, a grant by Offa, King of Mercia, to the church of Worcester, of land at Westbury and Henbury, Gloucestershire (AD 793–796) included in it the tribute/food rent of 7 oxen, 6 wethers, 40 cheeses, 30 ambers of unground corn to the royal estate (*EHD* 78). The Old English lease of Beddington, Surrey, by Denewulf, Bishop of Winchester, to King Edward the elder (AD 899–908) mentions 50 wethers (*EHD* 101), and an estate memorandum of tenth-eleventh century date mentions the fleece of a bellwether. The Irish law texts, contain more specific detail and state that all male lambs (apart from those few selected to act as serving rams) were castrated after weaning (Kelly 1997, 69). In the *Pactus Legis Salicae* (one tract of the Salic laws of the Franks), four of the five laws concerning the theft of sheep are solely to do with wethers (see Fischer Drew 1991), and in fact mentions fines for stealing upwards of 40–60 wethers.

Given the historical evidence for the obvious

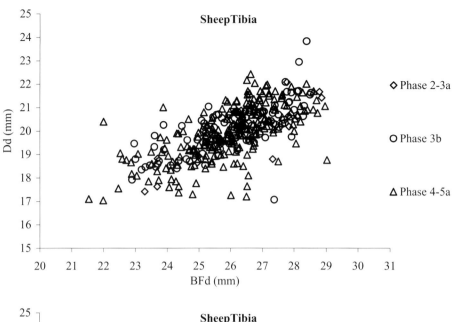

Fig. 7.50 *Sheep tibia – distal breadth (BFd) and distal depth (Dd) measurements (by phase).*

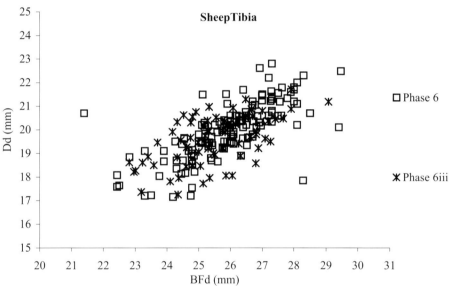

importance of wethers, it is likely that a significant proportion of the remains of sheep from Flixborough are indeed wethers.

Domestic fowl and the possible presence of capons

The vast quantity of chicken remains recovered from Flixborough attests to their obvious importance to the inhabitants of the site throughout all periods and, along with geese, their remains are commonly recovered from other sites of Anglo-Saxon date in England. They are rarely mentioned in Anglo-Saxon laws or wills, but were of obvious importance to the early Irish economy as they are frequently mentioned in law texts and portrayed in manuscripts (e.g. folio 67ʳ *Book of Kells*, where chickens feature more prominently than geese or ducks – Kelly 1997: 102). There is also mention of roosters and hens (along with domestic geese and ducks) in the *Pactus Legis Salicae* and their value is indicated by the fact that

the fine for stealing them is similar to that for sheep (i.e. 120 denarii or 3 solidi) (Fischer Drew 1991, 72).

The large assemblage of fowl bones from Flixborough has enabled the compilation of an extensive biometrical dataset that has provided an important opportunity to explore questions related to the exploitation of these birds. Transforming single measurements from the major long-bones into histograms produces bimodal distributions (e.g. for the tarsometatarsus, Fig. 7.52) suggesting the presence of two differently-sized populations of chickens throughout the represented phases.

Scatter plots of greatest length measurements against shaft circumference values for many of the elements again demonstrate the presence of two distinct groups, with, for some bones, a few points falling within the 'gap' between the groups (e.g. humerus – Fig. 7.53). This pattern does not vary significantly through time, and almost certainly reflects the differences in size between

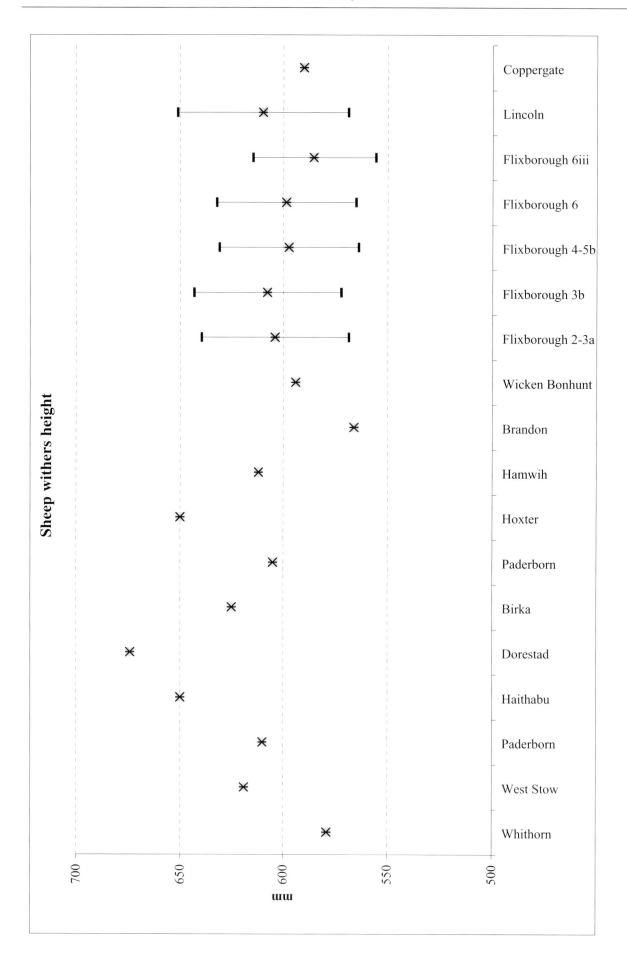

Fig. 7.51 Mean sheep withers heights values from the various Flixborough phases and comparative sites from England, Scotland and the Continent.

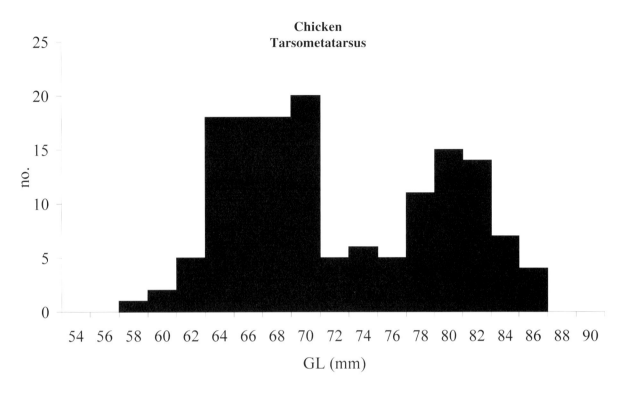

FIG. 7.52 Chicken tarsometatarsus greatest length (GL) measurements.

hens and cockerels, the smaller bones corresponding to the females and the larger to the males. As was the case for cattle (and to some degree for sheep), those values that do not fit the general pattern, i.e. those that are intermediate between large and small and those that represent the largest individuals), appear to be mainly from Phase 4–5b deposits. For most elements, proportions of males to females were roughly similar and little difference was discernible between phases.

A single element (the tarsometatarsus) can be used to specifically investigate the sex ratios in the assemblage, as well as perhaps being able to throw further light on the presence of capons (castrated cockerels). Tarsometatarsi are of importance because they provide another crucial indication for sex determination through the presence or absence of spurs on these bones. Although, much debate exists as to their interpretation (e.g. West 1982; 1985; Allison 1985; Sadler 1991), those bones with spurs or spur scars are, in general, interpreted as cockerels or capons, whilst it is suggested that those without represent females.

Measurements for tarsometatarsi were plotted according to one of three categories: those tarsometatarsi with spurs; those without; and those with spur 'scars' (see Appendix 4, TABLE A3). Histograms created using greatest length (GL) measurements (FIG. 7.54) show that most tarsometatarsi without spurs form a distinct group,

representing the smaller – presumably female – individuals. However, a small group of spur-less individuals is represented by some of the largest GL values obtained for Flixborough chickens. Those with spurs and spur scars represent exclusively larger (in fact taller) individuals, with little difference apparent in their range of values.

When greatest length values from tarsometatarsi are plotted against shaft diameter, a similar but somewhat more intriguing pattern emerges (FIG. 7.55). Once again the spur-less group are split between mostly shorter, less robust individuals, and a small group of taller, somewhat more gracile chickens, whilst the spurred bones and those with spur scars are all large, some being more robust and others more gracile. This would appear to be a slightly more complex picture than the simple interpretation of larger individuals as males and smaller ones as hens. This interpretation ignores a number of crucial points regarding the presence or absence of spurs or spur scars. Some hens, for example, can develop spurs, the lengths of which can vary considerably (Kozelka 1933). When present, they most often develop in older hens, but can sometimes be found on younger individuals (Allison 1985). In a normal population, it would be expected that these individuals would be of a similar size to other females, whether spurred or unspurred. Thus, the tarsometatarsi from Flixborough do not show any spurred

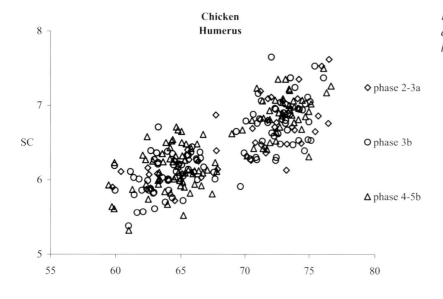

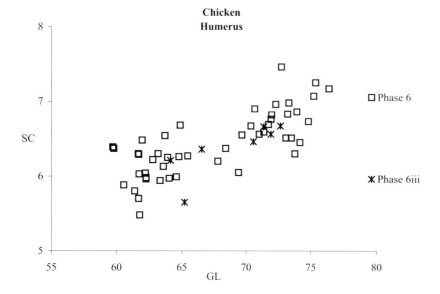

individuals amongst the group of smaller bones postulated to be female. Several of the smaller spurred bones do fall between the two distinct groups. These bones seem to represent more robust individuals than those of the 'female' group and it is more likely that these are males.

Figs 7.54 and 7.55 also include data for a number of unspurred tarsometatarsi that fall into the group representing larger individuals, and, in fact, two of the longest tarsometatarsi are without spurs. Bones with spur scars only are also found amongst this group, showing a range of sizes, with no specific concentration or pattern emerging. What do these bones represent – entire cockerels, young cockerels, or perhaps capons?

The development of the spur is a somewhat complicated procedure, but needs to be understood in order to interpret the possible sex composition of this assemblage. A fully developed spur is composed of a bony core (which

eventually fuses to the medial aspect of the tarsometatarsus), surrounded by a keratinous sheath. Gradual growth of the outer sheath begins soon after the chickens hatch (Allison 1985), but the bony core does not develop until the bird is approximately 7 months old, although this varies considerably between different birds and perhaps breeds (Louvier 1937). The bony core forms separately from the tarsometatarsus, growing towards the latter's shaft and the spur sheath tip. Research by Juhn (1952) has suggested that, once the spur core has reached a critical length, it stimulates the shaft of the bone to form bony swellings which represent the 'spur scar' or *socket primordium*. In due course, the core fuses to this point on the shaft. Fusion of the core to the shaft should only occur once the bird is skeletally mature (Juhn *op. cit*).

What implications, therefore, does the process of spur development have for the interpretation of bones with

Chicken Tarsometatarsus
Unspurred

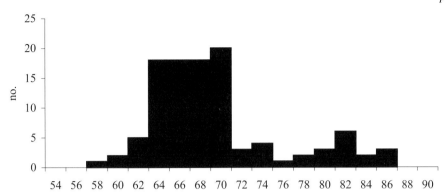

Chicken Tarsometatarsus
Spurred

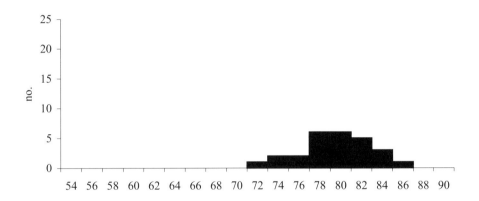

Chicken Tarsometatarsus
Spur scar

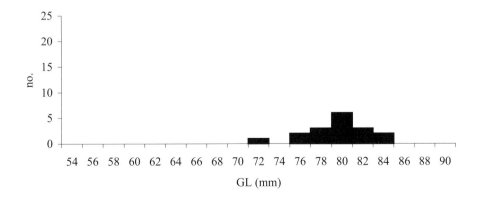

GL (mm)

spurs or spur scars? One significant point has been elucidated by Allison (1985) and Sadler (1991) – that spur development is such that there may be a period of time, prior to the bony core growing or inducing the formation of the socket primordium, when there is no evidence on the bone for its presence. The long-bone itself may be fused and appear, to all intents and purposes, fully developed. If spur development is slightly more advanced, then the spur scar may provide verification of the existence of a spur. The consequence of this is that the number of interpretative options for the large spurless tarsometatarsi increases – they could, for example,

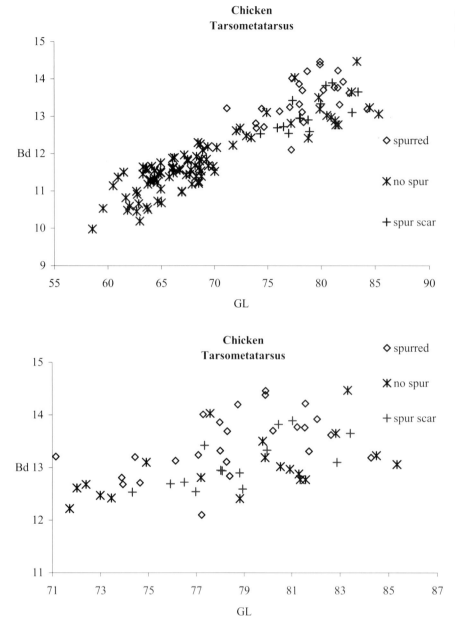

Fig. 7.55 Chicken tarsometatarsus distal breadth (Bd) and greatest length (GL).

indicate the presence of very large females of a different variety or breed. This seems unlikely, however, since there is no evidence from the Flixborough assemblage for a group of even larger males representing the cockerels of the same 'variety' as these putative unspurred large females.

On the basis of this evidence concerning spur development, the large spurless tarsometatarsi could represent males killed prior to the bony core of the spur reaching its optimum length for induction of the primordium socket. The line of epiphysial fusion at the proximal end of several of these bones (and a few of those with spur scars) was still visible, suggesting that, although these birds were adult, they were still young. Most of these larger bones (the unspurred and those with spur scars) also appear to be more gracile than those with spurs.

This perhaps again indicates younger individuals, killed before fusion of the spur core to the tarsometatarsus. A further possibility is that they represent males of a different variety who were spurless even when fully grown. There are some modern breeds where the males remain without spurs (Kozelka 1933).

And what of capons? Further complications occur when one considers the evidence for capons and how to recognise their presence within archaeological assemblages. Sadler (1991) argued that capons are probably under-represented in the biometrical records of archaeological material because they would be slaughtered before they were skeletally mature and unfused / immature bones are rarely measured. Quigley and Juhn (1951) established that spur cores of capons grow faster than those of cockerels. If fusion of the core is determined by its length rather than by the age of the bird (Juhn 1952), then those of capons would reach this critical length at an earlier age than cockerels, and their spurs would fuse to the shaft earlier (West 1985). Work undertaken by Hutt (1929) concluded that the major limb bones of capons were longer than those of cockerels. These factors and the additional information that caponisation delays epiphysial fusion led West (*ibid.*) to suggest that one would expect capons to be represented by long tarsometatarsi with spurs, whilst shorter tarsometatarsi with spur scars were probably from entire males.

Other workers (Masui and Hashimoto 1927; Landauer 1937), however, found that the skeletons of capons showed little size variation when compared with those of cockerels. They felt that the difference in size between cockerels and capons produced by Hutt's experiments were the result of his use of various types of Leghorns (a modern breed of chicken) from a number of different sources. On this basis, differentiating between capons and cockerels by size within archaeological material would be extremely difficult.

This conflicting evidence from modern experiments therefore makes the larger tarsometatarsi from Flixborough difficult to interpret. T-tests on the Flixborough biometrical data show slight (statistically insignificant) differences between spurred and spur scarred bones, whilst significant statistical differences were found between the spurred and unspurred bones. A number of different groups seem to be represented; these could include males killed at different ages and perhaps also capons. On the basis of the, at times, contradictory nature of all this evidence, it is difficult to be certain which group of bones is likely to represent capons. So what is the likelihood of capons being present within the Flixborough assemblage?

Cockerels were castrated because the resulting bird grew larger and the quality of the meat produced was better. Castration generally creates more docile birds, which are much less active and lack the desire to fight and behave in a territorial manner. The meat produced from entire cockerels gets tougher and rather 'stringy' with age, whilst caponised males accumulate more body fat (Jacob and Mather 2000). Although the first records in England of caponisation do not occur prior to the medieval period (Allison 1985), ancient authors like Aristotle (Barnes 1984) describe the practice. However, it is unclear from Roman authors, e.g. Columella and Varro, whether the birds were actually castrated (Forster and Heffner 1954; Hooper and Ash 1935). One recommendation involved using a hot iron to burn their spurs, which obviously did not caponize the birds, but presumably stopped fighting amongst cockerels. Most important in relation to the Flixborough assemblage, contemporaneous early Irish sources apparently make several references to capons – termed *gaillín* or *gaillén* (Kelly 1997, 102). Medieval documents and recipes mention capons and certainly, by the seventeenth century,

techniques of caponisation were well known (Lind 1963); Gervase Markham (1614) suggested that the process was easy and commonly undertaken. It was definitely an acquired skill as the testes of the cockerel are internal and have to be removed surgically. Open wounds are prone to infection. Additionally, care has to be taken not to damage the large blood vessels located between the two testes (Jacob and Mather 2000). Later, in the post-medieval period, caponisation was considered to be 'most barbarous and consequently frequently fatal character' (Tegetmeier 1867, 94).

Despite the fairly difficult nature of the operation, it does seem likely that true capons were present during the Saxon period. The effects and benefits of castration were understood, evinced by the more numerous contemporaneous historical references to wethers and oxen, and some zooarchaeological evidence for oxen (see biometrical and age at death evidence for cattle outlined above).

Geese: wild or domestic?

Goose remains are frequently recovered from British medieval archaeological sites, being particularly common in Anglo-Saxon assemblages. The corpus from Flixborough is no exception, with a total of 4557 identifiable fragments being recovered in total from the Saxon phases. These remains are likely to be individuals of one of six wild species found in the British Isles today (and almost certainly in the past): these are the grey geese – i.e. greylag (*Anser anser*), bean (*A. fabalis*), pink-footed (*A. brachyrynchus*) and white-fronted (*A. albifrons*) goose, and the black geese – i.e. barnacle (*Branta leucopsis*) and brent (*B. bernicla*) goose. In addition to wild geese, the numerous remains of domestic geese are also expected to be present.

Our current ability to identify the skeletal elements of, for example, ducks and geese to species on the basis of morphological and biometrical criteria is extremely problematic, severely limiting the interpretative potential of such a large dataset. The accurate identification of wild or domestic geese has important implications for the interpretation of economic activities at the site – for example, the presence of wild species indicates wild-fowling, and the types of species present may also provide information about the resources and environments being utilised, as habitat preferences vary between species (see Chapter 8). The presence of domestic geese indicates animal husbandry – a labour-intensive activity, but with obvious rewards (e.g. meat, eggs and feathers).

In reality, identification of most goose remains on the basis of morphological and biometrical criteria is not possible, since there are very few widely accepted distinguishing morphological features (Bacher 1967) and biometric measurements (Hutton-MacDonald *et al.* 1993) indicate a size-overlap between genera (*Branta* and *Anser*), species, and even sex.

Biometrical analysis of the goose remains from

Flixborough illustrates the point very well. Figs 7.56 and 7.57 show bivariate plots based on measurement values from goose humeri. It is more than obvious that there is a very wide and continuous range of data-points, with no evidence of distinct groups. We can thus only make general and rather speculative assumptions about what these data represent, for example:

– that there are probably large grey geese (probably the greylag, *Anser anser*) in the assemblage, the largest of which are probably domestic individuals;
– that the smallest geese are black geese (probably brent geese, *Branta bernicla*);
– that the vast proportion of datapoints towards the bottom of the distribution are probably barnacle geese (*Branta leucopsis*); and
– that those in the mid ranges could be smaller wild grey geese species.

Definitive identification by other means is, therefore, required; the recent development and application of biomolecular techniques to archaeological remains can now provide a powerful tool in addressing this problem.

In a previous study (Barnes 1998), modern and aDNA studies of geese resulted in the successful identification of a barnacle goose from the Romano-British (first century AD) site at Ulrome, East Yorkshire. In the same study, the discovery of a unique so-called 'domestic' sequence proved especially important, since it allowed for the first time the distinct possibility to explore the real (not implied) significance of goose domestication, husbandry and wildfowling strategies on any site with good aDNA preservation.

Barnes (*op. cit.*) studied several goose bones from two sites in Lincolnshire: Vicar's Court – a post-medieval garderobe deposit from Lincoln, and Flixborough – using DNA from the mitochondrial control region. Three domestic geese sequences were identified at Vicar's Court, whilst at Flixborough, two domestic geese and two pink-footed geese were identified. These results represented the first definitive biomolecular identifications of domestic and pink-footed geese in the archaeological record. The initial results from Flixborough highlighted the unreliability of biometrical analyses, since the measurements for the individuals of both species identified were shown to overlap considerably. The presence of both wild and domestic geese at Flixborough also confirmed that two very different activities (wildfowling and animal husbandry) took place in respect of geese.

Using the methodologies that had been developed in

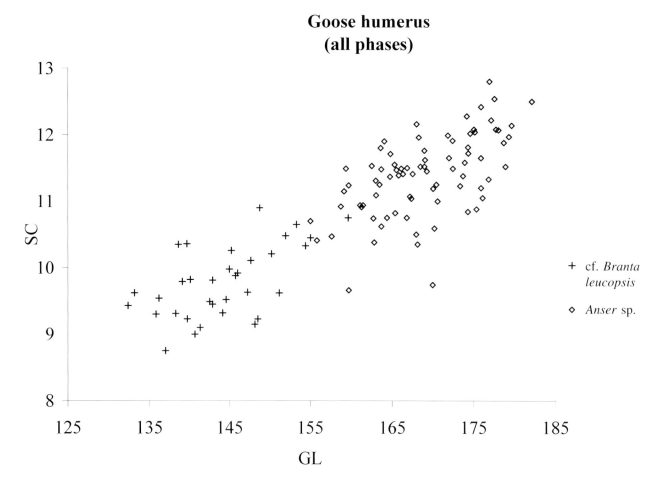

Goose humerus
(all phases)

Fig. 7.56 Greatest length (GL) and shaft diameter (SC) measurements of Anser *and* Branta *sp humeri. (all phases).*

the initial study, a much larger sample from Flixborough was examined in an attempt to systematically:

– identify the range of wild geese species present in the Flixborough assemblage
– establish the relative frequency of each wild species
– establish the relative proportions of domestic and wild individuals
– establish if different varieties of domestic geese were present

From the 323 archaeological goose humeri that were studied from Flixborough, 55 yielded positive results for the presence of amplifiable DNA (see Haynes 2001, table 4).

In addition to the identifications made in the initial study by Barnes (*op. cit.*), we have since confirmed the presence of an additional species (barnacle goose, *Branta leucopsis*) at Flixborough from two bone fragments. However, most of the identifications that were made were of domestic goose (22). A large number of sequences (15) appeared to carry two sequences (co-amplification) and these bones are also probably from domestic geese, but this could not be confirmed without further detailed analysis. A number of samples (11) failed to give useful sequence data.

Of the domestic sequences that were identified, there were two main genotypes, referred to as type 1 and 2. The majority (14) of the domestic geese were identical to type 1; five were identical to type 2. Three novel sequences were identified which were most similar to type 1, each differing from this reference at 1 position (see Haynes 2001, table 5).

The results show that both wild and domestic geese were definitively identified from the assemblage at Flixborough. If the aDNA sequences are representative of the overall, assemblage, then the vast majority of the geese consumed at Flixborough were domestic. Only two wild species of geese have been identified (barnacle and pink-footed) and they occurred in equal proportions (although sample numbers were small). The proportions of wild to domestic geese (1:6) suggest that domestic geese were of most economical importance to the inhabitants of the site. However, too few sequences were obtained to allow a more detailed evaluation of the apparent change in the ratio of wild to domestic birds previously noted during the ninth century (Phase 4–5b).

The combination of biometric and biomolecular data from the assemblage has also highlighted a wide size range for domestic geese (Figs 7.58 & 7.59). In terms of their mtDNA, the modern domestic breeds that we examined were identical but for one nucleotide position (1808), and this position divided the breeds into two

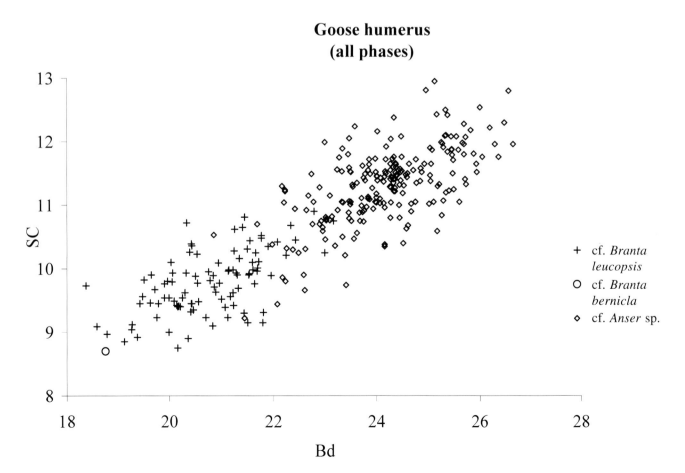

Fig. 7.57 Distal breadth (Bd) and shaft diameter (SC) measurements of Anser *and* Branta *sp. (all phases).*

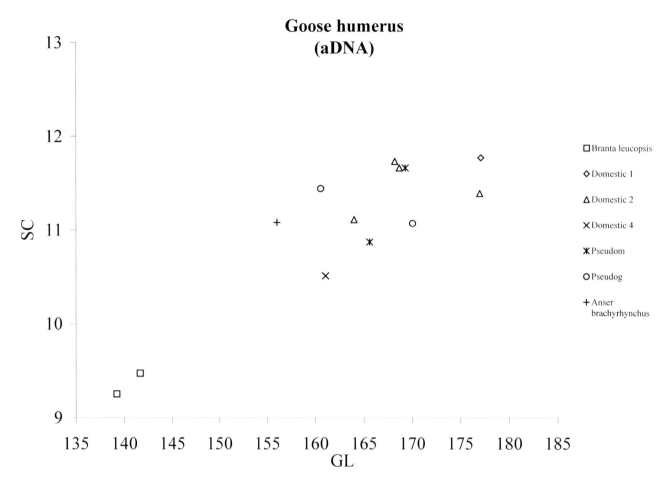

FIG. 7.58 *Goose aDNA identifications.*

groups (types 1 and 2). It is interesting to note that these two predominant genotypes are identical to the two common sequences that were observed in the Flixborough archaeological material. The presence of these 2 sequences at Flixborough may suggest the presence of two different domestic varieties at Middle–Late Saxon Flixborough. Type 1 and 2 genotypes correspond to representatives of the 2 breeds (Toulouse – type 1; Embden – type 2) described as 'monopolizing standards until recent times' and which were supposedly mentioned in the first book of standards (Hawksworth 1982, 328).

Although the presence of different varieties of any domestic animal on archaeological sites is practically impossible to prove using standard zooarchaeological techniques, the results from Flixborough tentatively suggest that DNA may be helpful in addressing such questions. However, further work on modern material, possibly with faster-evolving segments of DNA may shed further light on this issue.

Combined biomolecular and biometrical analysis of the Flixborough geese has provided a significant advance in our interpretation of Anglo-Saxon goose exploitation. It has for the first time definitively identified several species of wild geese, successfully separated some wild and domestic individuals, and tentatively indicated that at least two distinct varieties/breeds of domestic geese were already in existence at least 1200 years ago.

7.6 The use of bird eggs

Eggshell fragments were retrieved from the >4mm fraction of the sieved residues only. Fragments were recorded from 12% of the investigated samples and were most commonly recovered from samples representing post-hole fills and dump deposits. This amounted to 78 contexts, with 44% (34) of these deposits being dated to Phase 4–5b. In the absence of scanning electron microscopy, it was not possible to distinguish easily between the shell of eggs of different birds, although there did appear to be categories of fragments showing different shell thickness. Using some comparative material from the Environmental Archaeology Unit reference collection, the eggshell assemblage could be crudely divided into two broad categories: 1) 'thick' (assumed to be mostly from goose-sized eggs) and 2) 'thin' (assumed to be primarily from chicken-sized eggs). On the basis of this crude classification (simply counting fragments of shell), it would appear that most of the shell recovered from Flixborough probably

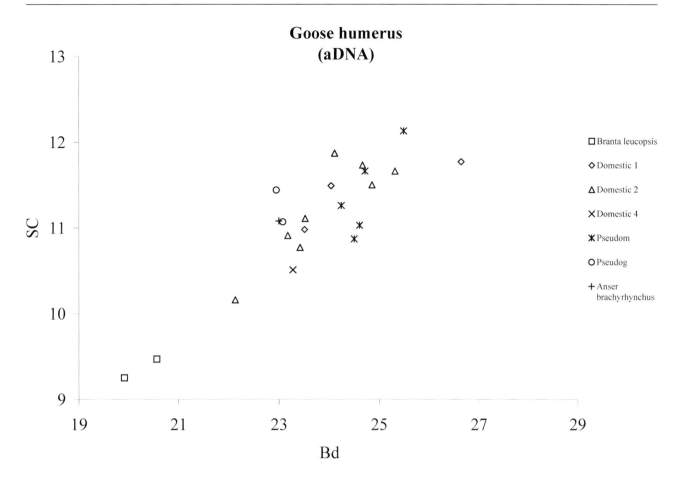

FIG. 7.59 *Goose aDNA identifications.*

represents chickens, with a smaller proportion being from domestic geese. This is not surprising, given that geese have a restricted laying period, traditionally from the beginning of February for 2 to 3 months and produce less than a quarter of the number of eggs in a year that chickens do. The possibility that eggshell fragments from wild geese or, indeed, from other bird species (e.g. duck) are also present cannot be ruled out.

Hens' eggs (and those of other wild birds) are frequently mentioned in the early Irish texts and were obviously important in early Irish diet where they are described as 'pearls of the household' (Jackson 1990, *Aislinge*, 39.1203–4).

7.7 Aspects of husbandry as indicated by non-metrical traits and pathology

In an assemblage of animal bones as large as that recovered from Flixborough, the presence of certain congenital traits and recognisable pathological conditions noted in the teeth and bones of some of the domestic species can provide important additional evidence regarding aspects of these animals' development and health. These kinds of data can help us draw useful

conclusions about aspects of husbandry in the past.

Mandibular non-metric traits

The specific non-metric traits recorded for the Flixborough assemblage included i) the presence (and location) of premolar foramina (see Dobney *et al.* 1996, 34 and plate 6b), ii) abnormalities of the mental foramen (see PLATE 7.3; *ibid.,* 34 and plate 6a), iii) absence of the lower second premolar and iv) absence (or reduction) of the hypoconulid on the lower third molar. The frequency of these traits was obtained by calculating the number of cases as a percentage of the total number of mandibles on which the trait could possibly have been noted (using the diagnostic zones present on each fragment).

FIG. 7.60 (TABLE 7.8) shows the frequency of the main mandibular non-metric traits listed above for cattle. In this case, the prevalence of the premolar foramen, absent P2s, and M3 hypoconulids was mostly less than 5% in all phases at Flixborough. However, it is worth noting that the highest frequency of absent premolar foramen was during Phase 4–5b (4.2%).

The absence of P2s and M3 hypoconulids has been recorded in material from many sites. For the Flixborough material overall, absent P2s were noted on 2.8% of the

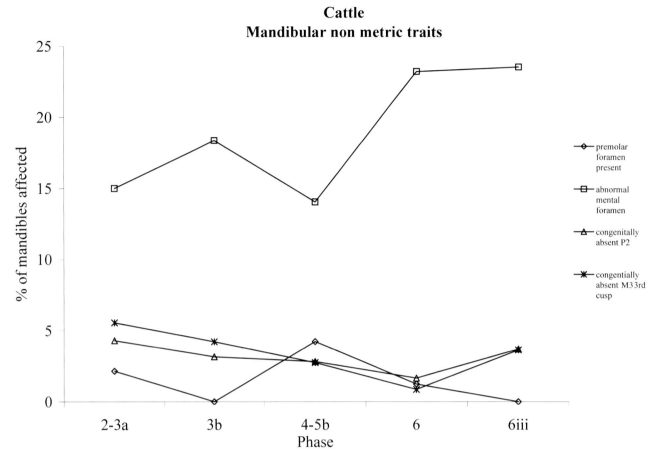

Fig. 7.60 Prevalence of selected cattle mandibular non-metrical traits.

	Premolar foramen		Abnormal mental foramen		Congenitally absent P2		Absent M3 hypocunulid	
Phase	*no*	*affected*	*no*	*affected*	*no*	*affected*	*no*	*affected*
2–3a	93	2	60	9	93	4	90	5
3b	317	0	256	47	317	10	166	7
4–5b	142	6	114	16	142	4	146	4
6	242	3	181	42	242	4	233	2
6iii	27	0	17	4	27	1	55	2
Total	821	11	628	118	821	23	690	20

Table 7.8 Cattle non-metrical traits.

mandibles. This is quite a low figure when compared with Anglo-Scandinavian Coppergate, York (where a prevalence of 6.8% was noted), and with Hamwih (where the frequency was recorded as 10.9%). It was particularly low in comparison with the very high frequency of 27% of mandibles affected reported at Haithabu. It is, however, very similar to the value (2%) observed at late Saxon Lincoln, a geographically much closer site. In addition, the frequency of reduced/absent hypoconulids at Lincoln was also very similar to that recorded from Flixborough (3% and 2.9% respectively).

In contrast to the figures for the premolar foramen, reduced hypoconulid of the M3, and absent P2, the frequency of mandibles with an abnormal mental foramen was considerably higher (between 14 and 25%) in all phases, and appeared to vary considerably between periods. The lowest frequency occurred during Phase 4–5b, followed by an obvious increase (of more than 9%) in frequency in Phase 6.

For sheep (Fig. 7.61, Table 7.9), the frequency of congenitally absent P2s was very low (less than 2% in phases. At Hamwih, a slightly higher figure of nearly 3%

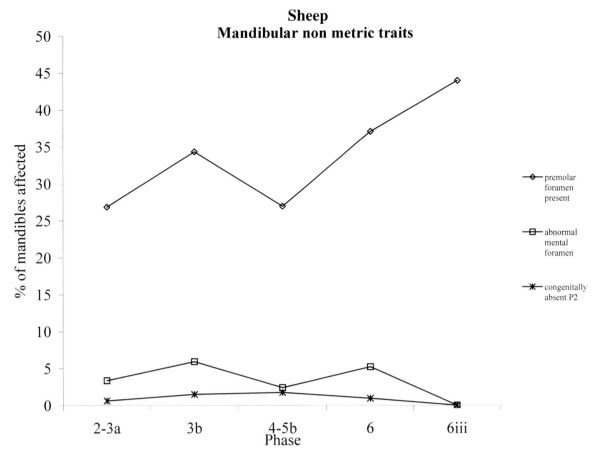

FIG. 7.61 Prevalence of selected sheep mandibular non-metrical traits.

Phase	Premolar foramen		Abnormal mental foramen		Congenitally absent P2	
	no	*affected*	*no*	*affected*	*no*	*affected*
2–3a	160	43	119	4	160	1
3b	335	115	237	14	335	5
4–5b	345	93	251	6	345	6
6	321	119	231	12	321	3
6iii	66	29	49	0	66	0
Total	1227	399	887	36	1227	15

Table 7.9 Sheep non-metrical traits.

is quoted, and at Coppergate the overall frequency was even higher at nearly 4%. In contrast to the cattle mandibles, abnormal mental foramina were relatively rare (4% overall) and premolar foramina prevalent (nearly 33% overall) in the sheep mandibles. The differences in frequencies of premolar foramina between phases appear quite marked, and follow almost exactly the same trend to that seen for the frequency of cattle abnormal mental foramen. Thus, once again, Phase 4–5b shows one of the lowest frequencies of this non-metrical trait, followed by a rise in frequency (10%) in Phase 6.

Oral pathology

The frequency of some commonly occurring pathological conditions of the jaw and teeth (namely dental calculus and periodontal disease) also produced some interesting patterns in the Flixborough dataset.

In cattle, periodontal disease (the ante-mortem loss of bone around the tooth roots) was observed in less than 4% of the recorded mandible fragments in any phase with variations between phases being subtle but not significant. The frequency of dental calculus (see Plate 7.4), on the other hand, was much more variable between

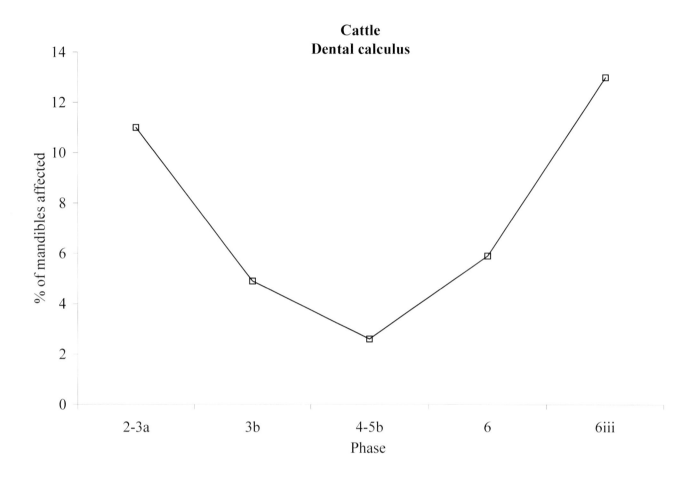

FIG. 7.62 Prevalence of dental calculus in cattle.

Phase	no. mands with teeth	no. with calculus	% affected
2–3a	118	13	11.0
3b	409	20	4.9
4–5b	151	4	2.6
6	323	19	5.9
6iii	23	3	13.0
Total	1024	59	5.8

Table 7.10 Cattle dental calculus.

phases. Phase 4–5b appears to have the lowest frequency, decreasing from 11% in Phase 2–3a to 2.6 % in Phase 4–5b, before rising again to 13% in Phase 6iii (FIG. 7.62 & TABLE 7.10).

In sheep, the frequency of calculus was quite low (2–6.5%) and the trends between phases were also different from those of cattle (FIG. 7.63 & TABLE 7.11). Periodontal disease was observed in around 4% of the mandibles until Phase 6, where it rose slightly to 6%, and then fell to 1.4% in Phase 6iii. However, these frequencies are quite high when compared with the single cases recorded at Hamwih and Coppergate.

Joint arthropathy – 'penning elbow'

Pathological changes associated with joints were relatively rare in the domestic animal assemblage from Flixborough. However, arthropathies of the proximal radius and distal humerus of sheep were quite common. These were characterised by the formation of bone spurs on the lateral side of the distal humerus (see PLATE 7.5) and proximal radius (PLATE 7.6) which, in advanced cases, formed a bridge between the two bones, limiting the range of motion of the elbow joint. In some cases, the area between the radius and ulna was also involved and the ulna became fused to the radius at its proximal end.

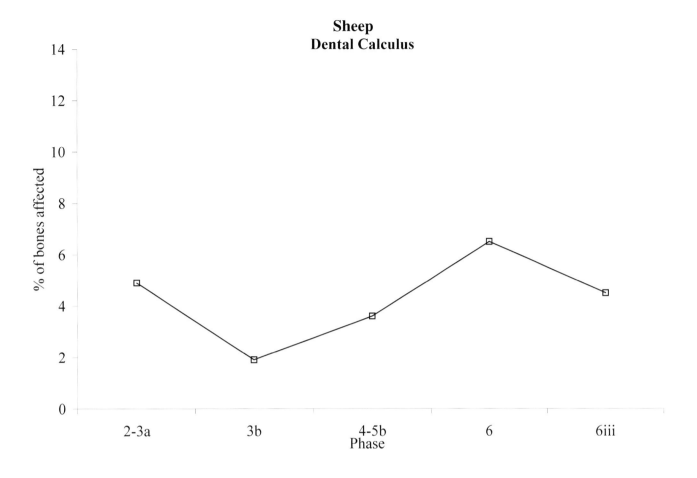

FIG. 7.63 *Prevalence of dental calculus in sheep.*

Phase	no. mands with teeth	no. with calculus	% affected
2–3a	142	8	5.6
3b	322	6	1.9
4–5b	360	14	3.9
6	321	22	6.9
6iii	67	3	4.5
Total	1212	53	4.4

Table 7.11 Sheep dental calculus.

This pathology has in the past been commonly termed 'penning elbow', and has been interpreted as damage caused by trauma (the result of either dislocation, sprain or an external blow) to the elbow joint during rough handling or confinement or penning of the animals. However, these specific causal factors are somewhat speculative and before a definitive aetiology for this condition can be identified, comparative studies on living populations need to be undertaken.

Although no cases of complete joint fusion were noted at Flixborough, ten (of the 57 cases) of bone spurs on the radius or humerus were recorded as 'extensive', and in three cases the involvement of the ulna was also described as 'extensive'. The remaining examples were either recorded as being 'slight' and 'moderate' in terms of their osteophytic bone growth.

The frequency of cases of 'penning elbow' through the phases produced an extremely interesting pattern (FIG. 7.64 & TABLE 7.12). It increased from 2.9% in Phase 2–3a to a maximum of 10.1% in Phase 4–5b, before decreasing again to 2.8% in Phase 6iii. A total of thirteen cases were noted from Anglo-Scandinavian Coppergate, whilst at Hamwih the condition was noted as the most prevalent sheep pathology. However, the frequency of

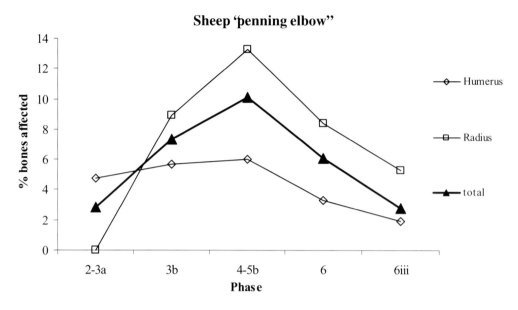

FIG. 7.64 Prevalence of "penning elbow" arthropathy in sheep.

humerus	phase	no overall	no with pen	% affected
	2–3a	21	1	4.8
	3b	53	3	5.7
	4–5b	149	9	6.0
	6	90	3	3.3
	6iii	53	1	1.9
	Total	366	17	4.6

radius	phase	no overall	no with pen	% affected
	2–3a	14	0	0.0
	3b	56	5	8.9
	4–5b	188	25	13.3
	6	107	9	8.4
	6iii	19	1	5.3
	Total	384	40	10.4

Table 7.12 'Penning elbow' arthropathy in sheep.

'penning elbow' at both these sites was not calculated, so direct comparisons with the data from Flixborough cannot be made.

An anomalous pathology of cattle calcanei

A possible pathology was noted on many of the cattle calcanei from the Flixborough assemblage. This condition was observed as an area of periosteal new bone growth on the medial aspect of the tuber calcis, above the sustentaculum, where the deep flexor tendon lies against the bone. The extent and thickness of this area of new bone varied considerably, but it almost always covered the posterior-distal quarter of the medial side of the tuber calcis (in more severe cases extending beyond the posterior edge). The bone was always well organised, with a smooth surface, and the proportion of calcanei affected was always over 10% in all phases, peaking at 34% in Phase 3b. Few other examples of this condition have been recognised from other sites, although a condition was noted on adult cattle calcanei from Haithbu which, from the limited description given, may be similar to that observed at Flixborough. Although it is possible that this condition could be tentatively linked to physical activity/stress, further observations on archaeological and modern comparative material is needed before its aetiology can be confirmed.

Evidence of physiological stress in the Flixborough pigs

Linear enamel hypoplasia (LEH) is a deficiency in (or in some cases a complete absence of) enamel thickness occurring during tooth crown formation. It is related to developmental stress, and is typically visible on a tooth's surface as one or more grooves or lines (see PLATE 7.7). A methodology for recording LEH on archaeological pig molars from the lower jaw has previously been published (Dobney and Ervynck 1998), along with a model for interpreting the chronological patterning observed in five archaeological assemblages of pigs from Belgium and Britain (Dobney and Ervynck 2000) and possible economic and environmental reasons for changes in the frequency of LEH between these assemblages (Ervynck and Dobney 1999).

Amongst the many pig remains at Flixborough was a large collection of mandibles (691) available for the analysis of LEH. Although a detailed account of LEH from the Flixborough pigs has already been published (Dobney *et al.* 2002), the following provides a brief summary of the results and interpretation of the data.

The chronology of linear enamel hypoplasia

The distributions of LEH on molar tooth crowns at Flixborough show peaks at the same heights as those observed in the material from the five sites previously studied (FIG. 7.65). The only marked difference is the consistent absence, in all phases, of what was considered in the original study to be the 'birth' peak in the distribution, the reflection of the frequent occurrence of LEH on the upper portion of the M1 crown. This absence can perhaps be explained by more severe wear of the occlusal and lateral surfaces of the teeth of the Flixborough pigs (obliterating LEH lines or depressions), compared with that in the other populations. This severe wear could be linked with the sandy soils at the site and could have been more influential for the analysis of the M1 compared to the M3 where, indeed, LEH markers were present on the upper part of the crown. It must be remembered that, at any given moment in life, the M1 has been present in the jaw for much longer than the M3.

An alternative explanation for the absence of LEH on the upper part of the M1 could be that birth was a less severe physiological trauma to the pigs at Flixborough than at the other sites studied. However, the possibility that the Flixborough pig population suffered less stress at birth seems to be contradicted by the almost complete absence of LEH (even of a minor LEH line) on the upper part of the tooth. It is expected that in all pig populations at least some individuals suffer from stress during the process of birth since, for a piglet, the event is stressful in itself, regardless of the condition of the sow.

Generally, the Flixborough data indicate that the chronology of stress presented in the earlier study remains valid, i.e. that weaning and first and second winters are distinct events represented by high frequencies of LEH on the lower portions of the M1, M2 and M3 respectively.

The relative frequency of linear enamel hypoplasia

The frequency of LEH at Flixborough changes little through time (FIG. 7.66) and suggests that environmental factors or husbandry regimes for pigs differed very little between periods. As a result, data from all phases were grouped together to produce a single frequency index value calculated for the site as a whole. When this overall value for Flixborough was compared with those from other sites previously studied, it was found to be similar to those for sites such as Durrington Walls, Wiltshire, and Wellin and Sugny in Belgium (see Dobney and Ervynck 2000; Dobney *et al.* 2002). These assemblages were interpreted as representing 'primitive' domestic pig populations, enjoying 'normal' living conditions, and kept under a traditional semi-natural husbandry regime in a woodland habitat offering suitable foraging opportunities (Ervynck and Dobney 1999, 7). A similar scenario is

therefore proposed for pig husbandry at Flixborough, with little or no change occurring through time.

Interpreting the non-metrical and pathological data

Interpretation of the possible meaning of changes in the frequency of non-metrical traits and pathological conditions in archaeological assemblages is problematic to say the least. The study of animal palaeopathology is still in its infancy, and is often still very much descriptive. Although there is a growing number of comparative datasets of the raw frequencies of conditions, there is still a distinct lack of studies of modern animals with which to compare data for ancient ones, as well as an almost complete absence of hypotheses to test. Nevertheless, some basic conclusions can be drawn from the Flixborough data.

As has been seen from much of the other broader zooarchaeological (and archaeological evidence) presented in this volume, Phase 4–5b appears to stand out in a number of ways. This general observation can also be applied to the non-metrical and pathological data. Could it be tentatively argued that the drop in frequency of cattle abnormal mental foramina seen in Phase 4–5b (compared to Phases 3b and 6) indicates a possible genotypic change in the cattle supplied to the site during the ninth century? The higher frequency of this trait in Phase 6 may indicate the introduction of new breeding stock during this period and/or the reinstatement of the supply lines from earlier periods. A similar argument could be made for sheep, on the basis of a similar trend observed in the changing frequencies of the premolar foramen. The obvious change in the frequencies of dental calculus in cattle may support this hypothesis. Many factors influence the formation of calculus, but genetics and diet are perhaps the most important. Therefore, the changes observed in the frequency of calculus in the Flixborough cattle may also reflect changes in either cattle genotype (once again most notable in Phase 4–5b) and/or changes in the diet (and husbandry) of these animals.

Evidence from the joint pathology known as 'penning elbow' (p. 184) also shows a peak in frequency during Phase 4–5b. This coincides with the period when sheep remains are at their most prevalent over the whole site, and with evidence of a shift towards fine textile working (see Walton Rogers in Volume 2 Chapter 9). The higher incidence of 'penning elbow' may, therefore, reflect a shift in one aspect of the sheep husbandry strategy during the ninth century, the result of a shift in economic activity at the site. Evidence from non-metrical traits in sheep from Flixborough (pp. 181ff), however, also hints at a possible change in the genetic make-up of sheep at this time. The increase in frequency of 'penning elbow' may, therefore, simply be another manifestation of the shift in origin of sheep in the ninth century, i.e. they came from other estate farms where some husbandry practices were different.

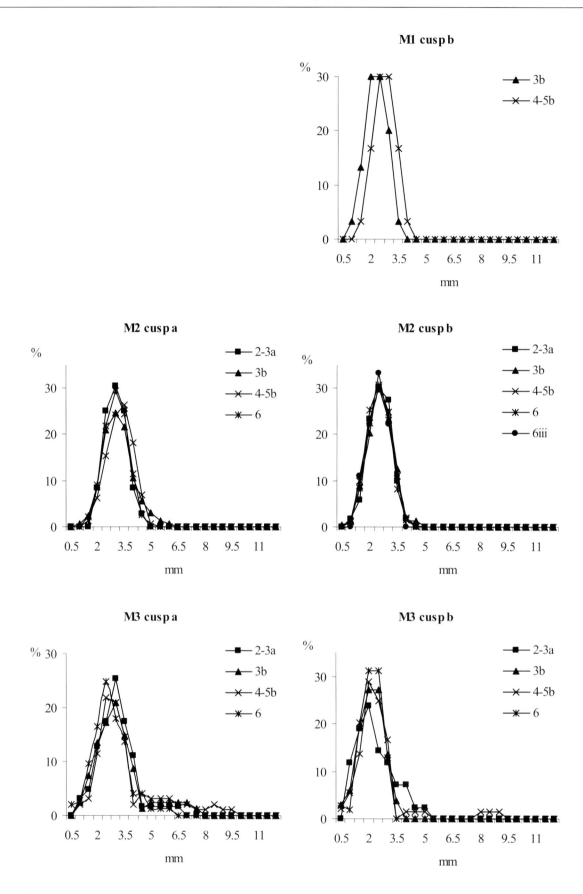

Fig. 7.65 *Frequency distribution of LEH heights for pigs per tooth and cusp (calculated as running means) for each chronological phase at Flixborough.*

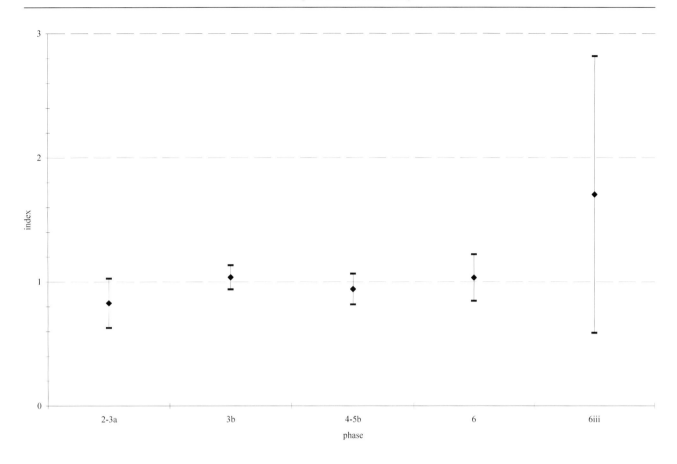

FIG. 7.66 Index comparing the average frequency of Linear Enamel Hypoplasia (LEH) in pigs for all the chronological phases at Flixborough, calculated for all molars combined.

Finally, if the condition noted on the cattle calcanei is indeed related to physical stress (perhaps as a result of the droving of animals over long distances), then perhaps the sharp decrease in its prevalence between Phases 3b and 4–5b could suggest that cattle were being moved on the hoof much shorter distances and from different areas during this later phase.

From the non-metrical and pathological evidence outlined above, it is postulated that the husbandry and origin of domestic ruminants (i.e. cattle and sheep) to Flixborough probably changed during the ninth century. This may reflect the animals' different genetic make-up and even possible differences in their diet (see also evidence from pig tooth wear discussed earlier). This may support the hypothesis of a dislocation of the manorial supply system during the ninth century, and its probable reinstatement during the tenth (see also Chapter 10). Alternatively, it could reflect a major agro-economic shift in the ninth century to a more intensive wool-grain system, where perhaps both the pasture and grazing terrain of domestic ruminants altered significantly (N. Sykes pers. comm. April 2005).

Whilst that may be true for cattle and sheep, analysis of incremental lines in pigs' teeth appears to indicate

that the same is not happening for them. Very little change in the chronology or the frequency of physiological stress was evident through time, and conclusions based on comparisons with data from other sites where similar detailed studies of LEH have occurred suggest that a primitive, 'semi-natural' domestic pig population was living in the vicinity of Flixborough throughout its Saxon occupation. These conclusions certainly fit well within the other zooarchaeological evidence recovered from the site and within what we understand of the historical and economic context of the first millennium AD (see also Chapter 10).

Notes

1   For the purposes of the following analyses and discussions, the category of remains comprising so-called 'major domesticates' include cattle, sheep and goat (collectively termed caprine), pig, chicken and 'large' geese (see Appendix 1 for details).

2   Although astragalus measurements are somewhat problematic in this respect, in that it is difficult to establish the presence of fully adult animals, these were the most commonly available published biometrical datasets that could be used for comparative purposes.

8 Exploitation of Resources and Procurement Strategies

Keith Dobney, Deborah Jaques, James Barrett, Cluny Johnstone, John Carrott, Allan Hall, Jerry Herman, Courtney Nichols, Gundula Muldner and Vaughan Grimes

8.1 Introduction

The direct and indirect lines of evidence reflecting the range of resources utilised by the inhabitants of Flixborough are many and varied and are extremely informative, as much through what is absent from the bioarchaeological record, as through what is actually present. The evidence for exploitation of these resources, and the ways in which they might have been procured, is outlined and discussed in more detail in this chapter.

8.2 Exploitation of the agricultural landscape

To maintain a viable farming unit, certain resources were essential, i.e. sufficient arable land for crops, pasture for animal grazing (including plough animals), meadows for hay, and woodland (for grazing, timber, and wood for fuel), are all basic requirements. It was, therefore, important to incorporate such resources within the boundaries of individual manors and wider estates (Hooke 1998). This is corroborated by the numerous surviving Anglo-Saxon charters and wills which almost always mention the presence of the fundamental economic agricultural units, i.e. fields, woods, meadows and pastures (e.g. *EHDs* 58, 67, 82, 100, 108, 113, 115, 117, 119, and 120). Some even include mention of fisheries, rivers and watercourses, springs, mills, and fowling and hunting grounds.

Woodland

Woodland was a valuable seasonal resource for pigs which, throughout the Saxon and later medieval periods, were turned out to forage in late summer and autumn on the fallen acorns or beech mast – *'the pannage season'*. The value of woodland pasture for swine husbandry is well illustrated by the seventh-century laws of Wessex, where a fine of 60 shillings was to be levied against those found cutting down a tree that could shelter 30 swine (Attenborough 1922). In eastern England, woodland was measured on the basis of how many pigs it could support, while in the South-East, it was expressed in terms of the amount of rent that was payable in return for the right of pannage (a certain amount for so many pigs) – i.e. 'swine render'. The large number of pigs represented throughout the sequence at Flixborough (and their apparent increase in importance during the ninth century) suggests that large tracts of woodland were available to and incorporated into the Flixborough estate (see archaeo-botanical evidence outlined below; Darrah, Volume 4, Chapter 3).

Woodland was also utilised for the pasturing of cattle, horses and even sheep (Hooke 1998, 143). The use of woodland for grazing livestock would have been seasonal, with stock being driven away from the arable land and hay meadows in late spring, whilst in late summer and early autumn, acorns and beech mast would have been foraged by pigs (see above and Hooke 1998). Utilising woodland for livestock grazing, however, obviously involved a delicate balance between wood pasture (*silva pastilis*) and woodland management. For example, on the one hand, the more trees there were, the less abundant the pasture would be, whilst on the other, the more animals that were sent in to graze, the fewer the saplings and coppice shoots that would survive (Rackham 1986, 120).

Woodland was also traditionally the preserve of the nobility for hunting game such as wild boar, deer, badger, wolf and bear, and large tracts of dense and relatively undisturbed 'wildwood' would be necessary to maintain viable populations of the larger wild game. In the case of

Flixborough, wild mammals made up a very small proportion of the overall assemblage (see Chapter 4), and of the species that were present, bones of roe deer were the most commonly identified (see also Chapter 5). The preponderance of roe deer over red deer is intriguing, and perhaps hints at the presence of enclosed wooded parkland (to which roe deer are more adapted), rather than open forest in which red deer congregate (Sykes 2006: 169).

Very few wild boar, and no wolf, bear or beaver bones were identified, perhaps supporting the idea that extensive swathes of dense woodland, undisturbed by humans, did not exist near the site. However, it may not be the lack of large areas of wildwood that account for the rarity or absence of these species at Flixborough. Alternative explanations may be that many large wild mammals were already rare in England by the eighth century AD, perhaps one of the reasons why certain wild animals had such important symbolic meaning in early medieval society.

On the basis of zooarchaeological and historical evidence, the bear appears to have disappeared from Britain very early in historic times, and the evidence of its presence in England is somewhat conjectural, often the subject of legend, and sometimes confused by the sport of bear-baiting (Clutton-Brock 1991) and the presence of dancing bears. It is probable that the brown bear was never abundant and post-Roman records for it are negligible (Yalden 1999, 112). The bear is well documented as being part of the Roman military diet (Davies 1971) whilst, during Anglo-Saxon times, Archbishop Egbert ruled that (when hunting) if a bear had started to consume a carcase then a Christian should not touch it. After the Norman Conquest, the Domesday Book records that the town of Norwich had to provide the king (Edward the Confessor) with one bear per year. However, being near to the coast, imports from mainland Europe would not have been difficult to obtain (Harting 1880). There is little evidence for bear in the post-glacial archaeological record of England. Several bear phalanges were identified from Anglo-Scandinavian levels at Coppergate, York, for example, but interpretation of the significance of this record in terms of the species' continued existence in the countryside around York is hampered by the possibility that these remains arrived in a bearskin – possibly imported from further afield.

Early evidence of the beaver's presence in the region is provided by the town of Beverley in Yorkshire, named in AD 710, literally translated as 'the stream of the beaver'(quoted in Harting 1880). Many earlier-named Welsh sites also bear the name of the beaver (translated as 'water dog'), but this was also the name for the otter, so it is unclear whether these sites refer to either or both species. The earliest written records of beaver fur are from AD 940. Their scarcity at this time in the country is illustrated by comparison of the monetary value of the pelts: a wolf pelt was worth '8d (pence)', whereas a beaver pelt was worth 120d. The medieval clergyman and chronicler, Giraldus Cambrensis, recorded a trip around Wales some 200 years later and claimed that in Wales only one beaver dam remained on the River Teifi (Harting 1880). There is very little archaeological evidence of the beaver in historic times from the region. Beaver remains were identified from the Roman military site of Corstopitum (Meek and Gray 1911), which may or may not indicate the presence of beaver in the catchment area of the site during the Roman period in Northumberland. The first records of the beaver from York (O'Connor 1991) were recovered (like the bear) from an early Saxon / Anglian pit at the supposed *wic* site of Fishergate and included a lower incisor and a number of post-cranial bones. Like the remains of bear from the site, these bones may have come from elsewhere, although the presence of larger post-cranial elements may imply a more local origin.

A few very large *Sus* fragments, tentatively ascribed to wild boar, were present in the Flixborough assemblage, but no large canid remains were found that may have been wolf (in fact almost no positively identified canid bones were found on the site). There is little zoo-archaeological evidence to suggest that the wolf and wild boar were particularly common in the region (or in much of England, for that matter) during or even after the early medieval period and this presents something of an interesting dichotomy between the historical and archaeological evidence. The word 'Eofer' means wild boar in the Anglo-Saxon tongue, and the Anglian name for the early trading settlement or *wic* at Fishergate in York was 'Eoferwic' (changed to Jorvik by the Viking settlers). The name 'Eofer' is considered to have been corrupted to 'Ever', so that numerous place-names such as Eversden and Eversley are taken to indicate the widespread presence of wild boar in the region during the Saxon period (Rackham 1986). The first literary appearance of wild boar is seen in the Welsh Laws written in AD 940, in which the hunting season of the animal was restricted to October and November. William I was a keen huntsman and in AD 1087, in order to preserve his hunting stocks, he ordered the blinding of anyone killing a boar (Harting 1880). Harting (*ibid.*) details an account by FitzStephen of the woodlands surrounding London in 1174, describing them as being full of boar. However, since medieval domestic pigs were probably very similar to their wild relatives (in appearance but perhaps not in size), it is conceivable that many of pigs hunted were perhaps hybrids or feral domestic animals. By the later Middle Ages the wild boar was rare in the region and the country and became an official 'beast of the king's forest'.

As far as archaeological evidence from the north of England is concerned, wild boar has only been recognised at a limited number of sites and is represented by only a few individual specimens. It is present in Roman deposits from York (at excavations in Blake Street, the 'General

Accident' site and Marygate), and at the ecclesiastical settlement at Lurk Lane, Beverley, from deposits of tenth-thirteenth century date (represented by loose canine teeth and mandibles) (Scott 1991). Wild boar was also reported throughout Anglo-Scandinavian and medieval deposits at Coppergate, York. These bones were larger than others found in the same deposits and, although they were not like those from previous studies, the authors were satisfied that they were wild specimens (O'Connor 1991; Bond and O'Connor 1999).

Prior to the Norman Conquest, there is very little documented evidence about the wolf and numbers can only be inferred from the lengths to which people are recorded as going in order to kill them. Alfred the Great hunted wolves and a number of Anglo-Saxon kings were named after them, as the wolf was associated with courage, ferocity and brute-strength. During the reign of Althestan (*c.* AD 938), a retreat was built at Flixton, near Filey, North Yorkshire, to be used by travellers as protection against wolves. It was during this period that the Welsh king Lundwall had to pay King Edgar 300 wolf skins per year as a pecuniary payment. However, after three years there were apparently no longer sufficient wolves in Wales to provide this annual levy. One significant historical account indicates that the dead were being consumed by wolves after the Battle of Hastings in 1066. In 1180, contrary to Forest Law, Puiset gave permission that dogs in Hardwick (Cambs.) no longer needed to be 'hambled' (the removal of the dog's three front claws to prevent harrying of the deer). In this region, the dogs' claws were for some reason necessary for wolf-hunts to protect the stock. The inference here is that, by 1180, wolves in the area were no longer a threat to livestock or managed game. As stock-keeping increased so did the encouragement to destroy wolves.

There are few positively identified bones of wolf from the north of England of any period. Canid bones exhibiting a range of sizes were reported from Anglo-Scandinavian levels at Coppergate, York, three bones being large enough to suggest they were from a wolf (O'Connor 1989). Although this is not conclusive evidence for their presence, it is probable that wolves were in the region (in small numbers) during Anglo-Saxon and Anglo-Scandinavian periods.

The social status of all these wild animals in relation to human activities and the changing nature of the landscape, render simple conclusions about their presence and absence of limited value. What is difficult to refute, however, is that the frequency and distribution of many vertebrate species was directly or indirectly brought about by the activities of humans. These activities included deforestation, greater farming efficiency, and an apparent decrease in the importance or emphasis on wild species (Tinsley 1981). When wild animals came into conflict with farmers they were hunted, and when the wildwood was destroyed, species such as wild boar, wolf and bear rapidly disappeared.

The overall picture of wild animal distribution, when relying on archaeological data, is inevitably distorted. Wild animals are only seen in human settlements if hunted, otherwise their remains are rarely preserved (Stuart 1982). Although inevitable, it is rather simplistic to equate the simple presence and absence of wild animal remains with local availability and habitat make up. Their absence may also hint at more complex socio-cultural factors which may have proscribed the hunting or exploitation of certain wild species for symbolic or even religious reasons. In this broader context, it is certainly the case that our primary data are somewhat obscure and incomplete.

The substantial (probably heavily managed) woodland controlled from the Flixborough estate was certainly large enough to support large herds of swine. It is, however, most likely that these tracts existed as 'islands' in the midst of larger areas of unimproved pasture, arable lands and areas of natural wetland. They were almost certainly heavily managed for wood, firewood, pannage and grazing, and thus heavily disturbed by humans and their livestock. That boar, bear, and wolf are absent from the Flixborough assemblage is unsurprising, since the available woodland utilised by the inhabitants of the site would not have supported and sustained viable populations which could have been actively and regularly hunted. The presence of moderate numbers of roe deer lends credence to this argument. Roe deer live in small groups and even today thrive in isolated pockets of managed woodland surrounded by arable fields and pastureland (see also Chapter 5).

One final remark concerns woodland or woodland edge wild plant resources which are likely to have been exploited by the inhabitants of the site at Flixborough. Remains identified from the archaeological deposits included hazel nuts (charred *Corylus* nutshell was recorded in 12 contexts), and various wild fruits (black-berry, *Rubus fruticosus* agg., identified in a single context, and wild plum, *Prunus domestica* ssp. *insititia*, recorded as charred fruit-stones from three contexts), but these few remains do not suggest large-scale or long-term exploitation, unless the nature of survival of plant material at this site is such that only a very little of the food waste discarded ever found its way into the fossil record.

Marshlands and coastal saltmarshes

These important areas were probably used as summer pastures, as well as for salt production, and for providing peat for fuel, thatching material, fish and fowl (Hooke, 1998, 173). The Lincolnshire fens provided rich pasture for stock during the summer months, and a number of monastic settlements were established on there (Hoskins and Dudley-Stamp 1963, 10–12).

Wetter, low-lying areas, such as the Lincolnshire Fens and Vale of York, favour cattle rearing, and there is little doubt that cattle were (by extrapolation from the bones) predominantly important at Flixborough throughout most of the occupation sequence. Sheep, on the other hand, would have thrived best on the drier, better-drained uplands of the Lincolnshire Wolds, since they suffer heavily from fluke infestation in wet pastures, a fact that must have been apparent to the shepherds of the region since Roman times or earlier (Dobney *et al.* 1996). Perhaps the stronger emphasis on sheep in the ninth century reflects, in part at least, the greater availability of suitable drier pasture in the region, rather than a shift in cultural preference.

However, saltmarshes, although very wet, contain salt, a factor that severely restricts the distribution of the small snail host of the sheep liver-fluke. Historical accounts indicate that the Lincolnshire marshland, particularly those saltmarshes of the coastal parishes, surpassed all other areas in the rearing and fattening of both cattle and sheep. It has been suggested that these areas were also important for intensive livestock grazing as early as the Roman period (Dobney *et al.* 1996). By the end of the sixteenth century, the Lincolnshire Fens and saltmarshes were specialising in the fattening of sheep bred on the neighbouring hill country, the animals being destined for droving to the meat market at Smithfield, London (Thirsk 1957, 137–8). By *c.* 1700 Lincolnshire was the largest wool-producing county in England and was particularly noted for long heavy wool (Munro 1978, 118–69). Similarly, the Romney Marshes (also largely saltmarsh) in Kent provided the bulk of sheep meat carcases to the London market during post-medieval times.

Another possibly beneficial effect of grazing cattle and sheep on saltmarshes is perhaps alluded to in the Irish Law texts (from the eighth to eleventh centuries AD) in which a passing reference indicates that salt or salted fodder was actually fed to livestock – particularly cattle (Kelly 1997, 19). Why was this done? Some classical authors (e.g. Virgil [Fairclough 1978] and Aristotle [Thompson 1910]) refer to the feeding of salted herbage to livestock in order to increase their milk yield. A passage in Virgil's *Georgics* (3.394–403) indicates that salt was added to the fodder of milch cows causing them to drink more and produce greater quantities of salt-flavoured milk, which was subsequently made into cheese. Aristotle in his *Historia animalium* (8.10) also refers to the practice of adding salt to the food of sheep, once again so that they drank more and thus increased their milk yield.

It is, therefore, most likely that the coastal saltmarshes and fenlands in southern and eastern Lincolnshire were extremely important landholdings of the major Saxon manorial estates in the region, providing high-quality, rich pasturelands for numerous head of sheep and cattle (both for meat and dairy purposes) owned by them or their tenants. Seasonal movements of livestock (particularly sheep) would also have occurred between the inland grazing grounds and more low-lying pastures (saltmarshes).

One intriguing pattern in the vertebrate data worthy of special note is what appears to be the simultaneous increase in importance of both sheep and duck remains during the ninth century. Assuming these ducks are mainly wild mallards,[1] the increase in sheep and wild ducks could be interpreted as indicating increased exploitation of the fens or saltmarshes at this period.

As previously mentioned (see Chapter 5 for details), more direct evidence of the exploitation of saltmarsh by the inhabitants of Flixborough was recovered from the wet-sieved samples in the form of plant and molluscan remains. It seems most likely these remains wholly or largely originated in an area of saltmarsh, perhaps from the middle parts of the vertical zonation (Rodwell 2000, 17ff.) if, for example, the plant association represented is the *Puccinellietum* (a rather species-poor community in which *Puccinellia* and *Plantago maritima* are prominent, (*ibid.*, 55ff.)) or the zonally slightly higher *Juncus maritimus-Triglochin maritima* or *Festuca rubra* communities (*ibid.*, 72–83). For reasons discussed by Adam (1990, 51) it is difficult to translate this precisely to a height in relation to Ordnance Datum, but these are plant communities which are likely to be flooded by seawater at least once or twice a day through much of the year. It is unfortunate, in this respect, that the charred rush capsules recovered from eighteen contexts have not been identified with certainty to species, though if *J. gerardi* is present, as suggested by the seed shown in PLATE 8.1 a–d, it would represent another typical denizen of middle and upper saltmarsh communities.

Strong corroborative evidence for saltmarsh as the principal source for the plant remains comes from the records for the snail *Hydrobia ulvae* (Carrott 2000), some, at least, of which had been charred. This species, typical of saltmarsh habitats, was found in four contexts, of which all also yielded remains of saltmarsh plants (table 10 of Hall 2000). An analysis of mollusc assemblages from these contexts using Canoco (FIG. 8.1) clearly separated three of them (a soakaway 4624, and two dumps 5369 and 5983) on the first axis of variation. The snail assemblages from these contexts were dominated by *H. ulvae* and this almost certainly indicates that the remains had been incorporated, along with other waste, by deliberate dumping. The more mixed assemblage from the post-hole fill, Context 10064, was also separated, though less markedly, perhaps indicating that waste material had been accidentally incorporated into the deposit.

If this explanation for the source of these saltmarsh plant and mollusc remains is correct, it is pertinent to ask how and why they were brought to the site and why they were burnt. A number of possibilities immediately spring to mind:

a) they arrived in cut vegetation for roofs or floors, or as hay, or bedding, or as packing for goods or live shellfish;

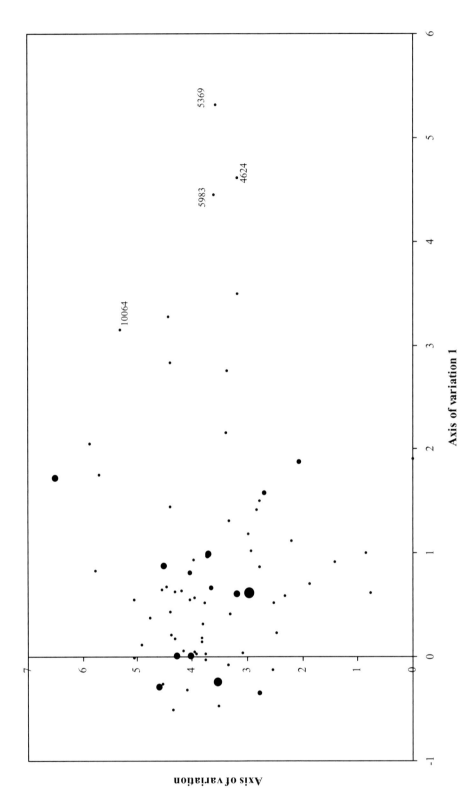

FIG. 8.1 Scatter plot showing detrended correspondence analysis of contexts containing terrestrial molluscs.

b) they arrived as remains brought with turves, or incidentally with or deliberately mixed in what was primarily mineral sediment intended, for example, to make daub;

c) they were present within vertebrate guts or in herbivore dung (the dung being collected deliberately for burning or some other purpose, or deposited by livestock at the site);

d) they represent organisms living at the site, remains of which were burnt incidentally underneath fires.

The last of these is perhaps the least likely. For the plant remains in question to have originated in vegetation growing at the site seems ecologically improbable. The generally well-drained sands at Flixborough are unlikely to have supported plants such as sea plantain which, in Britain today, is confined to maritime habitats. If the *Puccinellia* is correctly identified, this, too, would surely not have grown nearer Flixborough than the tidal reaches of the Humber, or perhaps the lowermost stretch of the Trent (though there are a few British records of it from inland habitats, always where there is a saline influence). It is true that the finer plant stems recorded might have come from a rush such as toad rush (*Juncus bufonius*), a species observed at the site in 1999 growing in quantity around shallow pools left by the excavation and sand extraction, but this does not help to explain the presence of the saltmarsh taxa.

The third explanation – at least so far as dung is concerned – also seems improbable, since the charred herbaceous plant material had evidently been charred when dried but uncompressed. Plant fragments from burnt dung might be expected to have collapsed prior to charring and, in particular, to have survived in clumps rather than as discrete charred plant fragments, often dispersed within lumps of ash. There is, otherwise, no reason to suppose the saltmarsh plants might not have been grazed by livestock; as Johnson and Sowerby (1862) observed, '*The sea plantain is so greatly relished by sheep that the Welsh call it* Llys y Defaid *– Sheeps-herb. In the time of Pennant [mid-eighteenth century] it was commonly cultivated in North Wales mingled with clover.*'

Another possibility, which ought to be explored further, however, is that these remains arrived in the crops of geese feeding on saltmarsh. Freshly ingested plant material, before it reached the gizzard, might well be present in a relatively undamaged state, though it would probably need to have dried before being charred to survive in the form recovered. The question remains, however, as to how such material became dispersed before charring (since clumps of plant fragments might be expected in this case, as with dung).

The arrival of the plant remains in cut vegetation as litter or thatch may probably also be discounted. The remains are from stems far too slender to have served for thatching themselves, and, if they are (for example)

flower stalks, one might have expected more of the larger material from the lower parts of the plants to have survived, too. There is also a notable absence of seeds from the kinds of taller-growing plants that might be found in hay meadows, reed-beds or in other places where vegetation suitable for cutting for this purpose might be collected. Moreover, the parts of saltmarshes most likely to have yielded these remains are traditionally grazed (when not immersed by the sea!) but they are not conventionally used to cut a 'hay' crop. On the other hand, the more heavily grazed swards might easily yield turves, and in this case one might expect a larger content of silt and clay in the deposits rich in ash containing these saltmarsh plant remains.

Insofar as the analyses permit this to be tested, with only one exception, all the contexts for which a crude measure of turbidity and fine sediment content were measured and from which remains of one or more saltmarsh plants were recorded, scored at least moderately well for levels of either turbidity and/or fine sediment content. Had turves been brought, however, one might expect more remains of the basal parts of the plants growing on them. Had the plant material arrived in saltmarsh clay for daub, or had they become incorporated into daub during mixing, in the way that straw is traditionally used, it is difficult to see how they might then become charred and freed from the daub matrix. (Material listed as daub, ?daub or baked clay/daub was frequently recorded – it was present in 25% of contexts, and at least moderately abundant in 4% – but charred plant remains were not noted from the lumps. Here, examination of clay lumps for diatoms or foraminiferans, for example, might have helped in indicating the location of sources for the clay).

On the other hand, we need to consider the records for fragments of charred rhizome/roots fragments (in six contexts) and charred fucoid seaweed lamina fragments (certainly in four, possibly as many as six, contexts). Unless they became charred within a living turf underneath a fire, the root/rhizome material may well have arrived in turves, being charred accidentally (e.g. in turves used in a building which was subsequently destroyed by fire), or because the turves had been used as low-grade fuel or in the construction of a hearth or oven. The seaweed may well have arrived incidentally with raw materials from the coast – it may become entangled in saltmarsh plants, for example, or grow in saltmarsh in its own right (Adam 1990, 97ff.; most of the taxa he lists are not the fucoids thought to be represented by the fossil material at Flixborough, however).

There is a further possibility: that the seaweed was brought as a resource in its own right as a source of alkali, or as fertilizer or animal feed (Newton 1951, Ch. II–III) (the last is a use also mentioned, for example, by Clark (1952, 90) with respect to the prehistoric period). In one case (a sample from Context 5369, a Period 2–3a dump), there were traces of what appeared to be spirorbid shells, likely to have arrived as seaweed epibionts (a similar association of charred seaweed and spirorbids has been recorded from Early Christian deposits at Deer Park Farms, Co. Antrim, N. Ireland (Kenward *et al.* 2000), also well inland.

For comparanda for the evidence from Flixborough for saltmarsh plants we may look to late prehistoric and early medieval coastal sites in the Netherlands and N.W. Germany, though at those sites preservation of plant remains by anoxic waterlogging was quantitatively much more important than was charring. Thus saltmarsh plants were abundant in deposits from the late Iron Age/early medieval Feddersen Wierde in N.W. Germany (Körber-Grohne 1967) and from a series of Iron Age and medieval sites in the northern Netherlands (van Zeist 1974). These habitation mounds (*terpen* or *Würten*) include many layers composed of sediment dug from the nearby saltmarsh, as well as layers rich in plant remains interpreted as stable manure or dung, of which a large proportion are uncharred remains of saltmarsh plants. No assemblages like those from Flixborough have been reported, however; samples rich in charred remains from the Feddersen Wierde contained quantities of crop weed seeds as well as cereal grains and chaff, though charred fossils from saltmarsh plants were present too (they were so widespread across the site during its life as to be incorporated into most of the deposits as they formed).

More recently, Buurman (1999) has described a rich assemblage of plant remains including many saltmarsh taxa (some of which were, again, charred) from the fill of a pit at a site at Schagen in North Holland. She concludes (p. 286) that the material was a mixture of 'dung, animal fodder, litter and household debris', with complete uncharred fruits and perhaps also stems of *Juncus gerardi* and fruit stalks and seed capsules of *Plantago maritima*, interpreted – along with many other taxa – as representing hay rather than being deposited in dung (since they would, she avers, have been changed by passage through the herbivore gut). Moreover, she records fragments of amorphous organic material which she suggests might be dung.

8.3 Wildfowling strategies

The vast majority of wild animal resources present in the Flixborough vertebrate assemblage were birds. The numerous bird bones, which represented a diverse range of species, attest to the important role wildfowling played in both the economic and social lives of the inhabitants (see Chapter 10 for more detailed discussion of birds as evidence of status). The hunting of wild birds (particularly waterfowl) has been important to humans for millennia and there are many historical references to wildfowling, both in terms of the species captured and the techniques used. A nineteenth-century treatise on wildfowling states: '*As different species of birds have different habits, so the method of taking them differs, in accordance with those*

habits. Such portions of the art as relate to the capture of wild-fowl and fen-birds, are by far the most attractive, varied and extensive...'' (Folkard 1859, 2). The following represents a brief and selective summary of some of these fowling techniques pertaining to the bird species identified at Flixborough.[2]

A contemporaneous and somewhat brief reference to the variety of techniques employed in wildfowling can actually be found in *Ælfric's Colloquy*. This set conversation piece between master and pupils was probably written for the novices at Cerne Abbas where Ælfric lived from AD 987–1002 (Swanton 1996, 169). In it, the wildfowler specifically states that '*I trap birds in many ways; sometimes with nets, sometimes with snares, sometimes with lime, by whistling, with a hawk or with a trap*'. Nets and snares, the form and function of which changed little from Saxon to early modern times, were perhaps the most common form of catching a wide variety of wildfowl. Nets (probably made of hemp) were especially good for capturing ground roosting birds. Black grouse, for example, '*fall easy prey to nets... and can be taken at night in the dead of winter*' (MacPherson 1897, 339). Nets have also been (and in some places are still) used for capturing wild geese and a variety of waders, including plovers. Present day field names containing the words cockshut or cockshoot (which means a glade where woodcocks were netted) are still common in parts of England (Smith 1964, cited in Hagen 1995).

Taking birds with snares (made of horse hair, the tendons of other large birds, and other similar materials) is very ancient in origin. According to Folkard (1859, 8) '*they were used by the Anglo-Saxons both by night and day and were employed in the fens as well as by the margins of lakes, rivers and pools, the snares being sometimes placed underwater*'. As was the case with nets, a wide range of bird species from small to very large could be caught this way. Snares were even employed for catching cranes. MacPherson (1897, 445) states that... '*[a] wary "Krannich" [crane] can be captured alive by means of ground snares. These are made with strong horsehair and are set in a circle*'.

An extremely common aid to catching wild birds was by the use of 'birdlime', a generic term for an ancient (and effective) adhesive which would be applied to branches upon which birds were likely to roost. When the birds alighted, they would quickly become stuck fast to await later collection by the hunter. The variety of recipes for birdlime attests to a diverse range of ingredients. Markham (1655 cited by Ray 1678, 49) indicates one should collect '*midsummer bark of holly (to fill a reasonable big vessel). Boil in running water till grey and white bark rise from the green. Take all green and lay it on the ground in a close place and on a moist floor covering with good thickness with docks, hemlocks and thistles. Or make up a heap with ferns. Then layer more of each. Leave for 10–12 days when it will rot and turn to slimey matter. Pound in a large mortar – till a uniform paste that may be wrought by hand like dough. Wash in running water to remove all filth. Put in close earthen pot and let it stand and purge (3–4 days) removing scum. Put in a clean vessel and wait to use. Mix with 1/3 part hogs/capons/goose grease set on a gentle fire and melt together stirring all the time. Let it cool. Warm the wooden rods in a fire to make lime easier to spread'.* Francis Willoughby, a seventeenth century ornithologist from Warwickshire, detailed a recipe for birdlime as follows, *'First collect large quantities of mistletoe berries. Leave to putrifie and macerate. Beat with round cudgel till it clears. Put in soot and cover with parchement. Add one ounce oil to 1lb lime. Mix over heat and add terpentine or water'* (Ray 1678, 50).

Birdlime is today commonly associated with the taking of small songbirds and passerines, but in the past was used to take a variety of prey of all sizes, including birds as large as geese. With the *'use of lime strings...a number of wildfowl of the largest species were taken at night at the moment of sweeping over the ground at very low flight, just before alighting. This method was particularly successful at taking plovers'* (Markham 1655, cited by Folkard 1859, 18).

Folkard (*op. cit.*) also states that lime twigs were used for catching geese in cereal fields. Reference to the catching of geese with lime twigs is also made by the ornithologist Francis Willoughby: *'Wild goose or bernacle set of your greatest rods upon green winter corn either wheat or Rie. Thet are very shie fowl therefore you must stand at a good distance'* (Ray 1678, 29–31).

Another way of catching wild birds was by the use of poisoned or drugged bait. This was a relatively simple way of catching geese and ducks by soaking the seeds and root of *'Belenge'* in water. When eaten by birds they are said to *'sleepe as if they were drunke'* (Helme 1614). An extremely early book on fowling and fishing, written originally in Flemish and printed in Antwerp in the year 1492, also describes the use of drugged bait as a method of catching birds ducks and other birds: *'First take a tormentilla and boil it in good wine, and afterwards boil therein corn or barley...when they eat the corn with the weed and become by that as if they were drunk, so that they cannot fly but fall on the earth'* (Boekske 1872).

Similar effects were had if barley meal and/or 'gall' were mixed together in a paste. They (birds) *'become too stupid, that they can no more fly and may be caught with the hands'.* The same effects were to be had *'from making a porridge of barley and toadstool'* (Boekske *op. cit.*).

Some birds could even be caught in a fashion similar to fish, i.e. by using a hook and lure. Folkard (1859, 194) indicates that herons could be caught by baiting a large hook with a live roach or eel, whilst a political poem dating from 1444 states that *'Bosard with botirflyes makith beytis for a crane'* which literally means cranes can be caught with the bait of an insect (Macpherson 1897).

Of course, individual birds could be killed using archery, although this method tended to be used only for larger species since large numbers could not be brought down at once. In medieval and post-medieval times, shooting large birds with the longbow was esteemed above all other methods for taking waterfowl. Such a degree of accuracy was attainable that the preferred target on large birds was the head, and birds killed in this way fetched higher prices since there was no wound to the body (Folkard 1859, 10).

Perhaps one of the most effective ways of capturing waterfowl (particularly ducks) in large numbers was to drive them into tunnel nets during their moult in the summer season. During late medieval times and later, it was a practice extensively resorted to in the fens of Cambridgeshire, Norfolk and Lincolnshire (Ray 1678; Folkard 1859, 22). In fact, in some areas, so many ducks were taken that legislation was enacted to restrict this method of fowling to conserve wildfowl stocks. The antiquity of decoys and tunnel nets is unknown but the limited numbers of duck bones identified in the Flixborough assemblage perhaps indicates that this particular method of wildfowling was not practised during Saxon times, at least within the coastal and fenland regions of the Flixborough estate holdings.

Finally, wild birds could have been hunted with hawks and falcons. It is certain that the art of falconry (catching wild game using tame birds of prey) was well known to the inhabitants of northern Europe from the sixth century onwards, and was a pastime associated with high-status individuals. As previously mentioned, the fowler in *Ælfric's Colloquy* describes the use of hawks as one means of catching birds. He goes on to describe their management... *'[Hawks] feed themselves, and me in winter; and in the spring I let them fly away to the woods; and in the autumn I take young birds and tame them...[they are released in the summer] since they eat too much'...* Master – *'Yet many feed the tamed ones throughout the summer, in order to have them already again'* (Swanton 1996, 172). There are various zoo-archaeological lines of evidence which might support the existence of falconry at Flixborough and other Anglo-Saxon sites in Britain (Dobney and Jaques 2002). These are discussed in more detail in Chapter 10.

Analysis of the bird remains have also provided a number of clues suggesting that Anglo-Saxon wild-fowling practices at Flixborough may have been targeted towards specific habitat types. The bones of what have been termed 'small geese' (most likely to be barnacle goose – and confirmed by aDNA analysis – see Chapter 7) appear to be the most abundant wild bird remains in the assemblage, whilst brent geese, in comparison, are poorly represented (a total of only nine fragments having been provisionally identified). This imbalance between the remains of brent and barnacle geese provides an important clue to exploitation. In short, if extensive wildfowling was being carried out in the saltmarshes of the Humber, one would expect to find more brent geese remains in the assemblage. Like barnacle geese and pink-footed geese, brent geese frequent the inter-tidal flats adjacent to the saltmarsh in similarly large numbers. Therefore, unless brent geese were being deliberately avoided, they should have been caught in equal numbers, particularly if they were being caught as flocks in nets. In this context, it is interesting to note that Old and Middle Irish texts (around AD 700–1000) distinguish between the barnacle and brent goose (Kelly 1997, 300). Interestingly, Meaney (2002) suggests that barnacle geese were already associated with Christian ideology as early as the Saxon period, perhaps indicating a broader symbolic significance to their presence at Flixborough beyond mere availability.

Wintering wildfowl tend be distributed according to their favoured food sources and the degree of safety from predation. Brent geese are very specific winter grazers, and their distribution depends on that of their favoured food, i.e. eel-grass, *Zostera* spp. (Percival and Evans 1997). Brent geese have been very numerous on the Humber in the recent past (in 1991 the area was designated as an internationally important site) and they can still occur in huge numbers in The Wash today (Prater 1981). Although sea-level rise and human disturbance have been blamed for their present-day changes in frequency and distribution (Percival *et al.* 1998), it seems more than likely that the Humber estuary would have had a very substantial brent goose population during Saxon and later medieval times.

As agriculture has intensified, many crops (such as winter wheat) are now sown in the autumn and this has led to some geese changing their feeding behaviour to move inland to feed upon arable land. As a result, most wild grey geese and the barnacle goose now rely on winter crops as their main winter food source, so much so that farmers now rate many populations as pests (Cranswick 1995). However, this is not the case for brent geese, although there has been a limited and small-scale shift towards the exploitation of arable fields by some brent geese populations; this mainly occurs in isolated pockets and in specific locations.

Inland, barnacle geese feed mainly on mosses, grasses and clover when arable land is not available (Black 1991) and are today only seen occasionally feeding on the saltmarshes at Blacktoft Sands, in the Humber Estuary. Historical texts appear to support these recent observations. Folkard (1859, 185) states that '*bernicle geese... spend their days at sea near sandy shores and banks and their nights inland, on fens and moors; as is the habit with many other of the wild goose species*'. There are, in fact, records of barnacle geese feeding on pastures and grasslands near the Humber from as early as the seventeenth century (WWT 1963). Markham (1655) observed that '*...they [barnacle geese] are infinitely delighted with green winter corn, as the blades of wheat or rye and, therefore they are ever, for the most part, to be found where such graine is sown especially where the*

ends of the land are much drowned...'. The idea that barnacle geese (known as '*claik geis*') were hatched from barnacles or grew on trees was still prevalent during the Elizabethan period (Folkard *op. cit.*, 186), something which allowed them to be considered as fish and, therefore, exempt from avoidance during periods of religious fasting. Indeed, Giraldus Cambrensis, during his travels in the 12th century tells us that in some parts of Ireland bishops and religious men ate barnacle geese during times of fasting on the grounds that they were not classified as '*fleshmeat*'.

The arable stubble of the Lincolnshire Wolds also supported the large numbers of pink-footed geese recorded during the 1960s on the Humber. Their numbers have greatly declined since then as a direct result of changes in the way winter crops are sown (Pashby 1992). Perhaps their numbers on the East Coast also fluctuated in the past. Folkard (1859, 190) noted that '*They are not very abundant but in sharp winters there are generally a few killed on the coast.*' He also observed that they were difficult to catch, stating that '*The sportsmen will invariably find these birds so wary that it is difficult to get in range* (ibid., 190).'

On the basis of the information presented above, the evidence from Flixborough would appear to suggest that most wildfowling for geese probably took place on the unimproved pastureland (which would have presumably been plentiful around the site during Saxon times) and not on the more distant saltmarshes and mudflats (the nearest saltmarshes are likely to have been at Whitton (Lillie 1998) some 7 km from Flixborough).

Evidence from other bird species may support this general hypothesis. For example, although the overall range of non-anseriform avian species from Flixborough include what can broadly be considered wetland species (e.g. crane, curlew, and plover), these species can also be found and caught in arable fields and pastureland. The curlew and plover species have very distinct habitat preferences, and (on the assumption that the plover remains represent mainly golden plovers, *Pluvialis apricaria*) can be found both wintering on coastal marshes, estuaries, fens and flood-meadows, as well as on upland moorland. The remains of woodcock (*Scolopax rusticola*) and the more numerous bones of black grouse (*Tetrao tetrix*) may lend further credence to this hypothesis, since today both are usually restricted to upland woodland or moorland habitats. They may, however, have been more commonly associated with wetland habitats in the past (Dobney *et al.* 1996). An interesting absentee from this list is the oystercatcher, a wading species which is also commonly found feeding inland in arable fields and pasture and a bird that was consumed and prized (among other coastal birds) at later medieval banquets.

Evidence from the wild avian remains may suggest that the vast and diverse wetland habitats within the region may not, in fact, have been heavily utilised for the purposes of wildfowling. At face value this appears somewhat strange since the coastal saltmarshes to the north and freshwater swamps to the west would have been havens for numerous wildfowl species, other than barnacle geese, all year round. It may indicate that these wetland areas were not easily accessible, although it is suggested above that at least the saltmarshes were probably heavily utilised for the purposes of grazing domestic cattle and sheep, if not also for the procurement of sods. Perhaps the most obvious explanation is that out on the mudflats the birds are usually dispersed when feeding, but when on unimproved grassland or arable fields they can congregate in large numbers, particularly in the evening when they roost. This is when they can be caught in large numbers. If they are hunted at night inland, the wildfowler has most of the daylight hours to set his nets and traps, whilst remaining unobserved by the birds feeding on and around the mudflats of the estuary.

8.4 The exploitation of marine and freshwater resources

Cetaceans

Perhaps one of the most interesting (and unusual) characteristics of the wild component of the vertebrate assemblage from Flixborough was the large number of cetacean remains identified (PLATE 8.2 & TABLE 4.1). The sheer quantity of cetacean fragments (over 600) found at the site is exceptional, since very few sites of similar or later date from Britain (or indeed Europe) have produced such a large collection of marine mammals. What is even more interesting is the fact that almost all of the fragments represent a single species, the bottlenose dolphin (*Tursiops truncatus*). The bones of this species are found throughout deposits in all phases which indicates their utilisation by the inhabitants of Flixborough over the entire sequence of occupation at the site. The only other species that have been identified from the site were minke whale (*Balaenoptera acutorostrata*, two specimens) and what may be a pilot or killer whale (*Globicephala melas/ Orcinus orca*, a single fragment). Bones of these larger whales do not appear in the assemblage until the ninth century (Phase 4–5b).

Skeletal element representation and butchery of cetaceans

A more detailed consideration of the skeletal element representation of the *Tursiops* remains by major period shows an obvious bias towards particular elements – i.e. selected vertebrae, rib and skull fragments (FIG. 8.2). There are also few cervical and no terminal caudal vertebrae present in the assemblage and a complete absence of elements from the flippers. Although meat was almost certainly the primary objective, the presence of cranial fragments may indicate that these animals were also utilised for their oil, which is particularly copious in

the 'melon' (the protuberance on the front of the head) and jaw. Evidence of butchery, in the form of cuts and chop marks, is present on many of the bone remains (FIG. 8.3). Transverse cuts across the spinal column are consistent with the separation of the dolphin carcases into manageable pieces, which must have aided transport from the coast to the site. Other marks are consistent with the removal of meat from the spinal column and ribs, and, in one case, the removal of the oil-bearing tissue from the skull. This evidence indicates that only the most useful parts were brought to the site where meat and oil were then removed. Moreover, from the representation of body parts and pattern of butchery evident on the bones, it can be concluded that bottlenose dolphins were being butchered away from the site. Only selected portions were reaching the settlement, i.e. those with a high meat or oil utility.

Of the three fragments of larger whale, the presence of the rostrum of a minke whale is difficult to explain in terms of utility value (there is no meat on this element, just skin). The presence (and obvious butchery) of a minke whale squamosal bone, however, probably reflects the removal of the mandible. This element is usually left attached to the soft tissue when removing the jaw, possibly for access to the very large and edible tongue. Thus its presence in the Flixborough midden indicates that it was probably brought to the site with the highly valued tongue.

Age and size profiles

In terms of the age profiles and size of the individuals represented, almost all of the *Tursiops* specimens were from sub-adult/adult animals, with few juveniles being present. All are from large animals of between 0.25m and 0.35m in length (FIG. 8.4), in fact most are larger than the numerous modern comparative specimens examined in the National Museum of Scotland's cetacean collection in Edinburgh. By contrast, all the large whale bones were from small juvenile specimens which, like *Tursiops*, could have either been hunted (in the estuary or inshore) or stranded on the coast (see below for a detailed discussion of the evidence for hunting versus stranding). These age profiles and size reconstruction data are extremely significant with respect to our proposed interpretation of cetacean exploitation at the site.

Biomolecular evidence from the bottlenose dolphins at Flixborough

Today, bottlenose dolphins found in waters surrounding Britain are the most northerly populations of this species and show a discontinuous distribution into discrete local populations. Despite the large number of bottlenose dolphin remains found at Flixborough, there is no population in waters near the site today. Genetic studies of the Flixborough bottlenose dolphin specimens, and comparisons with samples and reference sequences from elsewhere in the UK and around the world, have allowed insight

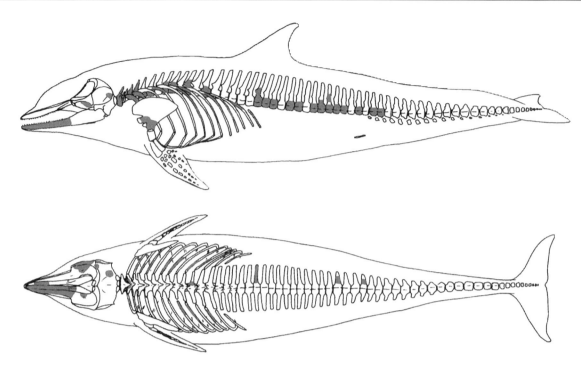

Fig. 8.2 Skeletal element representation of bottlenose dolphins at Flixborough (all periods combined).

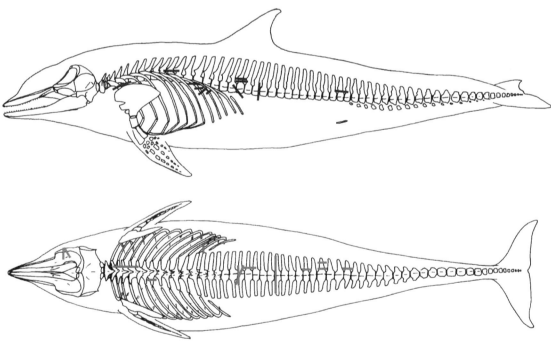

Fig. 8.3 Schematic representation of butchery observed on the bottlenose dolphin remains from Flixborough (all periods combined).

into the origin and possible redistribution or extinction of the animals found at Flixborough, as well as a better understanding of population dynamics of these animals around the UK (for full details see Nichols *et al.* 2007).

Mitochondrial DNA and microsatellite analyses show that the Flixborough animals are a genetically distinct group. They are significantly differentiated from all modern UK populations and, indeed, from all populations from other parts of the world. These results suggest that the Flixborough animals were from a distinct local population. This indicates that it is unlikely that these animals were hunted from other populations and imported to the Flixborough site. Low levels of variation suggest the possibility that the Flixborough population originated through a founding event. Additionally, shared genetic markers (alleles) suggest the founding of this group by a nearby British population. The genetic differentiation of these samples does not suggest that the present-day absence of a bottlenose dolphin population near the site is the result of a redistribution, as we would expect a close relationship of the Flixborough samples to another extant population if that were the case. So, it seems most likely that the bottlenose dolphin remains from Flixborough are from a founded, distinct, local population of animals that has since become extinct. The catholic feeding habits and cosmopolitan distribution of bottlenose dolphins suggest that, had the environment changed, these animals would have been able to redistribute. Therefore, the extinction of this group is likely to have resulted from excessive human predation.

Stable isotope analysis of cetaceans and fish from Flixborough

Carbon and nitrogen stable isotope analysis of bone collagen and oxygen isotope analysis of bone phosphate of cetaceans and fish from Flixborough were employed to assess whether the bottlenose dolphins were resident in the freshwater dominated upper reaches of the Humber

estuary, as might be suggested from the previously outlined results of the ancient DNA analysis that indicate a genetically distinct local population.

Carbon and nitrogen isotope analysis

It has long been recognised that the stable isotope ratios of carbon ($\delta^{13}C$) and nitrogen ($\delta^{15}N$) in bone collagen reflect those of the dietary protein consumed by a human or animal during life (see Schwarcz and Schoeninger 1991). Combined, the two isotopic systems usually allow terrestrial and marine organisms to be distinguished (Schoeninger and DeNiro 1984). Freshwater ecosystems are much more complex and isotopic values can be very variable between biotopes (Fry 1991; Dufour *et al.* 1999). Nevertheless, large differences in $\delta^{13}C$ ratios of freshwater and marine organisms have often been observed and are regularly used in modern ecological studies as proxies for feeding habitats and fish migration (e.g. Kline *et al.* 1998; Hobson 1999). Estuarine environments, where carbon from freshwater and marine sources mixes, are often characterised by intermediate $\delta^{13}C$ values (Fry and Sherr 1988).

In order to reconstruct the palaeoecology of the Flixborough cetaceans, bone collagen carbon and nitrogen isotope ratios of 42 samples of marine, freshwater and migratory fish from archaeological

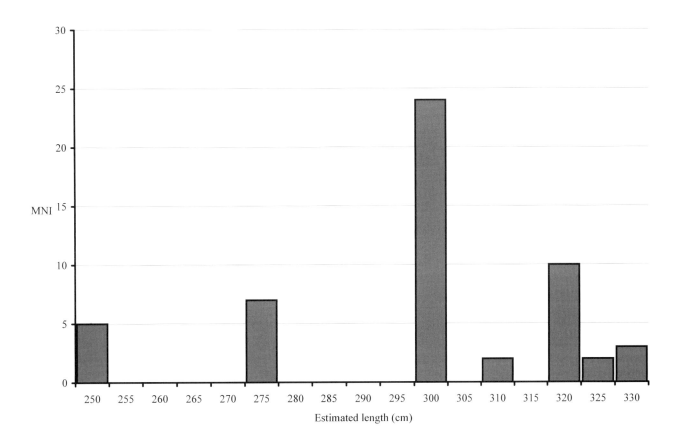

Fig. 8.4 Estimated length of bottlenose dolphins in the Flixborough assemblage (all periods combined).

contexts at Flixborough were analysed so as to establish an isotopic base-line for freshwater and marine organisms in the River Trent, the Humber estuary and the open sea. Comparison of these reference values with isotopic data obtained for 26 bottlenose dolphins (*T. truncatus*) and 2 minke whales (*B. acutorostrata*) and one possible minke whale from the Flixborough assemblage should make it possible to assess whether they spent considerable time during the year feeding in a freshwater environment.

Results (FIG. 8.5) show that the bottlenose dolphins form a rather tightly clustered group while isotopic values for the three minke whales spread more widely. This is consistent with the suggestion that the dolphins belonged to a single population while the whales were encountered as solitary individuals and hunted on an opportunistic basis.

The ranges of $\delta^{13}C$ values for freshwater and marine/outer estuarine fish species from Flixborough are exclusive and perfectly consistent with other collagen isotope data for riverine and marine fish from archaeological contexts in North-East England (Müldner and Richards 2005; Müldner 2005).[3]

The $\delta^{13}C$ ratios of the Flixborough cetaceans plot firmly in the marine range. With a mean $\delta^{13}C$ value of -12.1‰ ± 1.0 (2σ) and $\delta^{15}N$ ratio of 17.1‰ ±1.4 (2σ), the bottlenose dolphins are enriched in the heavy isotopes by several per mil over the Salmonidae and Pleuronectidae. These differences illustrate the higher trophic level of the dolphins, which have been shown to consume a wide range of fish species, including gadids and salmonids (see Pauly *et al.* 1998).

Using the widely accepted figures for trophic level

effects of around +1‰ for carbon and +2–5‰ for nitrogen (Rau *et al.* 1983; Minagawa and Wada 1984; see Bocherens and Drucker 2003), it may be suggested that the prey of the Flixborough dolphins had average $\delta^{13}C$ and $\delta^{15}N$ values of around -13‰ and +13‰. Based on the faunal background data presented here, this is consistent with the dolphins feeding almost exclusively in a marine or outer estuarine environment, although they may have followed anadromous fish (salmon) further upriver during their annual migrations. However, the isotope data does not suggest any measurable contribution of freshwater feeding species to the diet. It is therefore unlikely that the Flixborough dolphins spent prolonged periods of time in the upper reaches of the Humber estuary or the Trent.

Oxygen isotope analysis

The analysis of oxygen isotope ratios in biogenic phosphate ($\delta^{18}O_p$) from mammalian bone mineral is a well-established technique to obtain information about past climates, detect migration and identify animal habitat preference (Longinelli 1984; Fricke *et al.* 1995; Thewissen *et al.* 1996; White *et al.* 2004). The $\delta^{18}O_p$ values for many freshwater aquatic mammals are known to be strongly correlated with oxygen isotopes in precipitation ($\delta^{18}O_{precip}$), which result in wide isotopic variation. They are $\delta^{18}O$ depleted (more negative) due to environmental and geographic parameters (Dansgaard 1964), as well as diverse dietary preferences and physiology (Kohn 1996).

Marine mammals, however, should have higher and a more restricted range of $\delta^{18}O$ values than freshwater

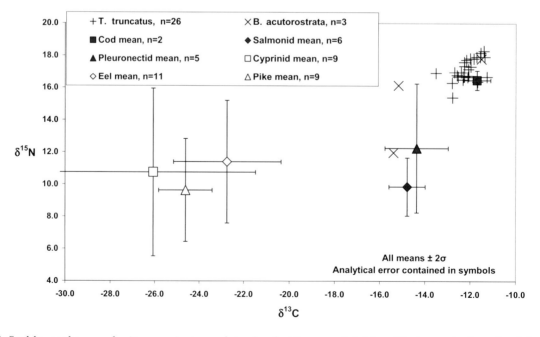

FIG. 8.5 *Stable carbon and nitrogen isotope data for bottlenose dolphins* (T. truncatus) *and minke whales* (B. acutorostrata) *in comparison with mean values for freshwater, marine and migratory fish species from Flixborough.*

mammals because their $\delta^{18}O_p$ signature primarily reflects the relatively homogenous ocean water (~0‰ ± 2‰) (Hui 1981; Kohn 1996). Even with the restricted range of marine mammal $\delta^{18}O_p$ values several studies on modern species have shown that this technique can be used to differentiate between habitats such as 'off shore', 'near shore', 'tidal', and 'estuarine', and verify that marine mammals generally have both higher and less variable $\delta^{18}O_p$ values than mammals that live exclusively in either semi-brackish or freshwater habitats (Yoshida and Miyazaki 1991; Roe *et al.* 1998; Clementz and Koch 2001).

Here, we analysed bone samples of *T. truncatus* (n=13) and *B. acutorostrata* (n=1) from Flixborough for their $\delta^{18}O_p$ values in order to address whether they were predominately marine living or spending significant amounts of time in the more freshwater influenced Humber estuary. It is important to note that there are currently no reference $\delta^{18}O$ values for water from the estuary available (Darling *et al.* 2003). However, based on the gradients of salinity observed in the Humber estuary (Marshall and Elliot 1998), we can reasonably assume that its upper reaches would have a mixture of ^{18}O depleted freshwater from the Ouse and Trent rivers and ^{18}O enriched ocean water.

Preliminary results of the $\delta^{18}O_p$ analysis from the Flixborough cetaceans, along with $\delta^{18}O_p$ values of modern marine and freshwater species taken from several literature sources, are shown in FIG. 8.6. The Flixborough cetaceans clearly fall within the range of $\delta^{18}O_p$ values for modern marine cetaceans and have a mean value (18.3‰) that is statistically indistinguishable from the modern

marine dataset (one factor ANOVA, *F*=4.027, *P*=0.940). Although they show slightly more within-group variation (±1.2‰, 1σ) than the modern marine cetaceans (±0.9‰, 1σ), this is likely to be due to differences in the size of the data-sets. The oxygen isotope results from Flixborough are therefore consistent with the cetaceans spending most of their year in a predominately marine environment, which may have included the outer regions of the Humber estuary. As such these data are in close agreement with the carbon and nitrogen isotope results presented above. In the absence of $\delta^{18}O$ values from potential prey species and the estuary itself, however, it is difficult to account for the variation seen within the oxygen isotope data and, ultimately, address the precise extent to which the estuary may have been utilised.

In conclusion, multi-isotopic analysis of cetacean bone from Flixborough produced values firmly within the range expected for mammals living in a marine environment. These results render it unlikely that the bottlenose dolphins were permanently resident in the upper, freshwater-influenced, reaches of the Humber estuary. However, the isotope data cannot exclude the possibility that they inhabited the outer estuary, nor that they spent limited periods of time upriver, for example preying on migratory fish during the spawning season.

A Saxon bottlenose dolphin fishery in the Humber estuary?

Porpoises and dolphins were collectively known as *marswin*, a term derived from the Old English (*mereswyn*), which translated literally means 'sea pig'. As a result, little differentiation is made between them in

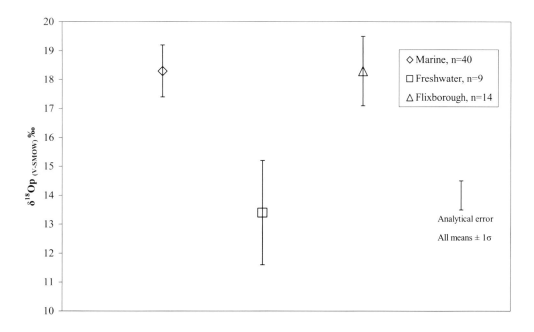

FIG. 8.6 *Phosphate oxygen isotope ($\delta^{18}O_p$) data for modern marine and freshwater cetaceans compared with bottlenose dolphins (*T. truncatus) *and a minke whale (*B. acutorostrata) *from Flixborough.*

the limited documentary sources from the Anglo-Saxon period. There is also confusion in the literature about the actual existence of cetacean fisheries in England during the Saxon and later medieval periods. Gardiner (1997) suggests that the Anglo-Saxons not only knew little of whales, but they seem to have had only slight knowledge of the practice of whaling. However, he cites the Venerable Bede, writing at the outset of his *Historia Ecclesiatica*, who claims that seals, dolphins and sometimes whales were, indeed, caught off the coast of Britain. In the year AD 828, the *Annals of Ulster* record a great slaughter of porpoises on the coast of Ard Ciannachta (present day County Louth) which was carried out (it is claimed) by 'Foreigners'. These are more likely to have been Norsemen than English fisherman (MacAirt and MacNiocaill 1983, sub anno 827).

Gardiner (1997) also cites *Ælfric's Colloquy* (written in the late tenth century) as a source for information about cetacean fishing. In it, the pupil (representing the fisherman) says that '*porpoises and sturgeon were caught among other fish, but whales were not, since they were dangerous and can sink the many boats sent to hunt them*'. However, the master presses the fisherman and states that '*...many catch whales... and make great profit by it*'.

In contrast to the evidence from Britain, the hunting of cetaceans was supposedly common along the Channel coast between Normandy and Flanders from at least the ninth century AD (Gardiner *op. cit*; Musset 1964; Lestocquoy 1948), as well as off the Biscay coast of France and Spain (Fischer 1881; Jenkins 1971). Documentary sources indicate that in AD 832 the Parisian Abbey of St Denis had a fishery on the Cotentin peninsula in Normandy for catching *crassi pisces* (porpoises or whales) (Tardif 1866, 85). In England, fishing for porpoises was supposedly well established by the eleventh century, with documented fisheries at Tidenham in Gloucestershire, where animals were presumably caught in the estuary of the River Severn (Sawyer 1968, no 1555).

How does the evidence from Flixborough fit into this somewhat confusing picture? The species that today most regularly occur in the North Sea include the common porpoise, the bottlenose dolphin and the minke whale. Porpoises and dolphins are often found close inshore, in small groups (of less than 10 and 25 respectively), and may enter estuaries and even rivers, while minke whales are often solitary but will also venture close inshore and into estuaries (Evans 1991; Watson 1981; Jefferson *et al.* 1993). There have been numerous inshore fisheries for these species around the world, which have used a variety of techniques including driving, netting and harpooning (Mitchell 1975).

Evidence from published stranding records since 1913 shows that bottlenose dolphins have only rarely been recorded near to the Humber Estuary (Harmer 1927; Kinze 1995). However, the records also suggest that there have been recent changes to the distribution of bottlenose

dolphins within the North Sea, and Kinze (*op. cit.*) has noted that bottlenose dolphins have tended to strand in Denmark during certain periods. Although the main concentrations of bottlenose dolphins are now found on the western coasts of the British Isles, and in the Moray Firth (Evans 1991), it seems likely that the remains from Flixborough indicate that concentrations of bottlenose dolphins were present around the Humber estuary during the eighth–tenth centuries.

There are several probable ways that the cetacean bones (particularly those of *Tursiops*) found their way into midden deposits at Flixborough. The animals could have been actively hunted (e.g. killed in the estuary or further out at sea or driven into shallow water or onto the shore where they were killed) as they were and still are today in Japanese dolphin fisheries. Alternatively, they could have been opportunistically acquired as accidentally stranded animals washed up locally on the shores of the estuary or East Coast.

Gardiner (1997) states that the main English source of cetaceans throughout the medieval period were probably those animals stranded or cast up on the shore. A famous passage from *The Life of St Godric* (twelfth century) describes the saint searching the shore, whereupon he came upon three stranded '*delphines*'. The two that were still living he returned to the sea, the third (dead individual) he cut up and carried home (Stevenson 1847, 26–7).

It might be expected that in the past (and as found today), family groups of bottlenose dolphins included juvenile, sub-adult and adult animals. Accidental live strandings of sick or disoriented animals should, therefore, include all of these age groups, with perhaps more juvenile and elderly animals expected (Fraser 1946, 36–7; Matthews 1978, 191). This is clearly not the case with the Flixborough assemblage, where a focus on fully-grown animals strongly indicates an element of selectivity in their acquisition (i.e. the targeted hunting of animals that have reached full adult size and the deliberate avoidance of smaller, more juvenile animals).

Corroborative evidence for this conclusion can be found by comparing the limited suite of cetacean species present at the site with modern stranding records. TABLE 8.1 shows the 19 species of cetacean which have been recorded from the North Sea (from stranding records and from Evans 1991). Some of these are resident; others may be seasonal or only rare visitors.

FIGS 8.7 and 8.8 show the number and frequency of the three most commonly stranded species – i.e. the common porpoise (*Phocoena phocoena*), bottlenose dolphin (*Tursiops truncatus*) and the minke whale (*Balaenoptera acutorostrata*) – recorded from the North Sea coast of Britain (Caithness to Straits of Dover, not including the Northern Isles) for the years 1913–1992. The records provide a reasonable (although by no means accurate) impression of which species might have been available after being washed ashore along the North Sea coasts in the past, although it must be remembered that cetacean distributions around the British Isles could well have changed over the last 1300 years.

What is extremely significant about these data is the consistently higher frequency of recorded porpoise strandings evident from all decades for which records exist, and the much lower (and very similar) numbers of minke whale and bottlenose dolphin strandings. If we make the rather sweeping assumption that the twentieth-century stranding data are what might have been expected during the eighth–tenth centuries AD, then we surely should expect similar frequencies of these three cetacean species to be represented in the Flixborough assemblage if the inhabitants were utilising stranded animals. Clearly this is not the case. Not a single common porpoise element has been identified from the vast vertebrate assemblage

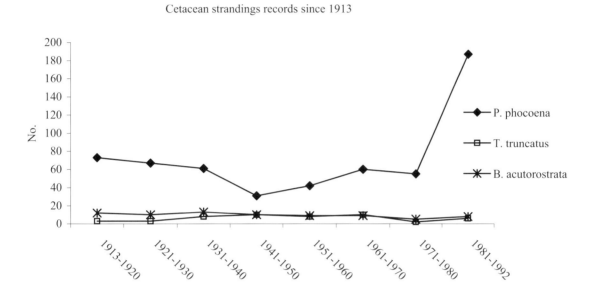

FIG. 8.7 *Number of three most commonly stranded cetacean species, i.e. the common porpoise, the bottlenose dolphin and the minke whale, recorded from the North Sea coast of Britain for the years 1913–1992.*

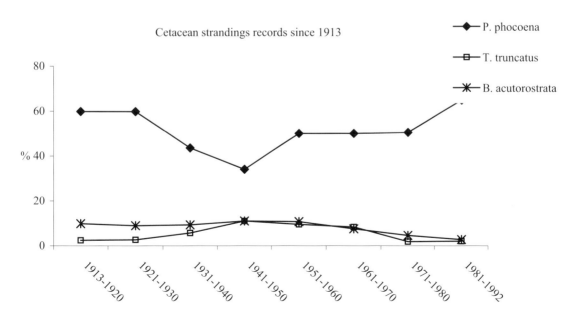

FIG. 8.8 *Frequency of three most commonly stranded cetacean species, i.e. the common porpoise, the bottlenose dolphin and the minke whale, recorded from the North Sea coast of Britain for the years 1913–1992.*

YEAR	1913–1920	1921–1930	1931–1940	1941–1950	1951–1960	1961–1970	1971–1980	1981–1992	Total
Phocoena	73	67	61	31	42	60	55	187	576
Delphis	2	1	11	3	3	2	3	3	28
Stenella coeruleoalba	0	0	0	0	0	0	0	2	2
Lagenorhyeus acutus	1	2	1	3	1	4	9	10	31
L. albirostris	11	15	19	5	6	17	15	43	131
Tursiops truncatus	3	3	8	10	8	10	2	6	50
Grampus griseus	1	1	2	1	3	1	0	1	10
Globicephala melas	3	0	2	7	4	7	4	13	40
Orcinus orca L.	1	3	1	9	1	3	2	0	20
Pseudorca crassidens	0	4	11	0	0	0	0	0	15
Mesoplodon bidens	2	1	3	0	3	4	6	5	24
Hyperoodon ampullatus	6	3	6	6	4	2	4	3	34
Physeter macrocephalus	2	0	1	0	0	0	3	5	11
Balaenoptera acutorostrata	12	10	13	10	9	9	5	8	76
B. physalus	5	1	0	2	0	1	0	2	11
B. musculus	0	1	0	0	0	0	0	0	1
B. borealis	0	0	0	2	0	0	1	0	3
Delphinapterus leucas	0	0	1	0	0	0	0	0	1
Monodon monoceros	0	0	0	2	0	0	0	0	2
Total	122	112	140	91	84	120	109	288	1066

TABLE 8.1 List of cetacean species recorded from the North Sea from stranding records for 1913–1992.

at Flixborough (despite careful sorting and identification of thousands of bones) and only two elements of minke whale are present. However, the low frequency of larger whalebones, compared with *Tursiops* remains, does not necessarily indicate that fewer minke whales were exploited. More minke whales could have been utilised by the inhabitants, but perhaps only the meat and blubber were arriving at the site. It would have been more efficient for these large cetaceans to be butchered and de-fleshed where they were washed up or beached and the heavy skeletal parts left behind.

Although the lack of bones of minke whale can be readily explained by their much larger size compared with either *Tursiops* or *Phocoena*, the complete absence of common porpoise remains is less easy to explain. These animals are very common in the waters around Britain today, and (as has been shown) were by the far the most commonly stranded cetacean recorded during the last century. If their present-day frequency and distribution can be projected back into the past, then they also ought to have been more common in waters around Britain during the Saxon period.

Porpoises are significantly smaller than bottlenose dolphins (reaching a maximum length today of approximately 1.5m). Like *Tursiops*, they frequent inshore and coastal waters, but are certainly more difficult to catch. However, it is hard to believe that small numbers of individuals were not occasionally encountered and successfully killed, unless they were being deliberately ignored during *Tursiops* hunting. An alternative explanation for their complete absence from the Flixborough middens in all periods could be that they were entirely absent from local waters in the past (something that is also hard to believe). If the cetacean remains at Flixborough were mainly or exclusively from stranded animals, we should expect a closer correspondence between the species there and the modern stranding records. It is, therefore, hard to explain why the remains of bottlenose dolphins are so frequent, whilst porpoises (which probably would have been plentiful), and white-beaked dolphins (which are commonly stranded and very similar in size to bottlenose dolphins) are entirely absent.

The answer may be that bottlenose dolphins were once common (and probably resident) in and around the Humber and Trent estuaries, probably following migratory fish that congregated in estuaries prior to moving upriver to spawn. A resident population in the estuary may have been easier to hunt than other cetacean species (particularly smaller porpoises) due to their propensity to come into very shallow waters and because of their extremely inquisitive nature, making them more approachable by boat (and therefore vulnerable). It is perhaps less likely that they were driven into shallow water or even ashore since they do not gather in large migratory groups; they are better adapted to shallow inshore waters, and they tend not to follow each other blindly to shore.

The nearest resident population of bottlenose dolphins today is to be found in the Moray Firth. There are none in the Humber estuary, nor are there any records of there ever having been any. The remains from Flixborough are, therefore, all the more intriguing in that they may indicate a once well-established (but now extinct) resident population living in the Humber estuary.

Overall, the data from Flixborough appear to provide incontrovertible evidence for the existence of a well-organised and active cetacean fishery on the east coast of Britain. It appears to have focussed almost exclusively upon a population of bottlenose dolphins that was present in the Humber estuary at least from the early to mid eighth century AD. Other, larger whales were probably hunted opportunistically when encountered, with fully-grown animals being deliberately avoided.

It is difficult to reconstruct in detail just how well organised, intensive or sustainable this exploitation might have been. The fact that there are no recent or historical records for the presence of a resident population of bottlenose dolphins in or around the Humber estuary may in fact indicate that their intensive exploitation in the past led to their eventual extinction from the region, and the genetic evidence outlined earlier certainly supports this view. It is unlikely that this suggested extinction occurred in the tenth century (numerous fragments are still present in Phase 6 dump deposits – some even in Phase 6iii dark soils). Interestingly, Musset (1964, 161) suggests that the zenith of whale hunting further south in the English Channel took place a little later, i.e. during the eleventh and early years of the twelfth century. Perhaps it could be argued that the unique evidence of Saxon exploitation suggested at Flixborough may have provided the initial crucial impetus, and that continued exploitation of the Humber bottlenose dolphins during subsequent Anglo-Norman times led to their eventual demise from the region.

The missing pinnipeds

One final intriguing point to explore in the discussion of marine mammal exploitation at Flixborough is the reason for the apparent absence of any pinniped (i.e. common or grey seal) remains from the Flixborough assemblage. Today there are large breeding colonies around the Humber (around Spurn point) and The Wash. If they were also present during the Saxon period, surely they would have represented a large and readily available additional marine resource. Does their absence from the Flixborough assemblage indicate that these large colonies were absent, or that they were just not exploited by humans (either deliberately avoided or not readily accessible)?

Evidence for fishing

The seven main fish taxa recovered at Flixborough could all have been caught in the nearby waters of the River Trent and its environs (Wheeler 1969; Whitehead *et al.*

1986a; 1986b; 1989; Maitland and Campbell 1992). Moreover, given the proximity of the Humber estuary, and independent evidence that the lower Trent was subject to brackish/marine incursion (Van de Noort and Ellis 1998, 289), the few marine specimens from the site may have been incidental catches from little further afield. Salmon typically spawn in the upper reaches of rivers, but are otherwise widely distributed. Smelt would have been available year-round in the Humber, but may have been harvested during their upriver spawning migrations. These runs typically occur between March and April, but within a single river system they may be restricted to only a few days during which smelt are a particularly easy catch. Eels are common in coastal waters, estuaries and all freshwater habitats. They are potentially a year-round resource, but are also most susceptible to capture during large-scale annual migrations (in this case the autumn progression of adult 'silver eels' to the sea).

Flounder, which probably account for most of the flatfish bones in the sieved material, routinely occupy freshwater. They could have been caught along the shores of the Trent or the Humber. However, they also figure largely in the diet of estuarine eels (Maitland and Campbell 1992, 248) and the archaeological remains may partly represent gut contents. Many of the specimens from Flixborough were small (from fish of less than 150mm total length). Most of the cyprinids from the site may also represent gut contents, particularly of the common piscivorous species, pike and perch (which would have been readily available in the lower Trent, typically inhabiting slow-flowing rivers and lakes). This observation is especially relevant from Phase 3b onwards, when most of the cyprinid specimens were from fish of less than 150mm total length. Some of the largest examples could, however, represent fish purposely caught in the Trent – particularly in Phases 1 and 2–3a.

The 'incidental' fish species recovered at Flixborough are equally consistent with very local use of the Trent and the Humber. Many small and uncommon fish, such as stickleback and burbot (the few bones of which that were recovered being from tiny individuals), may also have arrived on site as the gut contents of larger fish. Other taxa, such as the few herring, cod and haddock represented could conceivably represent long-range trade or fishing on the North Sea. Given their tiny numbers, however, they are more likely to derive from individuals caught in the Humber Estuary. The most common marine taxon, herring, is represented by only 11 specimens in an assemblage of over 6000 identified bones. Two ling specimens from Phases 3b and 4–5b of the hand-collected assemblage could conceivably have been traded from further north (cf. Wheeler 1977, 406), but are more likely to represent vagrants or even intrusive specimens.

In terms of diachronic change, the ratio of migratory to fresh water fish increased between Phases 2–3a and 3b (FIG. 8.9). This change was marked by increases in the

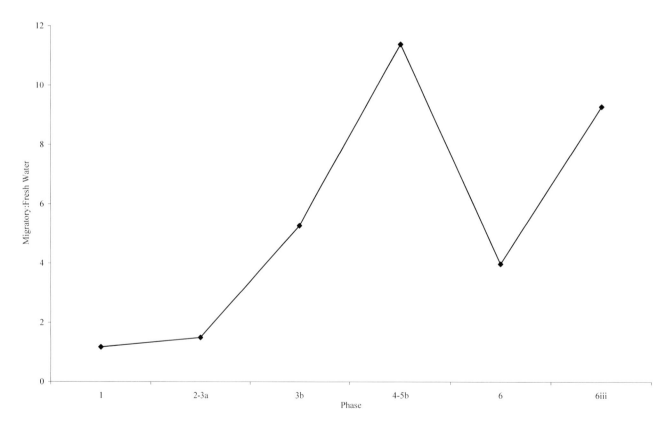

FIG. 8.9 Sieved fish: ratio of migratory to freshwater taxa by phase.

abundance of eel and flatfish at the expense of pike, perch and cyprinids (FIG. 8.10). It was paralleled by contemporaneous increases in the size of smelt and decreases in the size of cyprinids (TABLE 8.2) Preservation also improved from Phase 2–3a to Phase 3b (see chapter 6), which could conceivably be a biasing factor, but it is difficult to envisage how taphonomy could be responsible for the specific patterns observed.

It is tempting to interpret these diachronic trends as evidence for increasing emphasis on fishing in the Humber Estuary. However, the transition from Phase 2–3a to Phase 3b is also marked by a change in the context types from which the assemblage derives (see Chapter 4). Phase 1 is represented by post-holes and dumps and Phase 2–3a is dominated by soakaways. Conversely, Phases 3b, 4–5b and 6 are represented largely by dumps and Phase 6iii is predominately dark soils. This observation is important given that there are differences in the relative abundance of the seven dominant taxa between context types (chi-square = 949.16, df = 30, p = <0.001; see TABLE 4.13). Attempts to discern temporal trends across the entire assemblage may thus reflect differences in refuse disposal between feature types instead.

These broad trends represent a composite view, but they are heavily influenced by fluctuations in just four important taxa: pike, eel, smelt and flatfish. A decrease in pike (in most context types) and a profusion of flatfish (in dumps) increased the importance of migratory taxa in Phase 3b, whilst a vast quantity of eels (in dumps and occupation deposits) effected the same in Phase 4–5b. However, in Phase 6, a marked reduction in the numbers of smelt, eel and flatfish remains (principally in dumps) resulted in a low ratio of migratory to freshwater taxa for this period (See Chapter 4, FIGS 4a–4f).

These observations do not lend themselves to simple models of causation, but at least some trends (particularly in the abundance of pike and the size of smelt) may be consistent with the above-mentioned hypothesis that fishing extended from the nearby Trent to the Humber Estuary in Phase 3b. Alternative explanations could be that the lower Trent became more brackish in the mid eighth to early ninth centuries (see Van de Noort and

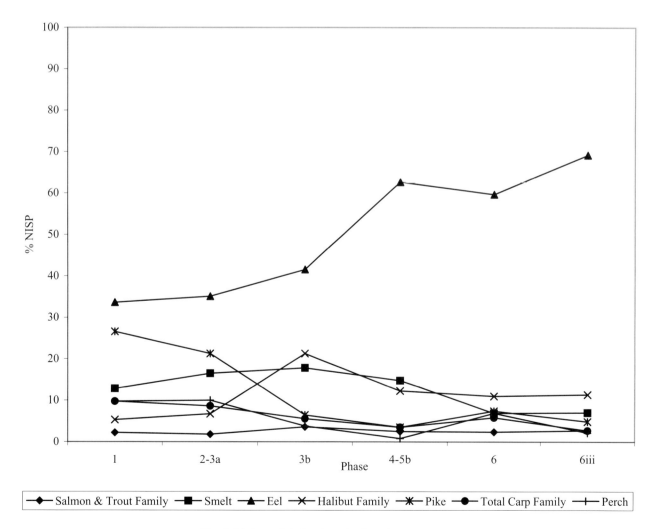

Fig 8.10 Sieved fish: % NISP by phase and taxon.

Common name	Size	Phase 1	Phase 2–3a	Phase 3b	Phase 4–5b	Phase 6	Phase 6iii	Total
Marine								
Haddock	50–80 cm				1			**1**
Migratory								
Salmon and trout family	<15 cm				3			**3**
	30–50 cm				1			**1**
	50–80 cm				1			**1**
	80–100 cm		1	1		1		**3**
Smelt	<15 cm	4	37	14	19	3		**77**
	30–50 cm	4	54	53	44	6		**161**
Eel	<15 cm				4			**4**
	15–30 cm	3	30	34	49	14	3	**133**
	30–50 cm		24	33	51	14	4	**126**
	50–80 cm		5	7	8	5	1	**26**
Flounder/plaice	<15 cm		3	26	11	2	1	**43**
	15–30 cm		8	46	19	8	1	**82**
	30–50 cm	1	3	5	6			**15**
Freshwater								
Pike	<15 cm						1	**1**
	15–30 cm		1	2	1			**4**
	30–50 cm	21	89	17	7	11	1	**146**
	50–80 cm		7	4	6	1		**18**
Cyprinids	<15 cm		21	17	12	3		**53**
	15–30 cm	1	15	1	6	1		**24**
	30–50 cm		5	1	2	1		**9**
Burbot	<15 cm		1		1			**2**
Perch	<15 cm			1	1			**2**
	15–30 cm	9	42	4	3	7	1	**66**
	30–50 cm	1	8	6	2			**17**
	50–80 cm	1						**1**
Other								
Stickleback family	<15 cm		8	3	1			**12**

TABLE 8.2 *Postulated size distribution of fish recovered from the bulk-sieved samples by phase.*

Ellis 1998, 289), that new fishing methods were employed, that food preferences changed, or some combination of these factors.

In the context of temporal trends, the most remarkable facet of the Flixborough assemblage is the fact that it does not reflect the increasing importance of marine taxa such as cod around the turn of the first millennium which is now documented throughout north-western Europe (e.g. Jones 1988; Barrett *et al.* 1999; Enghoff 1999; Perdikaris 1999; Enghoff 2000; Locker 2001, 281). One explanation is that the site pre-dates this development, with Phase 6iii ending in the early eleventh century. An alternative possibility is that this shift in emphasis was initially an urban rather than rural phenomenon (e.g. Ervynck 2004).

Fishing methods

The fish taxa identified at Flixborough could have been caught using a variety of methods, principally nets, lines and traps. Ælfric's fictional river fisherman (*c.* AD 987–1002) caught '*eels and pike, minnows and turbot [flounder?], trout and lampreys and whatever swims in the water*' (Swanton 1975, 110). When asked about his methods he replied '*I board my boat and cast my net into the river; and throw in a hook and bait and baskets*' (Swanton 1975, 110). Artefacts which may have been lead net weights have been found at Flixborough itself (C. Loveluck, pers. comm.) and Saxon fish weirs of wattle are known, at Colwick further up the River Trent, for example (Salisbury 1991). This specific example, comprising wattle fences forming a V-shaped enclosure with its mouth facing upstream, would have been particularly useful for catching eels in a terminal net or wicker basket during their autumn downstream migration (Salisbury 1991). However, similar technology facing in the opposite direction has been used to catch salmonids (principally salmon) during their upstream migrations. Inter-tidal traps placed in an estuarine setting could also have been employed to catch flatfish and marine taxa (Salisbury 1991).

In medieval England freshwater fish were often maintained in carefully managed ponds sponsored by monasteries and the aristocracy (Dyer 1988). Pisciculture of this kind was practised on the continent in the reign of Charlemagne (Hoffmann 1985, 73). However, it seems not to have been introduced to Britain until the eleventh and twelfth centuries (McDonnell 1981) and is unlikely to be the source of the freshwater fish recovered at Flixborough.

Evidence for seasonality

The seasonal cycle of scarcity and abundance may have created important niches for fish within the subsistence economy of Saxon Flixborough. Late winter, for example, was the traditional period of shortage in medieval Britain (Wilson 1973, 26). Fisheries for smelt during their upstream spawning run in March to April (Maitland and Campbell 1992, 165) may thus have been particularly valuable. Similarly, a fishery for adult eels during their seaward migration in September to October (Wheeler 1969, 228) could have produced huge catches in a matter of weeks or even days.[4]

The crucial role of seasonality in fish consumption may, however, have had more to do with Christian doctrine than ecology. The practice of Christian fasting formalised by St Benedict's Rule and subsequent monastic regulations (Dembinska 1986) was also applied to the English secular community by seventh century Kentish law (Swanton 1975, 3) (see also Chapter 10). Similar legislation was gradually adopted throughout Anglo-Saxon England. Examples include the ninth-century edicts of Alfred and Guthrum, Edgar's code at Andover (AD 959–963), and Canute's laws of the early eleventh century (Hagen 1992, 131). The precise number of fast days per year varied through time and according to the rigour of the community in question (Hagen 1992, 127–34). Nevertheless, the meat of quadrupeds would typically have been forbidden during 40 days of Lent, 40 days of Advent before Christmas, possibly 40 days following Pentecost and on the eves of Christian celebrations throughout the year (Hagen 1992, 127–31). This practice

is known to have had a major impact on the seasonal demand for fish in the later Middle Ages, particularly among the ecclesiastical and aristocratic elite who could afford the considerable expense (Dyer 1988). Some authorities dispute that fish were widely accepted as a component of fasts prior to the twelfth century (Dembinska 1986, 155). Although they were not explicitly excluded by St Benedict's Rule, fish may have been viewed as delicacies rather than staple fare by some Christian communities (McDonnell 1981, 22; Dembinska 1986, 155). Contrary to this view, however, King Ethelwulf is known to have granted a fishery on the North Devon coast to Glastonbury in the mid ninth century (Fox 2001, 47). It thus seems likely that fish were a part of monastic (and presumably secular) fasting by the late Saxon period (cf. Hoffmann 1996 regarding contemporaneous Continental practice).

These seasonal patterns may explain an apparent disparity between the limited number of fish bones from Flixborough and other Saxon sites (see Chapter 10), and references to the abundance of fish in some contemporaneous sources. Although Flixborough has produced one of the largest rural Saxon fish assemblages, even here the number of specimens is small in comparison with the mammal assemblage. Conversely, in AD 731 Bede observed that 'Salmon and eels are especially plentiful' (Sherley-Price 1968, 37). The fisherman of *Ælfric's Colloquy* (*c.* AD 987–1002) claimed '*I can't catch as many as I can sell*' (Swanton 1975, 110) and the *Laws of Æthelred* (code IV, *c.* AD 991–1002) set out tolls in London for boats containing fish (Robertson 1925, 73).

Poor recovery and preservation may explain this disparity in some cases, but these variables are unlikely to apply to Flixborough. Here, all relevant fish bone was sorted from a 2mm mesh and most specimens were reasonably well preserved. Across the phases, between 22% and 40% of the diagnostic elements were over 80% complete (Table 3.1). It seems probable that the historical importance of fish had more to do with the seasonal and ritual cycles of Anglo-Saxon Britain than with their absolute dietary contribution.

Shellfish exploitation

Oyster shell was by far the largest component of the molluscan assemblage recovered from all phases of the site. Evidence of the oysters having been opened using a knife or similar implement was represented by characteristic 'V'- or 'W'-shaped notches on the valve margins of approximately 40% of the remains. This percentage remains fairly consistent (36–47%) throughout all the phases of the site (apart from in Phase 1 where the 100% record is entirely misleading given that a total of only two valves and some shell fragments were recovered). These frequencies almost certainly indicate minimum values, as post-depositional, and indeed post-excavation, erosion and fragmentation of the shell are likely to have destroyed opening marks on some of the remains.

Where average values of oyster valve measurements by phase group could usefully be determined, these remained relatively consistent through time, suggesting that the oysters eaten at Flixborough were probably from 'cultivated' (or at least managed) rather than natural populations. From current evidence, the oysters could only have been imported to the site from the Kent, Essex or Suffolk coasts, or from the Firth of Clyde (Winder 1992 and pers. comm.). However, Kenward (1998) has speculated that exploitation of local (but as yet unlocated) oyster beds may well have been more widespread along the east coast of England. Certain organisms (e.g. *Polydora* spp. and barnacles) which infest oysters have known preferred habitats, and this might help to identify the source of the oysters. However, although evidence of the damage caused by these organisms was noted on some valves, the poor preservation of most of the shells prevented further exploration of this research avenue.

It seems likely that the few remains of other edible marine taxa were also derived from human food waste, with the extremely small number of 'non-edible' species probably having been collected accidentally. All of these taxa are still common off the coast of north-eastern England today. The fact that so few edible shellfish other than oysters are represented at Flixborough suggests that any other locally available seafood resources were not systematically exploited for consumption at the site. As was suggested for a number of the vertebrate species, a focus on oysters (to the exclusion of other locally available shellfish), may also reflect the overall high-status nature

and character of the settlement, or at least of some of those inhabitants responsible for the food waste recovered through excavation.

In terms of evidence for the changing nature of occupation through time from the molluscan data, it is interesting to note that a marked drop in the average weight of shell remains (mainly oysters) per context – in particular from 'dump' contexts – was observed in Phase 4–5b. In this regard, these data mirror similar changes previously noted for other zooarchaeological and broader archaeological evidence, and perhaps indicate some disruption at the site or an interruption in trading oysters from the estuary or coast.

Notes

1   There is no direct evidence of this except similarity in the size of the archaeological bones to those of modern wild mallards in the former Environmental Archaeology Unit's extensive comparative collection.

2   It does not include a detailed discussion of the possible evidence for falconry at the site, which is detailed in Chapter 10.

3   For the purpose of this study, the migratory taxa eel and Salmonidae can be classified as "freshwater" and "marine", since they feed almost exclusively in those respective environments (Maitland and Campbell 1992).

4   In small rivers, salmon are also a seasonal resource, tending to begin their upriver migrations around midsummer. In large rivers such as the Trent, however, they would have been present all year in variable numbers (Maitland and Campbell 1992, 105, 108).

9 Evidence for Trade and Contact

Keith Dobney, Deborah Jaques, James Barrett and Cluny Johnstone

9.1 Introduction

The numerous lines of evidence from the Flixborough finds assemblages show that the inhabitants had a wide variety of regional, national and international contacts, varying in scale and intensity through the different phases of occupation. From a zooarchaeological point of view, however, this evidence is (in the vast majority of cases) difficult to establish.

The very fact that Flixborough is undoubtedly a site of high-status character allows certain inferences to be drawn about the likely origins of the domestic and wild taxa recovered from the site. At a royal estate centre, many of the animal resources would have arrived as food rents from 'clients' (see Chapter 10). Maintenance of the personal ties of clientship at different levels ensured that there was considerable movement of property and transfer of ownership, especially of livestock and foodstuffs (McCormick 1992). Although many of these resources would probably have derived from neighbouring estates, access to goods that were rare or special would have been sought from farther afield (i.e. from far-flung estates, or even from overseas) in order to reinforce the social standing and identity of the élite inhabitants at Flixborough.

However, with the exception of the clearly exotic/imported species (see below), evidence for trade in livestock, domestic animal products or wild resources can be directly inferred in very few cases from the zoo-archaeological data.

9.2 The fish trade

Fish remains are one of the principal indicators of the growth of trade in staples, both local and long-range, in early historic Europe. There is now good evidence that cured gadids (members of the cod family) and herring were transported around the Continent from at least the eleventh century (e.g. Jones 1988; Barrett *et al.* 1999;

Enghoff 1999; Perdikaris 1999; Enghoff 2000; Locker 2001, 281). Local trade in herring was probably common several centuries earlier, to judge from the incidence of this species at inland urban sites of middle and late Saxon date (e.g. Locker 1989; O'Connor 1991, 263–7).

One might hypothesise that towns such as York (within easy reach by river transport) would have been supplied by rural estates on the Humber Estuary. However, there is little convincing evidence for fish trade from the Flixborough assemblage. Herring make up less than one percent of the sieved assemblage – only 11 bones of this species were recovered from the whole site. It is conceivable that the entire catch was consistently shipped directly to towns such as York (herring have not yet been noted in Saxon deposits from Lincoln) but, if so, any processing occurred 'off-site'. Butchering herring for storage and trade – which later involved removing the gill region – might be expected to leave a characteristic assemblage like that recognised by Enghoff (1996) at Selsø-Vestby in Denmark.

There is only a minute amount of evidence consistent with fish trade *to* Flixborough. The main freshwater and migratory taxa recovered, principally salmonids, smelt, eels, flounder or plaice, pike, cyprinids and perch, would all have been available in the lower reaches of the River Trent or in the Humber Estuary. Moreover, skeletal element distributions suggest that many fish were transported to the site prior to butchery (particularly in Phases 2–3a and 3b). Nevertheless, low ratios of cranial elements to vertebrae imply that some fish arrived after decapitation (particularly in Phase 1). These fish, or indeed whole fresh fish, may have been acquired by local trade or brought to the settlement as payments in kind. If Flixborough was a monastic community for part or all of its occupation (see Chapter 10), one can envisage the creation of satellite communities and patronage networks to serve its specific dietary requirements (cf. Fox 2001, 47), a process described as indirect subsistence rather than trade by Hoffmann (1996, 636–8). It is equally possible, however, that the inhabitants of Flixborough were self-sufficient in the provision of freshwater and migratory fish from the site's immediate hinterland.

Evidence for the import of marine taxa is equally ambiguous. The critical specimens are two ling bones and a caudal vertebra of cod, which has been cut in the transverse plane. Ling are more abundant in northerly waters (Wheeler 1977, 406; but see also Whitehead *et al.* 1986a, 703) and this kind of butchery mark can be characteristic of stockfish or klipfisk (being produced during removal of the anterior vertebrae; Barrett 1997). These bones could thus represent limited transport of dried fish – perhaps as traveller's rations – prior to the eleventh century date at which gadids are known to have been widely traded (see above). It is equally possible, however, that the ling bones represent an unusual catch (or even intrusive specimens) and that the relevant cut mark was caused during butchery of a locally caught fish.

9.3 Indigenous or imported? Evidence from the cattle

Differences in the sizes of domestic animals from different settlement types may, in some cases, be used to infer trade and contact (among other things) between them. It has already been suggested that the presence of particularly tall cattle at Flixborough in the earlier Mid-Saxon period could indicate the presence of 'improved' varieties or breeds (see Chapter 7, and also Chapter 10). Their absence from other sites in the region (particularly from the proto- and early urban centres of York and Lincoln) may further suggest that their origins may lie outside the region or perhaps even outside Britain. Therefore, can tentative links be drawn with sites far from Flixborough where similarly large-sized cattle have been reported?

There are, in fact, only a few sites in England where mean withers height values begin to approach those of Flixborough (see FIGS 7.46 & 7.47). These are: Six Dials and Hamwih, Southampton, and Vernon St, Ipswich (all *wic* sites), various London sites (including *wic*, ecclesiastical and early urban assemblages), Thetford, Norfolk (an early 'urban' centre), and Wicken Bonhunt, Essex (a high-status estate centre similar to Flixborough). There are also two sites on the Continent, Dorestadt (Prummel 1993) and Rijnsburg, both in the Netherlands, where large cattle have been reported. The presence of tall cattle at eighth-century Dorestadt, (near the mouth of the Rhine in Frisia) is particularly interesting, since evidence from the finds recovered from the site indicate that this is the area from which Flixborough is obtaining the bulk of its imported coinage and pottery. There are certainly no cattle of comparable size reported at sites such as, Haithabu and Feddersen Wierde, which all appear to have cattle that were much shorter in stature.

On the basis of this albeit limited dataset, the evidence

suggests that large varieties of cattle were introduced to the region either directly from the European mainland (probably from the Low Countries), or via the emporia or *wics* during the Mid-Saxon period. Perhaps the large animals recorded from Flixborough (and at the other sites in the east of England), represent an 'improved variety/ breed' of cattle, shipped specifically from the Continent to England and destined for the estates of high-status individuals (such as those of Flixborough and Wicken Bonhunt), in order to improve local stock.

9.4 Local or exotic?

At face value, the identification of certain wild species of mammal, bird and fish in the Flixborough assemblage (i.e. sturgeon, pine marten, crane and bottlenose dolphin, none of which are today found in the region), could also imply that the inhabitants of Flixborough had access to resources from much farther afield. However, major changes have occurred over the last 2000 years in the distribution and frequency of the great majority of our native species, mostly as a direct result of human impact. There is good evidence to suggest that these particular species were, in fact, present in the region 1000 years ago, some probably associated with wealth and status (see Chapter 10).

Thus, for example, although sturgeons are rare in British waters today, historical records indicate that they were found in the rivers of the Flixborough region, i.e. the Trent, Don, and Ouse (Bunting *et al.* 1974). Known as 'the King's fish' during the medieval period, these saltwater fish, which migrate into rivers to spawn, were (like many marine mammals) regarded as a delicacy for high-ranking members of society, and as such were highly sought after, commanding high prices (see also Chapter 10). Flixborough also produced several pine marten bones, mainly from Phase 3b deposits, and these potentially could be indicators of trade in furs. As already mentioned, at the site of Fishergate in York (O'Connor 1991), the remains of pine marten were identified from deposits of eighth–ninth century date. Here, all of the specimens were bones of the feet, and fine knife marks present on a calcaneum have been interpreted as evidence for the presence of pelts. The latter could have been imported from outside the region or could derive from animals caught locally. The bones from Flixborough were devoid of evidence of skinning and represented skeletal elements that suggested whole animals were present at the site, not just pelts or furs. This implies that the pine martens were more likely of local origin.

Although it is possible that both bottlenose dolphins and cranes were being sourced from further afield, detailed analysis of their rather numerous remains from Flixborough has suggested otherwise (see Chapter 8). In both cases, there is good evidence to support the idea that resident populations of these species were present in the region during the entire sequence of occupation at the site. In the case of bottle-nosed dolphins, it has been proposed that there was a local specialised dolphin fishery (perhaps in the Humber Estuary itself) supplying butchered carcases to the inhabitants of Flixborough (see Chapter 8). In the case of cranes, the Flixborough biometrical and aDNA data have helped to establish (we think) that the British population was quite distinct (larger than) to those from elsewhere in mainland Europe (Dobney *et al.* in prep.).

9.5 Long-term survival or accidental reintroduction? The case of the black rat

There is, in reality, only one element of the Flixborough vertebrate assemblage that categorically provides direct evidence of long-distance trade and contact. This is the large Muridae femur, identified as a black rat (*Rattus rattus*),[1] which was recovered from a well-sealed context of early–mid tenth century (Phase 6) date. The remains of this particular unwelcome exotic (which was almost certainly accidentally introduced to the site) provides an important insight into wider trade and exchange networks.

This specimen was originally recovered during hand-collection/dry-sieving procedures, and it was assumed that further black rat remains would be present in the extensive numbers of then unprocessed wet-sieved samples. However, despite the subsequent careful processing and sorting of the wet-sieved assemblage, no further specimens of black rat were recovered, leading to the present conclusion that black rats were extremely rare at Flixborough, and only present during the early-mid tenth century.

Although the fossil record for the black rat is very sketchy, it is generally assumed that this species originated in South-East Asia. During the Holocene, the black rat dramatically extended its distribution to incorporate most of Eurasia, establishing commensal populations in virtually all (non-arid) tropical and semi-tropical regions (Ervynck 2002). Until the late 1970's, when Rackham (1979) published details of black rat remains from a Roman well at Skeldergate in York, the black rat was generally accepted to have been a Norman introduction into England (Armitage *et al.* 1984).

Since then, further finds of this species in England have proven its more widespread presence in urban sites of late Roman date. For example, in northern England, Roman deposits containing the remains of black rat have been found at eight sites (Dobney and Harwood 1999). The most tightly dated and reliable of these come from York, Lincoln and the Roman fort at South Shields, Tyne and Wear. Interestingly, the temporal distribution of rat remains at South Shields perhaps provides tentative evidence of a decline in black rat numbers towards the end of the Roman period. Here, rat remains form 10% of the small mammal assemblage in a late third–early

fourth-century deposit, falling to 2% in a late fourth-century deposit from the same site (Younger 1994). The next oldest well-stratified record of black rat from the North of England is not found until the mid-ninth to early tenth centuries AD at Coppergate, York, coinciding with the establishment of the Viking town of Jorvik.

On the basis of this apparent hiatus in the record between the late fourth to early ninth centuries, Armitage (1994) has suggested that the black rat became extinct in northern Europe during the sixth to eight centuries AD. This was explained as being a direct result of the collapse of central Roman control over the northern frontier (including Britain), when large thriving urban centres (such as York and Lincoln) were progressively abandoned and subsequent settlement became more diffuse, rural and scattered. According to Armitage (*op. cit.*), the black rat, regarded as the ultimate obligate commensal in the colder climes of northern Europe, would not have survived the reduction of its mainly urban habitat. Reintroduction by the Vikings from the Continent into newly established and thriving urban centres thus saw it successfully re-established once again in England. Its apparent absence from the zooarchaeological record during the fifth to ninth centuries could, however, be an artefact, a direct result of the fact that archaeological vertebrate assemblages of Early and Mid-Saxon date are rare. This dearth of well-dated assemblages led Dobney and Harwood (1999) to propose that the black rat may have actually survived in England throughout the Saxon period.

An extensive sieving programme during excavations of eighth- to ninth-century deposits from Fishergate in York, however, also failed to recover any bones of black rat (O'Connor 1991). The site has been interpreted as the original *wic*, a Saxon trading settlement known as *Eoforwic*, situated a little outside the foci of the earlier Roman and later Viking and medieval cities. Although the precise nature of Anglian occupation at Fishergate may suggest intermittent occupation at certain times of the year – i.e. conditions unsuitable for obligate commensals (Dobney and Harwood 1999) – the absence of black rat remains serves to strengthen the hiatus hypothesis.

Finally, some 80km (50 miles) to the north of Flixborough, evidence from the rural site at West Heslerton, North Yorkshire, appears to show continuous occupation (of varying nature and degree) from the very late Roman through Early and Mid-Saxon periods (i.e. fourth to seventh centuries AD). Here, too, a vast collection of vertebrate remains has been recovered, along with bone from numerous sieved samples and, as at Flixborough and Fishergate, no *Rattus* remains (of either Roman or Saxon date) are reported (Jane Richardson pers. comm.).

The evidence from these recently excavated and sieved sites from the North of England is compelling, and does indeed appear to support the hypothesis that the black rat was absent from Britain from late Roman times until the early tenth century. The rarity of rat remains at Flixborough, even when it does eventually appear (during the early to mid tenth century), implies that no viable population was ever established at the site, despite the availability of large middens containing vast quantities of waste from animal carcases. It would, therefore, appear that it was the lack of truly 'urban' conditions (i.e. large concentrations of heated buildings, etc.), and not food availability, that was the limiting factor for the survival of the black rat in England during the Early and Mid-Saxon periods. In this respect, the rural and high-status nature of the assemblage from Flixborough is fundamental to our understanding of this particular question.

On the basis of the evidence previously discussed, it would appear that the single specimen from Flixborough represents a contemporaneous (but accidental) foreign import. This could indicate either direct or indirect links to the Continent (in the latter case perhaps via other urban centres within the region, where black rat populations were already established). Pottery of mid-late ninth- to tenth-century date from Flixborough indicates a purely regional exchange pattern. This contrasts with pottery evidence from earlier deposits which implies wider trading connections, i.e. with northern France and Belgium during the late seventh to early eighth centuries, and with the Rhineland during the early ninth century (Loveluck 1997).

In the light of evidence from pottery and other finds, the absence of black rat remains in all but early-mid tenth century deposits at the site also appears to indicate regional (not continental) links. This was most probably with the growing urban centres of the region, i.e. York or Lincoln (where black rat remains have also been found in Anglo-Scandinavian deposits). There is little doubt that the local and regional exchange of goods such as Torksey wares, almost certainly transported by boat, would have facilitated the accidental transportation of the black rat once it had begun to flourish again in the growing towns of the region.

In contrast to the evidence from the Roman period from the region (Dobney 2001), the vertebrate assemblages from Flixborough, and other Saxon/Anglo-Scandinavian sites in the region, provide little specific evidence for the importation of exotic or rare species. There is little or no direct evidence from the bones of any widespread trade and exchange in wild vertebrate resources beyond a local or perhaps even regional procurement network. The large cattle from Phase 2–3a are, therefore, perhaps the only possible evidence from the vertebrate remains of the importation of animals from beyond these shores.

Note

1   This was kindly identified by Dr Anton Ervynck at the Flemish Heritage Institute, Brussels, Belgium.

10   Zooarchaeological Evidence for the Nature and Character of the Settlement

Keith Dobney, Deborah Jaques, James Barrett and Cluny Johnstone

10.1 Introduction

In England, the 1st millennium AD witnessed the gradual and then rapid development of an ecclesiastical and secular settlement hierarchy, at the pinnacle of which were the residences of its peripatetic kings (Hodges 1982). During this time, élite organisations, which had been concerned primarily with the exchange of prestige items, used their position to administer and manage surplus. Therefore, royal patronage, which aimed to maximise the hitherto irregular trade in imported luxury goods, subsequently stimulated the evolution of trading centres (known as emporia *or wics*), where those essentially engaged in non-subsistence activities had to be fed and provisioned. The result of this evolution (which occurred in the matter of a few centuries – between the seventh and tenth centuries) was the inception of competitive markets, with an associated increase in economic specialisation, a fundamental part of the process of urbanisation and state formation (Hodges *op. cit.*, 130).

During this time, the establishment of large royal residences (each known as *villa regalis*), like those found at Yeavering and Milfield in Northumberland, led to the rearrangement of much of the rural settlement pattern. Royal and aristocratic estate centres, along with monasteries like Jarrow and Wearmouth, created new 'consumption centres' (Hinton 2001) which drew upon and utilised resources on a scale and of a diversity that reflected their 'special' status. In this respect, these 'special' settlements stimulated food production and economic specialisation, and the site of Flixborough appears to have been no exception.

Detailed analysis of the vertebrate assemblage outlined in previous chapters has already provided a wealth of evidence concerning broad aspects of, for example, the environment and the agricultural economy. However, the zooarchaeological assemblage can also provide both direct and indirect evidence as to the changing nature and character of the settlement from the middle of the eighth century to the end of the tenth century. Three pertinent themes are, therefore, discussed further in this chapter. These are:

- the possible impact of changes in land-holdings and the Viking raids/settlement during the ninth century;
- the possibility that there was a monastic phase of settlement; and
- the wealth and status of the inhabitants themselves.

However, before any of these questions can be systematically addressed, we must first examine the assemblage in the wider context of Anglo-Saxon animal exploitation, in order to establish how representative these data are in relation to other similar and contemporaneous sites of rural elite, religious and even urban type. When we simply compare the relative frequencies (based on NISP) of domestic and wild birds and mammals from the various phases at Flixborough to others of similar date organised by site type (TABLE 10.1, after Sykes 2007), it is immediately apparent just how unusual the vertebrate assemblage from Flixborough is. With the exception of Portchester Castle, few parallels exist, which at face value is both exciting and somewhat challenging, as it adds further levels of uncertainty to any comparison with other sites.

However, the obvious inter-site variation between Flixborough and almost all of the other site types in TABLE 10.1 appears to be largely a result of the large number of wild and domestic bird bones found at the site. Excavations at Flixborough represent one of the few examples of sites that have been extensively sieved and sampled. The dry sandy substrate, linked with a large-scale dry-sieving programme, ensured the collection of large quantities of smaller bones, which are likely to be seriously under-represented at other sites where hand-collection was standard practice. As a result, direct quantitative comparisons between the Flixborough data and other contemporaneous vertebrate assemblages may be

Phase/Site type (No of sites)	Domestic mammals	Wild mammals	Domestic Birds	Wild Birds
5th – mid-9th century				
Rural (n =28)	95.6	0.5	3.5	0.4
Urban (n=13)	95.5	0.2	4.1	0.2
Elite (n=11)	90.5	1.2	7.8	0.5
Religious (n=3)	97.3	1.0	1.4	0.3
Flixborough 2–3a	**59.4**	**0.3**	**29.3**	**11**
Mid-9th – mid-11th century				
Rural (n=5)	93.7	0.3	5.6	0.4
Urban (n=20)	95.0	0.6	4.0	0.4
Elite (n=9)	85.2	3.0	10.2	1.6
Religious (n=7)	86.9	3	9.1	1.0
*Portchester Castle	**65.6**	**4.1**	**23.1**	**7.2**
Flixborough 3b	**66.3**	**2.1**	**24.3**	**7.3**
Flixborough 4–5b	**81.5**	**0.2**	**16.5**	**1.8**
Flixborough 6	**73.2**	**0.4**	**21.6**	**4.8**
Flixborough 6iii	**88.4**	**0.3**	**10.2**	**1.1**
Mid-11th – mid-12th century				
Rural (n=3)	96.0	0.7	3.1	0.2
Urban (n=20)	90.8	0.4	8.4	0.4
Elite (n=15)	67.6	8.7	19.7	4.0
Religious (n=4)	91.0	2.0	6.4	0.6

TABLE 10.1 Comparison of relative proportions (%) of domestic and wild mammal and bird remains from fifth- to twelfth-century assemblages in England (classified by broad site type and calculated by total NISP) as a direct comparison with the different phases from Flixborough (data from Sykes, 2007, Appendix 1a:- reproduced here with kind permission of the author).

somewhat misleading. That said, however, a number of important questions relating to the nature and possible status of occupation at Flixborough can certainly be directly addressed using these and related data.

10.2 Vassals and Vikings: what happened in the ninth century?

What is clear from consideration of almost any aspect of the animal bone data discussed in the previous chapters, is that the zooarchaeological profiles relating to the settlement and its inhabitants during the eighth and tenth centuries are very different in many respects from those of the ninth century. Thus, the ninth century is the only time when the overall importance of cattle appears to be reduced in relation to sheep and pig, where morphometric traits perhaps indicate different source populations of cattle, and where dental and joint pathologies hint at different husbandry practices (see Chapter 7 for details). At the same time, exploitation of the nearby wetlands reached an all-time low within the overall Flixborough occupation sequence. The numerous wild geese, cranes and waders, evidently consumed in abundance in the eighth and tenth centuries, were very much reduced in number and variety in the ninth century. Instead, domesticated geese and ducks were exploited more extensively in this phase. Consumption and disposal patterns, as reflected by skeletal element representation, also show differences between the ninth century and the

earlier and later centuries. In fact, when detailed analysis of the various sub-phases of Phase 4–5b was undertaken, a shift in the pattern of skeletal element representation was apparent by the mid ninth century (i.e. in sub-phase 4ii, see Chapter 6).

Amongst the patterns of consumption and production observable within the artefact data for the ninth century are a number of traits which may be of direct relevance to the animal exploitation profiles. Within the same dumps of material containing large vertebrate assemblages, the largest quantity of debris from textile manufacturing was recovered from the entire occupation sequence, comprising fibre processing spikes, approximately 200 loom-weights, also spindle whorls, shears, and needles. In addition, it was apparent that a smaller loom-weight, thought to relate to the production of a finer quality textile, possibly for export, was used in this period (Loveluck and Dobney 2001; Walton Rogers, Volume 4, Chapter 6). Within this context, the predominance of sheep noted within the animal bone assemblage is likely to be related to the production of wool for this proposed specialist textile – perhaps even linked with the production of woollen habits and cowls. Other commodities, travelling along East-Coast communications routes at this date, included Ipswich ware pottery, from the emporium/nascent town in Suffolk.

The dumps from this period also contained the largest quantity and the greatest range of craft-working evidence. In addition to the artefacts representing textile manufacturing, tools relating to fine metalworking, leather-working and carpentry were also recovered, together with crucible fragments and iron-working debris. Other key stratified finds deposited for the first time between the early and mid ninth century included copper alloy, silver and iron styli, and window glass. An inscribed lead plaque with the names of seven individuals, both male and female, was recovered as a residual find in a later period; however, on palaeographic grounds it should also be ascribed to this period (Loveluck and Dobney 2001; Brown and Okasha, Volume 2, Chapter 3).

The array of evidence provided by the vertebrate remains of the ninth century suggests something of a dislocation from the resources of the surrounding landscape, and a possible commensurate intensification in production of the dominant domesticated livestock (particularly pigs). All the feast-related wild species of preceding periods are also much reduced. The decrease in the number of cattle could be explained by a change in both cattle husbandry and a lack of cattle renders to a settlement (and its associated territory) that could no longer call upon linked estate holdings of an earlier period. As a result, the focus shifted towards a more local and site-based production agricultural regime, relying much less on renders from far-flung estate holdings, which perhaps no longer existed. Such a dislocation from the resources of the wider landscape, and the absence of certain high-status foodstuffs, might both be explained by a combination of factors:

- as a result of the settlement becoming a family monastery, carved out of a larger family estate;
- through the wider socio-economic upheavals brought about by changes in landholdings in the ninth century; or
- the arrival and subsequent activities of the Viking 'Great Army' in AD 866 and their eventual conquering of the kingdom of Northumbria in 867.

The ninth century can be described as one of disruption and new impetus (Hinton 2001). Most scholars studying the Anglo-Saxon period in England concur that by the late ninth and tenth centuries a fairly radical change in settlement and farming occurred as a result of the development of the open field system, and this change may have occurred abruptly on some of the larger estates, perhaps as a result of deliberate planning (Hooke 1998, 115).

The area of open field in regions of high populations had to be extensive. This meant that the proportion of land available for common grazing was reduced, possibly leading to shortage of common grazing land (Thirsk 1967). This process coincided with major administrative changes and large-scale reorganisation which may both have resulted in the fragmentation of large estates into smaller ones. Newly-created independent small estates came under firm manorial control and were under even more pressure to increase both self-sufficiency and

revenues to the lords of the estate (Hooke 1998, 115). Possible evidence for estate fragmentation and subsequent dislocation from more distant resources can be postulated for Flixborough, beginning early in the ninth century. However, in this case it appears to have been a short-lived phenomenon (lasting perhaps 50–75 years) since, by the end of the ninth century and the beginning of the tenth century, the patterns of animal exploitation were virtually identical to those of the eighth century.

Viking armies in the late ninth century were '... *sharing out the land ... to plough and to support themselves in Northumbria, East Anglia and parts of Mercia'* (Hinton 2001, 70). The extent to which the Vikings were responsible for all or many of these changes is unclear and, although their influence can be exaggerated, equally they should not be underestimated (Hinton *op. cit.*). For example, the growth of York as an urban commercial centre within the Danelaw appears to have been more rapid than, for example, London or Winchester. Furthermore, the disintegration of the great churches within the Danelaw, resulted in major changes in the land-owning structure which gave the laity renewed ability to accumulate wealth and power (Hinton *op. cit.*, 81).

Although Viking raids no doubt caused much disruption and consternation, there is no evidence that they adversely affected population size and mobility. During the Danelaw, Anglo-Saxon culture continued to persist outside of Wessex (the only surviving English kingdom), '...*and trends towards a political system of royal authority over a manorially-based rural economy, eventually supported by market centres were maintained*' (Hinton 2001, 81). The important socio-economic role of Anglo-Saxon royal residences and other estate centres was obviously not lost on the new Scandinavian élite now in control. These centres (presumably now in their possession, or at least subject to them), appear to have maintained their earlier role within a wider economic framework, with food renders still brought to them by clients (Hinton *op. cit.*, 67).

Were one to look solely at the artefactual and structural evidence, then one might conclude that, in common with other sites within the Danelaw (e.g. Goltho and North Elmham), there was nothing obviously 'Danish' or 'Scandinavian' about the cultural material from Flixborough, and, hence, that the ethnic affinities of the inhabitants living there during the ninth and tenth centuries would appear to have changed very little; however, this would be an ill-founded judgement, as it would fail to take into account the abundant evidence from place-names for extensive Scandinavian influence within the Danelaw. It is possible that the maintenance of local Anglo-Saxon élites, and the economic systems already in place, was a deliberate policy of Anglo-Scandinavian overlords. However, one significant difference was the superimposition of another level of hierarchy, i.e. the establishment and development of urban centres such as York and Lincoln within the Danelaw. These became major catalysts for market development, particularly with regard to food supply.

The animal bone assemblage from Flixborough is perhaps one of the first to bear detailed witness to the major social and economic upheavals of the ninth century. The fine stratigraphic resolution allows us to see what may well be a period of disruption and resource dislocation beginning in the early ninth century and concluding towards the century's end. The tenth century pattern appears to return to that seen in the mid–late eighth century – both interpreted as periods of obvious high-status, where agricultural resources were drawn upon from far-flung estates and luxury goods from even further afield. Can the differences between the ninth and tenth centuries be regarded as indicating initial disruption as a result of Scandinavian influence, followed by the reintroduction and consolidation of well-established economic frameworks of Mid-Saxon times? It is tempting to draw that conclusion. However, other explanations are equally compelling and result in a more complex picture.

10.3 Monks or aristocrats: was Flixborough ever a monastery?

The Anglo-Saxon period in England saw the widespread re-adoption of Christianity and the beginnings of the monastic expansion. During the eighth and ninth centuries, monastic institutions flourished and became extremely widespread throughout England, although their exact nature and character during this time is uncertain (Holdsworth 1995). Many were granted lands by grateful and pious nobles/sub-kings who expected great rewards from such patronage (Holdsworth *op. cit.*). Viking raids saw many, like the great monasteries of the north of England, destroyed or decline in the ninth century, but the tenth century reformation led to a renewed growth in monastic houses (Hinton 2001). In fact, Domesday Book suggests that some tenth century monastic establishments enjoyed a wealthy and privileged lifestyle, with large revenues and vast tracts of land to support them (Hinton *op. cit.*). Thus, one of the principal questions associated with the study of all high-status Anglo-Saxon settlements is whether or not they were ever monasteries at any time during their occupation? This question cannot be addressed fully without exploring the evidence of diet, aspects of which may be linked with monastic food rules.

During the initial, early medieval, development of monasticism, many systems of behavioural rules were followed (Miccoli 1991). However, during the Carolingian period, the rule of Saint Benedict became adopted by all monasteries in Western Europe and, after that period, it stayed the most influential one within medieval Europe (Milis 1992). With it, came the prohibition against the consumption of the meat of four-legged terrestrial animals for monks who were not weak or ill (Schmitz 1945). This explains the near-absence of

mammal bones at monastic sites in Belgium (Ervynck 2004) and implies why, with regard to animal proteins, fish became an especially important commodity.

A number of Irish religious texts survive from the seventh to ninth centuries, which detail restricted diets. From these it follows that the rations of nuns and monks should have been meagre. Vegetarianism was optional; small amounts of meat were allowed, but only wild boar or venison. Fish were the most common source of animal protein consumed and, on special occasions, salted meat was also permitted. During Lent there were also periods of severe fasting, when even lay people were encouraged to abstain from fresh or salted meat (Kelly 1997; Ervynck 2004).

As previously discussed, the sheer quantity and variety of meat that was consumed throughout the entire Saxon occupation sequence at Flixborough certainly fails to tally with the descriptions above, suggesting that Flixborough was never a monastery – at least not during the eighth to tenth centuries AD. However, given the fact that we are still unsure of the exact nature of monastic settlements during Middle and Late Saxon times, this may be too simplistic a conclusion to draw. In fact a more detailed analysis of the animal bone assemblage by period (linked with other archaeological evidence) has provided some intriguing evidence in this regard.

The use of vertebrate 'signatures'

The range and frequency of wild and domestic species from archaeological excavations have long been used by zooarchaeologists in attempts to broadly classify sites, periods and even cultures. For the Saxon period in England, observations have been made regarding the nature and status of particular settlement types based upon the presence/absence of wild species, particularly birds. O'Connor (1991 and 2001), for example, has highlighted the paucity of evidence for wild species at so-called *wic* sites, the early trading emporia found on the navigable rivers and along the coasts of the North Sea area.

A survey of Anglo-Saxon vertebrate assemblages was undertaken in order to explore these observations further, and here we present the results, based on selected components of the mammal, bird and fish fauna represented at these sites. In the case of birds and mammals, there were obvious problems involved with the classification of wild and domestic representatives of the same species (e.g. geese and pigs) whose remains are usually common on Saxon sites. These problems can render any definitive statements regarding the overall importance of wild species somewhat problematic.

In the case of bird remains, species included in the survey were selected on the basis of their ease of identification and their inferred implications for settlement status, linked to consumption and/or specific activities (e.g. falconry), during later medieval times. Other avian species were also included because of their acknowledged and consistent occurrence in Saxon vertebrate assemblages (see TABLE 10.2 for full list of avian taxa included).

Before interpreting the patterns observed in the data, it is important to bear in mind the problems associated with such a generalised scheme. First and foremost, it is essentially chronological in nature – a result of the vagaries of excavation opportunities and, to some extent, of the history of Anglo-Saxon research interests in England. As a consequence, direct comparison of sites of different function or character is limited by the fact that, for certain periods, particular types of site predominate. Thus, most rural sites are Early to Mid-Saxon in date (*c.* late fifth to eighth centuries AD), whilst those classified as 'urban', are exclusively from the Late Saxon period (mid ninth to mid eleventh centuries), and (at least for the North of England) have the added complexity of direct Scandinavian influence. On the other hand, most high-status estate centres and *wics* are primarily of Mid-Saxon date (late seventh and eighth centuries), with ecclesiastical sites (usually regarded as monastic in nature) being primarily Middle to Late Saxon in date.

A second problem (related to the first) is the fact that such a broad classification inevitably masks a more complex reality. For example, ecclesiastical establishments and high-status estate centres must have included many people of lower status, whilst some high-status estate centres may well have associated with them a separate or integrated monastic element. The presence of these different components at sites may, therefore, provide higher levels of 'background noise' to any simple interpretation of site status and character. A third and final problem is that few Anglo-Saxon sites have provided long, well-stratified (and well-dated) sequences. In the rare instances, like Flixborough, where these do exist, the interpretative potential to explore some of the complexities outlined above is hugely increased.

Despite these drawbacks, it is our contention that certain data concerning vertebrate remains presented in this way can provide interpretable patterns which appear to reflect at least some broad aspects of the nature and status of sites and their inhabitants.

Domestic animal signatures

It has already been shown that the relative importance of some of the major domestic mammals and birds appears

Family	English name	Latin name
Phalacrocoracidae	cormorant	*Pholocrocorax carbo*
Ardeidae	grey heron	*Ardea cinerea*
	bittern	*Botaurus stellaris*
	heron	Ardeidae indet.
Ciconiidae	black stork	*Ciconia nigra*
Anatidae	swan	*Cygnus* sp.
	goose	*Anser* or *Branta* sp.
	duck	Anatinae indet.
Accipitidrae	red kite	*Milvus milvus*
	sparrowhawk	*Accipiter nisus*
	goshawk	*Accipiter gentilis*
	common buzzard	*Buteo buteo*
Falconidae	saker falcon	*Falco cherrug*
	gyrfalcon	*Falco rusticolus*
	peregrine falcon	*Falco peregrinus*
Tetraonidae	black grouse	*Tetrao tetrix*
	capercaillie	*Tetrao urogallus*
	peacock	*Pavo cristatus*
Gruidae	common crane	*Grus grus*
	crane	*Grus* sp.
Strigidae	eagle owl	*Bubo bubo*
Columbidae	pigeon or dove	*Columba* sp. or *Streptopelia* sp.

TABLE 10.2 Avian taxa included in the 'signature' study.

to change through time, and some of the possible reasons for this shift have been briefly outlined. How do these patterns at Flixborough compare with other Anglo-Saxon sites in England?

FIG. 10.1 is a tri-polar plot showing the proportions of cattle, sheep/goat and pig at a variety of Anglo-Saxon sites in England (see TABLE 10.3 for details). These data have been grouped into four broad categories (high-status, rural, urban and *wic*) that reflect current archaeological interpretations of the general nature of settlement at each site. The pattern that emerges, reflect the dominance of cattle and, to a lesser extent, sheep, at many of the sites and on closer inspection, several interesting points can be noted.

Firstly, it is apparent that a large proportion of sites classified generally as 'high-status' appear to show higher relative proportions of pig to cattle. Proportions of both cattle and pig at 'high- status' sites mostly fall between 15–40% (for pig, the proportions almost never exceed 50% of the total cattle : sheep : pig ratio). Assemblages from sites classified as 'urban' or '*wic*' are mostly characterised by high proportions of cattle (40–75%), with proportions of pig and sheep being similar to one another (15–40%). 'Rural' sites conversely seem to be characterised by their low relative proportions of pig (<20%).

The application of principal components analysis (PCA) to these data results in a similar pattern to that described previously. FIG. 10.2 shows a PCA plot of cattle/sheep/pig frequency data from the same sites shown in TABLE 10.3, grouped into the same broad settlement types. In this case, values for high-status sites are almost all influenced more strongly by proportions of pig and sheep (being mostly to the right of the vertical axis). Sites classified as *wics* appear to be mostly influenced by the frequency of cattle and then pig (falling below the horizontal axis), and the vast majority of rural sites are more strongly influenced by sheep and cattle (falling above the vertical axis). The large group of urban sites, however, shows little in the way of patterning, although most appear to be more strongly influenced by the frequency of cattle (falling to the left of the vertical axis).

Further refinement of the broad 'high-status' category was attempted in order to explore whether particular categories of so-called high-status sites could be characterised by the proportions of the major domestic mammals. FIG. 10.3 shows high-status sites further classified into those described as estate centres, those deemed to be ecclesiastical in nature and those described as palaces. As can readily be seen, there is little patterning in the data with which to further separate these site types on the basis of domestic animal proportions. However,

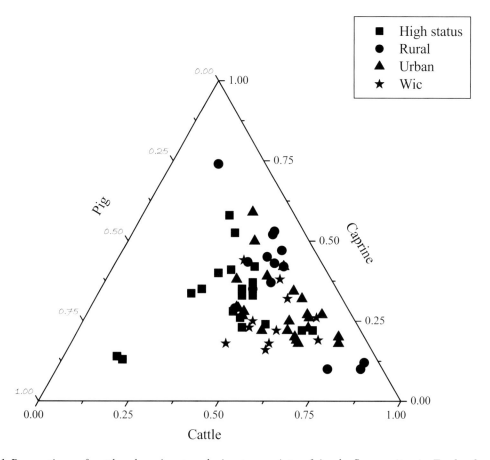

FIG. 10.1 *Proportions of cattle, sheep/goat and pig at a variety of Anglo-Saxon sites in England.*

Site	Broad type	Type	Date	Cattle %	Sheep/goat %	Pig	%
Fishergate	Urban	Urban	MS	53	34	12	
Caythorpe Pipeline	Rural	Ladder settlement	ES	13	74	13	
Maxey 60	Rural	Open settlement	ES	44	43	13	
West Heslerton	Rural	Rural	ES	44	47	9	
Spong Hill VII	Rural	Village	ES	84	12	4	
West Stow (animal husbandry)	Rural	Village	ES	41	45	14	
North Elmham	High status	Ecclesiastical	LS	31	45	24	
Westminster Abbey	High status	Ecclesiastical	LS	40	28	32	
Flixborough (Phase 6)	High status	High Status estate centre	LS	39	35	26	
Flixborough (Phase 6iii)	High status	High Status estate centre	LS	41	37	22	
Northampton	High status	High Status palace	LS	39	42	19	
Castle Mall AML 72/99	Urban	Urban	LS	51	22	27	
Flaxengate 72–6	Urban	Urban	LS	57	32	11	
Ipswich AML 3951	Urban	Urban	LS	63	18	19	
Lincoln sites (bones)	Urban	Urban	LS	61	27	12	
St Martin-at-Palace Plain	Urban	Urban	LS	41	29	30	
St Peters St (Nhtn) 73–6	Urban	Urban	LS	30	59	11	
The Green 83	Urban	Urban	LS	35	50	15	
Thetford 48–59	Urban	Urban	LS	57	25	18	
Thetford 73–80	Urban	Urban	LS	36	38	26	
Burystead 84–87 AML 71/92	Rural	Village	LS	46	37	17	
Haithabu	Wic	Wic	LS	48	38	14	
Barking Abbey	High status	Ecclesiastical	M/LS	28	35	37	
Ramsbury	Rural	Rural	M/LS	40	29	31	
Victoria and Berrington Sts (Hereford)	Urban	Urban	M/LS	39	24	27	
Birka	Wic	Wic	M/LS	43	18	39	
Flixborough (Phase 4–5b)	High status	High Status estate centre	MS	30	40	30	
North Elmham	High status	Ecclesiastical	MS	33	38	29	
St Alban's Abbey	High status	Ecclesiastical	MS	15	14	71	
Brandon	High status	High Status estate centre	MS	28	52	19	
Caister-on-Sea 51–5	High status	High Status estate centre	MS	62	22	16	
Flixborough (Phase 2–3a)	High status	High Status estate centre	MS	40	33	27	
Flixborough (Phase 3b)	High status	High Status estate centre	MS	43	33	24	
Wicken Bonhunt	High status	High Status estate centre	MS	17	13	70	
Cheddar	High status	High Status palace	MS	45	23	32	
Cheddar – period 1	High status	High Status palace	MS	43	26	31	
Northampton	High status	High Status palace	MS	24	58	18	
West Heslerton	Rural	Rural	MS	39	53	8	
St Peters St (Nhtn) 73–7	Urban?	Urban?	MS	34	48	18	
Dorestad – hand-collected	Wic	Wic	MS	68	19	13	
Fishergate	Wic	Wic	MS	64	26	10	
Hamwic	Wic	Wic	MS	53	32	15	
Ipswich AML 3952	Wic	Wic	MS	47	25	28	
Jubilee Hall	Wic	Wic	MS	55	22	23	
Maiden Lane	Wic	Wic	MS	55	16	29	
Peabody site	Wic	Wic	MS	47	23	30	
Ribe	Wic	Wic	MS	55	18	27	
National Gallery			MS	30	41	29	
Coppergate (16–22) (A/Scand bone)	Urban	Urban	AS	73	20	7	
Jarrow AML 80/87	High status	Ecclesiastical	SA	65	22	13	
Stonea 80–5		No site information	SA	40	51	9	
Mucking	Rural	Open settlement	SA	75	10	15	

TABLE 10.3 *Frequency of cattle, caprovid and pig remains from a variety of Early Medieval sites in England and the Continent (continued overleaf).*

Site	Broad type	Type	Date	Cattle %	Caprine %	Pig %
Nettleton Top	Rural	Open settlement	SA	84	10	6
Walton 73–4	Rural	Rural	SA	42	35	23
Berrington St 72–6	Urban	Urban	SA	62	19	19
Wharram 75	Rural	Village	SA	47	42	11
Castle Acre 72–7	High status	Castle	SN	26	34	41
Castle Mall AML 72/97	High status	Castle	SN	51	24	25
Goltho 70–5	High status	Manor	SN	33	41	26
Walton 73–5	Rural	Rural	SN	36	43	20
Coppergate (16–22) (A/Scand bone)	Urban	Urban	SN	58	22	20
Flaxengate 72–7	Urban	Urban	SN	47	42	11
Ipswich 74–88	Urban	Urban	SN	43	28	29
Skeldergate 73–5 (bone)	Urban	Urban	SN	65	27	8
St Martin-at-Palace Plain 81	Urban	Urban	SN	40	29	30
Thetford 64–70	Urban	Urban	SN	44	39	17
Mill Lane Thetford			SN	46	28	26
Coppergate (16–22) (A/Scand bone)	Urban	Urban	LS	62	26	12
Skeldergate 73–5 (bone)	Urban	Urban	LS	74	18	8
Treasury			MS	45	40	15
Porchester Castle	High status	High Status estate centre	M/LS	53	28	18
Porchester Castle	High status	High Status estate centre	EM	62	22	16
Porchester Castle	High status	High Status estate centre	LS	50	31	19

TABLE 10.3 continued.

when these high-status centres are grouped by broad chronological phase, Mid-Saxon high-status sites are much more variable in the proportion of cattle, sheep and pig than Late Saxon and Saxo-Norman ones (FIG. 10.4). This is difficult to interpret, but could reflect regional differences in food render, or evidence of a shift from a tribute to more market-based economy. Although the data for domestic mammals are difficult to interpret, there does seem to be a correlation between high frequencies of pigs and what are broadly termed here high-status settlements. Others have already highlighted the link between pigs and status (see below for further discussion).

Wild avian signatures

Perhaps a more interesting and interpretatively significant pattern is observed when considering the avian taxa. TABLES 10.4 and 10.5 and FIG. 10.5 show the presence/absence of selected birds identified at a number of Saxon sites in England. In all, data for 26 sites are represented, these ranging in date from the sixth to the eleventh centuries AD. They include a range of site types, again broadly classified rural, ecclesiastical, trading emporia (*wics*), high-status estate centres, industrial (represented by a single site) and urban.

A more detailed consideration of the data (represented in TABLE 10.5 and FIG. 10.5) shows that the presence (or indeed absence) of particular groups of birds or individual species is very different for certain categories of sites. All

consistently produce remains of Corvidae (crow family) or species of duck, but high-status estate centres and urban assemblages yield a much wider range of other taxa (i.e. Ardeidae, Tetraonidae, Accipitridae/Falconidae) than any of the other categories. They also show the only occurrences of species such as peacock and black grouse. Ecclesiastical sites, far from having a wide range of bird species have, in fact, perhaps the most restricted range of avian species of any site type, closely followed by sites classified as either rural or *wic*.

If we compare the patterns at those sites classified respectively as 'urban' and 'high-status estate centres', the similarities between the two are somewhat obvious. As previously mentioned, these two categories of site also reflect a chronological shift from mid–late Saxon, a fact which allows us to view changes through time. The data presented here suggest that no significant change in bird exploitation (in terms of the species selected in this study, at least) occurred between these site types and through time. The fact that the patterns are broadly similar for different site types can perhaps be explained by the probable presence of high-status elements of the population in the early urban centres of the Late Saxon period. One additional factor (which must be taken into account particularly when dealing with Saxon sites from the Midlands and North of England) is the influence of Norse/Viking settlers. Certainly urban centres in the North of England (e.g. York and Lincoln) were centres

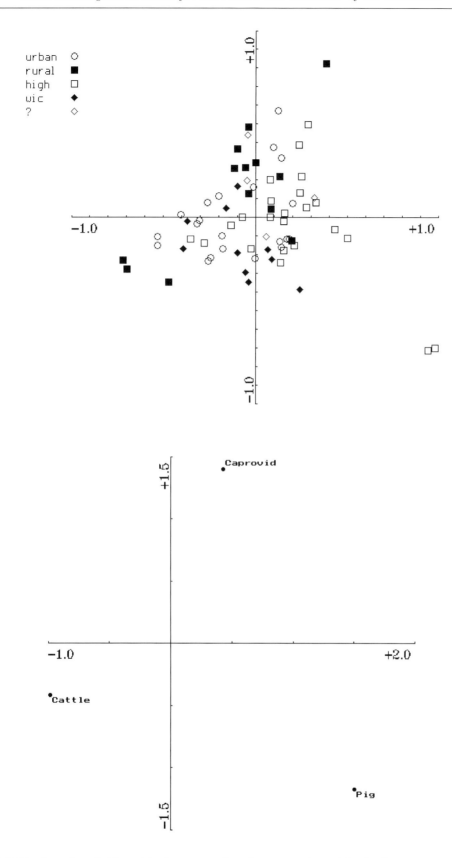

FIG. 10.2 PCA plot of cattle/sheep/pig frequency data from a variety of Anglo-Saxon sites in England.

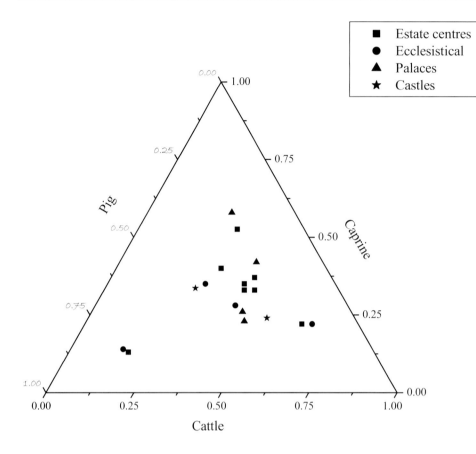

FIG. 10.3 Proportions of cattle, sheep/goat and pig from a selection of high status Anglo-Saxon sites in England.

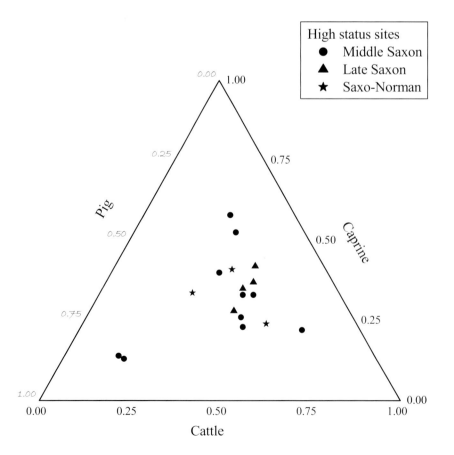

FIG. 10.4 Proportions of cattle, sheep/goat and pig from a selection of high status Anglo-Saxon sites in England by broad date group.

Rural	West Stow, Suffolk – Crabtree, P. 1989.
	West Heslerton, East Yorkshire – Richardson, J. pers. comm.
	Walton, Aylesbury – Noddle, B. 1976.
Wic	Ipswich, Suffolk – Crabtree, P. 1996; Jones, R. T. & Serjeantson, D. 1983
	Fishergate, York – O'Connor, T. P. 1991.
	London sites (Peabody and National Gallery) – West, B. (1989 issued 1993).
	Melbourne Street, Southampton – Bourdillon, J. & Coy, J. 1980.
Ecclesiastical	Holy Island, Northumberland – Allison, E., Locker, A. & Rackham, D. J. 1985.
	St Albans Abbey, Hertford – Crabtree, P. (Unpublished report – submitted1983).
	Barking Abbey and Westminster Abbey, London – West, B. (unpublished report – submitted 1989).
	Jarrow, Tyne and Wear – Noddle, B. A. 1987.
Industrial	Ramsbury, Wiltshire – Coy, J. (1980).
High Status Centre	Brandon, Suffolk – Crabtree, P. (Unpublished report – submitted 1991).
	Flixborough, North Lincolnshire.
	Wicken Bonhunt, Essex – Crabtree, P. (Unpublished report – submitted 1995).
	Caister-on-Sea, Norfolk – Harman, M. 1993.
	North Elmham Park, Norfolk – Bramwell, D. 1980.
	St Peter's Street, Northampton – Harman, M. 1979.
	Porchester Castle – Eastham, A. 1976.
	Goltho, South Lincolnshire – Jones, R. T. & Ruben, I. 1987
Urban	Thetford, Norfolk – Jones, G. G. 1984; Jones G. G. 1993.
	Saddler Street,Durham – Rackham, J. 1979.
	Chalk Lane, Northampton – Coy, J. 1981.
	Lincoln sites (Waterfront and Upper city) – Dobney, K., Jaques, D. & Irving, B. n.d [1996].
	Coppergate, York – O'Connor, T. P. 1989.
	Castle Mall, Norwich – Albarella, U., Beech, M. & Mulville, J. 1997.

TABLE 10.4 Sites from which data were used for 'avian signature' analysis.

of Viking influence and trade from the mid ninth century onwards and archaeological evidence reflects this to some degree. However, the avian zooarchaeological data used in this survey indicate that there was little or no change in bird exploitation from the eighth to the eleventh centuries.

Of course, it could be argued that the patterns outlined above simply reflect varying sample sizes between the different categories of site, so that larger assemblages would be expected to produce more bird taxa. However, at least some sites from all categories (with perhaps the exception of ecclesiastical ones) have produced large vertebrate assemblages, meaning that the patterns observed here must be explained by more than sample size alone. The data from Flixborough lend further support to this argument.

Interpreting the avian signatures at Flixborough

At Flixborough, the large (and systematically recovered) vertebrate and other finds assemblages, excavated from a series of tightly-dated phases, has allowed the exploration of the evidence for social and economic change at an unusually refined level. Therefore, this single multi-phase site provides an intriguing case-study on which to further test the application and validity of so-called vertebrate signatures. Although broadly classified as a high-status Saxon estate centre, the range and quality of the archaeological evidence from the site indicates that its nature and character changed significantly during approximately 300 years of occupation. As previously discussed, a wide range of archaeological evidence hints at the possibility of a significant change occurring at the site during the early ninth century.

The avian data from Flixborough indicate that the range (and quantity – except in the case of ducks) of wild bird species from the ninth century (Phase 4–5b) was lower when compared with the earlier mid–late eighth (Phase 3b) and the tenth centuries (Phase 6; TABLE 10.6). In terms of the selected species discussed above, the overall avian signature for Phase 4–5b at Flixborough appears to reflect that proposed for ecclesiastical sites (but perhaps also *wics* and rural sites) mentioned earlier.

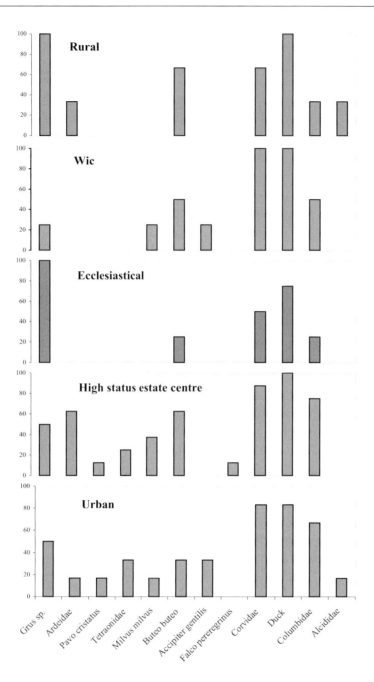

Fig. 10.5 Percentage of sites (by broad category) where selected bird taxa were present.

In contrast, the signatures from Phase 3b and Phase 6 compare best with those of high-status estate centres (see TABLE 10.5). This change in diversity at the site can be illustrated by the application of a simple biological statistic – Fisher's 'alpha' (Fisher *et al.* 1943), which uses the number of taxa and the minimum number of individuals for each to calculate an index of diversity. Fisher's alpha values (± the standard error) were calculated for the avian assemblage from Phases 3b, 4–5b and 6 from Flixborough (see Figure 10.6). Fisher's alpha for Phase 4–5b is revealed as the lowest of the values for the three phases.

On the basis of this limited evidence, it could be concluded that the composition of the avian fauna from

Flixborough corroborates the view that changes noted at the site during the ninth century were associated with the presence of a new (possibly monastic) component to the settlement. This appears to have been short-lived, since a very similar signature to that exhibited in Phase 3b (here interpreted as one associated with high-status) is also present in Phase 6.

Fish signatures

Fish bones are not common in English sites of Middle and Late Saxon date, even when large-scale sieving has been employed and preservation conditions are conducive to their recovery. This observation is particularly true of rural settlements. At the inland settlement of West

Site Category	Site name	*Grus* sp.	Ardeidae	*Pavo cristatus*	Tetraonidae	*Milvus milvus*	*Buteo buteo*	*Accipiter gentilis*	*Falco peregrinus*	Corvidae	Anatinae	Columbidae
Rural:	West Stow	**	*				*				**	
	West Heslerton	**					*			**	*	*
	Walton	*								*	*	
Wic:	Ipswich	*						*		*	**	*
	Fishergate				*		*			*	*	*
	London sites					*				*	*	
	Hamwic						*			*	**	
Ecclesiastical:	Holy Island	*										
	Jarrow									*	*	
	St Albans Abbey	*								*	*	
	Barking Abbey	**									**	
	Westminster Abbey	*					*			*	**	*
Industrial:	Ramsbury					*			*	*		
High status centre:	Brandon	**	*				*		*	**	***	
	Flixborough	***	*		**	*	**			***	***	***
	Wicken Bonhunt	**	*	*	*		*			**	**	**
	Caister-on-sea										**	*
	North Elmham Park	*	*			*	*			*	**	*
	Northampton									*	*	*
	Porchester Castle		*			*				*	**	**
	Goltho						*			*	**	
Urban:	Thetford	*		*		*	*			*	**	*
	Saddler St			*								
	Chalk Lane									*	*	
	Lincoln sites									*	**	*
	Coppergate	*			**		*			**	**	**
	Castle Mall	*	*				*	*		*	**	*

TABLE 10.5 Selected wild bird species identified from 27 Anglo-Saxon sites from England by broad site category. * = <10 fragments, ** = 10–99 fragments, *** = >100 fragments.

Heslerton, for example, only a single fish bone (pike) was recovered from an assemblage of over 80,000 identified specimens (Jane Richardson pers. comm.). In fact, Saxon fish assemblages of any size are rare outside urban contexts such as York (e.g. Jones 1988; O'Connor 1989; 1991), Ipswich (e.g. Locker and Jones 1985), London (e.g. Locker 2001, 181) and Southampton (e.g.

Bourdillon 1993). As one might expect, the few large rural collections of fish bones are from coastal and estuarine sites. Flixborough, with approximately 6000 identified specimens from the sieved samples, provides the largest assemblage known to the authors, followed by Sandtun, West Hythe (on the coast of Kent) with about 4000 specimens (Hamilton-Dyer 2002). A preliminary

Proposed character?	Date (phase)	*Grus* sp.	Ardeidae	*Pavo cristatus*	Tetraonidae	*Milvus milvus*	*Buteo buteo*	*Accipiter gentilis*	*Falco peregrinus*	Corvidae	Anatinae	Columbidae
High status estate centre:	Mid-late 8th century (Phase 3b)	***	*		**	**	**			**	**	**
Ecclesiastical ?:	9th century (Phase 4–5b)	**					*			**	***	**
High status estate centre:	10th century (Phase 6)	**			*	*	*			**	**	**

TABLE *10.6 Selected wild bird species identified from the different settlement phases at Flixborough.*

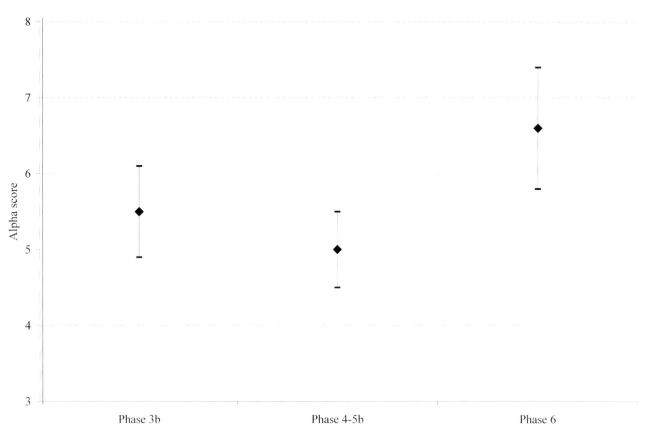

FIG. *10.6 Fisher's Alpha diversity index applied to the Flixborough bird assemblage.*

review of sieved Saxon assemblages from England has identified few other rural sites which have produced even 50 fish bones.

The first notable characteristic of the Flixborough assemblage is the relative abundance of fish for a 'non-urban' settlement of its date. This is not to say that they were common in an absolute sense. The ratios of fish to mammal bone at Flixborough range from less than 0.01 (Phase 6iii) to 0.15 (Phase 2–3a).[1] As a comparison, the equivalent ratio for broadly contemporaneous sites in northern Scotland ranges from 0.4 to 38.5 (Barrett *et al.* 2001, table 1). Nevertheless, within an English context, fish are well represented at Flixborough.

In contrast, taxonomic data indicate major differences between urban and 'non-urban' Saxon assemblages. FIGS 10.7 and 10.8 illustrate the results of a correspondence analysis based on the abundance by NISP of nine taxa at 13 Middle and Late Saxon sites (all pre- eleventh century) subdivided into 25 phase groups (see Barrett 2002 and references therein). Only sieved assemblages of 50 or more identified specimens were included. The first two axes (FIG. 10.7) differentiate inland, estuarine and coastal sites, largely based on the abundance of cyprinids (inland sites), herring (predominately inland sites), eel and flatfish (estuarine sites) and gadids (coastal sites only) (TABLE 10.7). Flixborough falls within the 'estuarine cluster', as one might expect.

Axes 2 and 3 (FIG. 10.8), however, differentiate urban and rural sites. The former are dominated by herring and eel, whilst the latter fall into two groups. The six phases of Flixborough (close to the Humber estuary) are characterised by smelt, flatfish, pike and perch. Conversely, the assemblage from Sandtun (on the coast of Kent) is dominated by gadids, whiting in particular. This latter distinction is probably related to the environmental contexts of the sites. Conversely, herring were transported to urban sites regardless of site location and they did not meet subsistence requirements in the countryside. This observation is reinforced by the fact that many rural Saxon sites have produced little or no fish bone of any species (e.g. Crabtree 1989; Albarella and Davis 1994; Richards 1999), and do not appear in the correspondence analysis. In sum, most settlements in the Saxon countryside were consuming few fish of any kind and those that did were apparently avoiding herring.

Flixborough clearly differed from contemporaneous urban sites, but the relative abundance of fish also distinguishes it from other non-urban settlements. Given the role of fish implied by St Benedict's Rule, this difference may be consistent with the possibility that at least some phases were monastic (Loveluck, Volume 4, Chapter 9). Unfortunately, few sieved ecclesiastical assemblages of any size are available for the Saxon period and in order to investigate this issue it is necessary to broaden the historical focus.

FIG. 10.9 illustrates axes 3 and 5 of a correspondence analysis based on the abundance by NISP of the same nine taxa considered above for 66 English assemblages dating from the sixth to sixteenth centuries (see Barrett 2002 and references therein). These results are influenced primarily by the abundance of smelt (axis 3), cyprinids (axis 3), herring (axis 3), flatfish (axes 3 and 5), pike (axis 5) and perch (axis 5) (TABLE 10.8). The number of ecclesiastical sites which meets the criteria necessary for consideration (sieving and 50 or more identified specimens) still remains small, with only eight

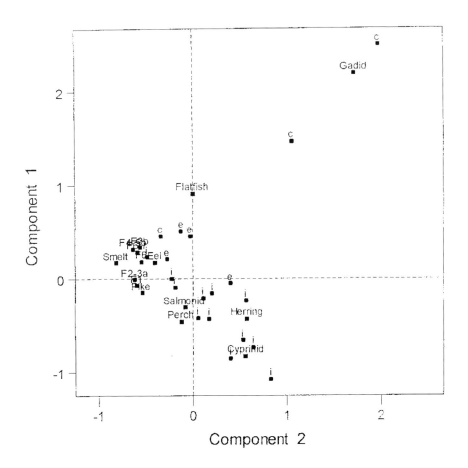

FIG. 10.7 Correspondence analysis plot of Saxon fish assemblages, Axes 1 and 2. Inland sites are coded "i", estuarine sites "e", and coastal sites "c".

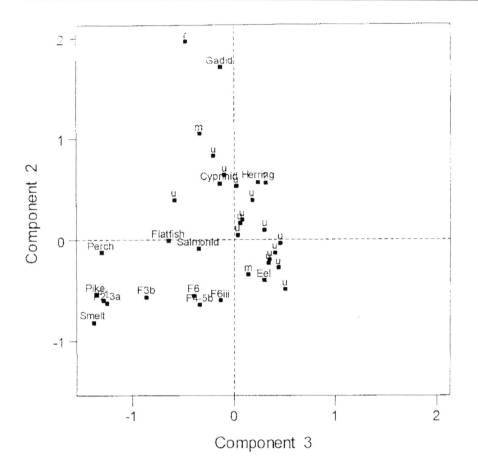

FIG. 10.8 Correspondence analysis plot of Saxon fish assemblages, Axes 2 and 3. Urban (including wic) sites are coded "u", rural sites "r", monastic sites "m", and the various phases of Flixborough "F", followed by the phase group.

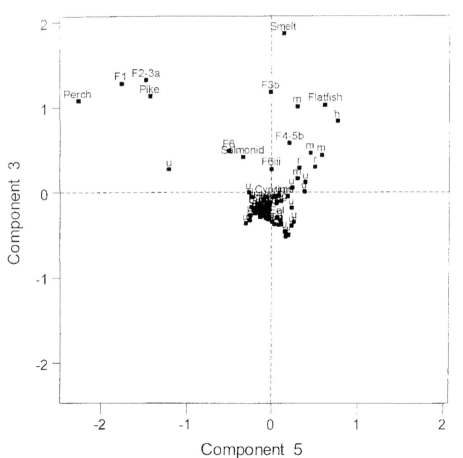

FIG. 10.9 Correspondence analysis plot of Saxon and medieval fish assemblages, Axes 3 and 5. Coding is that used in FIG. 10.8, with the addition of "h" for hospital sites.

Taxa	Axis 1	Axis 2	Axis 3
Herring	0.066	0.140	0.034
Salmonid	0.004	0.000	0.009
Eel	0.035	0.243	0.193
Gadid	0.476	0.357	0.003
Smelt	0.002	0.070	0.284
Pike	0.002	0.027	0.234
Perch	0.010	0.001	0.133
Cyprinid	0.299	0.163	0.016
Flatfish	0.106	0.000	0.094

TABLE 10.7 Column contributions of a correspondence analysis of 25 English Saxon fish assemblages.

Taxa	Axis 3	Axis 5
Herring	0.122	0.016
Salmonid	0.000	0.000
Eel	0.005	0.002
Gadid	0.022	0.002
Smelt	0.315	0.000
Pike	0.035	0.400
Perch	0.000	0.282
Cyprinid	0.235	0.087
Flatfish	0.266	0.210

TABLE 10.8 Column contributions of a correspondence analysis of 66 English Saxon and medieval fish assemblages.

monasteries and one hospital represented. Nevertheless, the resulting pattern is reasonably clear – monasteries, hospitals and all phases at Flixborough tend to be particularly rich in flatfish and smelt. Phases 1 and 2–3a of Flixborough are distinctive within this group in that they also have high levels of pike and perch. It is the data for Phases 3b, 4–5b, 6 and 6iii which most resemble those from the ecclesiastical assemblages.

With a few exceptions, English medieval (in the broadest sense) ecclesiastical sites tend to yield higher levels of flatfish and smelt than secular sites, be they rural or urban. With this observation in mind, it is worth returning to the intra-site data from Flixborough. The increase in flatfish noted in Phase 3b (FIG. 8.10), and perhaps the increasing size of smelt from Phases 2–3a to 3b (TABLE 8.2), could conceivably mark a monastic phase at the site. Repetition of this pattern in later phases could imply either continuity of site function or the re-deposition of residual material. The latter is most probable in Phase 6iii, which is represented by dark soils rather than primary features such as dumps.

Fish signatures broadly corroborate the evidence from

the wild bird assemblage in that both imply a possible non-secular/monastic phase existed at the site at some point during its occupation. However, the data for fish differ from those for birds in the timing of this characteristic occupation, which is difficult to explain. The necessity of using broader chronological comparanda for the fish may go some way towards explaining these differences, since the nature of monasticism must have changed between the Saxon and later Anglo-Norman and medieval periods. It may simply be, however, that these perceived 'signatures' merely reflect the changing availability of particular resources through time.

Comparative evidence for inter-/intra-site social differentiation

Although somewhat crude in its application and rather general in its assumptions, the use of so-called vertebrate signatures as a tool to aid the characterisation of Saxon sites in England appears, at a superficial level at least, to merit further exploration. Broad patterns do appear to exist in the data, which may reflect attributes linked to the nature and character of settlements and their inhabitants. In addition, diversity within the assemblage can also provide useful and complimentary information. However, in order to understand more fully what these 'vertebrate signatures' might mean, they must be viewed within a much wider archaeological interpretative framework of evidence, which certainly does exist for the site of Flixborough.

Excavations at the seventh–eleventh century AD poly-focal site of Karlburg, Germany, provided a unique opportunity to study different structural elements within settlements linked to royalty / high aristocracy and to a monastery, within the same broad settlement agglomeration for the early Middle Ages. Evidence from the vertebrate assemblage appears to indicate a contrast in the exploitation of domestic and wild animals between the castle of Karlburg (*castellum cum fisco regali* – constructed in the first half of the eighth century, possibly under the Carolingian 'Mayor of the Palace', Charles Martel), the valley-based settlement focus (villa) of the Karlburg estate, and a monastic settlement focus dedicated to St Mary, to the north of the 'villa' focus (Ettel 1998, 75–81).

Amongst the bones from the valley settlement, just under 1% were from wild animals, whilst in the castle (*Burg*), bones of wild/hunted animals (primarily red deer and European bison) accounted for just under 11 % of all vertebrate remains recovered. The higher proportions of wild animals present in assemblages excavated from the castle are thought to reflect the fact that a group of high-status individuals, who can be regarded as nobles (whether of royal or episcopal status, or otherwise) lived within the fortified settlement during the eighth to the tenth centuries (Ettel 1998, 83).

There also appears to be a sharp contrast in the exploitation patterns of domesticates between the *Burg* settlement and the valley settlement foci. Within the castle/*Burg* settlement, more 'luxury animals' (*Luxustiere*) occurred (i.e. geese, chickens and pigs) and most animals, such as the pigs, were slaughtered at a young age – up to three years of age. In contrast, evidence from the valley settlement indicates that, in general, the domesticates were killed at older ages. These differences between the castle settlement and the others are seen to reflect differentiation in social status between them, i.e. the greater number of wild species present, and the young age of the domesticates when they were slaughtered (and subsequently consumed) are thought to reflect the high-status of the occupants of the *Burg*. The valley settlement (although perhaps not the monastic focus) is thought to have provisioned the *Burg* high-status settlement focus (Ettel 1998, 83).

Ervynck's survey of zooarchaeological material from Flemish monastic sites (seven male communities and two nunneries, see Ervynck 1997b) shows that the remains of large animals were almost always absent, indicating that the meat of mammals was only occasionally consumed. Analyses of fine-sieved deposits from these sites indicate that higher frequencies of fish were consumed in monasteries compared with more secular sites (Ervynck 1997b, fig. 3). When meat was eaten within the abbey walls, this was almost exclusively beef or mutton and the remains of pigs were always extremely rare. These consumption patterns, however, did not imply that the diet at an abbey was necessarily austere. Even when the meat of mammals was not eaten, very rich banquets could be served, consisting, for example, of a wide variety of fish species (Van Neer and Ervynck 1996).

Manuscripts and monasticism: was vellum produced at Flixborough?

During the greater part of the Middle Ages, most books produced in northern Europe contained vellum (prepared from calf) or sometimes parchment (made from uncured sheep skins) (Bischoff 1986; 1990; Backhouse 1981). These materials would have been time-consuming and costly to produce, which is why those that survive are primarily religious texts produced by some of the most famous literate early medieval monastic communities in England and Ireland (e.g. the Lindisfarne Gospels and the *Book of Kells*).

The finest material for vellum is skin from still or new-born calves (Diderot and Alembert 1751–8). Skins of older animals can also be used and those that have been milk-fed are considered to have a finer grain than those raised on barley and hay (Reed 1972). Thus, animals killed in the spring (i.e. prior to weaning) would have been favoured.

Evidence from animal bone assemblages indicating the possible existence of vellum production in the past is scarce. However, some clues can be gleaned primarily from kill-off patterns and even the over-abundance of selected skeletal elements such as foot bones, which are

often left in the skins during initial processing (Serjeantson 1989). As previously mentioned, there are few early medieval sites in north-west Europe where the remains of very young calves attained high frequencies. However, from the Trädgårdmästaren quarter in Sigtuna (Sweden), nearly 40% of the cattle remains were from suckling calves, perhaps indicating parchment manufacture in the town (Wigh 2001, 105). Perhaps the most convincing case for vellum production has been made for some remains from Green Shiel, on the island of Lindisfarne, Northumberland (Scott 2000). Although there were some problems with dating, deposits considered to be of seventh-ninth century date produced a vertebrate assemblage dominated by the remains of cattle, approximately 50% of which were killed as suckling calves (31% killed younger than 1 month old – Scott *op. cit.* table 4.4). In addition, the absence from most of the cattle bones of evidence for butchery and the preponderance of distal limb elements recovered from building E (>90% being metapodials and phalanges), indicates that these individuals were killed for a specific purpose (Scott *op. cit.*, 21).

Lindisfarne (Holy Island) was one of the most important early medieval monastic communities in England. Founded in AD 635 by St Aidan of Iona (O'Sullivan and Young 1995), the home of St Cuthbert, and a place where finely illustrated manuscripts were produced – the most famous of which are the Lindisfarne Gospels. It is perhaps no coincidence that these are made of the finest quality vellum which, on the evidence outlined above, were probably produced at the outlying 'Monastic Grange' of Green Shiel (Scott 2000, 84). Although no such compelling evidence is to be found at Flixborough, there is perhaps some intriguing age at death data to be found in the material from the early-mid ninth century (sub-phases 4i–5a). Although the number of cattle mandibles is small (32), it is the only phase where high frequencies of neonatal and very juvenile animals are represented (FIG. 10.10). Could this represent small-scale vellum production?

Other archaeological and zooarchaeological evidence (Loveluck and Dobney 2001, and discussed previously) has been used to make the tentative suggestion that, during the early-mid ninth century at Flixborough, a non-secular (perhaps even monastic) element to society appeared. The presence of styli (for inscribing wax tablets) certainly indicates the presence of a literate component of the inhabitants at Flixborough during this time (either ecclesiastical or aristocratic in nature), so the production of other materials associated with writing should not be ruled out. Although a family monastery is hardly likely to have required extremely high-quality vellum in large quantities (as was the case at Lindisfarne), lower-quality vellum or parchment was almost certainly regularly used in the day-to-day production of less extravagant religious works, or perhaps even for the purposes of general estate management.

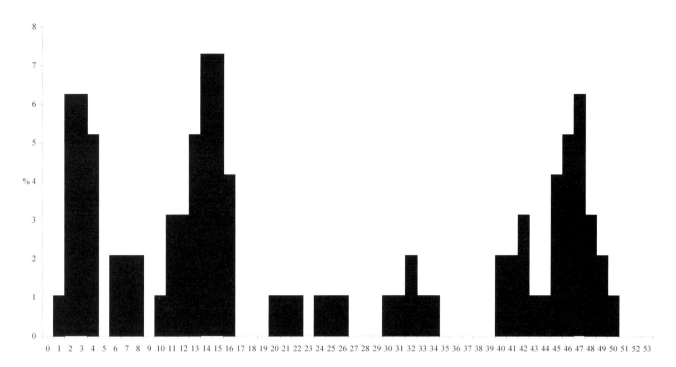

FIG. 10.10 Cattle mandible wear stage data (early-mid 9th century) showing numerous very young individuals.

Evidence for literacy on Mid-Saxon settlements, in the form of styli, has been viewed as *prima facie* evidence of monastic settlement character, but this is currently a matter of heated debate amongst historians, let alone archaeologists – especially as we have no knowledge of the extent to which clerics or priests were present at major secular estate centres and involved in estate administration. Nevertheless, the differences between the archaeological profiles between the ninth century and the mid–late eighth and the tenth centuries at Flixborough present a distinct contrast which could only be explained by a change in the character of the settlement. Whether this was caused by a change in the character of an element within the settlement's population is unclear. It is possible that we are observing the archaeological expressions of evolution from a secular estate centre to a family monastery, but it is at present unclear whether there would be any definable archaeological difference between a small monastery, and a secular estate centre with a church and a small number of resident clerics (Loveluck 2001).

The animal bones from Flixborough perhaps provide some intriguing evidence for the possibility of a monastic presence at the site sometime during the ninth century. This conclusion, it could be argued, might be supported by other archaeological evidence such as the presence of window glass, evidence of literacy, and the apparent intensification of craft production (particularly in relation to textiles). However, such a suggestion has to be balanced by the acknowledgement that we do not know to what extent major secular estate centres were producing commodities for export, whether within socially embedded contexts, such as gift exchange, or as products for trade (Loveluck and Dobney 2001).

10.4 Recognising wealth and status

Obviously, the vertebrate assemblage from Flixborough provides important information about the nature and character of the settlement, viewed within the broader context of major social and economic shifts that apparently occurred in Middle to Late Saxon England. However, what else can be gleaned from the animal bones about the nature of the inhabitants themselves, specifically within the socio-economic framework of the hierarchical society that existed? Simply put, can we recognize wealth and/or status from animal bones?

Taxes, tithes and renders

As previously mentioned (Chapter 7), most of the animals (and probably crop plants) utilised by the inhabitants of Flixborough, during Middle to Late Saxon times, were probably food rent paid by the servile classes to the aristocratic elite. The existence of such a system (which lay outside the traditional commercial market economy) is important within the study of archaeozoology, since it accommodated the widespread transfer of livestock and deadstock.

Society within the numerous petty kingdoms of England and Ireland during the sixth to tenth centuries comprised a rigid social hierarchy, which included the nobility, landed commoners, and the servile classes. Settlement was essentially rural in nature, and most commodities required for subsistence and everyday use were produced locally, so that market exchange was not important (McCormick 1992). Under such a system, however, considerable movement and transfer of goods, particularly in the form of agricultural products and wild commodities, still existed within and even between estate centres. Hierarchies within these exchange systems ensured personal ties of clientship, the extent and scale of which maintained and enhanced the status of individual nobles (of inferior or superior status) and their families. In return for land, livestock, and legal and military protection, the client provided the noble with a yearly supply of foodstuffs, a stipulated amount of labour and some military service, and undertook to entertain and feast the noble and his retinue (which could be very large) at specified times during the year (McCormick *op. cit.*). The scale and extent of this movement of resources depended upon the size and importance of the land-holdings and estates maintained by individuals. Flixborough was obviously an important (possibly royal) estate centre and, as such, certainly commanded tribute from a wide variety of sources. Estates would have paid their revenues (initially in kind) to the royal *vill* in a render known as the king's *feorm*. The nearest documented *vill* to Flixborough was to the north across the Humber, at Driffield (in 'the Kingdom of Northumbria': Sawyer 1983).

How this system functioned is difficult to ascertain from the zooarchaeological record alone, but some basic clues do exist in the animal bone assemblage. For example, the pattern of skeletal element representation of the major domestic animals (i.e. cattle, caprine and pig) appears to be significantly different in the ninth century at Flixborough, compared with earlier and later occupation phases at the site (see Chapter 6). A predominance of cattle cranial (head) and terminal limb (foot) bones during eighth and tenth century occupation sequence at Flixborough, is also found at other early and mid-Saxon élite sites such as Portchester Castle, the Cheddar Palaces, Wicken Bonhunt and Yeavering. This, it could be argued, relates to the re-distribution of meat whereby domestic animals brought to the site were killed, then butchered, with some meat bearing portions being then gifted to others down the social hierarchy. In contrast, a higher proportion of prime meat-bearing bones present during the ninth century at Flixborough appears similar to other non-elite and ecclesiastical sites such as Eynsham Abbey (Ayers *et al.* 2003), and possibly further support claims for a possible monastic presence at Flixborough during the ninth century (see previous this chapter).

If we now turn to Anglo-Saxon and other contemporaneous historical sources (principally from Ireland), they also provide much useful detail. There are various Anglo-Saxon, Irish, and Carolingian references which provide details of the nature and extent of clientship and the role of agricultural and wild-caught resources. Perhaps one of the most useful accounts of food rent associated with social ranking and occupation appears in an estate memorandum. This is a tract, drawn up during the tenth or eleventh centuries, which deals with aspects of estate management and specifically the duties and renders required from individuals of different social status (Swanton 1996). Thus, for example, the *geneat* (a tenant of some standing) was expected, amongst other duties, to provide one store pig per year. The *gebur* (the lowest rank of freeman) at Martinmas '*must pay 23 sesters of barley and two hens; at Easter one young sheep or twopence.*'

In this same document, much is written pertaining to the duties of the swineherd and to the management of pigs. For example, each tenant was also expected to give six loaves to the swineherd when he drove his herd to mast pasture (Swanton *op. cit.*, 27), and '*the taxable swineherd ought to pay for his butchering. On many estates it is the custom that he supply 15 pigs for killing every year; 10 old and 5 young. He is to have for himself whatever he rears beyond that; on many estates, a greater swineherds due pertains*'.

The estate memorandum also indicates the benefits that tenants and estate workers gained from these arrangements. For example, '*concerning a swineherd that goes with the property [i.e. he who keeps the estate herd], he ought to have a young pig to keep in a sty, and his prerequisites when he has prepared the bacon, and other rights which pertain to a slave.*' (Swanton *op. cit.*, 28). Similarly, '*concerning the oxherd – with his ealdorman's knowledge, the oxherd may pasture two or more oxen with the lord's herd on the common pasture – with that to earn shoes and gloves for himself. And his food-cow may go with the lord's oxen*' (Swanton *op. cit.*, 29).

The cowherd was allowed to keep and use milk from an old cow for seven days after she had newly calved. The shepherd was allowed twelve nights' dung at Christmas, one lamb from the year's young, one bellwether's fleece and the milk of his flock for seven days after the equinox, whilst the goatherd kept the milk of his herd after Martinmas and a one-year-old kid if he took good care of his herd. Tenants were also given '*for the occupation of the land; two oxen, and one cow and six sheep and seven sown acres on his piece of land*' (Swanton *op. cit.*, 28).

As we have already seen in the context of the chapter on the agricultural economy, a separate charter, a grant by Offa, King of Mercia, to the church of Worcester, of land at Westbury and Henbury, Gloucestershire (AD 793–796), provides details of the tribute or food rent that the king could draw from an estate as his farm. This included 7 oxen, 6 wethers, 40 cheeses and 30 ambers of unground corn and 4 ambers of meal (*EHD.* 78). The food rent required by the West Saxon King Ina included 2 full-grown cows, 10 wethers, 10 geese, 20 hens, 10 cheeses, a full amber of butter, 5 salmon and 100 eels (Hodges 1982). The King's food rent paid by the community at Berkeley, Gloucestershire, in AD 883 consisted of a render of clear ale, beer, honey, bullocks, swine and sheep (Sawyer 1968, 218; Birch 1885–1893 *Cartularium Saxonicum*, B551).

The Axbridge chronicle (a fourteenth to fifteenth century compilation which must be a copy of an earlier manuscript probably originating from London) also provides some detail about royal food rent. *'There shall be Governors in each Borough, who at that time were called Wardemen... Who in the name of the King were to supply victuals, to wit wheat, wine and barley, sheep and oxen and other cattle of the fields and fowls of the air and fishes of the waters for the time that the King with all his following ordered a stay in the appointed borough. But if it happened that the King did not come there, then all the supplies were to be sold in the market of the aforesaid Borough, and the money received there-from shall be carried to the King's treasury...' (Neale 1979).*

Texts concerned with a grant of land by King Eadwig to Bath Abbey in AD 956 provide some specific insights into renders due to the lord (see Swanton 1996, 17–18). In the description of this particular estate, numerous basket and grid weirs on the rivers Severn and Wye are mentioned and *'... at each weir, every alternate fish belongs to the landlord and each rare fish which is of value – sturgeon and porpoise, river or sea-fish; and nobody is to sell any fish for money when the lord is on the estate before telling him about it'*. Dues from his Tidenham estate also mention food rent paid in pigs *'... he who has 7 pigs shall supply 3, and thereafter always the tenth – and even so a mast levy when there is mast'*.

Other documents also indicate transactions of marine resources. Land leased by Abbot Ælfwig and all the Fellowship at Bath to Archbishop Stigand (AD 1061–5) included the sum of ten gold marks and twenty pounds of silver *'... and in addition 1 mark of gold and 6 porpoises and 30,000 herrings each year'* (Swanton 1996, 19).

In the Irish law texts of the seventh and eighth centuries, numerous animals (but mainly cattle, often referred to in terms of milch cows) were mentioned in relation to fines, tribute, bride prices, fosterage fees and other payments (Kelly 1997, 27). For example, one cow a year was due to the lord from the well-off farmer (or *bóaire*). One text, dealing with clientship (CIH ii 483.35–6), includes mention of the belly of a pen-reared (?) boar in the food rent paid by a client to his lord (*CIH* iii 920.20. *DIL* A 166.60). According to the *Cáin Aicillne*, a client's render included a pig, which was nine fists long and given to the lord in winter.

Conspicuous consumption

Bearing in mind the exceptional preservation of bone at the site and the fact that the vast refuse dumps of bone and other waste accumulated over at least three centuries,

it seems likely that considerable numbers of domestic animals were brought to Flixborough. One of the most important activities represented by the bones involved the extensive killing and butchering of livestock to provide primary products, including meat for direct consumption and possible re-distribution. Direct evidence of this primary consumption is to be found not only in the sheer quantity of remains of deadstock, but, more specifically, in the form of obvious disarticulation and butchery of skeletal elements (see Chapter 6). Such a large amount of remains indicates the conspicuous consumption of meat by the inhabitants of Flixborough throughout the period of occupation. The quantities involved, age at death profiles, and changes in the relative frequencies of the major domestic animals also provide clues about the status of the site and/or some of its inhabitants.

Feasting

Feasting was an important social activity for the higher-ranking members of society during early medieval times and one of the duties of the client was to feast his lord, together with his retinue. Conversely, the food rents, which a lord received from his clients, would enable him to provide regular feasts and thereby enhance his prestige. Although there is much more emphasis in Old English poetry on what is drunk than eaten, a few Anglo-Saxon documentary references do mention food at feasts, and it is also depicted in Anglo-Saxon art. For example, Alcuin of York condemns those who over-indulge in 'delicacies' and feasting, and feasting is also depicted on the Bayeux Tapestry (Magennis 1999, 32). Several Icelandic sagas conjure up images of warriors throwing large animal bones at each other in the hall (Magennis *op. cit.*, 31–2).

Feasting was very important in early Irish society and is mentioned in numerous legal and other sources (Kelly 1997, 358). There was much etiquette involved concerning where one sat and which cut of meat one received, both linked to individual status. Important guests, for example, were entitled to the best cuts, such as the tenderloin steak or haunch, whilst those of somewhat lower status got the shank or centre cut loin steak. Low-ranking people received inferior cuts such as the belly chine or shoulder fat (*ibid.*).

Although there is no direct evidence for feasting at Flixborough, the sheer quantity of meat that was apparently consumed throughout its occupation, as evinced by the large dumps of butchered mammal bones, and the variety of wild taxa (particularly birds associated with the medieval banqueting table), surely implies the feeding of large numbers of people. It is not too much of a leap of faith to conclude that at least a proportion of the domestic and wild animal remains on the site represent those that were prepared for and consumed at regular feasting events, perhaps instigated by the arrival of the royal retinue.

The significance of large cattle

Differences in the sizes of domestic livestock from different settlement types may also reflect the status and nature of those settlements, and their relationships with one another. For example, it has been argued that cattle bones from royal sites in Ireland tend to be larger than average, and this is taken to indicate competitive cattle breeding among the Irish aristocracy (McCormick 1987). Corroborative evidence for the importance of large cattle can also be found in the early Irish literature, where the size of cattle is continually emphasised (e.g. *TBC* LL 36.1323–6). These animals required more food and were sometimes difficult to handle, but at the same time they provided large carcases and were probably regarded as status symbols by their owners (Kelly 1997).

In Chapter 9 it was argued that the largest Anglo-Saxon cattle have been found on high-status sites in the East of England, and that these are most likely to have been introduced from the Continent, possibly the Low Countries. Comparisons of cattle bone measurements from a number of sites both here and on the Continent have shown that some of the largest cattle have in fact been recorded at Flixborough, particularly from Phase 2–3a. As has previously been mentioned, this 'improved' variety probably served a practical use – i.e. to improve the local cattle stock. However, as with access to other exotic and imported goods, these cattle (larger than local stock and probably of very different appearance) were perhaps yet another vehicle for reinforcing, emphasising and even increasing social rank.

The importance of pigs

The role of pigs within human society is something that is beginning to inform archaeologists about more than just their part in the general meat supply. For the medieval period particularly, as for so many agricultural activities, historical records portray the crucial role pigs played in the seasonal cycle of food supply. During the late autumn/early winter pigs were fattened; those in large herds were taken to woodland where they would gorge themselves on fallen acorns and beech mast (sometimes the swineherds would beat the trees to aid this process) – a system known as 'pannage'. One of the final agricultural tasks of the year was the winter killing of pigs. Scenes of pannage and pig slaughtering (PLATES 10.1 and 10.2) are common depictions in late Saxon and early medieval (twelfth and thirteenth centuries) calendars for the months of November and December (Perez-Higuera 1998). Many of these depictions provide detailed insight into the size and conformation of these animals (many show small animals with long pointed faces, their bodies covered with hair), as well as showing (in grisly detail) the stunning, slaughtering, bleeding and butchering of the animals. But what of the zooarchaeological evidence? Crabtree (unpublished 1994) has suggested that one explanation for the increasing numbers of pigs during the Saxon period may be the result of changing availability of access to woodland and pasture. Alternatively, she suggests that pigs may be a high-status dietary item brought into high-ranking sites. In fact an interesting pattern emerges when the frequency of pig remains is considered from a number of medieval sites in the region. Table 10.9 shows the ranked position of pig remains at sites where >500 fragments of identifiable mammal bones were recovered. Although at most sites, pig remains are typically the least numerous domesticate, several show an increase in their importance (i.e. to >20%). What is common about these sites is that all are interpreted as ecclesiastical in nature. Large monastic establishments would include in their holdings managed areas of woodland where pigs would be kept at certain times of the year, so on purely ecological grounds, pigs are likely to be more common at sites where there was access to this type of resource and it was actively managed.

In contrast to the English evidence, analyses of zooarchaeological assemblages from early medieval abbeys in Belgium indicate that meat from mammals was only occasionally consumed, and when it was, pig remains were always rare (Ervynck 1997b, fig. 4). On the other hand, high-status establishments such as castles have been linked with high proportions of pig bones. Using dental attrition data from pigs' teeth from these sites, Ervynck (1997a) has identified evidence for seasonal killing of pigs consistent with that indicated by historical sources. Data from one or two sites, however, suggest other non-seasonal pig slaughtering patterns, which may reflect different economic factors involved with changing husbandry.

However, what is most interesting is Ervynck's interpretation of status as indicated by pigs. As well as ecological factors involved with the abundant areas of managed woodland controlled by these large aristocratic estates, he suggests that the consumption of large quantities of pork was also a manifestation of wealth and position – a socio-economic divide used as a form of social identity (Ervynck 2004). Feudal lords and aristocrats constantly had to reaffirm their status, and they regularly could do this by showing the benefits of their privileges. One way was to be seen to serve and eat large quantities of meat, part of the Germanic tradition, reflecting power, well-being, virility and martiality (Montanari 1994).

Ervynck (2004) also suggests that, since domestic pigs retained a symbolic link with the 'wild' forest (because they were herded there), and because the medieval pig still largely resembled the wild boar (held in high esteem as the most dangerous hunted prey: Hainard 1948), these notional values were conferred upon those who controlled access to and ate large quantities of pork. He also raises the intriguing possibility that Roman culture and the army also played a major role in the composition of the medieval noble diet, particularly with regard to the importance of pigs.

Site Name	Period	Site Type	% Pig
Jarrow AML 80/87	High medieval	ecclesiastical	29.0
Dominican Priory (Beverley)	High medieval	ecclesiastical	23.0
Coppergate (16–22)	Saxo-Norman	urban	20.0
Dominican Priory (Beverley)	Early medieval	ecclesiastical	20.0
Coppergate (16–22)	Saxo-Norman	urban	18.6
Westgate Road 91	Medieval	urban	16.0
Coppergate (16–22)	High medieval	urban	15.8
Coppergate (16–22)	Early medieval	urban	15.7
St Giles by Brompton Bridge	High medieval	hospital	15.0
Coppergate (16–22)	10th Century AD	urban	13.6
Caythorpe Pipeline	Early Saxon	ladder settlement	13.0
Jarrow	Saxon	ecclesiastical	13.0
Queen St (Newcastle)	High medieval	waterfront dump	13.0
Coppergate (16–22)	10th Century AD	urban	12.1
St Giles by Brompton Bridge	Late medieval	hospital	12.0
Thrislington 73–4	Late medieval	deserted medieval village	12.0
General Accident	Early medieval	urban	11.0
Beeston Castle	Early 10th century AD	castle	10.0
Wharram	High medieval	deserted medieval village	9.0
Skeldergate	10th Century AD	urban	8.0
Coppergate (16–22)	9th century AD	urban	7.4
Castle Ditch Newcastle	Late medieval	castle	4.0

TABLE *10.9 Ranked frequency of pig remains recorded at medieval sites in the North of England.*

The theory of castles in Belgium as so called 'top-level predators' (Ervynck 1992) could perhaps also be postulated for high-status Anglo Saxon settlements in England, where the domestic pig may also have represented a symbol of wealth and prestige – an obvious way of separating the food of the elite and the commoner. The range of artefactual and structural evidence from most phases at Flixborough certainly supports this view. Many of the pigs consumed at Flixborough (and other contemporaneous sites) were mature adult animals, which might suggest that the preferences in the taste of the inhabitants at Flixborough (and other sites) favoured the production of leaner, more grainy meat with a heightened 'gamey' flavour – possibly akin to that of wild boar which, as previously mentioned, may have been scarce in the region. This would require the implementation of a somewhat less efficient and higher maintenance husbandry regime, favouring the extended development, raising and culling of older individuals. Or perhaps, the inhabitants were interested in large animals (or their tusks) for display purposes. The small numbers of very young pigs present in the Flixborough assemblage probably represent suckling pigs consumed by the few high-status inhabitants of the site. An alternative explanation to the apparent preference for mature pigs at many Anglo-Saxon sites might be that domestic pigs during this period were slower-growing/-maturing animals, which carried much less fat on them than pigs today. As a result, it is likely that these pigs did not attain full carcase weight until they reached advanced maturity.

Analysis of the vertebrate remains from three settlements in Westphalia, Germany – the Carolingian royal palace of Paderborn, the estate centres of the villas/estates of Soest (*vill* of the Archbishops of Cologne from the seventh century onwards), and Hoxter (royal Carolingian *vill*, given to the monastery of Corvey in AD 822/3) provide further contemporaneous evidence of the pig as an indicator of high-status (Doll 1999). At all these sites, remains of domestic stock (i.e. cattle, pigs, sheep, chickens, ducks and geese) and wild animals (mostly wild boar, red deer and hare) were present. Cattle are thought to have been the most important source of meat in the Carolingian period (AD 751/3 to 987), a fact certainly borne out by the assemblages from the estate centres of Soest and Hoxter. However, the assemblage from the palace at Paderborn indicated that pigs provided the majority (i.e. >50%) of the meat consumed. This suggests that the palace may have been receiving renders in the form of pigs, a hypothesis corroborated by documentary sources indicating the use of pigs as payments for tribute and taxation (Reuter 1985).

It is interesting to note that pig was the dominant domestic animal present in tenth–eleventh century assemblages from Dublin (McCormick 1991). Whether this implies a higher-status urban component to the inhabitants of Late Viking Dublin when compared with the contemporaneous lower-status tenements and artisans quarters excavated in Viking York, is difficult to ascertain. It could merely reflect different provisioning practices of urban centres, or the presence of different ecological conditions around each urban area (e.g. more woodland for pig breeding) favouring certain kinds of husbandry.

The fact that pig remains appear more common at what are considered to be high-status Anglo-Saxon sites in England appears to be corroborated somewhat by the eighth century Irish law text *Críth Gablach*. It refers to the boar 'which removes dishonour at every season' i.e. providing a feast for high-ranking individuals whenever they visit (*CIH* ii 563.27–8).

Wild animals and high-status

During medieval times in Western Europe, the hunting, procurement and consumption of wild fauna (e.g. birds and mammals) were directly linked to social identity and standing. Members of the aristocracy and nobility, if not directly engaged in the pursuit of wild animals, would certainly ensure that these were procured and consumed in varying quantities at feast times and religious festivals. Access to resources that added both quantity and diversity to the diet (which for the bulk of the population was probably severely limited in terms of meat – Albarella and Thomas 2002), as well as to animals that were considered exotic, rare and sometimes dangerous, afforded those of influence opportunities to display wealth, bravado and gain prestige befitting their social rank. This ensured that certain species and foodstuffs gained significance beyond mere calorific content or even taste (Dobney and Jaques 2002). The hunting of animals of limited availability during medieval times was restricted to an élite, so possession, control and consumption of these animals reinforced the social status of individuals or groups. Such beasts were generally consumed at banquets and provided suitable gifts to obtain influence with the powerful or to reward equals or social inferiors (Gardiner 1997, 186).

Although the link between certain animals and status is well known for the later medieval period, its origins are less well known. In Britain, for example, it is pertinent to question whether these ideas and practices may have been part of the legacy of the Norman Conquest after 1066, in which a foreign élite held sway over the main body of the indigenous Saxon population, or whether it already existed in some form, in the preceding Saxon period (Dobney and Jaques *op. cit.*). Was wild animal exploitation at all important during the immediate pre-Norman (Saxon/Anglian) times in England and, if so, did it change through time and from place to place? Was it influenced by the later arrival of Scandinavian ideas and settlement in Northern England?

The hunting of wild boar had specific social significance in early medieval society in Europe, being linked inextricably to warfare, masculinity and the elite warrior class. This can be seen in funerary objects such as the boar-crested helmets and tusk armlets recovered from numerous 'warrior burials' (Lucy 2000). Viewed in this context, its presence in the eighth- and tenth-century Flixborough assemblage, admittedly in very low frequencies, is hardly surprising given the proven high-status nature of the settlement and its inhabitants. Perhaps more significant) is the absence of wild boar remains from the very large (>12,000 identified fragments) ninth century excavated animal bone assemblage.

A recent study of cervid remains from early medieval sites in France and the U.K. has highlighted the preponderance of roe deer remains in the wild mammal assemblages of religious houses from the seventh to mid-twelfth centuries (Sykes 2006, fig. 11.5). Reasons given are either that ecclesiastics were often granted the right to hunt lesser game, or that roe deer held a symbolic significance to men of the cloth, being faithful, chaste and abstemious (Sykes *op. cit.*, 168). The remains of cervids, particularly roe deer, are the most common wild hunted mammal represented in the Flixborough assemblage (121 identified fragments) and are represented in all but the earliest phase. However, their presence and relative frequencies imply little or no significance, beyond their probable local or regional availability.

However, other elements of the wild vertebrate fauna from Flixborough do provide interesting and important information regarding both wealth and status.

Cetaceans

According to numerous historical texts, the social value given to cetaceans during the high and later medieval period, 'certainly exceeded their nutritional and other utilitarian worth...' (Gardiner 1997, 173). As Gardiner (*op. cit.*, 186) points out *'The possession and consumption of cetaceans was one arena in which social tensions and the aspirations of groups competing for power were worked out. Their symbolic value was considerably greater than their simple utility'*.

Was this also the case during early medieval/Saxon times in England? Sources indicate that in France the royal privilege of claiming stranded whales existed from at least the reign of Charles the Bald (AD 840–77). Since the documentary evidence for this practice in England does not appear before the Norman Conquest, (Gardiner 1997, 176), it has been claimed that during the Anglo-Saxon period until the eleventh century, stranded cetaceans were recovered by local communities for communal consumption (Gardiner *op. cit.*, 187). However, the unprecedented large numbers of bottlenose dolphin bones identified from the Flixborough animal bone assemblage appear to suggest that cetacean exploitation was indeed associated with high-status individuals during Middle to Late Saxon times in England, carrying wider meaning about the social context of the site.

Fish

In the high Middle Ages, freshwater fish (such as pike and bream) took on important status associations. They were costly components of élite diet, particularly during periods of fasting, and even served as the objects of gift exchange (Dyer 1988). It seems, however, that these taxa were consumed much more widely in the early historic period (see, for example, Enghoff 1999; 2000); thus most of the species recovered at Flixborough cannot be interpreted as indicators of wealth. Sturgeon, however, requires special comment. This taxon, present in Phases 2–3a through to 6 (inclusive), is rare in late prehistoric to medieval fish bone assemblages throughout north-western Europe (Enghoff 1999; 2000). A preliminary survey of English assemblages dating from the sixth to the fifteenth centuries has revealed only five other occurrences (Jones 1976; Thawley 1981; Locker 1989; O'Connor 1989; 1991). Like cetaceans, sturgeon were probably highly valued in the Saxon period (Hagen 1995, 167) and later came to be reserved as royal property in the Middle Ages (Hammond 1993, 21–2). Their presence at Flixborough is consistent with other ecofactual and artefactual evidence for high-status occupation (Loveluck 1997). This species could conceivably have been acquired by trade, but it does visit the lower reaches of large British rivers (Maitland and Campbell 1992, 91) and is more likely to represent a rare and highly-prized local catch.

The identification of salmon in the Flixborough fish bone assemblage may also point to the status of some of the inhabitants. In the Irish law codes, for example, the sheer number of references to salmon compared with any other fish species can be taken to indicate its prestige as a food item to the wealthy and powerful (Kelly 1997, 291). This position is highlighted (along with that of the pig), in the ninth century 'Triad', which lists the three deaths that are better than life as: the death of a salmon, a boar, and a robber (Meyer 1906, 12–18).

Birds

Dobney and Jaques (2002) have explored the evidence for wild bird exploitation in England during the Saxon period and illustrated how the utilisation of differences in the frequency and diversity of bird remains can be used to infer the nature and character of some Saxon settlements in England (see previous this chapter). They also used the presence of certain bird species to explore the possible origins of some specific high-status activities, and some interesting patterns emerged.

One example of this approach concerns the crane. Although during the later medieval period, the hunting and consumption of crane (like certain other wild species of mammal, bird, and fish) was considered to be an important symbol of wealth, prestige and status, evidence presented earlier appears to indicate that crane was perhaps a more common component of the diet during Anglo-Saxon times (see TABLE 10.5). The remains of common crane appear to have been identified from almost all categories of Anglo-Saxon site considered. They were present amongst the vertebrate remains at every ecclesiastical and rural site examined, at less than 50%

of estate centres and urban sites, though absent from all but one site classified as a *wic* (i.e. the site of Ipswich).

This picture may be biased by the relatively few rural and strictly ecclesiastical sites available for analysis (and the assumptions of high and low status assigned to each). Access to crane meat may in fact not have been a reflection of status in itself during Anglo-Saxon times. This may have been bestowed on individuals by the way the bird was hunted and captured and even perhaps tamed. In this respect, the presence of species of the Ardeidae family (i.e. bittern and grey heron) and red kite are perhaps even more enlightening (see TABLE 10.5). Unlike crane, their remains appear to be almost exclusively associated with high-status estate centres, and the reason for this may lie in the fact that they are also associated with the extremely high-status sport of falconry or hawking.

Anglo Saxon falconry

Evidence for falconry at Flixborough is certainly not at first site obvious from the zooarchaeological assemblage, i.e. no remains of falcons (e.g. peregrine) or hawks (e.g. goshawk) traditionally associated with this medieval high-status pastime, have been identified. However, on closer inspection, a number of secondary and somewhat circumstantial lines of evidence – i.e. the identification of other raptor species such as buzzards and red kite not traditionally perceived as hawking birds, and particular prey species of the falconer – provide significant clues in this regard. However, these can only be readily interpreted within the broader interpretative framework of historical and zooarchaeological evidence from Saxon England.

Although the antiquity and geographical origins of falconry are unclear (Dobney 2000, and 2002) has claimed that it could have arisen as early as 10,000 BP in the Near East), the art of hawking (catching wild game using tame birds of prey) was well known to the inhabitants of northern Europe from the sixth century AD onwards. The sixth century laws of some Germanic tribes make various indirect references to the importance of falconry through fines imposed for the theft or killing of a person's hawks (Epstein 1943), with the size of the fine depending upon the value of the bird based on its hunting prowess. It is apparent from slightly later literary sources that the sport of falconry was important to the Anglo-Saxon inhabitants of England. Oggins (1981), in his seminal paper on falconry in Anglo-Saxon England, illustrates a number of examples, the first being the earliest dated record of falconry in England. In a letter by St Boniface (an eighth century missionary to the Continent) written to King Ethelbald of Mercia (one of the Saxon kingdoms in southern Britain) around AD 745–6, he alludes to the gift of a hawk, two falcons, two shields and two lances. In a slightly later correspondence (AD 748–55), King Ethelbert of Kent wrote to St Boniface in Germany asking him to procure two hawks for crane hawking. He specifically asks for birds that should have '*skill and courage enough*' (Kylie 1911). It appears, however, that St Boniface objected to the recreational aspects of hawking, since in a letter written to Cuthbert, Archbishop of Canterbury, in AD 747, he states that ' *the servants of God we forbid to hunt and wander in the woods with dogs and to keep hawks and falcons*' (Kylie 1911, 178).

By the late eighth century, hawkers are recorded as established members of the Mercian royal household. A charter of King Burgred of Mercia of AD 855 exempted the minister at Blockley (Gloucestershire) from certain dues, including '*the feeding and maintenance of all hawks and falcons in the land of Mercians...*' (Sawyer 1968). This suggests that the maintenance of trained hunting birds was a significant drain on the purse of individuals, making their ownership all the more the preserve of the privileged. The absence of any references to falconry or hawking in the Old Irish texts, and the specific fact that the heroes of the eighth and ninth centuries are portrayed as having hounds but no hawks (Kelly 1997, 303), may well indicate that this sport was in fact introduced into England by the Saxon/Frisian aristocracy.

In all these literary sources, the birds that are mentioned or inferred are all hawks or falcons. The wildfowler in *Ælfric's Colloquy* mentions hawks as one of a range of methods of catching birds and mention is also made of a '*bigger hawk and a smaller one...*', although no indication of species is given (see translation by Swanton 1996, 111). The special falcons requested by King Ethelbert to undertake crane-hawking were almost certainly large gyrfalcons. All these references outlined above are exclusively linked with aristocrats, nobility and even the king, which indicates that the sport of falconry (as with certain other forms of hunting) held a special place in the social order during Saxon times. A full six centuries later, the 'Boke of St Albans' (dating from the fourteenth century) details how specific species of raptor were utilised by various ranks of nobility. The 'Egle', 'Bawtere' and 'Melowne' were birds used by an 'Emprowre', the 'Gerfawken' the bird used by a king, the 'Fawken Gentill' the bird used by a prince, and the 'Goshawke' that of a yeoman (quoted in Oggins 1989). It is probable, from the available literary sources, that social ranking (associated with the use of hawking birds) was already present in Anglo-Saxon England.

Little evidence from the archaeological record definitively shows the presence of trained birds of prey, and that which does exist, is somewhat circumstantial. Prummel (1997) outlines five types of evidence that could be used to infer the presence of hawking. The first is specific falconer's equipment, whilst the second is the direct association of raptor bones with the remains of humans (i.e. buried singly or together with their human masters). As far as we are aware, few or no elements of the small finds assemblages at any site from this period can be conclusively linked with the sport of falconry. However, birds of prey have been found in graves from

the fifth to seventh centuries in Thuringia, Germany (Muller 1993; Timpel 1990), and cremated remains of goshawks, peregrines and merlins have been found in cremation burials in Sweden dating from the sixth to ninth centuries AD (Sten and Vretemark 1988).

Prummel's third, fourth and fifth types of evidence are somewhat more circumstantial in nature, but likely to be more common in the archaeological record. These are: i) the presence of raptor bones from species that are traditionally associated with hawking, ii) a bias towards female birds (which are larger than their male counterparts and thus considered more useful at supplying food for the table), and iii) the bones of species that constituted their prey (i.e. numerous small and medium-sized birds and mammals).

At the mid eighth–late tenth century Slavonic castle of Oldenburg, in Ostholstein, Northern Germany, several of these lines of evidence are well represented (Prummel 1997). The remains of goshawk and sparrowhawk made up as much as 15% of the wild bird assemblage at this site and females of these two species outnumbered males by as much as 2:1 and 3:1 respectively. In addition, possible prey species associated with hawking were also recovered from the bone assemblage at Oldenburg and included members of the following families: Columbidae (doves and pigeons), Turdidae (blackbirds and thrushes), Corvidae (crows), Phasianidae (pheasants), Anatidae (ducks) and Leporidae (hares). Some larger bird species such as grey heron, goose, cormorant, black stork, bittern and swan were also identified.

How does the evidence from Anglo-Saxon England, and particularly Flixborough, relate to the lines of evidence outlined by Prummel (1997)? Hawking birds associated with human remains have been recognised on few sites in England. For example, two raptor terminal phalanges (species not indicated), have been identified from the Anglo-Saxon cemetery of Spong Hill, Norfolk, along with the cremated remains of a range of other wild and domestic animals. However, both had been perforated in order, presumably, to be worn as beads or amulets (Bond 1994, 134) and, therefore, may not reflect their principal use for hawking.

Also, few sites have produced the remains of what could be considered to be hawking birds themselves. In our survey of Anglo-Saxon sites, only five of the twenty-seven vertebrate assemblages studied contained the remains of goshawk or peregrine. Of these, only one (Brandon, Suffolk) is from a high-status estate centre. The remaining examples are from urban contexts: Coppergate, York (O'Connor 1989) and Castle Mall, Norwich (Albarella *et al.* 1997), a supposed iron-smelting site at Ramsbury, Wiltshire (Coy 1980), one from a *wic*, Ipswich (Crabtree 1996), but none from Flixborough. If we assume that these birds were indeed used for falconry, then (on the face of it) the zooarchaeological evidence for actual hawking birds does not tie in with the historical evidence for this as a high-status pursuit during Saxon times. If the evidence is considered in more depth, however, it may be more informative. For example, the occurrence of hawking birds in urban contexts is most easily explained by the fact that early urban centres must have comprised numerous individuals at every level of the social hierarchy. Thus, high-status individuals (with their hawking birds, etc.) may either have permanently resided or at least intermittently visited these early centres of commerce. Hawking birds were also probably bought and exchanged in urban centres, which may perhaps explain the presence of goshawk bones in assemblages from excavations of tenements at Coppergate, where much archaeological evidence for trade and commerce was also apparent.

Identification of the remains of peregrine falcon at the so-called iron-smelting site of Ramsbury is, at face value somewhat puzzling. This and other evidence however, indicates that its classification as 'industrial' is perhaps too simplistic. Only a small portion of the site was excavated and certainly much evidence of iron-smelting was recovered. However, a range of industrial processes (including iron-working) have also been identified from a number of estate centres (including Flixborough), indicating that a range of activities were carried out at these Middle and Later Saxon élite sites. Other vertebrate remains identified from Ramsbury include numerous wild animals, such as red deer and beaver which, like the peregrine falcon, support the conclusion that this was also a settlement of high-status.

As previously mentioned, Ipswich also appears to be the only so-called *wic* where remains of a hawking bird have been identified. It is thought that the *wics* (or emporia) were early trading centres, an expression of administered long-distance trade, encouraged and stimulated by royal patronage. It is thought that their evolution and development was aimed at maximising the hitherto irregular trade for import of luxury goods (Hodges 1982, 60). Perhaps some of those luxury goods were in the form of live falcons, gifts of which are mentioned in Anglo-Saxon texts (see earlier). Alternatively, it could be argued that the zoo-archaeological evidence from Ipswich may be reflecting the additional 'background noise' (briefly discussed earlier) associated with a settlement that was perhaps more complex in character.

TABLE 10.5 shows that there are only five sites where the remains of species traditionally used for hawking have been recovered. However, there are considerably more sites (a total of 14 including Flixborough) where the remains of several other types of raptor (specifically red kite and common buzzard) have been identified. The remains of scavenging birds such as buzzards and kites is usually and most simply explained by the killing (or natural deaths) of birds which were present in the vicinity of a site, and which were attracted by human waste and refuse (O'Connor 1993). The common occurrence of the remains of red kite in urban zooarchaeological assem-

blages (from the Roman and medieval periods), has led O'Connor (*op. cit.*) to infer that this bird formerly had a primarily commensal status in towns. The ornithologist Francis Willoughby (writing in the late seventeenth century) indicated that '*...they are noisome to tame birds, especially chickens, ducklings and goslings... Yea so bold are they that they affect to prey in cities and places frequented by men; so that the very gardens, and courts or yards of houses are not secure from their ravine. For which cause our good housewives are very angry with them, and of all birds hate and curse them most*' (Ray 1678, Book II, 75).

There may, however, be several additional or alternative explanations for their presence in Saxon elite centres such as Flixborough and other medieval sites.

Though not normally regarded as being suitable for falconry, the common buzzard can be (and were) trained by the novice to catch a limited range of prey (Oswald 1982, 50). Jameson, (1976, 95) commenting on the qualities of the common buzzard states that '*Anyone not acquainted with them in the field is apt to get the false impression that they are lethargic and not as graceful in flight as other hawks*'. He goes on to state '*They lack the finish of other hawks, but when on the wing they can be masters of aerial locomotion*'. Ford (1982, 39) suggests that '*the buzzard is a reasonably tough bird, which is able to withstand a certain amount of mismanagement in finding its flying weight. It is blessed with a relatively even temperament, and the work put in on manning is quickly rewarded. It is not easy to lose, working reasonably close to the falconer, and can, with much perseverance take rabbit, moorhen, hare and squirrel*'.

Remains of buzzard were noted from thirteen of the twenty-seven sites included in this survey, representing all site categories, although their highest incidence was from high-status estate centres, including Flixborough. Could these remains indeed be from birds used for the purposes of hawking? It is entirely plausible. The lower status of the buzzard as a hawking bird in later medieval times may explain the reason why this bird is found at such a wide variety of site types.

But what of the red kite, a number of bones of which were recovered from élite centres such as Flixborough? During later medieval times, they (like buzzards) were sometimes also employed as an essential part of particular wildfowling strategies. Tame red kites were traditionally used as decoys in order to prevent wildfowl/waterfowl from taking to the wing. '*Fowlers were wont to employ a trained kite to trap with their nets a covey while it lay fearful of their enemy above, the game being so terrified that they were heedless of any other possible danger*' (Jameson 1976, 100). The use of live-trained kites was later superseded by paper or cloth silhouettes (kites) in the shape of a bird of prey, which were kept aloft by the wind. Thus, while the soaring kite (real or virtual) kept the birds from taking flight, attendant fowlers could employ a range of techniques to catch numerous birds –

on the ground or on the water (Folkard 1859).

Alternatively, red kite remains may simply have been another prey species of the inhabitants at Flixborough (in common with a number of the other wild bird species previously discussed), but one which may once again reflect the very high status of the inhabitants. During the Tudor period, kite-hawking (i.e. the hunting of red kites with other birds of prey – either gyrfalcons or saker falcons) was regarded as perhaps the stateliest of all forms of falconry and the sport of princes (Harting 1898, 157). Henry VIII is said to have ridden out of London to the great heaths of Royston, Newmarket and Thetford for days or, in some cases, for several weeks of sport with gyrfalcons, which included the hunting of red kites. Harting (*op. cit.*, 157–67) describes the details of the hunt in which the kite was brought within range of the falcons. To avoid the kite soaring continually above the hunting falcons, a decoy was used to bring the kite to a lower altitude. This could be a tame eagle owl (called by the French *Le Grand Duc*, or by the Germans *Uhu*) which was released with a foxes '*brush*' (tail) tied to its jesses. The kite, thinking it was carrying prey, descended in order to rob it of its prize, whereupon the gyrfalcon would be slipped. According to Harting (*op. cit.*), the best description of kite-hawking is provided by the French falconer Charles d'Arcussia in his *Treatise on Falconry,* which describes kite-hawking with Louis XIII. This sport continued to be practised in England by the noble classes until 1773, when what was probably the last recorded kite-hawking took place with Lord Orford and Colonel Thornton's gyrfalcons, although the sport was certainly still practised in India with saker falcons at the turn of the eighteenth century (Harting *op. cit.*).

What of the zooarchaeological evidence for the red kite in the Saxon period? In our survey of Anglo-Saxon assemblages, the remains of red kite have been identified at only six out of twenty-seven sites including Flixborough. All except one are from high-status estate and urban centres (the individual from Ramsbury can perhaps also be considered high-status – see earlier), which seems a strange pattern if these were merely the remains of scavenging commensal animals.

Many more sites have produced vertebrate assemblages in which the remains of potential prey species of hawking birds have been identified. Unfortunately, many different mammals and birds could have been hunted and caught using falcons, but they could equally have been caught in a number of other ways (bird lime, snares, nets, drugged bait, etc. – see Chapter 8). The mere presence of a potential prey species at a site cannot, therefore, be used to as direct evidence of falconry. However, some species are perhaps of greater significance in this respect than others.

Many authors cite numerous pre-nineteenth century references to larger bird species being the preferred quarry of the nobility, particularly when hunting with goshawks and other large raptors (e.g. Lascelles 1892; Michell

1972; Mollen 1968; Evans 1973). These species included birds such as grey heron, goose, great bustard, and especially common crane, and even other raptors such as the red kite (see above). All these species (except bustard) were identified in the Flixborough vertebrate assemblage.

Hunting these birds with specially trained (and expensive) hawks (usually goshawks) was considered to be fine sport and the sole preserve of high-ranking individuals. Jameson (1976, 70) states that '*... the most formidable quarry (apart from the goose) was the crane. It is a wary animal, which requires careful stalking and attack. To place the hawk close enough for flight the falconer hid with the goshawk in a blind near where cranes were known to feed. The prospective prey was then baited and grain concentrated near the blind. When a crane ventured near, the hawk was slipped and the falconer hurried to aid the hawk since such a large prey could injure it. Egrets and herons were also hunted this way*'.

This form of hunting is depicted on one of the scenes from the *Cotton Tiberius Calendar* – the illustration for the month of October (PLATE 10.3). It clearly portrays a Saxon noble on horseback, with a large bird (most certainly a large raptor of some kind) on his right fist, riding towards an even larger, long-necked bird which appears to be oblivious to his approach. The overall shape, stance and characteristic cap of red plumage, leaves one in no doubt that this is a deliberate portrayal of the hunting of a common crane. Opposite the mounted noble is a person on foot, also with a large bird (presumably another raptor) on his right fist. This bird, with wings outstretched, is about to be 'slipped' (i.e. released) at the crane and/or the various (?) geese that are also depicted in and around a small pond/lake within the scene.

Other contemporaneous historical sources also indicate the élite nature and status of hawking and falconry, and the significance of certain quarry species. For example, the Chief Falconer (the fourth officer at the Welsh court – the tenth officer was the Chief Huntsman) was honoured with three presents on the day his hawk killed one of the three notable birds (i.e. a crane, grey heron or bittern, according to the Dimentian code, or crane, grey heron or curlew, in the Gwentian code). Is it coincidence that these species have been commonly identified from a number of the high-status Anglo-Saxon sites including Flixborough (detailed in TABLE 10.5), in addition to a range of other bird species which could also have been hunted (i.e. black grouse, wild geese, ducks, waders and pigeons)?

The case of the Ardeidae (herons and bitterns) in this survey is an intriguing one. As late as the nineteenth century, the heron was considered the favourite and 'noblest' quarry of the falconer (Folkard *op. cit.*, 11). As previously mentioned, unlike crane, their remains have been recorded almost exclusively from high-status sites, and it is also possible that heron and bittern were regarded as even higher-status game than crane during Saxon times. Sources from later medieval times indicate that herons were for many years protected by statute, and during the reign of Henry VII it was, in fact, prohibited to take herons by any other means than by hawking or long-bow (Folkard 1859, 194). As mentioned previously, heron is cited as one of the 'three notable birds' in both the Dimentian and the Gwentian codes, and they continued to feature in the banquets of the nobility and royal households well into the medieval period. They were esteemed as one of the daintiest luxuries of the dinner table and stood (with crane) at the head of the game course on every festive occasion. During the reign of Edward I (1272–1307) the prices of wildfowl assessed by the Mayor of London made the heron around 16 pence, among the highest price paid for waterfowl in those days (*vide Liber Albus Gildhallae,* introd., p. xxxiij: Folkard *op. cit.,* 194).

Although little traditional direct evidence for hawking or falconry has been identified from Flixborough, it is abundantly clear that a range of other information exists which can be used to argue a strong case for its existence at Flixborough and other élite Anglo-Saxon sites. If true, these data also indicate that many of the specific aspects of later medieval falconry and hawking, and their association with élite status of individuals or groups, have their origins in Anglo-Saxon times, and were unaffected by the later Norman Conquest.

Note

1   Based on the hand-collected assemblage (for which inter-class data are available).

Epilogue

As the previous chapters have, we hope, illustrated, the bioarchaeological evidence from Flixborough (in particular the animal bone assemblage) has provided a series of unique insights into many specific aspects of the settlement, as well as in more broader terms, of Anglo-Saxon life in England during the eighth to the tenth centuries. Ample detailed evidence has been elicited and conclusions drawn regarding the local and regional environment, many aspects of the agricultural economy, resource exploitation strategies and possible trade and exchange networks. However, perhaps the most important conclusions have been gleaned from the synthesis of these various lines of evidence, viewed in a broader archaeological context.

From a variety of different perspectives, it is clear that a major change occurred at Flixborough during the ninth century, which affected both the nature and character of the settlement. This corroborates other archaeological evidence from England (already highlighted by others), which points to a significant shift in social and economic aspects of wider Anglo-Saxon life. However, prior to the analysis of the Flixborough assemblage, this shift has never before been documented in such a detailed and systematic form from the bioarchaeological record. So, for the first time, data from Flixborough have contributed to this ongoing debate.

To what extent the influence of Scandinavian invaders and settlers had in producing these changes is still difficult to accurately assess. Major change appears to occur at the site early in the ninth century, supporting the view that these external factors were perhaps less important early on. However, a return in the tenth century to patterns of animal exploitation originally observed in the eighth century AD at Flixborough, perhaps (we suggest) provides good evidence for a later (elite) Scandinavian involvement in social and economic reform, which resulted in the re-establishment of at least some aspects of estate structure seen in earlier middle Saxon times. The bioarchaeological evidence from Flixborough also appears to corroborate other archaeological evidence indicating that, whilst it may not be the case that the site was actually a monastery during the ninth century, some elements associated with monastic life were indeed present during this time. Much of the bioarchaeological evidence from Flixborough also provides either direct or indirect evidence that some of the inhabitants commanded the power and influence that gave them either access to resources, or allowed them to participate in activities, commensurate with their elevated status within Anglo-Saxon society. This appears to be particularly true for the eighth and tenth centuries.

In conclusion, the Flixborough bioarchaeological assemblage is without doubt one of the most important datasets of the early medieval period, and one which has provided a unique insight into Anglo-Saxon life. This work provides both a solid foundation of current data, and a secure interpretative framework upon which any future research can be built.

Appendix 1. Recording Protocol for Mammal and Bird Remains

The enormous potential of the hand-collected assemblage of vertebrate remains from Flixborough was recognised during the assessment phase of this project. As a consequence, a two-stage approach for the recording and analysis of the material was outlined by Loveluck (1996 project design), based on documentation supplied by Dobney. The following is an account of the protocol adopted for the project. A purpose-built electronic input system (using *Paradox* software) was used to record data from the vertebrate remains directly into a series of tables.

Stage 1

1. Preservation and fragmentation

For each context, subjective records were made of the state of preservation, colour of the fragments, and the appearance of broken surfaces ('angularity'). Additionally, semi-quantitative records were made of fragment size, and of burning, butchery, fresh breakage and dog gnawing. TABLE A1.1 gives a breakdown of the categories which were recorded for each field and the criteria for each category. This information was recorded into a single table in the *Paradox* database. More detailed notes were made for each of the above categories if unusual or mixed material was encountered.

2. Identification of fragments

Fragments were identified to species or species group using the reference collection at the former Environmental Archaeology Unit (EAU), University of York. Selected elements ('A' bones) were recorded using the diagnostic zones method described by Dobney and Rielly (1988). Illustrations of the zones for each element can be found in FIGS A1.1–7. Remaining elements which could be identified to species ('B' bones) were counted. Other fragments, (classified as 'unidentified') were, where possible, grouped into the following categories: large mammal (assumed to be horse, cow or large cervid), medium-sized mammal 1 (assumed to be sheep, pig or small cervid), medium-sized mammal 2 (assumed to be cat, dog or hare), small mammal (assumed to be voles, mice, shrews, rats, etc.), unidentified bird, unidentified

fish and unidentifiable. The 'unidentified' categories were initially re-boxed according to fragment size categories until the second stage of recording commenced.

Identification criteria

Distinctions between sheep and goat bones were undertaken using comparative material at the EAU, with reference to Boessneck (1969), and Payne (1985) for mandibular teeth. The following elements are those where distinctions were routinely attempted: horncore, Dp4, distal humerus, distal radius, distal tibia, calcaneus, astragalus, metacarpal, metatarsal and phalanges.

Some of the canid remains (of which there were very few) could not be confidently identified as dog, being of a size which could represent fox or dog. These have been recorded as canid.

Problems can exist in the identification of closely related galliformes e.g. differentiating between chicken, pheasant and black grouse. With adequate modern reference material (coupled with the vast numbers of galliforme remains represented in this assemblage), morphological variations on a number of elements proved distinct enough for identification to species to be confidently made. On the basis of those elements that could be positively identified, it is, therefore, likely that the vast bulk of the galliforme remains from Flixborough were chicken.

The numerous goose fragments were recorded as *Anser* sp. or cf. *Branta leucopsis*, largely on the basis of size and it would probably be more accurate to call these two groups 'large' and 'small' geese. There is little morphological variation between the different geese species and it is equally difficult, if not completely impossible, to determine whether the larger individuals were wild or domestic or a mixture of the two. Fragment counts have assumed that those bones recorded as *Anser* sp. represent mainly domestic individuals, whilst most of the smaller geese are assumed to be wild and thus have been included in counts for wild birds.

Research undertaken by two PhD students (Barnes and Haynes) obtained DNA sequence data from modern samples of the six geese species (greylag, white-fronted, pink-footed, bean, barnacle and brent) most likely to occur

Field	Categories	Recorded as
Preservation	Good, Fair, Poor, Variable	>90% of fragments in one category otherwise recorded as variable
Angularity	Spiky, Rounded, Battered, Variable	>90% of fragments in one category otherwise recorded as variable
Colour	Dark Brown, Brown, Ginger, Fawn, Beige, White, Variable	>90% of fragments in one category otherwise recorded as variable
Fragmentation	Fragment sizes <5 cm, 5–20 cm and >20 cm	in each category record proportions as None, 0–10%, 10–20%, 20–50%, 50+%
Butchery	–	proportions: None, 0–10%, 10–20%, 20–50%, 50+%
Dog gnawing	–	proportions: None, 0–10%, 10–20%, 20–50%, 50+%
New breaks	–	proportions: None, 0–10%, 10–20%, 20–50%, 50+%
Burning	–	proportions: None, 0–10%, 10–20%, 20–50%, 50+%

TABLE A1.1. *Categories and criteria for recording preservation, etc.*

in bone assemblages from British archaeological sites. Ancient DNA techniques were employed to extract DNA from goose bones recovered from the excavations at Flixborough. The results of this work enabled the certain identification of pink-footed and domestic species. The remains of pink-footed and domestic geese could never have been confidently identified without this pioneering research because of the limited morphological differences and the large overlap between species encountered in biometrical analyses.

The remains of ducks were quite numerous, but most could only be distinguished as 'mallard-sized'. Only those bones which were morphologically and biometrically distinct, such as those of teal, could be identified to species. Fragment counts for wild species include duck bones but, realistically, it is not possible to determine whether they represent wild mallards or domestic stock.

Although the reference collection at the EAU had a number of wader species, some specimens, morphologically similar to the Charadridae, could not be confidently identified to species and these were recorded as wader sp. A great number of the waders recorded were plovers, but it was not possible to distinguish between grey and golden plover, with the result that these bones were recorded as *Pluvialis* sp.

Corvid remains of a certain size category were recorded as crow/rook. Species identifications were not made, although examination of reference material for comparison was undertaken. It was not felt that morphological differences were distinct enough for positive identifications to be made.

All fragments recorded as Columbidae were of a size consistent with modern wood pigeon reference specimens. No smaller species were represented.

3. Recording the' identifiable' mammal fragments ('A' bones)

For cattle, caprines and pigs, the following selected elements (with relevant zones present) were usually the only ones recorded. These were selected on the basis of providing the most useful zooarchaeological information. Each fragment was recorded separately and given a unique number generated by the computer. This enabled information about a particular fragment to be linked between several different tables. The species, element and side are recorded, along with the diagnostic zones reflecting the portions of the bone surviving (Dobney and Rielly 1988). Information regarding epiphysial fusion, mandibular tooth wear, butchery, pathology and measurements were also recorded as described below. Any additional information pertaining to individual bones was recorded in a notes field.

Horncores: All horncore fragments which can definitely be identified to species.

Isolated mandibular teeth: Incisors, Dp4, P4, M1, M2 and M3, where more than half of the tooth is present.

Mandible: All mandibles with at least one identifiable tooth present will be recorded. Mandible fragments with no teeth are recorded if at least 2 zones (>50%) are present.

Scapula: Where at least 2 zones (>50%) from the glenoid region (i.e. zones 1, 2 or 3) are present.

Humerus: Where at least 2 zones (>50%) from the distal portion (i.e. zones 3, 4, 5 and 6) are present (zones 7 and 8 if distal epiphysis is unfused).

Radius: Where at least 2 zones (>50%) from the proximal or distal portion (i.e zones 1 and 2 or 3 and 4) are present (zone 5 or 9 and 10 if the epiphysis is unfused).

Metacarpal/Metatarsal: Where at least 1 zone (>50%) from the distal condyles (i.e. 3 or 4) are present (also zone 7 or 8 if distal epiphysis unfused) or where (>50%) zones 1 and 2 are present. Some fragments cannot be distinguished and will therefore be recorded only as 'metapodials'.

Pelvis: Where at least 1 zone (>50%) from the acetabulum rim (i.e. zones 1, 2, or 3) is present

Femur: Where at least 2 zones (>50%) from the distal portion (i.e. zones 9, 10 and 11) are present (zones 7 and 8 if distal epiphysis unfused).

Tibia: All tibia fragments where at least 2 zones (>50%) from the proximal portion (i.e. zones 1–4) are present and/or where at least 2 zones (>50%) from the distal portion (i.e. zones 5 and 6) are present (zone 7 or 10 if epiphyses unfused).

Calcaneum: All calcaneum fragments which can be definitely identified and where at least 2 zones (>50%) are present.

Astragalus: All astragalus fragments which can be definitely identified and where at least 2 zones (>50%) are present.

Phalanges: Where >50% of zone 1 is present (zone 2 if unfused).

4. Recording mandibular tooth wear stages

During this first process, mandibular tooth wear stages for both *in situ* and for isolated teeth were recorded for the major domesticates. Caprine (sheep and goat) mandibular teeth (Dp4, P4, M1/M2 and M3) were assigned eruption and wear-stages after Payne (1973 and 1987) and Grant (1982), whilst for cattle and pig mandibular teeth, only the stages of Grant (1982) were used. Cattle, pig and caprine mandibles were allocated general age categories as outlined by O'Connor (1988 and 1989) and, additionally for caprines, age profiles detailed by Payne (*op. cit*). The sex of pig lower canines was also noted where possible.

5. Additional selected age-at-death data (epiphysial fusion)

The state of epiphysial fusion was recorded for all identified fragments. These were either 'fused' or 'fusing' (mature) or 'unfused' (sub-adult, juvenile, neonatal). 'Fusing' was defined when spicules of bone were formed across the epiphysial plate joining metaphysis to epiphysis

but where a fusion line was still clearly visible. 'Fused' was recorded when no fusion line was visible. 'Neonatal' was defined where there was an obviously spongy and porous texture to the bone and it was very small. 'Juvenile' was recorded where there was an obviously porous appearance to the bone but it was not small enough to be neonatal. 'Unfused' was recorded where the epiphyses were unfused but the diaphysis appeared to be adult in texture. All other fragments, where species identification was made but with no epiphyses present, were assigned general age categories (i.e. neonatal, juvenile, sub-adult, or adult) where appropriate. Horn-cores were assigned general age categories following Armitage (1982). Epiphysial fusion data were presented using categories based on O'Connor 1989.

6. Recording identified bird fragments

A similar system to that used for mammal bones was employed to record the bird bone fragments. Identifications were made to species or to family group using the reference collection at the EAU. Bird elements which were routinely identified included: coracoid, scapula (proximal articulation), humerus (distal articulation), ulna (proximal articulation), carpo-metacarpus (proximal articulation), femur (proximal articulation), tibio-tarsus (distal articulation), tarso-metatarsus (distal articulation). The diagnostic zone system used for recording bird bones is shown in FIG. A1.4.

7. Recording of other, less common, mammals

For other mammal species, all identifiable fragments were recorded using a simplified version of the diagnostic zone system (see FIG. A1.3). Fusion information is usually also recorded for long bones.

8. Measurements

For the main domestic mammals and bird species, selected measurements (see TABLE A1.2) were taken using digital callipers to the nearest 0.1 mm. Measurements followed those of von den Driesch (1976), Davis (1992) and those outlined by Dobney *et al.* 1996. All are listed in TABLE A1.2 and those not following von den Driesch are also illustrated in FIGS A1.8–12. Withers heights were estimated using calculations devised by Foch (1966) and Matolsci (1970) for cattle, Teichert (1975) for caprines, Kieswalter (in von den Driesch and Boessneck 1974) for horses. Withers height for horses is expressed in hands (hh), where 1 hand = 4 inches = 101.6 mm.

9. Pathology and non-metrical traits

Evidence of these was routinely and quantitatively recorded where present on all recorded diagnostic zones and teeth. Significant evidence on fragments not included in the original protocol was noted separately. Enamel hypoplasia for pigs was recorded following the protocol of Dobney and Ervynck (1998).

Element	Cattle	Caprovid	Pig	Horse	Bird
Horncore	BC (=vdd 44) 45, 46, 47	BC (=vdd 40) 41, 42, 43	–	–	–
Teeth	M3, Length and breadth	M3, Length and breadth	see Fig 1.	Length and breadth, P2-M3	–
Humerus (HT & HTC see Fig. 2)	GLC ,SD, BT, HTC	GLC ,SD, BT, HT, HTC	GLC, SD, BT, HTC	GLC, GLl, SD, BT, HT	GL, SC, Bd, Dip
Radius	GL, SD, Bp, BFp	GL, SD, Bp, BFp	GL, SD, Bp	GL, Ll, SD, Bp, BFp, Bd, BFd	–
Metacarpal (see Fig. 5)	GL, SD, Bp, Dp, BFd, Dd, Dem, Dvm, Dim	GL, SD, Bp, Dp, BFd, Dd, Dem, Dvm, Dim	GL, Bp, Bd	GL, GLl, Ll, SD, Bp, Dp, BFd, Dd,	–
Femur	–	–	–	–	GL, SC, Bd, Dd, Dp
Tibia (SD see Fig. 3 except horse)	GL, SD, Bd, Dd	GL, SD, Bd, Dd	GL, SD, Bd, Dd	GL, Ll, SD, Bd, Dd	–
Astragalus	GLl, Bd, Dl	GLl, Bd, Dl	GLl, GLm	GH, GB, LmT, BFd	–
Calcaneum (see Fig. 4)	GL, DS, C, C+D	GL, DS, C, C+D	GL, DS, C+D	GL	–
Metatarsal (see Fig. 5)	GL, SD, BFp, DFp, BFd, Dd, Dem, Dvm, Dim	GL, SD, BFp, DFp, BFd, Dd, Dem, Dvm, Dim	GL, Bp, Bd (only GL for m/t II & V)	GL, GLl, Ll, SD, Bp, Dp, BFd, Dd	–
Coracoid	–	–	–	–	GL, BF, Bb, Lm
Ulna	–	–	–	–	GL, Did, Dip, Bp, SC
Carpometacarpus	–	–	–	–	GL, Bp, Did, L
Tibiotarsus	–	–	–	–	GL, Bd, Dip, Dd, La
Tarsometatarsus	–	–	–	–	GL, SC, Bp, Bd

Table A1.2. The measurements routinely taken from vertebrate remains. Unless illustrated all measurements are taken according to von den Dreisch (1976). (Key: vdd = von den Dreisch).

Stage 2

'Not identified' material

As outlined above, a two stage approach to recording the material was undertaken. Once all the vertebrate remains had been sorted, and the identified fragments had been recorded, a decision was made as to which material designated as 'not identified' was to be recorded. Contexts selected for analysis were chosen to reflect the major periods and feature types encountered at the site and on the basis of information recovered from Stage 1 and additional stratigraphic and phasing details provided by the excavator.

'Not identified' vertebrate remains from sixteen deposits, from which more than 500 identified fragments had already been recorded, were chosen (see Table A1.3). Most of these contexts, representing all but one of the main phasing groups, were dump deposits, with two pit fills and a single trench fill also represented.

For each of these contexts, the number of boxes of large mammal and medium-sized mammal 1 fragments were noted, to allow a proportion of each to be selected for recording. A random selection of boxes of each fragment size category were chosen and weighed to enable an average box weight to be calculated. The material was sorted for specific elements (see below) to identify and record. Only those which could be definitely identified as cattle, caprine or pig were recorded – except ribs which were sorted where possible into cattle size and caprine/pig size. Any other information that was deemed worthy of comment, e.g. butchery marks, was also noted.

Butchery

Butchery was recorded on individual identifiable bones which had been removed from the identified fragments. Details that were recorded included whether knife/chop/saw marks were evident, zone/s in which they occurred and the 'aspect' of the mark. Additional keywords such as 'split' (where bones have been obviously split

Context
3610
3758
3891
4323
5139
5193
5369
5391
5503
5617
5871
5983
6235
6300
6710
12057

Table A1.3. List of contexts from which material was used for Stage 2 analysis.

longitudinally) and 'hook' where a hole or damage to the blade was suggestive of hanging the leg or joint on a hook were noted. These details were recorded by a simple text description and by marking the position of the butchery on representations of individual elements.

Bulk-sieved sample methodology

During excavation at Flixborough, an extensive and systematic programme of sampling and on-site 'bulk' sieving was undertaken, mainly for the recovery of biological remains. A total of 1759 samples, representing 1273 contexts, were collected and available for investigation. Following a detailed assessment, 790 samples were selected for further analysis. Selection was determined by the nature of the feature type and by the 'tightness of dating' and, obviously, by the results of the assessment.

All residues were first sieved into three fractions, >4mm, 2–4mm and <2mm, and then sorted according to the procedure outlined by Mainland *et al* (1999). To summarise, all bone (mammal, bird, fish, amphibian) and eggshell fragments were retrieved from the >4mm fraction, as were any mollusc shells (marine and terrestrial) and large fragments of charcoal. For the smaller fractions, the sorting concentrated on the recovery of identifiable mammal, bird, fish and amphibian remains. The 2–4mm and >2mm components were examined for the retrieval of small mammal, amphibian and bird fragments which could be identified to skeletal element. All fish bones were recovered with the exception of vertebrae spine and rib fragments without articulatory facets. A record was made for each sample of all material

recovered. A more detailed methodology for fish can be found in Appendix 3.

Recording of the vertebrate remains recovered from the residues was restricted to a specific suite of elements (see below) for the major domesticates (cattle, caprine, pig, chicken and goose), whilst remains representing the more minor domesticates, wild mammals, wild birds and small mammals were mostly routinely identified and recorded. Total weights were noted for the major domestic mammals.

Mammals

Counts were made of phalanges, incisors and dP4s and tooth wear records were made for all dP4s.

Birds

For chicken and geese only carpometacarpals and phalanges were recorded. Remains of other species were recorded regardless of skeletal element.

Small mammals

Mandibles and teeth were recorded species level where possible. Counts were made of selected postcranial fragments (humerus, ulna, femur, tibia and pelvis). The latter were identified to family level only (i.e. vole/mouse/rat/shrew).

Amphibians

Pelves were identified to species where possible. Counts were made of all skeletal elements recovered.

References

Armitage, P. (1982) A system for ageing and sexing the horn cores of cattle from British post-medieval sites (17th to early 18th century) with special reference to unimproved British longhorn cattle. In: B. Wilson, C. Grigson and S. Payne (eds.), *Ageing and sexing animal bones from archaeological sites*, BAR British Series 109: 37–54.

Boessneck, J. (1969) Osteological differences between sheep (*Ovis aries* Linné) and Goat (*Capra hircus* Linné). In: D. Brothwell and E. S. Higgs (eds.), *Science in Archaeology*. London: Thames and Hudson: 331–358.

Davis, S. J. M. (1992) A rapid method for recording information about mammal bones from archaeological sites. *Ancient Monuments Laboratory Report* 19/92. London.

Dobney, K. and Ervynck, A. (1998) A protocol for recording enamel hypoplasia on archaeological pig teeth. *International Journal of Osteoarchaeology* 8 (4), 263–273.

Dobney, K. and Rielly, K. (1988) A method for recording archaeological animal bones: the use of diagnostic zones. *Circaea*, 5(2): 7996.

Dobney, K., Jaques, D. and Irving, B. (1996) Of butchers and breeds. Report on vertebrate remains from various sites in the City of Lincoln. *Lincoln Archaeological Studies* 5, vi + 215 pp.

Foch, J. (1966) *Metrische Untersuchungen an Metapodien einiger europäischer Rinderrassen*. Unpublished dissertation, University of Munich.

Grant, A. (1982) The use of tooth wear as a guide to the age of domestic ungulates. In: B. Wilson , C. Grigson and S. Payne (eds), *Ageing and sexing animal bones from archaeological sites*, BAR British Series 109: 91–108.

Loveluck C. (1996) *The Anglo-Saxon settlement and cemetery remains from Flixborough: revised and summarised assessments and updated project design.* Unpublished document for Humber Archaeology Partnership.

Mainland, I., Alcock, J. and Chambers, E. (1999) *Preliminary analysis of the environmental samples from Flixborough: an outline of the methodologies employed in sample sorting and a brief description of the material retrieved from the sample residues.* Unpublished report for the Environmental Archaeology Unit.

Matolsci, J. (1970) Historische Erforschung der Körpergröße der Rindes auf Grund von ungarischem Knochenmaterial. *Zeitschrift für Tierzüchtung und Züchtungsbiologie* 87, 89–137.

O'Connor, T. P. (1988) Bones from the General Accident Site, Tanner Row. *The Archaeology of York* 15 (2), 61–136 + plates III–VII. London: Council for British Archaeology.

O'Connor, T P. (1989) Bones from Anglo-Scandinavian levels at 16–22 Coppergate. *The Archaeology of York* 15 (3), 137–207 + plates VII–XI. London: Council for British Archaeology.

Payne, S. (1973) Kill-off patterns in sheep and goats: the mandibles from Asvan Kale. *Anatolian Studies*, 23: 281–303.

Payne, S. (1985) Morphological distinctions between the mandibular teeth of young sheep, *Ovis* and goats, *Capra*. *Journal of Archaeological Science*, 12: 139–147.

Payne, S. (1987) Reference codes for wear stages in the mandibular cheek teeth of sheep and goats. *Journal of Archaeological Science*, 14: 609–641.

Teichert, M. (1975) Osteometrische Untersuchungen zur Berechnung der Widerristhohe bei Schafen, pp. 51–69 in Clason, A. T. (ed.), *Archaeological studies*. Amsterdam: Elsevier.

von den Driesch, A. (1976) *A guide to the measurement of animal bones from archaeological sites*. Peabody Museum Bulletin 1, Cambridge Mass., Harvard University.

von den Driesch, A. and Boessneck, J. (eds) (1974) Kritische Anmerkungen zur Widerristhöhenberechnung aus Längenmassen vor- und frühgeschichtlicher Tierknochen. *Säugetierkundliche Mitteilungen* 22, 325–48.

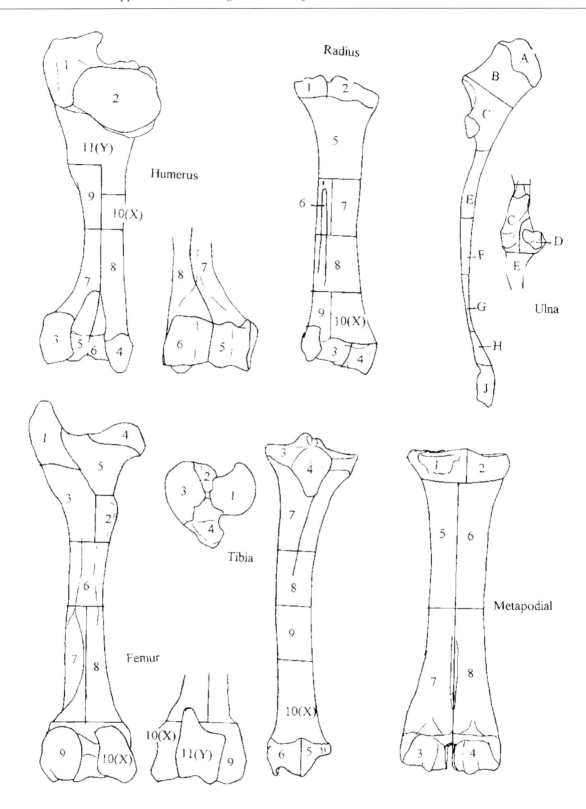

F*IG.* A1.1 *Diagnostic zones used for recording the long bones of large and medium-sized mammals (medium-sized mammal 1) (after Dobney and Rielly 1988).*

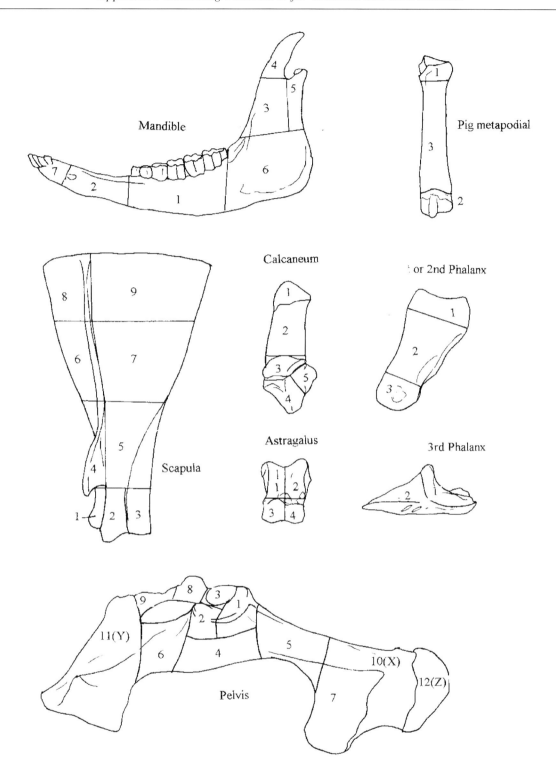

Fig. A1.2 Diagnostic zones used for recording other bones of large and medium-sized mammals (medium-sized mammal 1) (after Dobney and Rielly 1988).

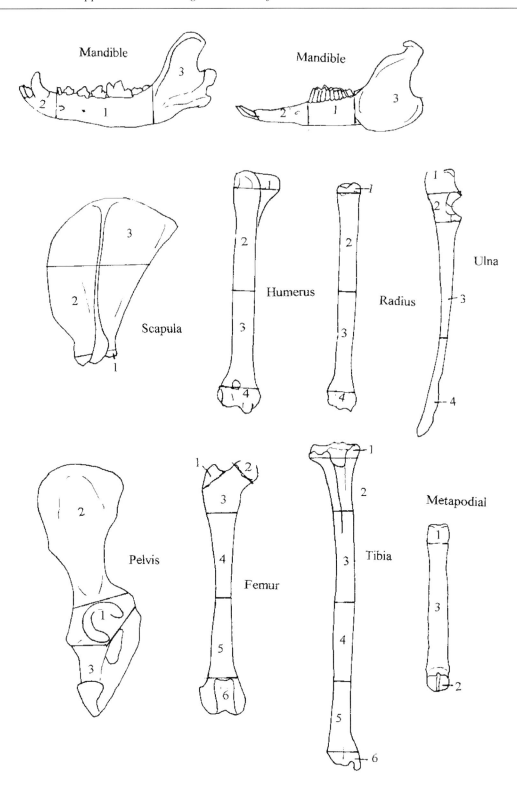

FIG. A1.3 *Diagnostic zones used for recording medium-sized mammal 2 bones.*

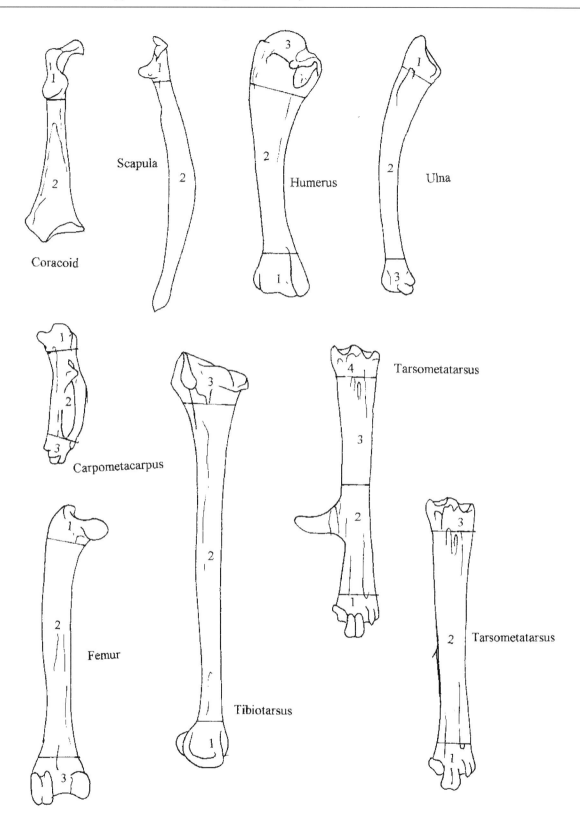

Fig. A1.4 Diagnostic zones used for recording bird bones.

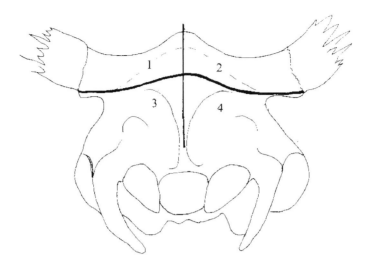

FIG. A1.5 *Zones used for recording cattle cranial fragments.*

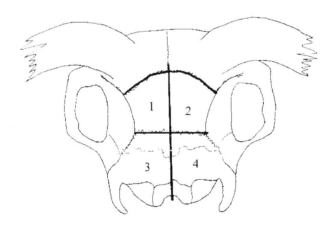

FIG. A1.6 *Zones used for recording caprovid cranial fragments.*

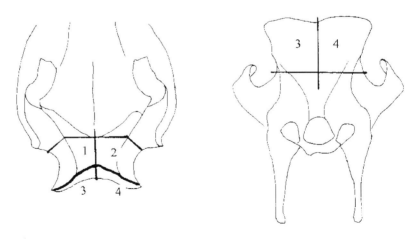

FIG. A1.7 *Zones used for recording pig cranial fragments.*

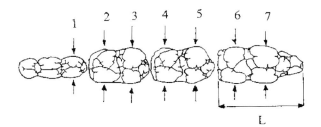

Fig. A1.8 Pig tooth measurements.

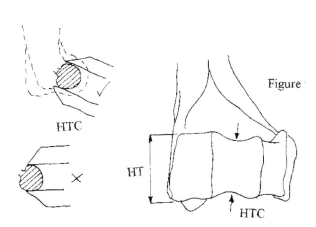

Fig. A1.9 Additional measurements of the humerus.

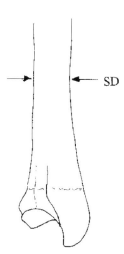

Fig. A1.10 Tibia shaft diameter for caprovids, cattle and pigs ONLY, measured in the anterior-posterior plan as shown.

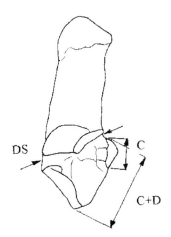

Fig. A1.11 Additional measurements of the calcaneum.

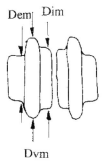

Fig. A1.12 Additional measurements of the distal metapodial.

Appendix 2. Methodology and Protocol for Sediment Samples, Plants and Molluscs

For more details see – Hall, A. 2000 and Carrott 2000.

Sampling in the field and the laboratory

The site was well sampled: there were, in all, 1759 samples of whole sediment, of which 1086 were BSs (*sensu* Dobney *et al.* 1992) and 673 GBAs. BS samples were processed on site, but in most cases a 2 kg 'voucher' of a BS sample was retained and these sometimes served to stand as GBAs for contexts where no GBA had been collected or where a GBA could not be retrieved from store.

The 1759 samples represented 1274 contexts and 341 phase/feature type combinations; for some contexts, several samples had been collected to represent different parts of an extensive feature. Most samples were from deposits eventually assigned to the Anglo-Saxon phases of occupation (only 63 samples, from the same number of contexts, were either of earlier or later date, or of uncertain date). Moreover, at the time of the latest analyses, a total of 401 GBAs and 676 BS/GBAs (61% of all the samples taken together, representing 741, or 58%, of the contexts) were designated as having a narrowly-defined phase (e.g. '1', '6'), the remainder being phased more broadly, or with some degree of uncertainty (e.g. '1–4', '5a/6?') – though from a wider chronological perspective they were still quite narrowly dated as 'mid-late Saxon'.

Such a large number of phase/feature type combinations made selection of material for assessment of plant (or indeed other) remains very difficult, the more so because, in the hand, most of the samples consisted of unconsolidated sand, varying mainly in colour but little in texture. Their very variable content of charcoal, ash, and bone often only became apparent when disaggregation commenced. A system of assigning priorities on the basis of tightness of dating and nature of context was employed to facilitate selection.

In addition to the BS/GBA samples, a small number of 'spot' finds, mostly of charcoal, were examined.

Two key problems were associated with the systematic recovery of bioarchaeological remains during excavation – associated with the wet- and dry-sieving procedures.

These should be borne in mind when considering both the analysis and interpretation of the data:

1. Unfortunately during excavation, recovery of the vast majority of charred plant remains was undertaken using a 1mm mesh, rendering the assemblage somewhat biased in favour of larger fragments.

2. Extensive on-site dry-sieving was carried out on large quantities of sediment matrix to recover artefacts and ecofacts. However, all material from this separate dry-sieving recovery programme was subsequently and mistakenly re-bagged together with relevant hand-collected material from the same contexts. As a result, no comparative quantitative analysis of recovery techniques could be satisfactorily undertaken between the hand-collected and dry-sieved assemblages – a problem perhaps most significant in the vertebrate assemblage. However, simple quantitative comparisons of the datasets remain relevant.

Methods

Plants remains were examined from a total of 560 samples (or sub-samples) of various kinds, representing 386 contexts. The types of sample investigated were:

– dried wash-overs and residues from samples of 4–25 kg (but usually of about 20 kg) bulk-sieved to 1 mm during excavation; these samples are designated 'BS', and bear the sub-sample coding /BS or /BS2 in the data tables in the archives; these represent sub-samples examined during the assessments and 'main phase', respectively;

– sub-samples of unprocessed sediment of 0.75–5 kg (but usually of 1–3 kg) from the GBA samples or BS 'vouchers' (see above) sieved in the laboratory to 300 μm; these bear the sub-sample coding /T or /T2, representing sub-samples examined during the assessments and 'main phase', respectively;

– charcoal and other remains collected on site ('spot' finds), with the sub-sample coding /SPT, or material collected during sorting for bone from certain BS samples which was not examined otherwise for plant remains.

Techniques for examining the plant remains and other components in the samples broadly followed those of Kenward *et al.* (1980), using a 'wash-over' from the GBA sub-samples to concentrate plant material. Material was examined using a binocular microscope, with a scanning electron microscope used to obtain photomicrographs and look for diagnostic superficial tissues.

In all cases, records of plant remains and of other components of the samples (at the level of 'sand', 'ash concretions', 'bone fragments', and so on), were entered into a computer database during or shortly after recording, with a subjective quantification as follows: for BS and spot samples, a three-point scale from 1 (one or a few fragments or individuals) to 3 (many individuals or a significant component of the deposit); and for the GBA sub-samples, an equivalent four-point scale. Note that, for samples examined earlier in the project, recording of non-plant material is likely to be less detailed than for samples examined latterly, and that for the bulk-sieved samples it was usually the wash-over alone which was examined closely for plant remains, the residues having been found, during assessment, usually to contain no more than a little charcoal.

To investigate the nature of the sediments at Flixborough a little further, some additional tests were carried out on a series of 105 GBA samples during the second stage of assessment. After making a detailed description of the nature of the sediment (colour, texture, obvious inclusions), sub-samples of about 50g of unprocessed sediment were disaggregated in about 0.5 litre of water in a 1 litre measuring cylinder and a semi-quantitative measure (on a four-point scale from 0 to 3) made for a number of parameters after allowing the sediment to settle for a few minutes: the quantity of charcoal floating at the meniscus, the quantity settling, the quantity of fine (probably smaller than fine sand grade) sediment settling, and the degree of turbidity of the column of water. Degree of calcareousness of the unprocessed sediment was also measured on a similar scale, via the effervescence resulting from addition of a few cm^3 of dilute hydrochloric acid.

Comments on some of the plant and non-plant components in the sediment samples

A number of items recorded from the samples during the analysis of plant remains require comment or explanation. The first group are all thought to be associated with burning of plant material and comprise plant remains themselves, 'ash beads', ash concretions, and 'char' (some of this material was previously noted by Canti (1992) during examination of sediments at this site). The 'glassy slag', in lumps as big as 60 mm may also be related to this. The second comprises other kinds of concretions.

A) 'Charred herbaceous detritus'

At an early stage in the examination of the wash-overs from the bulk-sieved samples from Flixborough, it was noted that many 'wash-overs' contained needle-like charred plant stems, mostly no more than a millimetre in diameter (and often as little as 0.3–0.5 mm in diameter) and up to about 10 mm in length. Some clearly bore stem nodes and were variously recorded as being from grasses and/or cereals (altogether these were recorded in 12 contexts, always at an abundance of '1'). Some other specimens were recognised as having a characteristic 'pinching' at one end, presumably at the point of attachment of the structure to another organ or at a stem node. Exceptionally, examples were found with an intact branched structure.

Microscopic examination with reflected light and using a scanning electron microscope failed to demonstrate the survival of any distinguishing epidermal characters though it seemed most likely that the material came from rushes (*Juncus*), spike-rushes (*Eleocharis*) or grasses (Gramineae).

Although a comprehensive examination of specially prepared charred reference material of grasses, rushes and other possible candidates was impractical, it was found that the bases of some rush stems were narrowed at the point of attachment to the roots whilst the branching stalks of rush inflorescences were narrowed somewhat at their point of insertion with the culm (main stem), around the whole circumference. Given the slender nature of the 'pinched' stems, the culms of larger rushes such as *Juncus effusus*, *J. conglomeratus* or *J. inflexus*, or even mud rush, *J. gerardi*, can probably be discounted. The fossils are, however, rather similar to modern reference material of the inflorescence stems of *J. gerardi* or the culms of small rushes like toad rush, *J. bufonius*, charred in the laboratory to mimic the fossils. (It should be noted, however, that none of the charred rush capsules and seeds resembled those of *J. bufonius*.)

Though no definitive identification of the fragments with branches was been possible, they were found to be rather similar to culm material of the salt-marsh grass *Puccinellia maritima* and, indeed, it is possible that the 'pinched' stems with a flattened end also belong to this plant. (*P. maritima* is characterised by having many rather procumbent shoots, as well as creeping stolons, with leaves tending to arise from the upper side.)

Where these plant stem fragments had no particular characteristic they were simply recorded as 'charred herbaceous detritus'; this category was present in 7% of contexts. As for the other stem material, it lacked any epidermis which might give a clue as to their taxonomic affinities but again seemed most likely to be from rushes or grasses (none had the three-sided conformation characteristic of most members of the sedge family, Cyperaceae).

B) 'Silicified' material

This category includes exocarp of spike-rush (*Eleocharis palustris* s.l.) nutlets (from two samples from the same context), and silicified herbaceous detritus (from a third). Such material is also the product of burning, though the precise circumstances under which silicification occurs remain obscure (it is discussed by Robinson and Straker 1990); it seems likely that such delicate tissues are reduced to a siliceous skeleton only where they are well protected within the sediment in which they are buried.

The 'ash beads' consisted of small (usually <3 mm), more or less spherical vesicular structures, which must have been liquid at some point. They are probably formed when plant material is burnt as silica becomes fused in the presence of alkalis from plant tissues, to judge from the results of X-ray diffraction on a sample of the beads undertaken by M. Canti (*in litt.*).

The concretions (found in 8% of the contexts examined, sometimes in large amounts) comprised amorphous lumps of brittle greyish or whitish material often with small fragments of charred plant material visible, including the plant stems mentioned above. Indeed, of the 30 contexts in which these concretions were recorded, 17 also yielded one or more of charred herbaceous detritus, 'pinched' stems, or remains of sea plantain, *?Puccinellia*, *Suaeda* or *Juncus*. Indeed, in several cases, one or more of 'ash beads', ash, or ash concretions, and these charred plant remains were well represented; certainly deposits rich in 'ash' of some kind were also productive of charred plant remains including material likely to have originated in salt-marsh.

C) 'Char'

A term used for amorphous fragments of charred organic material which, in some cases (though not here), represents bituminous exudate from the burning of coal. Another likely source for such material is wood and, at this site at least, seaweed might be another. There were two records of 'char', both from Phase 5b deposits (but both in trace amounts only). Other unidentified but clearly charred material was recorded from two dump contexts, one from Phase 4ii, the other Phase 56–6i; this was listed as ?charred bread, but its identification has not been pursued. In a sample from one of the dumps, it reached an abundance of '2' on a three-point scale.

Concretions other than those clearly formed of ash were noted in many contexts, occasionally in modest or significant amounts. Some, listed as 'lime' concretions – from 72 deposits – may be fragments of tufa (itself noted in 7+?7 cases, with a further four instances where 'lime/tufa' was recorded), or lime mortar, or slaked lime which had re-crystallised. There were also some examples of material recorded simply as 'concretions' or 'concreted sediment' and, in two cases, as tentatively identified faecal concretions. The last were from Contexts 4748 (a Phase 3bi–3bv post-hole fill associated with building 1b) and 534, a Phase 7 'dark soil' layer.

Methodology and protocol for snails and hand-collected shell

Remains of snails were examined from bulk sediment samples ('BS' samples *sensu* Dobney *et al.* 1992) processed either on site or later in the laboratory. In most cases, the remains were concentrated in the wash-overs from processing but small numbers of remains recovered from the residues were also included where present. All complete fossils and distinctive fragments were identified as closely as possible though, in many cases, key diagnostic features had been lost (through damage to the shells) or were obscured by concreted sediment in the shell openings (attempts to remove such material generally led to the destruction of the shell and so were abandoned at an early stage of the study). Counts of minimum numbers of individuals (MNI) were recorded. Principal sources for the biology of the recorded species were Kerney and Cameron (1979) and Evans (1972). Phase groups for the contexts were defined as for the vertebrate remains (Table 1). The manuscript lists were entered to a *Paradox* database using a system written by the author. *Paradox*, *Microsoft Excel, and Microsoft Powerpoint* were used to investigate and produce summary presentations of the data. The statistical software package *Canoco* was also used to investigate the data using detrended correspondence analysis.

Fourteen boxes (each of approximately 16 litres) of hand-collected shell (representing material from 336 contexts of which 27 were from later deposits (Phase 7 or later), unphased, or too broadly phased for classification) were recorded. All of the remains were identified as closely as possible using the EAU comparative collection and reference works – a low-power binocular microscope was employed to assist the identifications where necessary. The preservational condition of the shell was recorded using two four-point scales for erosion and fragmentation – scale points were: 0 – none; 1 – slight; 2 – moderate; 3 – high. The weight (in grammes) of remains from each context was recorded. The data were initially recorded on paper and later entered into a series of *Paradox* data tables for subsequent interrogation.

References

Canti, M. G. (1992). Research into natural and anthropogenic deposits from the excavations at Flixborough, Humberside. *Ancient Monuments Laboratory Report* 53/92.

Carrott, J. (2000). Technical Report: Mollusc remains (other than shellfish) recovered from bulk sediment samples from excavations at Flixborough, North Lincolnshire (site code: FLX89). *Reports from the Environmental Archaeology Unit, York* 2000/55.

Dobney, K., Hall, A. R., Kenward, H. K. and Milles, A. (1992). A working classification of sample types for environmental archaeology. *Circaea, the Journal of the Association for Environmental Archaeology* 9 (for 1991), 24–6.

Evans, J. G. (1972) *Land snails in archaeology.* London and New York: Seminar.

Hall, A. (2000) Technical Report: Plant remains from excavations at Flixborough, N. Lincolnshire (site code: FLX89). *Reports from the Environmental Archaeology Unit, York* 2000/56, 107pp.

Kenward, H. K., Hall, A. R. and Jones, A. K. G. (1980) A tested set of techniques for the extraction of plant and animal macrofossils from waterlogged archaeological deposits. *Science and Archaeology* 22, 3–15.

Kerney, M. P. and Cameron, R. A. D. (1979) *A field guide to the land snails of Britain and north-west Europe*. Glasgow: William Collins Sons and Co. Ltd.

Robinson, M. and Straker, V. (1990) Silica skeletons of macroscopic plant remains from ash, pp. 3–13 in Renfrew, J. M. (ed.), *New light on early farming. Recent developments in palaeoethnobotany*. Edinburgh: University Press.

Appendix 3. Recording Methods for Fish Remains

Nineteen diagnostic elements (quantification categories 1 and 2 – see below) were identified to the finest taxonomic level possible and used for routine quantification. First anal pterygiophores of flatfish were also identified to species, but are unique to this group and are treated separately. Other bones were classed as unidentified unless they exhibited cut marks, charring, carnivore gnawing or other taphonomic alterations (for which all specimens were examined). These specimens are grouped with unidentified elements except where bone modification is of specific concern. Fragmentation was assessed by estimating the percent completeness (Barrett 1997: 629) of all diagnostic elements except vertebrae. Bone texture was assessed using a four point scale (see below). Fish size was estimated by comparison with reference skeletons from specimens of known total length. Selected osteometrics (after Morales and Rosenlund 1979; Jones 1991; Butler 1993; Enghoff 1994) were recorded. All material was weighed to 0.01g.

The category to which the nineteen diagnostic elements can be identified differs between taxonomic groups. For cyprinids, species identification was only attempted routinely for the basioccipital and infrapharyngeal. The remaining diagnostic elements were grouped at the family level. Pleuronectidae vertebrae were also identified only to family. In this case, however, the other diagnostic elements of the group suggest that most derive from flounder or plaice (probably flounder).

Fish taxonomy follows Whitehead *et al.* (1986a; 1986b; 1989) and Maitland and Campbell (1992). Latin names for the taxa mentioned are provided below. Fish anatomical terminology follows Wheeler and Jones (1989). All statistical procedures were conducted using SPSS Release 10.0.7 and MINITAB Release 13.1.

The following tables (pp. 265–269) list the definitions for abbreviations, codes and measurements.

References

Barrett, J. H. (1997) Fish trade in Norse Orkney and Caithness: A zooarchaeological approach. *Antiquity* 71, 616–638.

Butler, V. L. (1993) Natural versus cultural salmonid remains: Origin of the Dalles Roadcut bones, Columbia River, Oregon, U.S.A. *Journal of Archaeological Science* 20,1–24.

Enghoff, I. B. (1994) Fishing in Denmark during the Ertebølle Period. *International Journal of Osteoarchaeology* 4, 65–96.

Jones, A. K. G. (1991) The fish remains from excavations at Freswick Links, Caithness. D.Phil, University of York.

Maitland, P. S., and Campbell, R. N. (1992) *Freshwater Fishes of the British Isles*. London: Harper Collins Publishers.

Morales, A., and Rosenlund, K. (1979) *Fish Bone Measurements: An attempt to standardize the measuring of fish bones from archaeological sites*. Copenhagen: Steenstrupia.

Wheeler, A., and Jones, A. K. G. (1989) *Fishes*. Cambridge: Cambridge University Press.

Whitehead, P. J. P., Bauchot, M. L., Hureau, J. C., Nielsen, J., and Tortonese, E. (eds) (1986a) *Fishes of the North-eastern Atlantic and the Mediterranean Volume 2*. Paris: United Nations Educational, Scientific and Cultural Organization.

Whitehead, P. J. P., Bauchot, M. L., Hureau, J. C., Nielsen, J. and E. Tortonese (eds) (1986b) *Fishes of the North-eastern Atlantic and the Mediterranean Volume 3*. Paris: United Nations Educational, Scientific and Cultural Organization.

Whitehead, P. J. P., Bauchot, M. L., Hureau, J. C., Nielsen, J., and Tortonese, E. (eds) (1989) *Fishes of the North-eastern Atlantic and the Mediterranean Volume 1*. Paris: United Nations Educational, Scientific and Cultural Organization.

Wilson, C. A. (1997) *Food and Drink in Britain*. London: Constable.

Taxon

Marine

Abbreviation	Taxon	Common Name
ch	*Clupea harengus*	Atlantic Herring
cc	*Conger conger*	Conger Eel
gad	Gadidae	Cod Family
gm	*Gadus morhua*	Cod
ma	*Melanogrammus aeglefinus*	Haddock
pv	*Pollachius virens*	Saithe
mm	*Molva molva*	Ling
ss	*Scomber scombrus*	Atlantic Mackerel
ac	*Aspitrigla cuculus*	Red Gurnard
sod	Soleidae	Sole Family
sv	*Solea vulgaris*	Sole

Migratory

Abbreviation	Taxon	Common Name
as	*Acipenser sturio*	Sturgeon
a	*Alosa alosa/Alosa fallax*	Allis Shad/Twaite Shad
af	*Alosa fallax*	Twaite Shad
sld	Salmonidae	Salmon & Trout Family
oe	*Osmerus eperlanus*	Smelt
aa	*Anguilla anguilla*	Eel
dl	*Dicentrarchus labrax*	European Seabass
pfp	*Platichthys flesus/Pleuronectes platessa*	Flounder/Plaice

Freshwater

Abbreviation	Taxon	Common Name
el	*Esox lucius*	Pike
cpd	Cyprinidae	Carp Family
bar?	*Barbus barbus?*	Barbel?
tnt	*Tinca tinca*	Tench
blb?	*Blicca bjoerkna?*	Silver Bream?
se	*Scardinius erythrophthalmus*	Rudd
se?	*Scardinius erythrophthalmus?*	Rudd?
rr	*Rutilus rutilus*	Roach
rr?	*Rutilus rutilus?*	Roach?
lcl	*Leuciscus*	Chub/Dace
lc	*Leuciscus cephalus*	Chub
lel	*Leuciscus leuciscus*	Dace
cbd	Cobitidae	Loach Family
lot	*Lota lota*	Burbot
pfl	*Perca fluviatilis*	Perch
gyc	*Gymnocephalus cernua*	Ruffe

Other

Abbreviation	Taxon	Common Name
cld	Clupeidae	Herring Family
gad	Gadidae	Cod Family
gsd	Gasterosteidae	Stickleback Family

het	Heterosomata	Flatfish Order
pld	Pleuronectidae	Halibut Family
ui	Unidentified	Unidentified

Element and Quantification Code (Q)

Abbreviation	Element	Quantification Code (Q)
ac	Acanthotrich	0
bb	Basibranchial	0
bpt	Basipterygium	0
cd	Coracoid	0
e	Ethmoid	0
ecp	Ectopterygoid	0
eh	Epihyal	0
ex	Exoccipital	0
f	Frontal	0
ih	Interhyal	0
io	Interopercular	0
la	Lacrimal	0
lhh	Lower Hypohyal	0
opo	Opisthotic	0
pf	Prefrontal	0
pl	Parietal	0
pro	Prootic	0
pto	Pterotic	0
soc	Supraoccipital	0
sph	Sphenotic	0
sy	Symplectic	0
uh	Urohyal	0
uhh	Upper Hypohyal	0
a	Articular	1
bo	Basioccipital	1
ch	Ceratohyal	1
cl	Cleithrum	1
d	Dentary	1
hy	Hyomandibular	1
iph	Infrapharyngeal	1
mx	Maxilla	1
o	Opercular	1
pa	Palatine	1
par	Parasphenoid	1
po	Preopercular	1
pt	Posttemporal	1
px	Premaxilla	1
qd	Quadrate	1
scl	Supracleithrum	1
scp	Scapula	1
vo	Vomer	1
av	Abdominal Vertebra	2
av1	Abdominal Vertebra Group 1	2
av2	Abdominal Vertebra Group 2	2
av3	Abdominal Vertebra Group 3	2
cv	Caudal Vertebra	2
cv1	Caudal Vertebra Group 1	2

cv2	Caudal Vertebra Group 2	2
fv	First Vertebra	2
mvc	Mineralized Vertebral Centrum	2
puv	Penultimate Vertebra	2
sct	Scute	2
uv	Ultimate Vertebra	2
v	Vertebra	2
osa	1st Anal Pterygiophore	4
ot	Otolith	4

Side

Abbreviation	Definition
l	Left
r	Right
m	Midline or Indeterminate

Diagnostic Zones Present (Part)

Based on Barrett (1997). Details available from the author.

Element Percent Completeness (%)

Abbreviation	Definition
20	0–20% Complete
40	21–40% Complete
60	41–60% Complete
80	61–80% Complete
100	81–100% Complete

Texture

Abbreviation	Definition
1	Excellent: bone surface appears fresh or even slightly glossy over most or all of the element. If flaky or powdery patches are present they are very localized.
2	Good: bone surface lacks fresh appearance, but is otherwise solid. If flaky or powdery patches are present they are very localized.
3	Fair: bone surface solid in places, but flaky or powdery areas may cover up to 49% of the specimen.
4	Poor: bone surface flaky or powdery over >50% of the specimen.

Size

Abbreviation	Definition
t	0–150mm
s	151–300mm
m	301–500mm
l	501–800mm
x	801–1000mm
xx	>1000mm

Maximum Linear Dimension (MLD)

Measured along the longest axis to 0.01mm

Burning

Abbreviation	Definition
char	Brown, Grey or Black
cal	White

Other Taphonomic Alterations

Abbreviation	Definition
kn	Knife Marks (<c.2mm Deep)
ch	Chop Marks (>c.2mm Deep)
tp	Transverse Plane
sp	Sagittal Plane
crush	Crushed
tooth	Carnivore Tooth Impressions
path	Pathological

Measurements M1 and M2

After Butler (1993), Enghoff (1994) and Jones (1991).
Measured to 0.01mm

Context Types

After Dobney & Loveluck (pers. comm.)

Abbreviation	Definition
DCH	Ditch Fill
DKSL	Dark Soil/ Occupation Deposit
DUMP	Dump
GLY	Gully Fill
GRAVE	Grave Cut or Fill
HARD	Hardstanding
OCC	Occupation Deposit
OVEN	Dump-Oven Related
PH	Post Hole Fill
PIT	Pit Fill
SLOT	Slot Fill
SOAK	Soakaway Fill
TCH	Trench Fill
UNKN	Unknown

Appendix 4. Detailed Datasets for Fish and Bird Bones

Common Name	Element[1]	1	2–3a	3b	4–5b	6	6iii	Total
Marine								
Atlantic Herring	av				3		1	4
	cv				5		1	6
Conger Eel	cv						1	1
Cod Family	fv			1				1
	cv1		3					3
Cod	cv1			1				1
	cv2				1			1
Haddock	o				1			1
	av3				1			1
Migratory								
Sturgeon	sct				2			2
Allis Shad/Twaite Shad	av		1		1	1		3
	cv			1	2		1	4
Salmon & Trout Family	a				1			1
	ch				1			1
	d				1			1
	qd		1		2	1		4
	scp			1				1
	fv				1			1
	av	1	8	20	15	11	2	57
	cv	3	14	29	26	6	2	80
	puv		1		1		1	3
	uv	1		3				4
	v		1		1			2
Smelt	a		10	9	9	2		30
	bo		4	5	1			10
	ch		7	6	6	2		21
	d	5	23	21	13	2		64
	hy		4		2			6
	mx	2	23	11	9	1		46
	o		4	1	5			10
	pa			1				1
	par		3	1	1	2		7
	po	1	3	3	5			12
	px			1				1

TABLE A4.1 Flixborough sieved fish-element distribution by taxa and phase (continued opposite).

Common Name	Element[1]	1	2–3a	3b	4–5b	6	6iii	Total
	qd		3	4	4			11
	vo				1			1
	cl		7	4	7			18
	fv	2	7	5	3	2		19
	av	12	64	108	126	18	9	337
	cv	7	65	80	98	23	4	277
	uv		1	3				4
Eel	a		1	2	5	2		10
	bo		6	8	12	1		27
	ch		7	8	12	4	2	33
	d		12	19	23	5	2	61
	hy		1	3	7	1	1	13
	mx		5	5	4	1		15
	o	1	5	7	10	1		24
	par		4	7	7	2	1	21
	qd		1	1	4	2	1	9
	vo		8	7	7	6	1	29
	cl	2	9	7	21	8		47
	fv	2	2	3	2			9
	av	40	242	293	573	231	49	1428
	cv	31	182	243	542	187	71	1256
	v				1			1
Total Halibut Family	a			8		5	1	14
	bo		1	5	1			7
	ch		1	3	2	1		7
	d		1	6	5			12
	hy		1	7	5	1		14
	iph			3	2			5
	mx	1	2	10	7			20
	o		1	5	3			9
	pa				2			2
	par			1				1
	po		1	10	6			17
	px			5	1	1		7
	qd		1	6	4	1	1	13
	vo		1	2	2			5
	pt			3	3		1	7
	scl		1	3	1	2		7
	cl		6	10	1	1		18
	fv		1	3	6	1		11
	av	1	13	73	47	17	4	155
	cv	9	59	147	142	53	12	422
	uv	1	3	4	1		2	11
Fresh Water								
Pike	a	1	7	1	4	2		15
	bo	1	3		1		2	7
	ch	1	2	1		1		5
	d	2	10	6	2	2		22
	hy		6					6

TABLE A4.1 continued.

Common Name	Element[1]	1	2–3a	3b	4–5b	6	6iii	Total
	mx	3	8	3	1	1		16
	o		1					1
	pa	1	12	2	1	1		17
	par		3	2	1	1		7
	po	2	8	3	1			14
	px		2					2
	qd	3	9	2	1	2		17
	vo	1	1					2
	pt	2	4					6
	scl		5					5
	cl	4	16	3	2	2		27
	fv		2	1	1			4
	av	31	114	57	35	26	7	270
	cv	8	78	14	19	18		137
	puv		2					2
	uv		1					1
Carp Family	a		1		1			2
	ch		1					1
	d	1	3	2	1			7
	hy		2	1	2			5
	iph	1	5	2	3	1		12
	mx					1		1
	o		9		2			11
	par		2	1				3
	po		3	2	3	1		9
	qd			1				1
	cl		6	2	4	1		13
	scp		1					1
	fv			2	2			4
	av	5	22	22	20	21	2	92
	cv	15	53	36	24	15	3	146
	uv					1		1
Barbel?	bo				1			1
Tench	bo		1					1
	iph		1					1
Rudd?	iph		1					1
Roach	bo				1	1		2
	iph			3				3
	o		1					1
Roach?	iph		1					1
Chub/Dace	iph		5	2	2			9
Chub	bo				1			1
	iph			3	1			4
Dace	bo				1			1
	iph		1	3		2		6
Loach Family	cv			1				1
Burbot	a				1			1
	mx		1					1
	av2			1	1			2
	cv1		3	1	3			7

TABLE A4.1 continued.

Common Name	Element[1]	1	2–3a	3b	4–5b	6	6iii	Total
Perch	a		3	1		3		7
	ch	1	2	2		1		6
	d	1	2			1		4
	hy	1	3					4
	iph				1			1
	mx	1	4					5
	o	2	5					7
	pa		2				1	3
	par		2					2
	po	1	3	5				9
	px	1	6	1	3	1		12
	qd		6		1			7
	pt		2	2	1	1		6
	scl	2	3					5
	cl	1	6					7
	scp		1					1
	fv		1	1	1	1		4
	av	6	44	29	2	29	2	112
	cv	5	43	15	7	15	1	86
Other								
Herring Family	av		1		1			2
Stickleback Family	o		3	1				4
	po		2					2
	cl		3	2	1			6
	av		1	1				2

[1] See Appendix 3 for key to element abbreviation

TABLE A4.1 continued.

Common Name	Element[1]	DUMP	PH	SOAK	OCC	PIT	DKSL	TCH	UNKN	DCH	GLY	SLOT	OVEN	Total
Marine														
Atlantic Herring	av	2	1		1									4
	cv	4			1					1				7
Conger Eel	cv						1							1
Cod Family	fv	1					1							1
	av3									1				1
	cv1		3											3
Cod	cv1	1												1
	cv2	1												1
Haddock	o	1												1
	av3									1				1
Migratory														
Sturgeon	sct	2												2
Allis Shad/Twaite Shad	av	1	1		1									3
	cv	3					1							4
Salmon & Trout Family	a	1												1
	ch	1												1
	d	1												1
	qd	2	1		1									4
	scp	1												1
	fv	1												1
	av	32	12	2	5	2	2	1	3					59
	cv	53	11	7	4	2	3							80
	puv	1	1				1							3
	uv	3	1											4
	v		1	1										2
Smelt	a	19	3	2	1	1			5					31
	bo	3	1	2	3	1								10
	ch	7	4	2	4	1		3						21
	d	29	10	13	4	5	2		2			1		66
	hy	2		3				1						6

TABLE A4.2 Flixborough sieved fish-element distribution by taxa and context type (continued opposite and overleaf).

Common Name	Element[1]	DUMP	PH	SOAK	OCC	PIT	DKSL	TCH	UNKN	DCH	GLY	SLOT	OVEN	Total
	mx	23	7	6	5	2		1	4					48
	o	4	1	2		1			2					10
	pa	1												1
	par	4	1	1	1					1				8
	po	8	1		1	2			2					14
	px				1									1
	qd	5	1	2	1	2								11
	vo	1												1
	cl	11	2	4					1					18
	fv	10	2	2	2	1		1	1					19
	av	202	42	25	34	22	8	8	4	3			3	351
	cv	153	27	32	22	24	4	10	4	9	2	1	2	290
	uv	1		3										4
Eel	a	5	2	1		3								11
	bo	11	4	2	8	2		2						29
	ch	17	6	1	2	3	2	2	1					34
	d	24	8	5	6	7	3	4	2	3				62
	hy	7		1	2	1	1	1						13
	mx	5	4	3	2				1					15
	o	10	5	1	3	1	1	2	1					24
	par	7	3	2	3		1	4	1					21
	qd	4	1		1	1	1						1	9
	vo	14	3	2	3	3	2	2						29
	cl	22	7	2	5	3	1	3	3	1				47
	fv	5	2	1	1				1	1				11
	av	639	254	97	172	116	77	68	20	18	4	11	2	1478
	cv	562	219	53	159	112	90	55	16	24	17	4	2	1313
Total Halibut Family	v				1									1
	a	6			1	2	4	1						14
	bo	5	2											7
	ch	4			1	2								7
	d	8	2		1	1								12
	hy	11	1		2	1								15
	iph	5								2				7
	mx	13	6		1	1			1					22

TABLE A4.2 continued.

Common Name	Element[1]	DUMP	PH	SOAK	OCC	PIT	DKSL	TCH	UNKN	DCH	GLY	SLOT	OVEN	Total
	o	6			3									9
	pa					1		1						2
	par	1												1
	po	13	1			3								17
	px	7												7
	qd	7	1	1	1	1	2							13
	vo	4		1										5
	pt	4			2									7
	scl	3	1		1	1	1							7
	cl	12	1	3	1								1	18
	fv	5	3		2	1								11
	av	115	8	5	11	3	5	8		1				156
	cv	278	40	18	35	21	27	8	1	2		1	1	432
	uv	5	3	1			2							11
Fresh Water														
Pike	a	7	1	4	2	2								16
	bo	1	1	3			2							7
	ch	2	1	2										5
	d	8	2	8	3			1						22
	hy		2	4										6
	mx	4	3	7	1							1		16
	o			1										1
	pa	6	1	10										17
	par	4		3										7
	po	3	3	6	2									14
	px			1					1					2
	qd	4	4	7	1			1						17
	vo	1	1											2
	pt		2	2	2									6
	scl		1	3	1									5
	cl	7	5	9	3	1			2					27
	fv	2		1	1									4
	av	94	51	84	22	8	7	2	3	1				272
	cv	42	11	56	22	4	1	2		1				139

TABLE A4.2 continued.

Common Name	Element¹	DUMP	PH	SOAK	OCC	PIT	DKSL	TCH	UNKN	DCH	GLY	SLOT	OVEN	Total
	puv		1	1										2
	uv			1										1
Carp Family	a				1			1						2
	ch				1									1
	d	3	2		1				1					7
	hy	2	2	2	1									5
	iph	5	2		4				2					13
	mx	1												1
	o	2	2	4	3									11
	par	1		1	1									3
	po	5		3		1								9
	qd				1									1
	cl	4	2	2	4				1					13
	scp			1										1
	fv	3	1											4
	av	38	16	14	13	4	5	3	1				1	94
	cv	59	28	31	18	7	4	1	1	3		1		153
	uv	1												1
Barbel?	bo	1												1
Tench	bo			1										1
	iph				1									1
Rudd?	iph			1										1
Roach	bo	1	1											2
	iph	3												3
	o								1					1
Roach?	iph		1											1
Chub/Dace	iph	4	2		1				1			1		9
Chub	bo	1												1
	iph	3			1									4
Dace	bo							1						1
	iph	5		1										6
Loach Family	cv	1												1
Burbot	a	1												1
	mx								1					1
	av2	2												2

TABLE A4.2 continued.

Common Name	Element[1]	DUMP	PH	SOAK	OCC	PIT	DKSL	TCH	UNKN	DCH	GLY	SLOT	OVEN	Total
Perch	cvl	2	2		3									7
	a	4		2	1									7
	ch	4	1	1										6
	d	1	1	2										4
	hy		1	3										4
	iph					1								1
	mx		1	4										5
	o		2	5										7
	pa			2			1							3
	par			2										2
	po	5	1	3										9
	px	6		5		1								12
	qd	1		6										7
	pt	4		2										6
	scl		2	3										5
	cl		1	6										7
	scp			1										1
	fv	2		1						1				4
	av	56	10	39	4	2	2							113
	cv	36	6	32	9	1	1	1	1					87
Other														
Herring Family	av	2								1				3
Stickleback Family	o	2							2					4
	po								2					2
	cl	2		2					2					6
	av	1							1					2

[1] See Appendix 3 for key to element and context type abbreviations

Table A4.2 continued.

Species	Element	Bone id	GL	Bd	Notes
fowl	tarsometatarsus	758	63.74	11.18	No spur
fowl	tarsometatarsus	759	68.68	12.25	No spur
fowl	tarsometatarsus	760	72.4	12.68	No spur
fowl	tarsometatarsus	761	85.33	13.06	No spur
fowl	tarsometatarsus	763	66.11	11.48	No spur
fowl	tarsometatarsus	764		12.17	No spur
fowl	tarsometatarsus	1752	64.34	11.54	No spur
fowl	tarsometatarsus	1753	67.67	11.44	No spur
fowl	tarsometatarsus	1754	78.82	12.41	No spur
fowl	tarsometatarsus	1755	68.56	11.62	No spur
fowl	tarsometatarsus	1756	68.5		No spur
fowl	tarsometatarsus	1757	63.96	11.25	No spur
fowl	tarsometatarsus	1758	83.31	14.47	No spur
fowl	tarsometatarsus	1759	68.31		No spur
fowl	tarsometatarsus	1762			No spur
fowl	tarsometatarsus	1763			No spur
fowl	tarsometatarsus	1764			No spur
fowl	tarsometatarsus	1765			No spur
fowl	tarsometatarsus	1766			No spur
fowl	tarsometatarsus	1767			No spur
fowl	tarsometatarsus	1768			No spur
fowl	tarsometatarsus	1769			No spur
fowl	tarsometatarsus	1770			No spur
fowl	tarsometatarsus	1771			No spur
fowl	tarsometatarsus	1772			No spur
fowl	tarsometatarsus	1773		11.12	No spur
fowl	tarsometatarsus	1774		11.33	No spur
fowl	tarsometatarsus	1775		13.64	No spur
fowl	tarsometatarsus	1776		10.61	No spur
fowl	tarsometatarsus	1777		10.89	No spur
fowl	tarsometatarsus	1778		12.35	No spur
fowl	tarsometatarsus	1779		11.57	No spur
fowl	tarsometatarsus	1781	81.36	12.77	No spur
fowl	tarsometatarsus	1782	79.78	13.5	No spur
fowl	tarsometatarsus	1783	62.89	10.66	No spur
fowl	tarsometatarsus	1785			No spur
fowl	tarsometatarsus	1786			No spur
fowl	tarsometatarsus	1787		10.71	No spur
fowl	tarsometatarsus	1788		11.07	No spur
fowl	tarsometatarsus	1789		13.02	No spur
fowl	tarsometatarsus	1790		11.54	No spur
fowl	tarsometatarsus	2372	63.63	11.6	No spur
fowl	tarsometatarsus	2373	66.08	11.63	No spur
fowl	tarsometatarsus	2374	63.74	10.5	No spur
fowl	tarsometatarsus	2375	57		No spur
fowl	tarsometatarsus	2376	68.13		No spur
fowl	tarsometatarsus	2377	62.83		No spur
fowl	tarsometatarsus	2378			No spur
fowl	tarsometatarsus	2380			No spur
fowl	tarsometatarsus	2381			No spur
fowl	tarsometatarsus	2382		13.16	No spur
fowl	tarsometatarsus	2389	65	10.68	No spur

TABLE A4.3. Flixborough chicken tibiotarsus spur sex and related biometry data (continued overleaf).

fowl	tarsometatarsus	2390	68.46	12.29	No spur
fowl	tarsometatarsus	2391	63.3	11.64	No spur
fowl	tarsometatarsus	2392	64.6	11.23	No spur
fowl	tarsometatarsus	2394			No spur
fowl	tarsometatarsus	2395	59.55	10.53	No spur
fowl	tarsometatarsus	2396			No spur
fowl	tarsometatarsus	2397			No spur
fowl	tarsometatarsus	2398		10.74	No spur
fowl	tarsometatarsus	2399		12.23	No spur
fowl	tarsometatarsus	2400		13.16	No spur
fowl	tarsometatarsus	2986	70.02	11.52	No spur
fowl	tarsometatarsus	2987	60.5	11.14	No spur
fowl	tarsometatarsus	2988	72.99	12.47	No spur
fowl	tarsometatarsus	2989	65.65		No spur
fowl	tarsometatarsus	2990	64.75	11.45	No spur
fowl	tarsometatarsus	2991	63.65		No spur
fowl	tarsometatarsus	2992			No spur
fowl	tarsometatarsus	2993		13.05	No spur
fowl	tarsometatarsus	2994		11.24	No spur
fowl	tarsometatarsus	2995		11.22	No spur
fowl	tarsometatarsus	2996			No spur
fowl	tarsometatarsus	2997			No spur
fowl	tarsometatarsus	2998			No spur
fowl	tarsometatarsus	3001		11.29	No spur
fowl	tarsometatarsus	3002		11.33	No spur
fowl	tarsometatarsus	3312			No spur
fowl	tarsometatarsus	3313		14.83	No spur
fowl	tarsometatarsus	3740	67.14	11.96	No spur
fowl	tarsometatarsus	3741	68.32	11.92	No spur
fowl	tarsometatarsus	3742	67.27		No spur
fowl	tarsometatarsus	3744			No spur
fowl	tarsometatarsus	3745		11.59	No spur
fowl	tarsometatarsus	3746			No spur
fowl	tarsometatarsus	3747		11.84	No spur
fowl	tarsometatarsus	3748		10.88	No spur
fowl	tarsometatarsus	3749		10.79	No spur
fowl	tarsometatarsus	3750		12	No spur
fowl	tarsometatarsus	3751		11.13	No spur
fowl	tarsometatarsus	3754	63.51	11.58	No spur
fowl	tarsometatarsus	3755	61.5	11.5	No spur
fowl	tarsometatarsus	3756	77.2	12.81	No spur
fowl	tarsometatarsus	3757	67.33	11.43	No spur
fowl	tarsometatarsus	3758	61.69	10.82	No spur
fowl	tarsometatarsus	3759	85.28		No spur
fowl	tarsometatarsus	3760			No spur
fowl	tarsometatarsus	3761			No spur
fowl	tarsometatarsus	3762			No spur
fowl	tarsometatarsus	3763			No spur
fowl	tarsometatarsus	3764			No spur
fowl	tarsometatarsus	3765			No spur
fowl	tarsometatarsus	3766			No spur
fowl	tarsometatarsus	3767			No spur
fowl	tarsometatarsus	3770		13.04	No spur
fowl	tarsometatarsus	4608	81.58	12.77	No spur

TABLE A4.3 *continued.*

fowl	tarsometatarsus	4609	68.89	12.09	No spur
fowl	tarsometatarsus	4610	64.89	11.49	No spur
fowl	tarsometatarsus	4611	68.78	11.39	No spur
fowl	tarsometatarsus	4612	70.21	12.16	No spur
fowl	tarsometatarsus	4613	68.78	11.85	No spur
fowl	tarsometatarsus	4614	68.29	11.39	No spur
fowl	tarsometatarsus	4615			No spur
fowl	tarsometatarsus	4616	63.59		No spur
fowl	tarsometatarsus	4618	68.63	11.8	No spur
fowl	tarsometatarsus	4619	62.75	10.91	No spur
fowl	tarsometatarsus	4620			No spur
fowl	tarsometatarsus	4621			No spur
fowl	tarsometatarsus	4623			No spur
fowl	tarsometatarsus	4624			No spur
fowl	tarsometatarsus	4625			No spur
fowl	tarsometatarsus	4626		13.5	No spur
fowl	tarsometatarsus	4627		11.6	No spur
fowl	tarsometatarsus	4628		11.49	No spur
fowl	tarsometatarsus	4629			No spur
fowl	tarsometatarsus	4633	68.53	11.25	No spur
fowl	tarsometatarsus	4634	67.49	11.8	No spur
fowl	tarsometatarsus	4635	63.96	11.3	No spur
fowl	tarsometatarsus	4636	62.02	10.59	No spur
fowl	tarsometatarsus	4637	62.99	10.19	No spur
fowl	tarsometatarsus	4638	81.3	12.88	No spur
fowl	tarsometatarsus	4639	58.55	9.98	No spur
fowl	tarsometatarsus	4640	67.47	11.84	No spur
fowl	tarsometatarsus	4641		11.12	No spur
fowl	tarsometatarsus	4643			No spur
fowl	tarsometatarsus	4644			No spur
fowl	tarsometatarsus	4645			No spur
fowl	tarsometatarsus	4646			No spur
fowl	tarsometatarsus	4647		11.85	No spur
fowl	tarsometatarsus	4648		10.45	No spur
fowl	tarsometatarsus	4649		10.67	No spur
fowl	tarsometatarsus	4650		13.07	No spur
fowl	tarsometatarsus	4651		11.14	No spur
fowl	tarsometatarsus	5132			No spur
fowl	tarsometatarsus	5134		11.4	No spur
fowl	tarsometatarsus	5395			No spur
fowl	tarsometatarsus	5396		12	No spur
fowl	tarsometatarsus	5397	66.04	11.87	No spur
fowl	tarsometatarsus	5398	64.18	5.36	No spur
fowl	tarsometatarsus	5400			No spur
fowl	tarsometatarsus	5401		10.39	No spur
fowl	tarsometatarsus	5583			No spur
fowl	tarsometatarsus	5585	69.38	12.18	No spur
fowl	tarsometatarsus	5586		13.94	No spur
fowl	tarsometatarsus	5587	62.7	10.45	No spur
fowl	tarsometatarsus	5588		12.43	No spur
fowl	tarsometatarsus	5589		11.87	No spur
fowl	tarsometatarsus	5871			No spur
fowl	tarsometatarsus	5873			No spur
fowl	tarsometatarsus	6042	68.52	11.2	No spur

TABLE A4.3 continued.

fowl	tarsometatarsus	6043	69.87	11.65	No spur
fowl	tarsometatarsus	6044	67.88	11.18	No spur
fowl	tarsometatarsus	6045	67		No spur
fowl	tarsometatarsus	6046		11.44	No spur
fowl	tarsometatarsus	6049			No spur
fowl	tarsometatarsus	6056	64.89	11.51	No spur
fowl	tarsometatarsus	6058			No spur
fowl	tarsometatarsus	6059			No spur
fowl	tarsometatarsus	6061		11.31	No spur
fowl	tarsometatarsus	6064		10.43	No spur
fowl	tarsometatarsus	6212			No spur
fowl	tarsometatarsus	6403			No spur
fowl	tarsometatarsus	6452	69.43	11.67	No spur
fowl	tarsometatarsus	6453	60.97	11.37	No spur
fowl	tarsometatarsus	6454		11.66	No spur
fowl	tarsometatarsus	6458	64.96	11.49	No spur
fowl	tarsometatarsus	6459	68.73	11.53	No spur
fowl	tarsometatarsus	6460		13.29	No spur
fowl	tarsometatarsus	6559	66.21	11.89	No spur
fowl	tarsometatarsus	6562	79.88	13.19	No spur
fowl	tarsometatarsus	6563		13.61	No spur
fowl	tarsometatarsus	6566		12.55	No spur
fowl	tarsometatarsus	6567			No spur
fowl	tarsometatarsus	6568			No spur
fowl	tarsometatarsus	6569			No spur
fowl	tarsometatarsus	6572	66.13	11.62	No spur
fowl	tarsometatarsus	6574	64.34	11.28	No spur
fowl	tarsometatarsus	6576		11.29	No spur
fowl	tarsometatarsus	6577		12.87	No spur
fowl	tarsometatarsus	6578			No spur
fowl	tarsometatarsus	6579			No spur
fowl	tarsometatarsus	6580			No spur
fowl	tarsometatarsus	6749	64.11	11.66	No spur
fowl	tarsometatarsus	6750	65.73	11.38	No spur
fowl	tarsometatarsus	6751			No spur
fowl	tarsometatarsus	7116			No spur
fowl	tarsometatarsus	7149	80.52	13.02	No spur
fowl	tarsometatarsus	7150	67.79	11.56	No spur
fowl	tarsometatarsus	7376			No spur
fowl	tarsometatarsus	7378			No spur
fowl	tarsometatarsus	7411		11.08	No spur
fowl	tarsometatarsus	7435	77.58	14.03	No spur
fowl	tarsometatarsus	7438		13.53	No spur
fowl	tarsometatarsus	7533	68.18	11.68	No spur
fowl	tarsometatarsus	7764	74.91	13.1	No spur
fowl	tarsometatarsus	7765	62.68	10.99	No spur
fowl	tarsometatarsus	7766			No spur
fowl	tarsometatarsus	7795	84.5	13.23	No spur
fowl	tarsometatarsus	7905	64.66	10.73	No spur
fowl	tarsometatarsus	8134			No spur
fowl	tarsometatarsus	8156			No spur
fowl	tarsometatarsus	8211	66.91	10.97	No spur
fowl	tarsometatarsus	8222		10.59	No spur
fowl	tarsometatarsus	8234	82.82	13.65	No spur

TABLE A4.3 continued.

fowl	tarsometatarsus	8325	69.26	11.84	No spur
fowl	tarsometatarsus	8336	66.65	11.58	No spur
fowl	tarsometatarsus	8440		11.35	No spur
fowl	tarsometatarsus	8854		11.14	No spur
fowl	tarsometatarsus	8857		10.62	No spur
fowl	tarsometatarsus	9177		13.7	No spur
fowl	tarsometatarsus	9232	66.91	10.99	No spur
fowl	tarsometatarsus	9245	72.02	12.61	No spur
fowl	tarsometatarsus	9264	64.39	11.34	No spur
fowl	tarsometatarsus	9266		11.62	No spur
fowl	tarsometatarsus	9328	64.94	11.75	No spur
fowl	tarsometatarsus	9329			No spur
fowl	tarsometatarsus	9346			No spur
fowl	tarsometatarsus	9347		12.3	No spur
fowl	tarsometatarsus	9387			No spur
fowl	tarsometatarsus	9400	63.28	11.45	No spur
fowl	tarsometatarsus	9486			No spur
fowl	tarsometatarsus	9584	63.64	10.56	No spur
fowl	tarsometatarsus	9585	61.84	10.48	No spur
fowl	tarsometatarsus	9677		11.71	No spur
fowl	tarsometatarsus	9678			No spur
fowl	tarsometatarsus	9728	66	11.6	No spur
fowl	tarsometatarsus	9729	64.07		No spur
fowl	tarsometatarsus	9795			No spur
fowl	tarsometatarsus	9885			No spur
fowl	tarsometatarsus	10166			No spur
fowl	tarsometatarsus	10427	80.74		No spur
fowl	tarsometatarsus	10448		12	No spur
fowl	tarsometatarsus	10553			No spur
fowl	tarsometatarsus	10564	80.92	12.97	No spur
fowl	tarsometatarsus	10595			No spur
fowl	tarsometatarsus	10667		12.1	No spur
fowl	tarsometatarsus	10672		10.7	No spur
fowl	tarsometatarsus	10673			No spur
fowl	tarsometatarsus	10685		12.99	No spur
fowl	tarsometatarsus	10709			No spur
fowl	tarsometatarsus	10771	73.46	12.42	No spur
fowl	tarsometatarsus	10876		9.64	No spur
fowl	tarsometatarsus	10935	64.95	11.05	No spur
fowl	tarsometatarsus	10983	66.73	11.55	No spur
fowl	tarsometatarsus	10994	71.72	12.22	No spur
fowl	tarsometatarsus	11034		13.72	No spur
fowl	tarsometatarsus	11065			No spur
fowl	tarsometatarsus	11065		11.47	No spur
fowl	tarsometatarsus	11070		13.2	No spur
fowl	tarsometatarsus	11071		11.19	No spur
fowl	tarsometatarsus	11184			No spur
					No spur
fowl	tarsometatarsus	1761			Spur scar
fowl	tarsometatarsus	1791		11.88	Spur scar
fowl	tarsometatarsus	2370	83.42	13.65	Spur scar
fowl	tarsometatarsus	2371	76.98	12.54	Spur scar
fowl	tarsometatarsus	2387		13.63	Spur scar
fowl	tarsometatarsus	2388			Spur scar

TABLE A4.3 continued.

fowl	tarsometatarsus	2999	78.08	12.94	Spur scar
fowl	tarsometatarsus	3000	81.03	13.89	Spur scar
fowl	tarsometatarsus	4631	76.49	12.72	Spur scar
fowl	tarsometatarsus	5131	80.44	13.82	Spur scar
fowl	tarsometatarsus	5133			Spur scar
fowl	tarsometatarsus	5872			Spur scar
fowl	tarsometatarsus	6048		14.36	Spur scar
fowl	tarsometatarsus	6052	79.96	13.33	Spur scar
fowl	tarsometatarsus	6054		11.96	Spur scar
fowl	tarsometatarsus	6055	78.94	12.59	Spur scar
fowl	tarsometatarsus	6560		12.91	Spur scar
fowl	tarsometatarsus	6561	82.87	13.1	Spur scar
fowl	tarsometatarsus	6571		12.9	Spur scar
fowl	tarsometatarsus	6573	78.02	12.95	Spur scar
fowl	tarsometatarsus	6575		13.43	Spur scar
fowl	tarsometatarsus	7098			Spur scar
fowl	tarsometatarsus	7115			Spur scar
fowl	tarsometatarsus	7299	78.11		Spur scar
fowl	tarsometatarsus	7410	78.81	12.9	Spur scar
fowl	tarsometatarsus	7436			Spur scar
fowl	tarsometatarsus	7437			Spur scar
fowl	tarsometatarsus	7532	70.75		Spur scar
fowl	tarsometatarsus	7763			Spur scar
fowl	tarsometatarsus	7906	81.25		Spur scar
fowl	tarsometatarsus	7984			Spur scar
fowl	tarsometatarsus	8856	75.91	12.69	Spur scar
fowl	tarsometatarsus	9265	74.33	12.53	Spur scar
fowl	tarsometatarsus	10458	77.35	13.42	Spur scar
fowl	tarsometatarsus	756	84.28	13.19	Spurred
fowl	tarsometatarsus	757	79.9	14.46	Spurred
fowl	tarsometatarsus	762	79.89	14.38	Spurred
fowl	tarsometatarsus	2379		12.85	Spurred
fowl	tarsometatarsus	2385	77.98	13.86	Spurred
fowl	tarsometatarsus	2386	81.57	14.22	Spurred
fowl	tarsometatarsus	3739	74.44	13.2	Spurred
fowl	tarsometatarsus	3753	81.23	13.77	Spurred
fowl	tarsometatarsus	4605	82.05	13.92	Spurred
fowl	tarsometatarsus	4606	74.65	12.71	Spurred
fowl	tarsometatarsus	4607	82.62	13.62	Spurred
fowl	tarsometatarsus	4622			Spurred
fowl	tarsometatarsus	4632	80.21	13.7	Spurred
fowl	tarsometatarsus	4642			Spurred
fowl	tarsometatarsus	5582	78.29	13.69	Spurred
fowl	tarsometatarsus	6047	83.09		Spurred
fowl	tarsometatarsus	6053	77.09	13.24	Spurred
fowl	tarsometatarsus	6211	81.72	13.31	Spurred
fowl	tarsometatarsus	6990	78	13.32	Spurred
fowl	tarsometatarsus	7078	77.29	14.01	Spurred
fowl	tarsometatarsus	7409	78.73	14.2	Spurred
fowl	tarsometatarsus	7722	71.15	13.21	Spurred
fowl	tarsometatarsus	7983	81.55	13.76	Spurred
fowl	tarsometatarsus	8233	76.12	13.13	Spurred
fowl	tarsometatarsus	8508	78.39	12.84	Spurred
fowl	tarsometatarsus	8527	78.26	13.11	Spurred

Table A4.3 continued.

fowl	tarsometatarsus	10524	73.94	12.68	Spurred
fowl	tarsometatarsus	10680		11.67	Spurred
fowl	tarsometatarsus	10829		11.55	Spurred
fowl	tarsometatarsus	10989	73.89	12.81	Spurred
fowl	tarsometatarsus	11045		13.49	Spurred
fowl	tarsometatarsus	11096	77.23	12.1	Spurred

TABLE A4.3 continued.

Bibliography

Abbreviations

CIH   *Corpus iuris hibernici* i–vi (ed. Binchy, D. A., Dublin 1978).
EHD   English Historical Documents (ed. Whitelock, D. London 1979).
TBC LL *Táin Bó Cúalnge* from the book of Leinster (ed. O'Rahilly, C., 1967).
LTNC   Lincolnshire Trust for Nature Conservation.
DIL   (Contributions to a) Dictionary of Irish language (ed. Quin 1913–1976).
WWT   Wildfowl and Wetland Trust.

Adam, P. (1990) *Saltmarsh Ecology*. Cambridge: Cambridge University Press.

Addyman, P. V. (1964) A Dark-Age settlement at Maxey, Northants. *Medieval Archaeology* 8, 20–73.

Albarella, U. and Davis, S. (1994) The Saxon and medieval animal bones excavated 1985–89 from West Cotton, Northamptonshire. *Ancient Monuments Laboratory Report* 17/94. London.

Albarella, U. and Thomas, R. (2002) They dined on crane: bird consumption, wild fowling and status in medieval England. Proceedings of the 4th meeting of the ICAZ Bird Working Group, Kraków, Poland, 11–15 September, 2001. *Acta Zzoologica Cracoviensia* 45 (Special Issue), 23–38.

Albarella, U. Beech, M. and Mulville, J. (1997) The Saxon, medieval and post-medieval mammal and bird bones excavated 1989–91 from Castle Mall, Norwich, Norfolk. *Ancient Monuments Laboratory Report* 72/97. London.

Allison, E. P. (1985) *An archaeozoological study of bird bones from seven sites in York*. Unpublished PhD thesis, University of York.

Allison, E., Locker A. and Rackham, D. J. (1985) 'The animal remains', pp. 83–85, in O'Sullivan, D., "The excavation in Holy Island Village 1977". *Archaeologia Aeliana* 13, 27–116.

Armitage, P. L. (1994) Unwelcome companions: ancient rats reviewed. *Antiquity* 68, 231–240.

Armitage, P. L., West, B. and Steedman, K. (1984) New evidence of the black rat in Roman London. *London Archaeologist* 4, 375–383.

Attenborough, F. L. (1922) *The Laws of the earliest English Kings*. Cambridge: Cambridge University Press.

Ayers, K., Locker, A. and Serjeantson, D. 2003. Phases 2f–4a in the Medieval Abbey: Food Consumption and Production, pp. 360–406, in A. Hardy, A. Dodd and G. Keevil (eds) *Aelfric's Abbey: Excavations at Eynsham Abbey, Oxfordshire 1989–92* (Thames Valley Landscape Volume 16). Oxford: Oxford University School of Archaeology.

Bacher, A. (1967) *Vergleichend morphologische Untersuchungen an Einzelknochen des postkranialen Skeletts in Mitteleuropa vorkommender Schwäne und Gänse*. Unpublished dissertation, University of Munich.

Backhouse, J. (1981) *The Lindisfarne Gospels*. Oxford: Phaidon.

Bain, C. G. (1992) Ornithological survey of Thorne and Hatfield moors. *Thorne and Hatfield Moors Papers* 2, 19–31.

Barnes, I. (1998) *The Molecular Identification of Goose Species in Archaeozoological Assemblages*. Unpublished PhD thesis, University of York.

Barnes, I., Dobney, K. M. and Young, J. P. (1998) The molecular palaeoecology of British geese species: a progress report on the identification of archaeological goose remains using DNA analysis. *International Journal of Osteoarchaeology* 8, 280–287.

Barnes, J. (ed.) (1984) *The Complete Works of Aristotle*, 2 vols. Princeton: Princeton University Press.

Barrett, J. H. (1997) Fish trade in Norse Orkney and Caithness: a zooarchaeological approach. *Antiquity* 71, 616–638.

Barrett, J. H. (2002) *The fish bone from excavations at Saxon Flixborough, Lincolnshire*. Unpublished report, Department of Archaeology, University of York.

Barrett, J. H., Nicholson, R. A. and Cerón-Carrasco, R. (1999) Archaeo-ichthyological evidence for long-term socio-economic trends in northern Scotland: 3500 BC to AD 1500. *Journal of Archaeological Science* 26, 353–388.

Barrett, J. H., Beukens, R. P. and Nicholson, R. A. (2001) Diet and ethnicity during the Viking colonisation of northern Scotland: evidence from fish bones and stable carbon isotopes. *Antiquity* 75, 145–154.

Bergin, O. (1946) White red-eared cows. *Eriu* 14, 170.

Binchy, D. A. (ed.) (1978) *Corpus iuris hibernici: ad fidem codicum manuscriptorum recognovit. i–vi.* Dublin: Institiúid Ard-Léinn Bhaile Átha Cliath.

Birch, W. de G. (1885–1893) *Cartularium Saxonicum.* London: Whiting & Co.

Bischoff, B. (1986) *Paläographie des römischen Altertums und des abendländischen Mittelalters* (2nd ed.). Berlin: E. Schmidt.

Bischoff, B. (1990) *Latin Palaeography, Antiquity and the Middle Ages.* Cambridge: Cambridge University Press [= English edition of Bischoff (1986), by D. Ó Cróinín and D. Ganz]

Black, J. M. (1991) Foraging behaviour and site selection of the barnacle goose, *Branta leucopsis* in a traditional and newlycolonised spring staging habitat. *Ardea* 79, 349–358.

Blumenschine, R. J., Marean, C. W. and Capaldo, S. D. (1996) Blind tests of inter-analyst correspondence and accuracy in the identification of cut marks, percussion marks and carnivore tooth marks on bone surfaces. *Journal of Archaeological Science* 23, 493–507.

Bocherens, H. and Drucker, D. 2003. Trophic Level Isotopic Enrichment of Carbon and Nitrogen in Bone Collagen: Case Studies from Recent and Ancient Terrestrial Ecosystems. *International Journal of Osteoarchaeology* 13, 46–53.

Boekske, K. (1872) *A Literal Translation into English of the Earliest Known Book on Fowling and Fishing Written Originally in Flemish and Printed at Antwerp in the Year 1492.* Privately printed for Alfred Denison. London: Chiswick Press.

Boessneck, J., von den Driesch, A., Meyer-Lempennau, U. and Weschler-von Ohlen, E. (1971) Das Tierknochenfunde aus dem Oppidum von Manching. *Die Ausgrabungen in Manching* 6. Wiesbaden.

Bond, J. (1994) 'Appendix 1. The cremated animal bone', in J. McKinley The Anglo-Saxon cemetery at Spong Hill, North Elmham. Part VIII: The cremations. *East Anglian Archaeology Report* 69, 121–135. Norwich: Norfolk Museums Service.

Bond, J. M. and O'Connor, T. P. (1999) Bones from medieval deposits at 16–22 Coppergate and other sites in York. *The Archaeology of York* 15(5), 299–429. York: Council for British Archaeology.

Bourdillon, J. (1993) 'Animal bones', in M. F. Garner, Middle Saxon evidence at Cook Street, Southampton (SOU 254). *Proceedings of the Hampshire Field Club Archaeological Society* 49, 116–120.

Bourdillon, J. and Coy, J. (1980) 'The animal remains', in P. Holdsworth, *Excavations at Melbourne Street, Southampton 1971–76*, 79–121. London: Council for British Archaeology Research Report 33.

Bramwell, D. (1980) 'Identification and interpretation of the bird bones', in P. Wade-Martins, North Elmham Park. Volume II. *East Anglian Archaeology Report* 9, 409–412.

Buckland, P. C. and Dinnin, M. H. (1997) The rise and fall of wetland habitat: recent palaeoecological research on Thorne and Hatfield moors. *Thorne and Hatfield Moors Papers* 4, 1–18.

Bunting, W., Hanson, M., Howes, C. A. and Kitchen, A. (1974) The history and distribution of fish in the Doncaster district. *The Naturalist* 99, 41–55.

Buurman, J. (1999) Plant remains from an early medieval site at Schagen, the Netherlands, in H. Sarfatij, W. J. H. Verwers and P. J. Woltering (eds) *In discussion with the past. Archaeological studies presented to W. A. van Es.,* 279–290. Zwolle/Amersfoort: Foundation for the Promotion of Archaeology (SPA)/Rijksdienst voor het Oudheidkundig Bodemonderzoek.

Cameron, K. (1998) *A Dictionary of Lincolnshire Place-names.* Nottingham: English Place-name Society.

Canti, M. G. (1992) Research into natural and anthropogenic deposits from the excavations at Flixborough, Humberside. *Ancient Monuments Laboratory Report* 53/92. London.

Carrott, J. (2000) Technical Report: Mollusc remains (other than shellfish) recovered from bulk sediment samples from excavations at Flixborough, North Lincolnshire (site code: FLX89). *Reports from the Environmental Archaeology Unit, York* 2000/55. York.

Chandler, J. (1993) *John Leland's Itinerary – Travels in Tudor England.* Stroud: Sutton.

Church. L. E. and Johnson, L. C. (1964) Growth of the longbones in the chicken. *American Journal of Anatomy* 114, 521–538.

Clark, J. G. D. (1952) *Prehistoric Europe: the Economic Basis.* London: Methuen.

Clementz, M. T. and Koch P. L. (2001). Differentiating aquatic mammal habitat and foraging ecology with stable isotopes in tooth enamel. *Oecologia* 129(3), 461–472.

Clutton-Brock, J. (1991) Extinct mammals, in G. B. Corbet and S. Harris, *The Handbook of British Mammals* (3rd ed.), 571–575. Oxford: Blackwell Scientific Publications.

Cohen, A. and Serjeantson, D. (1986) *A Manual for the Identification of Bird Bones from Archaeological Sites.* London: Alan Cohen.

Colson, I. B., Bailey, J. F., Vercauteren, M. and Sykes, B. C. (1997a) The preservation of ancient DNA and bone diagenesis. *Ancient Biomolecules* 1, 109–117.

Colson, I. B., Richards, M. B., Bailey, J. F., Sykes, B. C. and Hedges, R. E. M. (1997b) DNA analysis of seven human skeletons excavated from the Terp of Wijnaldum. *Journal of Archaeological Science* 24, 911–917.

Coppack, G. (1986) St Lawrence's Church, Burnham, South Humberside: the excavation of a parochial chapel. *Lincolnshire History and Archaeology* 21, 39–60.

Corbet, G. B. and Harris, S. (1991) *The Handbook of British Mammals* (3rd edn.). Oxford: Blackwell.

Coy, J. (1980) The animal bones, pp. 41–51, in J. A. Haslam, Middle Saxon iron smelting site at Ramsbury, Wiltshire. *Medieval Archaeology* 24, 1–68.

Coy, J. (1981) Bird bones from Chalk Lane [Northampton]. Ancient *Monuments Laboratory Report* 3450. London.

Crabtree, P. J. (1989) West Stow, Suffolk: early Anglo-Saxon animal husbandry. *East Anglian Archaeology* 47. Ipswich: Suffolk County Planning Department.

Crabtree, P. J. (1996) Production and consumption in an early complex society: animal use in Middle Saxon East Anglia. *World Archaeology* 28, 58–75.

Crabtree P. Unpublished report – submitted 1983. *Report on the animal bones from the Chapter House at St. Alban's Abbey.*

Crabtree, P. Unpublished report – submitted 1991. *The faunal remains from Brandon.*

Crabtree, P. Unpublished report – submitted 1994. *The animal bone remains from Ipswich, Suffolk recovered from sixteen sites excavated between 1974 and 1988.*

Crabtree, P. Unpublished report – submitted 1995. *Animal bones recovered from Wicken Bonhunt, Essex.*

Cranswick, P. A. (1995) National Waterfowl Counts 1991–92, in S. Carter, *Britain's Birds in 1991–92.* Thetford: British Trust for Ornithology.

Dansgaard, W. (1964). Stable isotopes in precipitation. *Tellus* 16(4), 436–468.

Darby, H. C. (1952) *The Domesday Geography of Eastern England.* Cambridge, Cambridge University Press.

Darby, H. C. (1987) Domesday Book and the Geographer, in Holt, J. C. (ed.) *Domesday Studies,* 101–119. Woodbridge: Boydell Press.

Darling, W. G., Bath A. H. and Talbot, J. C. (2003). The O & H stable isotopic composition of fresh waters in the British Isles. 2. Surface waters and groundwater. *Hydrology and Earth System Sciences* 7(2), 183–195.

Davies, R. W. (1971) The Roman military diet. *Britannia* 2, 122–142.

Dembinska, M. (1986) Fasting and working monks: regulations of the fifth to eleventh centuries, in A. Fenton, A. and E. Kisbán (eds) *Food in Change: Eating Habits from the Middle Ages to the Present Day,* 152–160. Edinburgh: John Donald.

Diaz, M., Gonzalez, E., Munoz-Pulido R. and Naveso M. A. (1996) Habitat selection patterns of common cranes (*Grus grus*) wintering in holm oak (*Quercus ilex*) dehesas of Central Spain: effects of human management. *Biological Conservation* 75(2), 119–23.

Diderot, D. and Alembert, J. D. (1751–8) *Encyclopédie; ou Dictionnaire raisonné des Sciences* 6. Paris, Briasson etc.

Dobney, K. (2000) *Ancient Falconry.* www.firstscience.com Internet Science Recruitment website.

Dobney, K. (2001) *A place at the table: the role of zooarchaeology within a Roman research agenda,* in S. James and M. Millett (eds) Britons and Romans: advancing an archaeological agenda, 36–45. York: Council for British Archaeology Research Report 125.

Dobney, K. (2002). Flying a kite at the end of the Ice Age: The possible significance of raptor remains from epipalaeoloithic and early neolithic sites of the Middle East, in H. Buitenhuis, A. Choyke, M. Mashkour & A. H. Al-Shiyab (eds), *Archaeozoology of the Near East: Proceedings of the 5th International Symposium on the Archaeozoology of Southwestern Asia and Adjacent Areas.* Groningen: ARC-publications 62.

Dobney, K. and Ervynck, A. (1998) A protocol for recording enamel hypoplasia on archaeological pig teeth. *International Journal of Osteoarchaeology* 8(4), 263–273.

Dobney, K. and Ervynck, A. (2000) Interpreting developmental stress in archaeological pigs: the chronology of linear enamel hypoplasia. *Journal of Archaeological Science* 27, 597–607.

Dobney, K. Ervynck, A. and La Ferla, B. (2002). Assessment and further development of the recording and interpretation of linear enamel hypoplasia in archaeological pig

populations. *Environmental Archaeology* 7, 35–46.

Dobney, K., Hall, A. R., Kenward, H. K. and Milles, A. (1992) A working classification of sample types for environmental archaeology. *Circaea, the Journal of the Association for Environmental Archaeology* 9 (for 1991), 24–26.

Dobney, K. and Harwood, J. (1999) Here to stay? Archaeological evidence for the introduction of commensal and economically important mammals to the North of England. In N. Benecke (ed.), *The Holocene history of the European vertebrate fauna: Modern aspects of research,* 373–387. Berlin: Deutsches Archäologisches Institut. Archäologie in Eurasien 6.

Dobney, K. M., Jaques, S. D. and Irving, B. G. (1996) Of Butchers and Breeds: report on vertebrate remains from various sites in the City of Lincoln. *Lincoln Archaeological Studies* 5. Lincoln: City of Lincoln Archaeology Unit.

Dobney, K. and Jaques, D. (2002) Avian signatures for identity and status in Anglo-Saxon England. Proceedings of the 4th Meeting of the ICAZ Bird Working Group, Kraków, Poland, 11–15 September, 2001. *Acta Zoologica Cracoviensia,* 45 (Special Issue), 7–21.

Dobney, K., Jaques, S. D., Panithianarak, T., Searle, J. B., Stewart, J. and von den Driesch, A. (in prep.). The giant cranes of England: zooarchaeological and biomolecular evidence for the status of *Grus* in Britain during the Holocene.

Doll, M. (1999) 'Im Essen jedoch konnte er nicht enthaltsam sein....Fleischverzehr in der Karolingerzeit', in C. Stiegemann and M. Wemhoff (eds), *799-Karl der Große und Papst Leo III in Paderborn: Kunst und Kultur der Karolingerzeit. Beiträge zum Katalog der Ausstellung,* 445–449, Mainz: Philipp von Zabern.

Dudley, H. E. (1931) *The History & Antiquities of the Scunthorpe & Frodingham District* (1975 edition). Scunthorpe: Scunthorpe Borough Council.

Dufour, E., Bocherens, H. and Mariotti, A. (1999) Palaeodietary implications of isotopic variability in Eurasian lacustrine fish. *Journal of Archaeological Science* 26, 617–627.

Dyer, C. (1988) *The consumption of freshwater fish in medieval England,* in M. Aston (ed.) *Medieval fish, fisheries and fishponds in England.* Part i. 27–38. Oxford: British Archaeological Reports, British Series 182(i).

Eastham, A. (1976) *The animal bones,* In B. W. Cunliffe *Excavations at Portchester Castle, Volume II: Saxon.* Report of the Research Committee of the Society of Antiquaries of London 33. 287–296. London: Society of Antiquaries.

Ellis, S. (1998) Physical background to the Ancholme and Lower Trent Valleys, In R. van de Noort and S. Ellis (eds) *Wetland Heritage of the Ancholme and Lower Trent Valleys: an archaeological Survey,* 9–14. Hull: Humber Wetlands Project, Centre for Wetland Archaeology, The University of Hull.

Enghoff, I. B. (1996) A medieval herring fishery in eastern Denmark. *Archaeofauna* 5, 43–47.

Enghoff, I. B. (1999) Fishing in the Baltic region from the 5th century BC to the 16th century AD: evidence from fish bones. *Archaeofauna* 8, 41–85.

Enghoff, I. B. (2000) Fishing in the southern North Sea region from the 1st to the 16th century AD: evidence from fish bones. *Archaeofauna* 9, 59–132.

Epstein, H. J. (1943) The origin and earliest history of falconry. *Isis* 34(6), no. 98.

Ervynck, A. (1992) Medieval castles as top-predators of the feudal system: an archaeozoological approach. *Château Gaillard. Etudes de Castellologie médiévale* 15, 151–159. Caen.

Ervynck, A. (1997a) Detailed recording of tooth wear (Grant, 1982) as an evaluation of the seasonal slaughtering of pigs? Examples from medieval sites in Belgium. *Archaeofauna* 6, 67–79.

Ervynck, A. (1997b) Following the rule? Fish and meat consumption in monastic communities in Flanders (Belgium), in G. de Boe and F. Verhaeghe (eds) *Environment and subsistence in Medieval Europe. Papers of the 'Medieval Europe Brugge 1997' Conference Volume 9* (I.A.P. Rapporten 9). 67–81. Zellik: Instituut voor het Archeologisch Patrimonium.

Ervynck, A. (2002) Sedentism or urbanism? On the origin of the commensal black rat (*Rattus rattus*), in K. Dobney and T. P. O'Connor (eds) *Bones and the man: Studies in Honour of Don Brothwell*, 95–109. Oxford: Oxbow Books.

Ervynck, A. (2004) *Orant, pugnant, laborant*. The diet of the three orders within the feudal society of medieval Europe, in S. J. Jones O'Day, W. van Neer and A. Ervynck (eds) *Behaviour behind bones*, 215–223. Oxford: Oxbow Books.

Ervynck, A. and Dobney, K. (1999) Lining up on the M1: a tooth defect as a bio-indicator for environment and husbandry in ancient pigs. *Environmental Archaeology: The Journal of Human Palaeoecology* 4, 1–8.

Ettel, P. (1998) 'Karlburg – Entwicklung eines königlich-bischöflichen Zentralortes am Main mit Burg und Talsiedlung vom 7. bis zum 13. Jahrhundert', *Chateau Gaillard Etudes de Castellologie médiévale* 18 (for 1996) Caen: University of Caen.

Evans, H. (1973) *Falconry*. Edinburgh: John Bartholomew.

Evans, J. G. (1972) *Land Snails in Archaeology*. London: Seminar Press.

Evans, P. G. H. (1991) Cetacea, in G. B. Corbet and S. Harris (eds) *The Handbook of British Mammals*, 299–350. Oxford: Blackwell Scientific Publications.

Eversham, B. G. (1991) Thorne and Hatfield moors: implications for land use change for nature conservation. *Thorne and Hatfield Moors Papers* 2, 3–14.

Fairclough, H. R. (1978) Virgil *(1): Eclogues, Georgics, Aeneid 1–6* (The Loeb Classical Library). Cambridge: Cambridge (Massachusetts) and London 1916, repr. (1978).

Fischer, P. (1881) Cétacés de sud-ouest de la France. *Actes Société Linnéenne de Bordeaux*, 4th series 35, 5–219.

Fischer Drew, K. (1991) *The Laws of the Salian Franks*. Philadelphia, University of Pennsylvania Press.

Fisher, R. A., Corbet, A. S. and Williams, C. B. (1943) The relation between the number of species and the number of individuals in a random sample of an animal population. *Journal of Animal Ecology* 12, 42–58.

Folkard. H. C. (1859) *The Wild-Fowler: a Treatise on Ancient and Modern Wild-Fowling, Historical and Practical* (1st edn.). London: Piper.

Ford, E. (1982) *Birds of Prey*. London: Batsford.

Forster, E. S. and Heffner, E. H. (1954) *Columella: De re Rustica*, Volume 2. London.

Foster, C. W. and Longley, T. (1924) *The Lincolnshire Domesday and the Lindsey Survey*. Lincoln Record Society 19. Horncastle.

Fox, H. (2001) *The Evolution of the Fishing Village: Landscape and Society along the South Devon Coast, 1086–1550*. Oxford: Leopard's Head Press.

Fraser, F. C. (1946) *Report on Cetacea stranded on the British Coasts from 1933–1937*. 12. London: British Museum (Natural History).

Fricke, H. C., O'Neil, J. R., Lynnerup, N. (1995) Oxygen-isotope composition of human tooth enamel from Medieval Greenland – linking climate and society. *Geology* 23(10), 869–872.

Fry, B. (1991) Stable isotope diagrams of freshwater food webs. *Ecology* 72: 2293–2297.

Fry, B. and Sherr, E. B. (1988) $\delta 13C$ Measurements as indicators of carbon flow in marine and freshwater ecosystems. In: P. W. Rundel, J. R. Ehleringer and K. A. Nagy (eds), *Stable Isotopes in Ecological Research*, 196–229. New York: Springer.

Fuller, R. J. (1982) *Bird Habitats in Britain*. London: T. and A. D. Poyser.

Gardiner, M. (1997) The exploitation of sea-mammals in medieval England: bones and their social context. *Archaeological Journal* 154, 173–195.

Gaunt, G. D. (1975) The artificial nature of the river Don north of Thorne, Yorkshire. *Yorkshire Archaeological Journal* 47, 15–21.

Gaunt, G. D. (1997) *Geological Profile of Flixborough Area*. Unpublished typescript in the Flixborough archive.

Gautier, A. (1984) How do I count you, let me count the ways? Problems of archaeozoological quantification. In C. Grigson and J. Clutton-Brock (eds) *Animals and Archaeology 4: Husbandry in Europe*, 237–251. Oxford: British Archaeological Reports, International Series 227.

Grant, A. (1975) The animal bones, in B. W. Cunliffe *Excavations at Portchester Castle I. Roman*, 378–408. Report of the Research Committee of the Society of Antiquaries of London 32. London: Society of Antiquaries

Grant, A. (1976) Faunal remains, in B. W. Cunliffe *Excavations at Portchester Castle II. Saxon*. 262–296. Report of the Research Committee of the Society of Antiquaries of London 33. London: Society of Antiquaries.

Grant, A. (1982) The use of tooth wear as a guide to the age of domestic ungulates, in B. Wilson, C. Grigson and S. Payne (eds) *Ageing and sexing animal bones from archaeological sites*, 91–108. Oxford: British Archaeological Reports, British Series 109.

Hagelberg, E., Bell, L. S., Allen, T., Jones, S. J. and Clegg, J. B. (1991) Analysis of ancient bone DNA: techniques and applications. *Philosophical Transactions of the Royal Society of London Series B* 333, 399–407.

Hagen, A. (1992) *A Handbook of Anglo-Saxon Food: Processing and Consumption*. Middlesex: Anglo-Saxon Books.

Hagen, A, (1995) *A second Handbook of Anglo-Saxon Food and Drink: Production and Distribution*. Norfolk: Anglo-Saxon Books.

Hainard, R. (1948) *Les Mammifères sauvages d'Europe. I: Insectivores, Chiroptères, Carnivores*. Neuchâtel: Delachaux et Niestlé.

Hall, A. (2000) Technical Report: Plant remains from excavations at Flixborough, N. Lincolnshire (site code: FLX89). *Reports from the Environmental Archaeology Unit, York* 2000/56.

Hall, A. and Milles, A. (1993) Material assessment of hand-collected non-vertebrate remains from Flixborough. *Reports from the Environmental Archaeology Unit, York* 93/27.

Hamilton-Dyer, S. (2002) *Bird and fish remains*, pp. 255–261, in Gardiner, M., Cross, R., and Riddler, I. (eds) Continental trade and non-urban ports in Middle Anglo-Saxon England: excavations at Sandtun, West Hythe, Kent. *Archaeological Journal* 158, 161–290.

Hammond, P. W. (1993) *Food and Feast in Medieval England.* Dover, Alan Sutton Publishing.

Harding, P. and Peterken, G. F. (1975) Woodland conservation Eastern England: comparing the effects of changes in three study areas since 1946. *Biological Conservation* 8, 279–298.

Harmer, S. F. (1927) *Report on Cetacea stranded on the British coasts from 1913–1926.* 10. London: British Museum (Natural History).

Harman, M. (1979) *The mammalian bones*, in J. H. Williams, *St Peter's Street Northampton, excavations 1973–1976*, 328–32. Northampton: Northampton Development Corporation Archaeological Monographs 2.

Harman, M. (1993) *The animal bones*, in M. Darling and D. Gurney, *Caister-on-Sea. Excavations by Charles Green 1951–5.* Gressenhall: Norfolk Museums Service. East Anglian Archaeology Report 60.

Harting, J. E. (1898) *Hints on the Management of Hawks and Practical Falconry.* London: Horace Cox (facsimile reprint of 2nd ed. 1970, London: Tabard Press.).

Harting, J. E. (1880) *British Animals Extinct within Historic Times.* London, Trübner.

Harvey, B. (1993) *Living and Dying in England 1100–1540: the Monastic Experience.* Oxford: Clarendon Press.

Hatting, T. (1991) The archaeozoology, in M. Bencard, L. B. Jorgensen and H. B. Madsen (eds) *Ribe excavations 1970–76.* 3. 43–58. Esbjerg, Sydjysk Universitetsforlag.

Hawksworth, H. (1982) *British Poultry Standards* (4th edn). Frome & London: Butler & Tanner.

Haynes, S. (2001) *The palaeoecology of ancient geese, house mice and shrews as shown by the biomolecular record.* Unpublished PhD thesis, University of York.

Haynes, S., Bretman, A. J., Searle, J. B. and Dobney, K. M. (2002) Bone preservation and ancient DNA. The application of screening methods for predicting DNA survival. *Journal of Archaeological Science* 29, 585–592.

Hedges, R. E. M., Millard, A. R. and Pike, A. W. G. (1995) Measurements and relationships of diagenetic alteration of bone from three archaeological sites. *Journal of Archaeological Science* 22, 201–209.

Helme, J. (1614) *A Jewell for Gentrie.* London. [cited in H. C. Folkard 1859.]

Hinton, D. A. (2001) *Archaeology, Economy and Society: England from the fifth to the fifteenth century.* London: Routledge.

Hobson, K. A. 1999. Tracing origins and migration of wildlife using stable isotopes: a review. *Oecologia* 120, 314–326.

Hodges, R. (1982) *Dark Age Economics: the Origins of Towns and Trade AD 600–1000.* London: Duckworth.

Hoffmann, R. C. (1985) Fishponds. In J. R. Strayer (ed.) *Dictionary of the Middle Ages* 5, 73–74. New York: Charles Scribner's Sons.

Hoffmann, R. C. (1996) Economic development and aquatic ecosystems in medieval Europe. *The American Historical Review* 101, 631–669.

Holdsworth, C. (1995) Bishoprics, monasteries and the landscape *c.* AD 600–1066, in D. Hooke and S. Burnell (eds) *Landscape and Settlement in Britain AD 400–1066*, 27–49. Exeter: University of Exeter Press.

Hooke, D. (1998) *The Landscape of Anglo-Saxon England.* London: Leicester University Press.

Hooper, W. D. and Ash, H. B. (1935) *Cato and Varro: on Agriculture.* London.

Hoskins, W. G. and Dudley-Stamp, L. (1963) *The Common Lands of England and Wales.* London: Collins.

Hudson, P. J. and Rands, M. W. (1988) *Ecology and Management of Game-birds.* Oxford: University Press.

Hui, C. A. 1981. Seawater consumption and water flux in the common dolphin *Delphinus delphis. Physiological Zoology* 54, 430–440.

Hutt, F. B. (1929) Sex dimorphism and variability in the appendicular skeleton of the leghorn fowl. *Poultry Science* 8, 202–218.

Hutton-MacDonald R., MacDonald, K. C. and Ryan, K. (1993) Domestic geese from medieval Dublin. *Archaeofauna* 2, 205–218.

Jackson, K. (ed.) (1990) *Aislinge Meic Con Glinne.* Dublin: School of Celtic Studies, Dublin Institute for Advanced Studies.

Jacob, J. and Mather, F. B. (2000) *Capons. Factsheet PS-54.* Department of Animal Sciences, Cooperative Extension Service, Institute of Food and Agricultural Sciences, University of Florida, Gainesville, FL, 32611. (http://edis.ufl.edu)

Jameson, E. W. (1976) *The Hawking of Japan: the History and Development of Japanese Falconry.* California: Davis.

Jefferson, T. A., Leatherwood, S. and Webber, M. A. (1993) *Marine Mammals of the World. FAO species identification guide.* Rome: Food and Agriculture Organisation.

Jenkins, J. T. (1971) *A History of Whale Fisheries.* Port Washington (New York): Kennikat.

Johnson, C. P. and Sowerby, J. E. (1862) *The useful Plants of Great Britain.* London: Robert Hardwicke.

Jones, A. (1976) The fish bones, pp. 170–176, in G. Black, Excavations in the sub-vault of the misericorde of Westminster Abbey. *Transactions of the London and Middlesex Archaeological Society* 27, 135–178.

Jones, A. K. G. (1988) Provisional remarks on fish remains from archaeological deposits at York, in P. Murphy and C. French (eds) *The exploitation of wetlands*, 113–127. Oxford: British Archaeological Reports. British Series 186.

Jones, G. G. (1984) Animal bones. In A. Rogerson and C. Dallas, *Excavations in Thetford 1948–59 and 1973–80*, 187–192. Gressenhall: Norfolk Archaeological Unit. East Anglian Archaeology Report 22.

Jones G. G. (1993) Animal bone, in C. Dallas, *Excavations in Thetford by B. K. Davison between 1964 and 1970*, 176–191. Gressenhall: Field Archaeology Division, Norfolk Museums Service East Anglian Archaeology Report 62.

Jones R. T. and Serjeantson, D. (1983) The animal bones from five sites at Ipswich. *Ancient Monuments Laboratory Report* 3951. London.

Jones R. T. and Ruben I. (1987) Animal bones, with some notes on the effects of differential sampling, in G. Beresford, *Goltho: the development of an early medieval manor* c. *850–1150.* London: English Heritage. English Heritage Archaeological Reports 4.

Juhn, M. (1952). Spur growth and differentiation in the adult thiouracil-treated fowl. *Physiological Zoology* 25, 150–162.

Kelly, F. (1997) *Early Irish Farming: a study based mainly on the law-texts of the 7th and 8th centuries AD.* (Early Irish Law Series IV) Dublin: School of Celtic Studies, Dublin Institute for Advanced Studies.

Kenward, H. K. (1998) *Invertebrates in archaeology in the north of England* (unpublished draft).

Kenward, H., Hall, A. and Carrott, J. (2000) Draft publication text. Environment, activity and living conditions at Deer Park Farms, Co. Antrim, N. Ireland: evidence from plant and invertebrate remains. *Reports from the Environmental Archaeology Unit, York* 2000/57. York.

Kinze, C. C. (1995) Danish whale records 1575–1991 (Mammalia, Cetacea). Review of whale specimens stranded, directly or incidentally caught along the Danish coasts. *Steenstrupia* 21, 155–196.

Kline, T. C., Wilson, W. J. and Goering, J. J. (1998) Natural isotope indicators of fish migration at Prudhoe Bay, Alaska. *Canadian Journal of Fisheries and Aquatic Sciences* 55, 1494–1502.

Kohn, M. 1996. Predicting animal δ18O: accounting for diet and physiological adaptation. *Geochimica et Cosmochimica Acta* 60(23), 4811–4829.

Körber-Grohne, U. (1967) Geobotanische Untersuchungen auf der Feddersen Wierde. *Feddersen Wierde* 1. Wiesbaden.

Kozelka, A. W. (1933) Spurlessness of the White Leghorn. *Journal of Heredity* 24, 71–78.

Kruse, S. E., (1992) Late Saxon balances and weights from England. *Medieval Archaeology* 36, 67–95.

Kylie, E. (1911) *The English Correspondence of St Boniface.* London, Chatto and Windus.

Landauer, W. (1937) Studies on the creeper fowl. XI. Castration and length of bones of the appendicular skeleton in normal and creeper fowl. *Anatomical Record* 69, 247–253.

Lascelles, G. (1892) (repr. 1971). *The Art of Falconry.* London: Neville Spearman.

Latimer, H. B. (1927) Post-natal growth of the chicken skeleton. *American Journal of Anatomy* 40(1), 1–57.

Leahy, K. (1995) The Middle Saxon site at Flixborough, North Lincolnshire. In J. Hawkes and S. Mills (eds), *Northumbria's Golden Age,* 87–94. Stroud: Sutton Publishing.

Lernau, O., and Ben-Horris, M. (1994) Taphonomic curve and index: a preliminary exploration of a new concept, in W. Van Neer (ed.) *Fish exploitation in the past. Proceedings of the 7th meeting of the ICAZ fish remains working group.* 17–24. Tervuren: Musée Royal de l'Afrique Centrale.

Lestocquoy, J. (1948) Baleine et raitaillement au Moyen Age. *Revue du Nord* 30, 39–43 (repr. in Lestocquoy, J., *Etudes d'histoire urbaine: villes et abbayes, Arras au Moyen-Age,* 114–17 Arras: Commission Départmentale des Monuments Historiques de Pas-de-Calais).

Lillie, M. (1998) The palaeoenvironmental survey of the lower Trent Valley and Winterton Beck, in R. van de Noort and S. Ellis (eds) *Wetland Heritage of the Ancholme and Lower Trent Valleys: an archaeological Survey,* 33–72. London: English Heritage.

Limbert, M. (1986) The extraction of peat at Thorne [moors]. *Old West Riding* 6, 9–16.

Limbert, M. (1992) Records of the black grouse on the Yorkshire-Lincolnshire border. *Thorne and Hatfield Moors Papers* 3, 77–85.

Limbert, M. (1994) The importance of Thorne and Hatfield moors for vertebrate fauna. *Thorne and Hatfield Moors Papers* 4, 39–49.

Lind, L. R. (1963) (trans.) *Aldrovandi on Chickens. The Ornithology of Ulisse Aldrovandi (1600) Vol. 2, Book XIV.* Norman: University of Oklahoma Press.

Locker, A. (1989) *The evidence from London sites of the importance of fish in the Saxon period.* Unpublished report for the Museum of London.

Locker, A. (2001) *The role of stored fish in England 900–1750 AD: The evidence from historical and archaeological data.* Sofia: Publishing Group Limited.

Locker, A. and Jones, A. (1985) Ipswich: the fish remains. *English Heritage Ancient Monuments Laboratory Report* 4578. London.

Long, A. J., Innes, J. B., Kirby, J. R., Lloyd, J. M., Rutherford, M. M., Shennan, I. and Tooley, M. J. (1998) Holocene sea-level change and coastal evolution in the Humber estuary, eastern England: an assessment of rapid coastal change. *Holocene* 8(2), 229–247.

Longinelli, A. 1984. Oxygen isotopes in mammal bone phosphate: a new tool for paleohydrological and paleoclimatological research? *Geochimica et Cosmochimica Acta* 48, 385–390.

Louvier, R. (1937) *Histogénèse des Appendices cutane céphaliques et de l'Ergot du Coq domestique.* Unpublished PhD thesis, University of Paris.

Loveluck C. (1996) *The Anglo-Saxon Settlement and Cemetery Remains from Flixborough: Revised and Summarised Assessments and Updated Project Design.* Unpublished enabling document for Humber Archaeology Partnership.

Loveluck, C. (1997) Flixborough – the character and economy of a high status Middle Saxon settlement in northern England, in G. de Boe and F. Verhaeghe (eds) *Rural settlements in Medieval Europe. Papers of the 'Medieval Europe Brugge 1997' Conference* 6 (I.A.P. Rapporten 6). 179–194. Zellik: Instituut voor het Archeologisch Patrimonium.

Loveluck, C. P. and Dobney, K. (2001) A match made in heaven or a marriage of convenience? The problems and rewards of integrating palaeoecological and archaeological data, in U. Albarella (ed.) *Environmental archaeology: Meaning and Purpose,* 149–176. Dordrecht: Kluwer Academic.

Loveluck, C. P. and McKenna, B. (1999) *The site of Normanby Steelworks – assessment of potential of archaeological remains.* Humber Archaeology Report No. 45. Hull: Hull City Council.

LTNC (1998) *Lincolnshire Trust for Nature Conservation: Habitat Surveys.* Unpublished report.

Lucy, S. 2000. *The Anglo-Saxon Way of Death: Burial Rites in Early England.* Stroud: Sutton.

MacAirt, S. and MacNiocaill, G. (eds) (1983) *The Annals of Ulster 1: Text and Translation.* Dublin: Dublin Institute of Advance Study.

McCormick, F. (1987) *Stock-rearing in Early Christian Ireland.* Unpublished PhD thesis, Queen's University, Belfast.

McCormick, F. (1991) The effect of the Anglo-Norman settlement on Ireland's wild and domestic fauna, in P. Crabtree and K. Ryan (eds) *Animal Use and Culture Change,* 41–52. Philadelphia: University of Pennsylvania, Museum of Archaeology and Anthropology Research Papers in Science and Archaeology (MASCA) 8.

McCormick, F. (1992) Exchange of livestock in early Christian Ireland, AD 450–1150. *Anthropozoologica* 16, 31–36.

McCormick, F. and Murphy, E. (1998) The animal bones, in P. Hill, *Whithorn and St Ninian: the excavation of a monastic town, 1984–91*, 605–613. The Whithorn Trust/Stroud: Sutton.

McDonnell, J. (1981) Inland fisheries in medieval Yorkshire 1066–1300. *Borthwick Papers* 60. York: University of York, Borthwick Institute of Historical Research.

Macpherson. H. A. (1897) *A History of Fowling*. Edinburgh: D. Douglas.

Magennis, H. (1999) *Anglo-Saxon Appetites: Food, Drink and their Consumption in Old English and related Literature*. Dublin: Four Courts Press.

Maitland, P. S. and Campbell, R. N. (1992) *Freshwater Fishes of the British Isles*. London: Harper Collins.

Markham, G. (1614) *Cheape and good Husbandry for the Well-ordering of all Beasts, and Fowles, and for the generall Cure of their Diseases*. London: Roger Jackson.

Markham, G. (1655) *Hungers Prevention: or, the Whole Arte of Fowling by Water and Land, etc.* London.

Marshall, S. and Elliot, M. 1998. Environmental Influences on the fish assemblage of the Humber Estuary. *Estuarine, Coastal and Shelf Science* 46, 175–184.

Masui, K. and Hashimoto, S. (1927) Studies on the physiology of reproduction in the domestic fowl. 2. On the effect of caponisation on the growth of the body and the weight of various organs. *Imperial Zootechnical Experimentation Station, Chiba-Shi, Japan, Research Bulletin* 21.

Matthews, L. H. (1978) *The Natural History of the Whale*. London: Weidenfeld and Nicolson.

Meaney, A. L. (2002) Birds on the stream of conciousness: riddles 7 to 10 of the Exeter Book, *Archaeological Review from Cambridge* 18, 120–52.

Meek, A. and Gray, R. A. H. (1911) Animal remains, pp. 220–267 in Forster, R. H. and Knowles, W. H. (eds), Corstopitum. *Archaeologia Aeliana* (3rd series) 7, 143–267.

Meyer, K. (ed.). (1906) *The Triads of Ireland* (Todd Lecture Series XIV, Dublin, repr.). Dublin: Hodges, Figgis; London: Williams & Norgate.

Miccoli, G. (1991) De monniken. In J. Le Goff (ed.) *De Wereld van de Middeleeuwen*. 43–79. Amsterdam, Agon. (translation of *L'Uomo Medievale*. Bari: Laterza. 1987).

Michell, E. B. (1972). *The Art and Practice of Hawking*. London: Holland Press.

Milis, L. (1992). *Angelic Monks and earthly Men: Monasticism and its Meaning to Medieval Society*. Woodbridge/Rochester, New York: Boydell Press.

Millard, A. R. (1993) *Diagenesis of archaeological bone: the case of uranium uptake*. Unpublished PhD. thesis, University of Oxford.

Minagawa, M. and Wada, E. 1984. Stepwise enrichment of 15N along food chains: Further evidence and the relation between δ15N and animal age. *Geochimica et Cosmochimica Acta* 48, 1135–1140.

Mitchell, E. (1975) Porpoise, dolphin and small whale fisheries of the world. Status and problems. *IUCN Monograph* no. 3. Morges: IUCN.

Montanari, M. (1994) *Honger en Overvloed*. Amsterdam, Agon

(translation of *La Fame et l'Abbondanza: Storia dell'Alimentazione in Europa*. Roma: Laterza. 1993).

Mortimer, J. R., (1905) *Forty Years' Researches in British and Saxon burial Mounds of East Yorkshire*. London: A. Brown and Sons.

Müldner, G. (2005) *Eboracum – Jorvik – York: A diachronic study of human diet in York by stable isotope analysis*. Unpublished PhD Thesis, University of Bradford

Müldner, G. and Richards, M. P. (2005) Fast or feast: reconstructing diet in later medieval England by stable isotope analysis. *Journal of Archaeological Science* 32, 39–48.

Mulkeen, S. and O'Connor, T. P. (1997) Raptors in towns: towards an ecological model. *International Journal of Osteoarchaeology* 7, 440–449.

Müller, H. H. (1993) Falconry in central Europe in the Middle Ages. In [editors?] *Exploitation des animaux sauvages à travers le temps. L'Homme et l'Animal (Colloque international 4)*, 431–437 Juans-les-Pins: Editions APDCA.

Munro, J. H. (1978) Wool price schedules and the qualities of English wools in the later middle ages. *Textile History* 9, 118–169.

Musset, L. (1964) Quelques notes sur les baleiniers Normands de Xe au XIIIe siècle. *Revue d'Histoire Economique et Sociale* 42, 147–161.

Neale, F. (1979) The relevance of the Axbridge Chronicle, in P. Rahtz, *The Saxon and Medieval Palaces at Cheddar*, 10–12. Oxford: British Archaeological Reports, British Series 65.

Newton, L. (1951) *Seaweed Utilisation*. London: Sampson Low.

Nichols, C., Herman, J., Geggiotti, O. E., Dobney, K. M., Parsons, K. and Hoelzel, A. R. (2007) Genetic isolation of a now extinct population of bottlenose dolphins (Tursiops truncatus). *Proceedings of the Royal Society. Biology*. 274, 1611–1616.

Nicholson, R. A. (1992) Bone survival: the effects of sedimentary abrasion and trampling on fresh and cooked bone. *International Journal of Osteoarchaology* 2, 79–90.

Nicholson, R. A. (1996) Fish bone diagenesis in different soils. *Archaeofauna* 5, 79–91.

Noddle, B. (1976) *Report on the animal bones from Walton, Aylesbury*, pp. 153–290, in Farley, M., Saxon and Medieval Walton, Aylesbury: excavations 1973–4. *Records of Buckinghamshire* 20, 153–290.

Noddle, B. A. (1980) Identification and interpretation of the mammal bones. In P. Wade-Martins (ed.) *Excavations in North Elmham Park*. 375–409. pop*. East Anglian Archaeology Report 9.

Noddle B. A. (1987) Animal bones from Jarrow. 3rd Report. *Ancient Monuments Laboratory Report* 80/87. London: English Heritage.

O'Connor, T. P. (1982) Animal bones from Flaxengate, Lincoln c. 870–1500. *The Archaeology of Lincoln* 8(1). London: Council for British Archaeology.

O'Connor, T. P. (1989) Bones from Anglo-Scandinavian levels at 16–22 Coppergate. *The Archaeology of York* 15(3), 137–207. London: Council for British Archaeology.

O'Connor, T. P. (1991) Bones from 46–54 Fishergate. *The Archaeology of York* 15(4), 209–298. London: Council for British Archaeology.

O'Connor, T. P. (1993) Birds and the scavenger niche. *Archaeofauna* 2, 155–162.

O'Connor, T. P. (2001) On the Interpretation of Animal Bone Assemblages from *Wics*, pp. 54–60, in D. Hill and R. Cowie (eds) *Wics: The Early Medieval Trading Centres of Northern Europe*. Sheffield: Sheffield Academic Press.

O'Rahilly, C. (ed.) (1967) *Táin Bó Cúalnge from the Book of Leinster*. Dublin: Dublin Institute for Advanced Studies. (repr.1984).

Ó Riain, P. (ed.) (1985) *Corpus genealogiarum Sanctorum Hiberniae*. Dublin: Dublin Institute for Advanced Studies.

O'Sullivan, D. and Young, R. (1995) *Book of Lindisfarne, Holy Island*. London: Batsford.

Oggins, R. S. (1981) Falconry in England in the Anglo-Saxon period. *Mediaevalia* 7, 173–208.

Oggins, R. S. (1989) Falconry and Mediaeval social status. *Mediaevalia* 12, 43–55.

Ordnance Survey (1966) *Land Utilization Survey of Britain*. London: Lovell Johns.

Orson, R. A., Warren, R. S. and Niering, W. A. (1998) Interpreting sea level rise and rates of vertical salt marsh accretion in a southern New England tidal salt marsh. *Estuarine Coastal and Shelf Science* 47, 419–429.

Oswald, A. (1982) *The History and Practice of Falconry*. Jersey: Neville Spearman.

Ottaway, P. (1996) 'The ironwork', in Hall, R. A. and Whyman, M., Settlement and monasticism at Ripon, North Yorkshire, from the 7th to 11th centuries. *Medieval Archaeology* 40, 99–114.

Owen, M. (1976) Factors affecting the distribution of geese in the British Isles. *Wildfowl* 27, 143–147.

Pääbo, S. (1989) Ancient DNA: extraction, characterization, molecular cloning and enzymatic amplification. *Proceedings of the National Academy of Sciences USA* 86, 1939–1943.

Panithanarak, T. (2004). *Molecular Studies of Races, Raciation, Speciation and Species Identification*. Unpublished PhD thesis, University of York.

Parker, A. J. (1988) The birds of Roman Britain. *Oxford Journal of Archaeology* 7, 197–226.

Pashby, B. S. (1992) The Humber Wildfowl Refuge: an experiment in wildfowl conservation. *The Naturalist* 117, 81–98.

Pauly, D., Trites, A. W., Capuli, E. and Christensen, V. (1998) Diet composition and trophic levels of marine mammals. *ICES Journal of Marine Science* 55, 467–481.

Payne, S. (1973) Kill-off patterns in sheep and goats: the mandibles from Asvan Kale. *Anatolian Studies* 23, 281–303.

Payne, S. (1985) Morphological distinctions between the mandibular teeth of young sheep, *Ovis* and goats, *Capra*. *Journal of Archaeological Science*, 12: 139–147.

Payne, S. (1987) Reference codes for the wear state in the mandibular cheek teeth of sheep and goats. *Journal of Archaeological Science* 14, 609–614.

Percival, S. M. and Evans, P. R. (1997) Brent Geese *Branta bernicla* and *Zostera;* factors affecting the exploitation of a seasonally declining food resource. *IBIS* 139, 121–8.

Percival, S. M., Sutherland, W. J. and Evans, P. R. (1998) Intertidal habitat loss and wildfowl numbers: applications of a spatial depletion model. *Journal of Applied Ecology* 35, 57–63.

Perdikaris, S. (1999) From chiefly provisioning to commercial fishery: long-term economic change in Arctic Norway. *World Archaeology* 30, 388–402.

Perez-Higuera, T. (1998) *The Art of Time: medieval Calendars and the Zodiac*. London: Weidenfeld and Nicholson.

Peterken, G. F. (1975) Woodland conservation in Eastern England comparing the effects of changes in three study areas since 1946. *Biological Conservation* 8, 279–299.

Peterken, G. F. and Game, M. (1984) Historical factors affecting the number and distribution of vascular plant species in the woodlands of Central Lincolnshire. *Journal of Ecology* 72, 155–182.

Pethick, J. S. (1990) The Humber Estuary, pp.54–67, in S. Ellis and D. R. Crowther (eds) *Humber Perspectives: a Region through the Ages*. Hull: Hull University Press.

Prater, A. J. (1981) *Estuary Birds of Britain and Ireland*. London: T. and A. D. Poyser.

Prummel, W. (1983) Excavations at Dorestad 2. Early medieval Dorestad: an archaeozoological study. *Nederlandse Oudheden* 11. Amersfoort, Rijksdienst voor het Oudheidkundig Bodemonderzoek.

Prummel, W. (1997) Evidence of hawking (falconry) from bird and mammal bones. *International Journal of Osteoarchaeology* 7, 333–338.

Quigley, G. D. and Juhn, M. (1951) A comparison of spur growth in the cock, slip and capon. *Poultry Science* 30, 900–901.

Rackham, D. J. (1979) Animal resources, pp. 47–54, in Carver, M. O. H., Three Saxo-Norman tenements in Durham City. *Medieval Archaeology* 23, 1–80.

Rackham, O. (1980) *Ancient Woodland: its History, Vegetation and Uses in England*. London: Arnold.

Rackham, O. (1986) *The History of the Countryside: the full fascinating Story of Britain's Landscape*. London: Dent.

Rau, G. H., Mearns, A. J., Young, D. R., Olson, R. J., Schafer, H. A. and Kaplan, I. R. (1983) Animal 13C/12C correlates with trophic level in pelagic food webs. *Ecology* 64, 1314–1318.

Ray, J. (1678) *The Ornithology of Francis Willughby of Middleton in the County of Warwick...* London: Royal Society.

Reed, R. (1972). *Ancient Skins, Parchment, and Leathers*. London: Seminar Press.

Reichstein, H. (1972) Einige Bemerkungen zu den Haustierfunden auf der Feddersen Wierde und verleichbarer Siedlungen in Nordwestdeutschland. *Die Kunde* 23, 142–156.

Reuter, T. (1985) Plunder and tribute in the Carolingian empire. *Transactions of the Royal Historical Society* 35, 75–94.

Richards, J. D. (1999) Cottam: an Anglian and Anglo-Scandinavian settlement on the Yorkshire Wolds. *Archaeological Journal* 156, 1–110.

Robertson, A. J. (ed.) (1925) *The Laws of the Kings of England from Edmund to Henry I*. Cambridge: Cambridge University Press.

Robinson, M. (1985) Nature conservation and environmental archaeology. In G. Lambrick, *Archaeology and Nature Conservation*, 11–17. Oxford: University of Oxford, Department for External Studies.

Rodwell, J. (ed.) (2000) *British Plant Communities 5. Maritime Communities and Vegetation of open Habitats*. Cambridge: Cambridge University Press.

Roe, L. J., Thewissen, J. G. M., Quade, J., O'Neil, J. R., Bajpai, S., Sahni, A. and Taseer Hussain, S. (1998) Isotopic approaches to understanding the terrestrial-to-marine transition of the earliest cetaceans, in J. G. M. Thewissen, (ed.), *The Emergence of Whales*, 399–422. New York: Plenum Press.

Sadler, P. (1991) The use of tarsometatarsi in sexing and ageing domestic fowl (*Gallus gallus* L.), and recognizing five-toed breeds in archaeological material. *Circaea* 8, 41–48.

Salisbury, C. R. (1991) Primitive British fishweirs, in G. L. Good, R. H. Jones, and M. W. Ponsford (eds) *Waterfront Archaeology: Proceedings of the Third International Conference*. 76–87. London: Council for British Archaeology Research Report 74.

Sawyer, P. H. (1968) *Anglo-Saxon Charters: An Annotated List and Bibliography*. London: Royal Historical Society.

Sawyer, P. H. (1983) The royal Tun in pre-Conquest England, in P. Wormald (ed.) *Ideal and Reality in Frankish and Anglo-Saxon Society,* 273–99. Oxford: Blackwell.

Schmitz, P. (1945) *Sancti Benedicti Regula Monachorum*. Maredsous: Editions de Maredsous.

Schoeninger, M. J. and DeNiro, M. J. 1984. Nitrogen and carbon isotopic composition of bone collagen from marine and terrestrial animals. *Geochimica et Cosmochimica Acta* 48, 625–639.

Schwarcz, H. P. and Schoeninger, M. J. 1991. Stable isotope analyses in human nutritional ecology. *Yearbook of Physical Anthropology* 34, 283–321.

Scott, S. (1991) The animal bones, in P. Armstrong, D. Tomlinson and D. H. Evans. *Excavations at Lurk Lane, Beverley, 1979–82*, 216–233. Sheffield: Sheffield Excavation Reports 1.

Scott, S. (2000) *The Animal Bones from Green Shiel, Lindisfarne*. Unpublished Masters thesis, University of Durham.

Serjeantson, D. (1989) Animal remains and the tanning trade, in D. Serjeantson and T. Waldron (eds) *Diet and crafts in towns. The evidence of animal remains from the Roman to the post-medieval periods*, 129–146. Oxford: British Archaeological Reports, British Series 199.

Serjeantson, D. (2002) Goose husbandry in medieval England, and the problem of ageing goose bones. Proceedings of the 4th meeting of the ICAZ Bird Working Group, Kraków, Poland, 11–15 September, 2001. *Acta Zoologica Cracoviensia* 45 (Special Issue), 39–54.

Sherley-Price, L. (1968) *Bede: a History of the English Church and People*. Harmondsworth: Penguin.

Silver, I. A. (1970) The ageing of domestic animals, in D. R. Brothwell and E. S. Higgs (eds) *Science in Archaeology* (2nd edn.), 283–302. New York: Praeger Publishing.

Simoons, F. J. (1994) *Eat not this Flesh: Food Avoidances from Prehistory to the Present* (2nd ed.). Wisconsin: University of Wisconsin Press.

Smith, A. E. (1975) The impacts of lowland river management. *Bird Study* 22, 249–254.

Smith, A. H. (1964) *The Place Names of Gloucestershire, Parts 1–3*. Cambridge: Cambridge University Press.

Snow, D. W. (ed.) (1971) *The Status of Birds in Britain and Ireland.* (prepared by the Records Committee of the British Ornithologists' Union). Oxford.

Starck, J. M. (1994) Quantitative design of the skeleton in bird hatchlings: does tissue compartmentalization limit post-hatching growth rates? *Journal of Morphology* 222, 113–131.

Sten, S. and Vretemark, M. (1988) Storgravsprojektet –

osteologiska analyser av yngre jernalderns benrika brandgravar. *Fornvanen* 83, 145–176.

Stevenson, J. (ed.) (1847) *Libellus de Vita et Miraculis S. Godrici*. London: Nichols, etc. Surtees Society Publications 20.

Stuart, A. J. (1982) *Pleistocene Vertebrates of the British Isles*. London: Longman.

Swanton, M. (1975) *Anglo-Saxon Prose*. London: Rowman and Littlefield.

Swanton, M. (1996) *Anglo-Saxon Prose.* London/Vermont: Everyman.

Sykes, N. J. (2006) The impact of the Normans on hunting practices in England, in C. Woolgar, D. Serjeantson and T. Waldron (eds) *Food in medieval England: history and archaeology*. Oxford: Oxford University Press

Sykes, N. J. (2007) *The Norman Conquest: A Zoo-archaeological Perspective*. British Archaeological Reports, International Series. Oxford: Archaeopress.

Tams, A. (2002) *Reassessing Age at Death in Archaeological Pigs from Tooth Wear and Crown Height Measurement.* Unpublished undergraduate dissertation (Z0135969), University of Durham.

Tardif, J. (ed.) (1866) *Monuments Historiques: Archives Nationales de l'Empire, Inventaires et Documents*. Paris: J. Claye.

Tegetmeier, W. B. (1867) *The Poultry Book*. London: Routledge.

Thawley, C. R. (1981) The mammal, bird and fish bones, in J. E. Mellor and T. Pearce (eds) *The Austin Friars, Leicester*, 173–175. London: Council for British Archaeology Research Report 35.

Thewissen, J. G. M., Roe, L. J., O'Neil, J. R., Hussain, S. T., Sahni, A. and Bajpal, S. 1996. Evolution of cetacean osmoregulation. *Nature* 381(6581), 379–380.

Thirsk, J. (1957) *English Peasant Farming. The Agrarian History of Lincolnshire from Tudor to Recent Times*. London: Routledge and Kegan Paul.

Thompson, D'A. W. (trs.) (1910) *Historia animalium*. The works of Aristotle 4. (ed. Smith, J. A. and Ross, W. D.) Oxford: Clarendon Press.

Thompson, M. (2001) The pine marten in north-east Yorkshire. *Voice of the Moors* 66. (North Yorkshire Moors Association magazine.)

Timpel, W. (1990) Das frankische Gräberfeld von Alach, Kreis Erfurt. *Alt-Thuringia* 25, 61–155.

Tinsley, H. M. (1981). The Bronze Age, in I. G. Simmons and M. J. Tooley (eds) *The Environment in British Prehistory*, 210–49. London: Duckworth.

Tutin, T. G, Heywood, V. H., Burges, N. A., Moore, D. M., Valentine, D. H., Walters, S. M. and Webb, D. A. (eds) (1964–80) *Flora Europaea* 1–5. Cambridge: Cambridge University Press.

Van Neer, W. and Ervynck, A. (1996) Food rules and status: patterns of fish consumption in a monastic community. *Archaeofauna* 5, 155–164.

Van de Noort, R. and Ellis, S. (eds) (1998) *Wetland Heritage of the Ancholme and Lower Trent Valleys: an archaeological Survey*. Hull: Humber Wetlands Project, Centre for Wetland Archaeology, The University of Hull.

Van Zeist, W. (1974) Palaeobotanical studies of settlement sites in the coastal area of the Netherlands. *Palaeohistoria* 16, 223–371.

Von Mensch, P. J. A. (1974) A Roman soup kitchen at Zwannesdam? *Berichten von de Rijkdienst voor het Oudheidkundig Bodemondarzoek* 24, 159–65.

Vonkanel, A. (1981) Winter feeding ecology of wigeon at the Ouse washes, England. *IBIS* 123, 438–449.

Wade, K., (1980) A settlement at Bonhunt Farm, Wicken Bonhunt, Essex, in D. G. Buckley (ed.) *Archaeology in Essex to AD 1500*. 96–102. London: Council for British Archaeology Research Report 34.

Watson, L. (1981) *Sea Guide to Whales of the World*. London: Hutchinson

West, B. (1982) Spur development: recognising caponized fowl in archaeological material, in B. Wilson, C. Grigson and S. Payne (eds) *Ageing and sexing animal bones from archaeological sites*, 255–261. Oxford: British Archaeological Reports, British Series 109.

West, B. (1985) Chicken legs revisited. *Circaea* 3, 11–14.

West, B. (1993) Birds and mammals from the Peabody site and National Gallery, pp. 150–168, in Whytehead, R. L., Cowie, R. and Blackmore, L., Excavations at the Peabody site, Chandos Place and the National Gallery. *Transactions of the London and Middlesex Archaeological Society* 40 (for 1989), 35–176.

Wheeler, A. (1969) *The Fishes of the British Isles and North-West Europe*. London: Macmillan.

Wheeler, A. (1977) Fish bone, in H. Clarke and A. Carter (eds) *Excavations in King's Lynn 1963–1970*. 405–409. London: Society for Medieval Archaeology Monograph Series No. 7.

Wheeler, A. and Jones, A. (1989) *Fishes*. Cambridge: Cambridge University Press.

White, C. D., Spence, M. W., Longstaffe, F. J. and Law, K. R. (2004) Demography and ethnic continuity in the Tlailotlacan enclave of Teotihuacan: the evidence from stable oxygen isotopes. *Journal of Anthropological Archaeology* 23(4), 385–403.

Whitehead, P. J. P., Bauchot, M. L., Hureau, J. C., Nielsen, J. and Tortonese, E. (eds) (1986a) *Fishes of the North-eastern Atlantic and the Mediterranean* 2. Paris: United Nations Educational, Scientific and Cultural Organization.

Whitehead, P. J. P., Bauchot, M. L., Hureau, J. C., Nielsen, J. and Tortonese, E. (eds) (1986b) *Fishes of the North-eastern Atlantic and the Mediterranean* 3. Paris: United Nations Educational, Scientific and Cultural Organization.

Whitehead, P. J. P., Bauchot, M. L., Hureau, J. C., Nielsen, J. and Tortonese, E. (eds) (1989) *Fishes of the North-eastern Atlantic and the Mediterranean* 1. Paris: United Nations Educational, Scientific and Cultural Organization.

Whitelock, D. (ed.) (1979) *English Historical Documents* (2nd edn). London: Methuen.

Whitton, B. A. and Lucas, M. C. (1997) Biology of the Humber Rivers. *The Science of the Total Environment* 194/195, 247–262.

Whitwell J. B. (1994) *Flixborough Middle Saxon Settlement Excavations 1988–91, Material Assessment Report*. Humberside Archaeology Unit Report for English Heritage.

Wigh, B. (2001) Animal husbandry in the Viking Age town of Birka and its hinterland. *Birka Studies* 7. Stockholm.

Wildfowl and Wetland Trust (1963) *Wildfowl of Great Britain*. London, HMSO.

Williams, D. and Vince, A. (1997) The characterisation and interpretation of early to middle Saxon granitic tempered pottery in England, *Medieval Archaeology* 41, 214–220.

Wilson, C. A. (1973) *Food and Drink in Britain*. London: Constable.

Winder, J. M. (1992) *A Study of the Variation in Oyster Shells from Archaeological Sites and a Discussion of Oyster Exploitation*. Unpublished PhD thesis, University of Southampton.

Yalden, D. (1999) *The History of British Mammals*. London: T. and A. D. Poyser.

Yoshida, N. and Miyazaki, N. 1991. Oxygen isotope correlation of cetacean bone phosphate with environmental water. *Journal of Geophysical Research-Oceans* 96(C1), 815–820.

Younger, D. A. (1994) [Report on bones], In Van der Veen, M., Report on the biological remains, pp. 243–68, in P. Bidwell and S. Speak (eds) *Excavations at South Shields Roman fort*. Newcastle-upon-Tyne: Society of Antiquaries of Newcastle upon Tyne (with Tyne and Wear Museums) Monograph Series 4.

Zohar, I. and Cooke, R. (1997) The impact of salting and drying on fish bones: preliminary observations on four marine species from Parita Bay, Panama. *Archaeofauna* 6, 59–66.

Index

PLATE 2.1 *View of excavation showing sandy substrate and concentrations of dark ash (Humber Field Archaeology).*

PLATE 2.2 *Section of central ditch showing dark ash fill with concentrations of bone (courtesy of Terry O'Connor).*

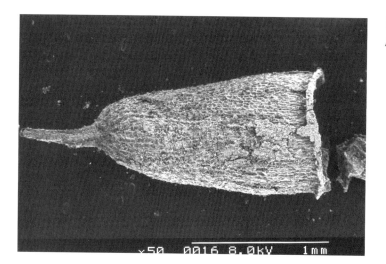

PLATE 3.1 Charred capsule remains of sea plantain, Plantago maritima L.

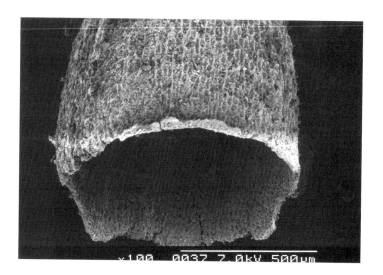

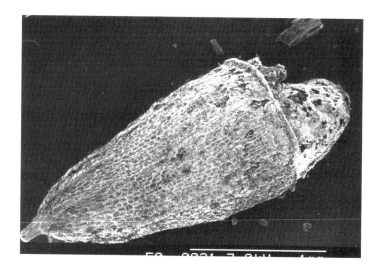

PLATE 7.1 *Cattle distal tibiae showing size differentiation linked with sexual dimorphism.*

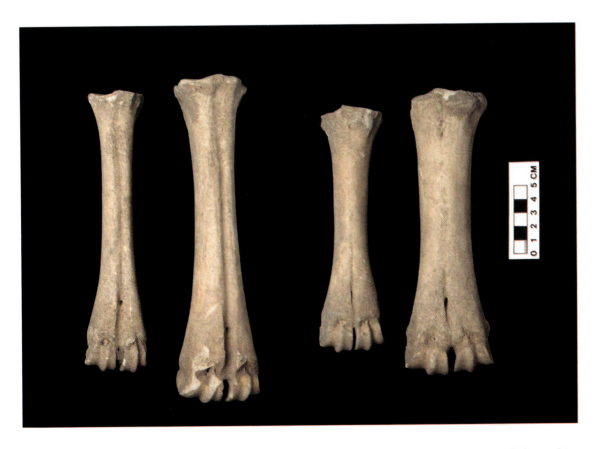

PLATE 7.2 *Cattle metatarsals and metacarpals showing size differentiation linked with sexual dimorphism.*

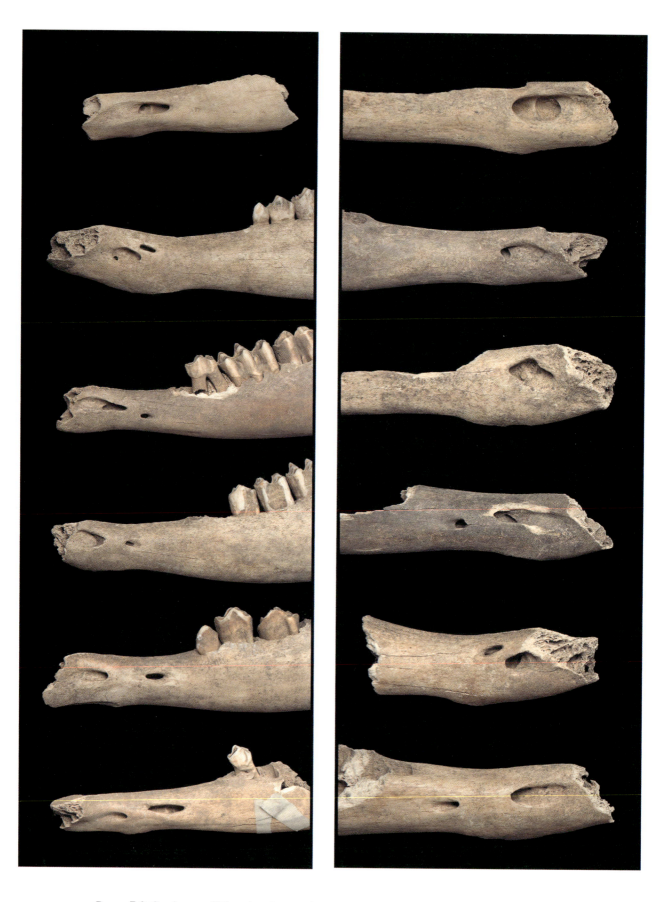

PLATE 7.3 *Cattle mandibles showing variation in conformation of the mental foramen.*

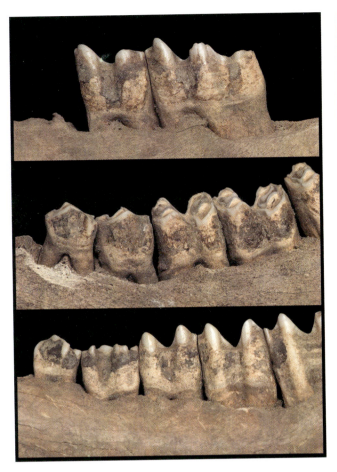

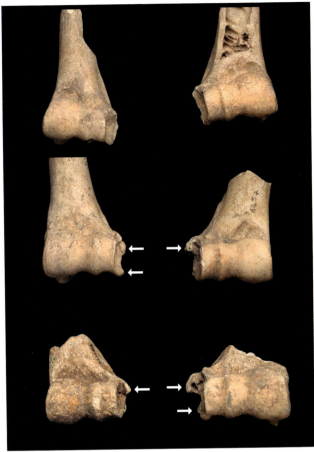

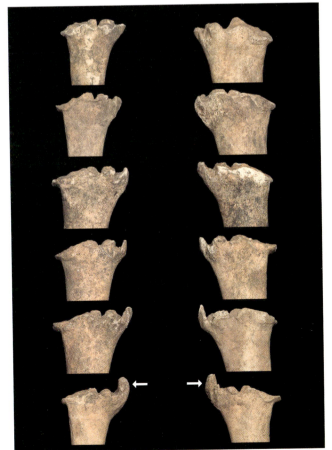

PLATE 7.4 (top left) Cattle mandible tooth rows showing deposits of dental calculus present on the tooth crowns.

PLATE 7.5 (top right) Sheep distal humeri showing changes to the joint characteristic of 'penning elbow'.

PLATE 7.6 (bottom left) Sheep proximal radii showing changes to the joint characteristic of 'penning elbow'.

PLATE 7.7 *Linear enamel hypoplasia (LEH) on the lingual surface of a pig mandibular 2nd permanent molar (M_2).*

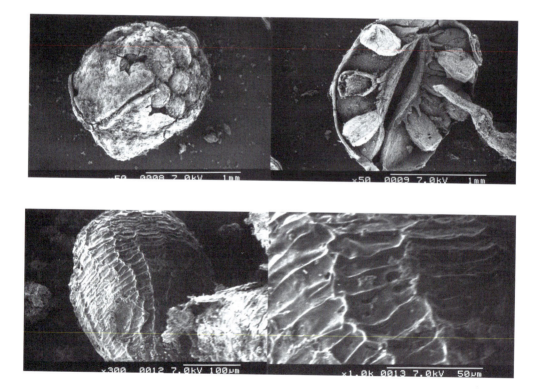

PLATE 8.1 *Charred capsule and seeds of a rush,* Juncus, *probably mud rush,* J. gerardi *Loisel.*

PLATE 8.2 Bottlenose dolphin (Tursiops truncatus) *remains from Flixborough.*

PLATE 10.1 Pig slaughtering at the beginning of winter – source: Historische, chronologische, astronomische Schriften (lat.). Salzburg vor 821 *[copyright Austrian National Library, picture archive, Vienna: Cod. 387, fol. 9v].*

PLATE 10.2 Pig butchery – source: Annales, Computus, Kapiteloffiziumsbuch *from the former monastery of Zweifalten, about 1162 [copyright Württembergische Landesbibliothek Stuttgart, Cod. hist. fol. 415, 17v].*

PLATE 10.3 Falconry and fowling scene depicted in the Cotton Tiberius Manuscript B.V., Part 1, page folio no. f.7v (October). [Courtesy of the British Library]